Ngambouk Vitalis Pemunta (ed.)

Concurrences in Postcolonial Research

Perspectives, Methodologies, and Engagements

Beyond the Social Sciences

Edited by Michael Kuhn, Hebe Vessuri, Shujiro Yazawa

ISSN 2364-8775

1 Michael Kuhn, Shujiro Yazawa *(eds.)*
   Theories about and Strategies against Hegemonic Social Sciences
   ISBN 978-3-8382-0586-1

2 Michael Kuhn
   How the Social Sciences Think about the World's Social
   Outline of a Critique
   ISBN 978-3-8382-0892-3

3 Michael Kuhn, Hebe Vessuri *(eds.)*
   The Global Social Sciences
   —Under and Beyond European Universalism
   ISBN 978-3-8382-0893-0

4 Michael Kuhn, Hebe Vessuri *(eds.)*
   Contributions to Alternative Concepts of Knowledge
   ISBN 978-3-8382-0894-7

5 Kazumi Okamoto
   Academic Culture: An Analytical Framework
   for Understanding Academic Work
   A Case Study about the Social Science Academe in Japan
   ISBN 978-3-8382-0937-1

6 Ngambouk Vitalis Pemunta *(ed.)*
   Concurrences in Postcolonial Research
   Perspectives, Methodologies, and Engagements
   ISBN 978-3-8382-1154-1

Ngambouk Vitalis Pemunta (ed.)

CONCURRENCES IN POSTCOLONIAL RESEARCH

Perspectives, Methodologies, and Engagements

ibidem-Verlag
Stuttgart

Bibliografische Information der Deutschen Nationalbibliothek
Die Deutsche Nationalbibliothek verzeichnet diese Publikation in der Deutschen Nationalbibliografie; detaillierte bibliografische Daten sind im Internet über http://dnb.d-nb.de abrufbar.

Bibliographic information published by the Deutsche Nationalbibliothek
Die Deutsche Nationalbibliothek lists this publication in the Deutsche Nationalbibliografie; detailed bibliographic data are available in the Internet at http://dnb.d-nb.de.

∞

Gedruckt auf alterungsbeständigem, säurefreien Papier
Printed on acid-free paper

ISSN 2364-8775

ISBN: 978-3-8382-1154-7

© *ibidem*-Verlag
Stuttgart 2018

Alle Rechte vorbehalten

Das Werk einschließlich aller seiner Teile ist urheberrechtlich geschützt. Jede Verwertung außerhalb der engen Grenzen des Urheberrechtsgesetzes ist ohne Zustimmung des Verlages unzulässig und strafbar. Dies gilt insbesondere für Vervielfältigungen, Übersetzungen, Mikroverfilmungen und elektronische Speicherformen sowie die Einspeicherung und Verarbeitung in elektronischen Systemen.

All rights reserved. No part of this publication may be reproduced, stored in or introduced into a retrieval system, or transmitted, in any form, or by any means (electronic, mechanical, photocopying, recording or otherwise) without the prior written permission of the publisher. Any person who does any unauthorized act in relation to this publication may be liable to criminal prosecution and civil claims for damages.

Printed in the EU

Dedication

To all martyrs fighting for the restoration of the independence of the former British Southern Cameroons (BSC), aka Ambazonia
Those imprisoned in bunkers for no crime other than being Anglophones,

Those speaking truth to power and standing up against the Frenchification, and in defence of their Anglo-Saxon identity as they engage the French-backed Yaounde puppet regime in concurrent discourses in their quest for the restoration of the independence of the BSC.

Acknowledgements

On behalf of the co-organizers—Margareta Wallin Wictorin and Hans Hägerdal—of the interdisciplinary conference 'Concurrences in postcolonial research-perspectives, methodologies, engagements', which took place 20–23 August 2015 at Kalmar, held by the Centre for Concurrences in Colonial and Postcolonial Studies of Linnaeus University (LNU), Sweden, I would like to fervently thank the following sponsors—the Swedish Research Council, The Crafoord Foundation and the Vice Chancellor at LNU for their generous sponsorship. We, the organizers are equally grateful to all the participants of the conference as well as the contributors to this volume for their patience in responding to comments and bringing this work to fruition. We would also like to unreservedly thank Åse Magnusson, the Centre's coordinator for enthusiastically taking care of the general organizational aspects of that great come together. I would personally like to thank the anonymous reviewers for their forensic scrutiny of multiple versions of various papers that make up this collection and the authors for their patience in reworking their various contributions.

Ernest A. Pineteh would like to sincerely thank the American Council of Learned Societies through its African Humanities Program for sponsoring the broader research project on Cape Town-based Somali victims of xenophobia that forms the basis of his contribution. His contribution was put together during a one-month visiting research fellowship at the Centre for Concurrences in Colonial and Postcolonial Studies at LNU in Sweden. During the fellowship, he received financial support and was provided with office space, the internet and library access. He would like to express his deepest gratitude to the Centre for hosting him.

Cristina Sá Valentim is immensely grateful to all her interlocutors, in Portugal and Angola, especially to Catele Jeremias and Mateus Segunda Chicumba for their generosity and friendship in helping her with the complex meanings of one of the Angolan national languages—the Cokwe language. This chapter is drawn from her ongoing research done for a PhD dissertation at the University of Coimbra, Portugal. A visiting fellowship at the Center for Concurrences in Colonial and Postcolonial Studies, LNU, Växjö from August to September 2015 that preceded the conference afforded her a chance to rework her article for publication. She extends a profound gratitude to Åse Magnusson and Professors Gunlög Fur, Hans Hägerdal and Margareta Wallin Wictorin, for all kindness, hospitality, and logistical support at Växjö, as well to her doctoral scientific advisors Dr Catarina Martins (CES-FLUC) and Dr Ricardo Roque (ICS-IUL), for their incisive comments to early reflections that preceded this paper, and for the encouragement to proceed with this PhD research.

On behalf of *ibidem*-Verlag, I heartily wish to thank Jakob Horstmann and Florian Bölter as well as their entire staff for their tireless efforts, time-consciousness and professionalism. It was wonderful working with all of them!

To Emilia Nkoyo Otang: Thank you for keeping the night virgil with me all through as I worked hecticly to bring this project to fruition.

Ngambouk Vitalis Pemunta
Lessebo, August 31, 2017

Contents

Acknowledgements 7

Contributors 11

**Towards Global Connections
and Multiple Entanglement** 15
Ngambouk Vitalis Pemunta

**Concurrent Subjectivities and Coevalness
in Saidiya Hartman's *Lose Your Mother*** 53
Nicklas Hållén

**Autofiction as a Postcolonial Strategy: Guilherme
Mendes da Silva's *The Moods of Mister Utac* (De
humeuren van meneer Utac) and Junot Díaz'
*The Brief Wondrous Life of Oscar Wao*** 73
Kristian Van Haesendonck

**Moments of Suffering, Pain and Resilience:
Somali refugees' Memories of Home and
Journeys to Exile** 101
Ernest Angu Pineteh

**Homosexuality as "UnAfrican":
Heteronormativity, Power, and Ambivalence
in Cameroon** 125
Ngambouk Vitalis Pemunta

**Concurrent contestations: Framing,
and Naming the 'queer' in art from Africa** 175
Melanie Klein

Queer Visibility and Visual Resistance against Homophobia at Dak'Art, The Biennial Exhibition of Contemporary African Art in Dakar 2014 199
Margareta Wallin Wictorin

Entangled Voices, Lived Songs. *Mwambwambwa*, a Cokwe Song recorded in 1954 at Colonial Lunda, Angola 217
Cristina Sá Valentim

A Contradictory Encounter: Swedish Missionaries and the Local Population in the Congo Free State ... 261
Pia Lundqvist

"Lest the punishment of Ahab fall upon you": The Psychic Impact of Concurrent Narratives in the Hawaiian Missionary Legacy 291
Catherine E. Hoyser

Policy Lending or Imposition: An Assessment of the World Bank's Education Policy influence on Development in Africa 315
Terry Y. Yong

Contributors

Ngambouk Vitalis Pemunta holds a D. Phil. in Sociology and Social Anthropology from the Central European University (CEU) Budapest, Hungary. Apart from teaching stints at the Universities of Yaounde1, Cameroon, CEU, and University College Dublin, (Ireland), he has recently completed postdoctoral research at Linnaeus University, Växjö, Sweden. He is also a consultant for several NGOs in both his native Cameroon and abroad-thereby cross-pollinating between the fields of anthropology and development. He is the country expert on asylum for Cameroon for the United Kingdom-based Rights in Exile Programme. He has conducted extensive ethnographic fieldwork in, and published on Cameroon, Chad, South Africa and Sierra Leone. His research interests include gender, reproductive health, HIV/AIDS, environmental policy, ethnography, medical sociology/anthropology, social science and medicine, colonialism and postcolonialism.

Nicklas Hållén is a postdoctoral researcher at Concurrences in Colonial and Postcolonial Studies at Linnaeus University, Sweden and is currently working on a research project called African Street Literatures and the Future of Literary Form at the Department of English at Uppsala University, Sweden. He was awarded his PhD in 2011 (Umeå University). His research interests include African literature and travel literature about Africa.

Kristian Van Haesendonck is a research fellow at the University of Antwerp and works on Latin American, Caribbean and Lusophone African literatures. He is the author of ¿Encanto o espanto? Identidad y nación en la novela puertorriqueña actual (Frankfurt-Madrid: Vervuert-Iberoamericana), editor of Going Caribbean! New Perspectives on Caribbean Literature and Art (Lisbon: Humus), and co-editor of Caribbeing: Comparing Caribbean Literatures and Cultures (Amsterdam-Atlanta: Rodopi). His book Postcolonial Archipelagos: essays on Hispanic Caribbean and Lusophone African Literatures is forthcoming at Peter Lang.

Ernest A. Pineteh is senior lecturer and researcher in the Unit for Academic Literacy in the Faculty of Humanities at the University of Pretoria, South Africa. He obtained his PhD from the

University of the Witwatersrand in Johannesburg, for an interdisciplinary research project on the life testimonies of a group of asylum seekers and refugees. He has written and published several articles on the experiences of African migrants in South Africa. His current research interests include but are not limited to xenophobia, migrant narratives, African transnational students and academic literacies.

Melanie Klein held a fellowship as a postdoctoral researcher in the DFG Research Group "Transcultural Negotiations in the Ambits of Art. Comparative Perspectives on Historical Contexts and Current Constellations" at Freie Universitaet Berlin from 2011 to 2017. She studied Art History and Economics in Heidelberg, London and Berlin and completed her thesis on "Masculinity contested. Strategies of resistance in the art from South Africa and the oeuvre of Wim Botha" at the Academy of Visual Arts in Leipzig in 2008. She was Visiting Associate at the Centre for African Studies in Cape Town with a scholarship from the German Academic Exchange Service and held a two-year research position at the Graduate College "Identity and Difference. Gender Constructions and Interculturality" at the University of Trier. Her research interests include modern and contemporary art from Southern and Eastern Africa, art education and perspectives on Gender issues.

Margareta Wallin Wictorin has a PhD in Art history and visual studies from the University of Gothenburg, Sweden. She is Reader in Art history and visual studies at Linnaeus University in Växjö, Sweden, and has a position as senior lecturer in Cultural Studies at Karlstad University. She is affiliated to Linnaeus University Centre for Concurrences in Colonial and Postcolonial studies. Since 2008 she has been on several research trips to Senegal and Kenya to study contemporary art and visual culture, especially at Dak'Art, The Biennial Exhibition of Contemporary African Art In Dakar.

Cristina Sá Valentim is a cultural and social anthropologist with a BA and MA from the University of Coimbra, Portugal. The main areas of her research are related with anthropology and postcolonial studies concerning social differentiation, identitary processes, migration, power, agency, resistance, subjectivity, colonial relations, image and music. She is a PhD candidate in Sociology in the doctoral programme 'Postcolonialisms and Global Citizenship' at the Centre for Social Studies (CES), School of Economics of Coimbra University (FEUC). Currently she is studying the colonial category of 'indigenous folk music' within the Cokwe people, during the Portuguese colonialism at Lunda, northeast of Angola. To this project she did fieldwork in Portugal and Angola through oral history survey and on colonial archives. She is an associated researcher at the Centre for Research in Anthropology (CRIA), and recently collaborated with the Institute of Ethnomusicology – Center for Studies in Music and Dance (INET-md). She is the back office manager of the website "Diamang Digital" (www.diamangdigital.net).

Pia Lundqvist is a researcher in history at University of Gothenburg, Sweden. Her doctoral thesis (2008) contains a study on peddling in Sweden in the 18th and 19th centuries. Her main research interests lie in the areas of the history of consumption with a particular focus on textiles and material culture, migration, and cultural encounters. Her current research project, Equals or subordinates? Male and female Swedish missionaries in the Congo Free State, 1886–1908, draws attention to the complexity of different missionary identities and power hierarchies of gender, race, and class within the mission. The project is financed by the Swedish Research Council and started in 2014.

Catherine E. Hoyser is Professor of English and Director of Women's and Gender Studies at the University of Saint Joseph in West Hartford, Connecticut, USA. Her doctorate is in Victorian Studies with a minor in Women's Studies. She teaches postcolonial literature, British cultural studies, detective fiction, gender studies, and feminist theories. Publications include an anthology of women writers and an overview of the novelist Tom Robbins as well as scholarly articles. She is also a published poet. Her research in Hawaii focuses on the impact of U. S. 19th century settler colonialists and royal Hawaiian connections to Victorian England.

Terence Y. Yong holds the degree of MPhil in Higher Education from the University of Oslo, Norway. He is a doctoral researcher with Higher Education Group, School of Management, University of Tampere, Finland. The focus of his doctoral research is in the regulatory framework of governments in higher education. He also researches the influence of global policy ideas on African national university systems. He focuses on neoliberal tendencies relating to the organization and management of universities in Africa. Consequently, he stretches his research interest to assessing the impacts of universities on African economic development.

Towards Global Connections and Multiple Entanglement

Ngambouk Vitalis Pemunta
Centre for Concurrences in Colonial
and Postcolonial Studies,
Linnaeus University, Växjö, Sweden

One of the central preoccupations of postcolonial studies is "to recover the voice and agency of the subaltern to find alternative articulations to monolithic imperial representations. Universalizing perspectives obscure their origins and threaten to silence alternatives, regardless of their validity or influence" (Fur et al., 2014: 1253). The methodological and theoretical process of recovering alternative voices in space and time while factoring in our conflicting analysis and claims regarding culture, history and identity is no easy feat. The difficulties are because either one individual academic discipline or grand theory can fruitfully explain concurrent encounters. This difficulty is rather an invitation to open our eyes to the permeability of academic disciplines, concepts and methods as captured by the idea of "travelling concepts". Concerning perspectives in research, Doris Bachmann-Medick invites us not only to take a critical look "at the differences between cultural semantics, knowledge traditions, and knowledge gaps. [Nevertheless to also] concentrate on smaller units of social interaction, on misunderstandings, or even battles over interpretation" (Bachmann-Medick 2014: 130–131). It is also an invitation to journey into the seemingly unfamiliar, a space in which to reflect upon the travels of concepts, beyond disciplinary boundaries, using widely different theoretical and methodological approaches. Stated otherwise, methodological nationalism has been shown to be inadequate in accommodating these challenges. What then is this intellectual elephant called concurrences; is it just another synonym for the concept of globalization in its various guises?

Concurrences is a complex, all-inclusive, multidisciplinary concept that describes ongoing, simultaneous cultural processes and encounters—one that gives voice to, and in which dominated populations challenge representations that play upon and legitimize racial and cultural differences (Nicholas, 1994). Challenging structures of power and actions that silence alternative, subaltern voices by recovering these voices constitute concurrent views. It is about capturing multiple voices in our analysis and demonstrating the multiple capillaries of power and myriad forms of collective and individual acts of resistance.

This interdisciplinary collection of essays explores the multiplicity of paradigmatic meanings that the all-encompassing concept of concurrences connotes. We focus on concurrent, but hierarchical relationships between the colonized and the colonizer, and between subaltern and dominant groups. We examine how these relationships are challenged through different forms of resistance by the subaltern in both colonial and postcolonial contexts. In a sense, this collection demonstrates the complexities and contradictions inherent in these relationships regarding ideas and practices, but also regarding discourses between the colonized and the colonizer as well as the powerful and the powerless. One hallmark of colonial relations that is worthy of note is that the subjects of colonial rule are never directly and totally against the colonizer. Bill Ashcroft speaks to these ambivalent relations thus "ambivalence suggests that complicity and resistance exist in a fluctuating relation within the colonial subject" (Ashcroft, 1998: 12–13). These encounters involve cultural otherness, the coming together of conflicting and competing facts, narratives and counter-narratives about capitalist benevolence that mask exploitation. The same events are narrated in different ways thereby challenging the accounts of various social actors as mere fabrications. Can social agents objectively recount their encounters with each other? Why do various actors narrate the same events in different ways? Can the subaltern speak?

While the volume attempts to elicit connections between different, and sometimes disparate, instances of concurrences, it also maintains their contextual specificities. Scholars have put to question contemporary theories that portray colonialism as monolithic in character, purpose, and efficacy throughout the world (Fur et al., 2014, Nicholas, 1994). In Nicholas Thomas' view, colonialism is not so much a discourse but rather a project—a project in which the interactions among colonizing and colonized people are far more variable and reveal greater ambivalence than is imagined (Nicholas, 1994). Thomas further concedes that "Even colonialism as a concept is not a unitary project but a rather fractured one, riddled with contradictions and exhausted as much by its internal debates as by the resistance of the colonized" (Nicholas, 1994: 51, Fur et al. 2014, 2017). The apparent humanitarian gestures of descendants of missionaries in Hawaii and of the Swedish Missionary Society (SMS) in the Congo Free State are all self-interested acts. In the same light, colonial injustice as perpetrated on the native Hawaiians cannot be whitewashed as regrettable, but understandable in its specific historical moment.

At the same time, the contradiction of compulsory freedom is palpable and omnipresent. Essays under the rubric of homophobia and the transnationalization of homosexuality raise the question of how readily Western countries should intervene or dictate the social practices of other societies. The international outcry against the persecution of same-sex partners in African countries and the competing discourses of human rights and cultural autonomy raise the issue of whether Western nations must impose the "UnAfrican practice" of same-sex relationships in the name of universal human rights. The linking of aid (a form of inter-governmental benevolence) by Western nations as a benchmark of civilization or modernity seems uncalled for and smacks of material and discursive imperialism. It leads us to question what human rights as a hegemonic discourse is really about. Human rights can, of course, not be assumed as normative, static and universal—a standard to which non-Western countries must assimilate and adhere to, to continue receiving Western development aid. As expected, African nations are resisting this Western imposition by continuing to adopt anti-homosexuality laws. Same-sex relationships in African societies go beyond sexuality, it is also intertwined with magico-religious practices, the quest for social mobility and serves as a mechanism for deflecting criticisms of bad governance and unbridled corruption among the ruling elites.

Core to this book is the recognition of the multiple understandings of concurrences and cultural encounters, and how power relationships are negotiated as well as shaping these battles across space and time. It is also, about how to simultaneously analyze these relationships and power fields by capturing the multiplicity of voices and positionalities embedded in them. While these concerns have traditionally been at the forefront of postcolonial theory, we seek to reopen and deepen these debates and find the underlying cause of its inherent ambivalences and contradictions. Through the result of new empirical, interdisciplinary studies, we engage with the voices of individuals and groups in different cultural encounters as well as how these encounters (re)shape their identities (McCorrmak, 2014, Goebel & Schabio 2013, Spivak, 1988). As a response to the incessant debates that characterize postcolonial studies, this collection emphasizes the lived experiences of social agents taking part in cultural encounters. The papers draw from a wide range of methodological traditions—autoethnography, participant observation, autobiography, individual in-depth interviews, storytelling, archival sources, and literary analysis. They also draw on various cultural archives—formal and informal, traditional and digital, fiction and documentary text, and different methodological traditions, present different disciplinary viewpoints and engage with a variety of geographical locations in order to explore the multiplicity and diversity of experiences, which can be brought together under the concept of "current encounters".

To situate concurrent encounters within the fluid geographic, historic, temporal and cultural context they operate within is significant for two main reasons. First and foremost, social and cultural context and power fields/relationships matter in the experiences of subjects in concurrent encounters. Secondly, different contexts open up different possibilities for both resistance and subaltern agency. Accordingly, only a multiplicity of disciplinary lenses and not one overarching theorization can encompass the complex and varied cultural encounters that appear in this collection. Concurrences is a shorthand description for a wide range of theoretical concepts that reoccur in debates about cultural encounters, cultural productions and social experiences. Most of these concepts, including among others—identity, xenophobia, sociology of absences, contact zones, colonialism, imperialism, cultural genocide, white supremacy, deviant sexualities, sexual minorities, discursive dichotomies, invisibilities, queer, autobiography, autofiction, "divergent modernities", temporalities, coevalness, concurrent subjectivities, diaspora, slavery, and alienation—have originated in sociology, anthropology, history, English studies, arts history, virtual art, refugee studies, literary, and historical studies. In the course of debates on the human condition, they have traversed into other academic disciplines. While these concepts are significant in capturing concurrent encounters, they require revision and contextualization to reflect lived experiences and the reasoning of social agents involved in cross-cultural encounters. This explains why they are sometimes used differently in different disciplines.

This collection is part of a larger long-term project at Linnaeus University. It seeks to expand current scientific debates on the specificity of concurrent encounters (see Fur et al. 2014, 2017), by revisiting previous discussions on xenophobia, homophobia, the layering of temporalities—nation time, diasporic time, and time of slavery that are coeval and facilitates the encounter between concurrent subjectivities, the renegotiation of relations between past and present as well as the ambivalence and contradictions that is inherent in the various encounters that these scholars individually engage with in their papers.

At the Linnaeus University interdisciplinary Centre for Concurrences in Colonial and Postcolonial Studies, an interdisciplinary group of researchers is preoccupied with refining the methodological and theoretical framework for engaging with the simultaneity of claims and counterclaims about culture, history and identity.[1]

For more than a decade, these humanities and social science scholars have collaborated around investigations of colonialism, archives and cultural encounters. In 2011 the Swedish Research Council awarded the group funding for four years to investigate a

---

[1] I adopt heavily from my blog post titled "Researching the Entangled Web of Humanity: the Case for rigorous theoretical and methodological encyclopaediasm" published on the concurrences website which has now been taken down.

range of cultural archives, and develop methodologies to map multiple, simultaneous, and concurring claims of reality, experience, and meaning in time and place. The conference at which most of the papers in this anthology were presented in their draft forms was one of the greatest milestones in the history of the Centre.

Concurrences as a Multifaceted Concept: Temporality and the co-production of the past

The concept of concurrences evokes many things: It is a multifaceted concept. It is an all-encompassing concept that is at the centre of cross-border thinking and intersectionality. It can be deployed alongside a wide range of concepts to approach a multiplicity of experiences and understandings such as intersectionality, transnationality, contact zones, temporality, power inequalities, resource colonialism, multiple identities, modern and local knowledge, entangled histories and connected sociologies, border thinking, contrapuntal perspectives, and transnational ethnography among others. As a methodology, Concurrences recognizes both confluence and competition, alliance and conflict, and insists that any understanding of the world must take into account both entanglements and tension between equally weighty jurisdictions. Concurrences suggest that different perspectives and locations are always and inescapably entangled and human beings constantly negotiate the different and sometimes incompatible demands arising out of these concurrent conditions.

The issues in this anthology are framed around three interconnected themes—temporality, homophobia and the transnationalization of homosexuality, entanglement and colonial encounters. Coevalness runs through most of the essays. Although the critical term 'coeval' speaks to and engages with Achille Mbembe's (2001) widely cited 'temporality of entanglement' in *On the Postcolony*, Nicklas Hållén instead chooses to compare the two. Through this comparison, he articulates the notion of multiple temporality—nation time, diasporic time, and time of slavery. Hållén's notion of multiple temporality is analogous with what philosophers variously refer to as entangled times, temporal heterogeneity, timeknots, hetero-temporality, etc. Even the present or the now is marked by plurality. It is about the idea of worlding the world, which allowed the slaves in Sidiya Hartman's book, *Lose Your Mother: A Journey Along the Atlantic Slave Route* that Hållén analyzes the possibility of recognizing the plurality of co-existing temporalities—nation, diasporic and slavery times, in her book Hartman's search is for 'a method of renegotiating the relations between past and present, history and identity' (Hartman, 2007: 4). This temporal co-existence is competing and simultaneously conflictual. The various themes connect past and present, disparate places as well as competing and co-operating social agents who influence each other and are involved in the co-production of ideas and identities.

Whatever transpires in one part of the globe reverberates in other parts of the world. Europe is facing the adverse effects of bad governance, mismanagement, unemployment, climate change and Islamic fundamentalism from the Middle East and Africa as refugees flood into the continent leading to homophobic reactions. In the fall of 2015, Europe's fortress walls got shattered, putting to question attempts such as barbed wire along the Hungarian border and detention camps offshore of Australia. Scores of refugees escaping violence and threats from climate change flooded the shores of the continent seeking safety. It is no longer possible—if it ever was—to ignore "the global" in whatever shape it enters the consciousness. Scholarly disciplines in the humanities and social sciences are failing short in grappling with these simultaneously local and global challenges. The process of migration brings together multiple temporalities and is often fraught with xenophobia from the host society, victimization and concurrently, resilience from refugees. In fact, even places such as "home" tend to have multiple meanings. Methodological nationalism has been shown to be inadequate in accommodating the challenges of multiple temporalities that the process of migration involves.

Similarly, autofiction gives a semblance of truth to the multiple but concurrent voices of different characters that allow an author to express multiple personalities, temporalities and the cultural complexity involved in diasporic lives. Through autofiction, the autobiography of an individual is written across different characters representing the narrator and the author concurrently. Characterized simultaneously by ambiguities and contradictions, autofiction shows the multiplicity of the author's self, and multiple voices that create the effect of verisimilitude and authenticity (see Kristian Van Haesendonck this volume)

Travel writing scholar Nicklas Hållén appropriates the concepts of home, temporality and identity to explore the inaccessibility, coevalness and concurrent intersection of multiple temporalities. Also, he explores how they tend to differentially shape places and human life. Hållén explores the concurrent opposition and rupture between past and present as captured in the complexity involved in the relations between Africa and the black Western subject through Saidiya Hartman's travelogue *Lose Your Mother: A Journey Along the Atlantic Slave Route* to signal distance and difference rather than closeness and sameness. The group of travellers with whom Hartman interacts, he argues, have juggled identities. They are simultaneously American pilgrims, the ancestors of contemporary Ghanaians and African Americans who escaped slavery. They exist, like Hartman, in time of slavery insofar as it shapes their world and identity as a people of refugees, but they are at the same time, free from the constraints of this horizon-less temporality. The layering of temporalities is paradoxical, and results into multiple, concurrent temporalities—nation time, diaspora time and the time of slavery. This entanglement of temporalities makes the travellers coeval with Hartman and the reader and facilitates the encounter between concurrent subjectivities. In the spirit of Paul Gilroy (1993), Hållén points to the need to consider space and time as relational in their underarticulation with racialized being. As concepts, past and present and its impacts on the lived experience of the diaspora creates connections between the living and dead, traditional and modern.

The past and ongoing he argues, merge and become coeval and concurrent since they achieve a kind of encounter between the two subjectivities. This encounter is, however, characterized by fictitiousness, because in this textual moment more than one past and one present intersect. Hartman is faced with resolving the ambiguities and contradictions of the coexistence of a sense of belonging and a personal sense of loss and uprootedness. He demonstrates how the language of love and kinship and that of domination and ownership of property are simultaneously intertwined in the discursive history of the slave trade. Central in this language are relationships embedded in the temporal and spatial concepts of coevalness and closeness. They are central because the relationship is threatened by the slave's and child's departure and estrangement from their people. In negotiating relations between past and present, history and identity, Hartman finds herself in some sought of a dilemma as she attempts to stage an encounter between the self and an entangled past and present that, nonetheless remains distant and unreachable. Hållén concedes that Hartman is seeking to approach the history that has been severed from the present not by the ordinary passage of time, but by the rupture of the middle passage and forced amnesia under slavery. In his analysis of Hartman's work, Hållén connects places and multiple temporalities by chronicling the forced journeys from the homeland to the Americas and the journey back in time as a voyage back in the date of slavery. The journey back in the date of slavery is contrasted with diasporic time, temporality and history that is discontinuous and fractured. Diasporic time is simultaneously compared with nation time, which tends to exclude and is only accessible to those having a privileged and largely uncontested position within the narrative of the Western country. Unlike diaspora time that emphasizes "… Breaks and continuities," in a march toward Western style progress, nation time "links past, present and future". Hållén highlights the enmeshed histories and hyphenated African-American identity that creates a rupture between past and current.

Combining the concepts of the politics of violence and resilience, academic literacy and migration scholar Ernest A. Pineteh demonstrates how the social and political violence experienced by Somali refugees in Cape Town, who are fleeing Al-Qa'ida orchestrated violence in their home country shape the experiences of the xenophobic violence they face in post-apartheid South Africa. Pineteh unearths the multiple meanings of home and flight as well as multiple temporalities. Somalis' reconstruction of home as resembling post-apartheid South Africa renders the concept of home as concurrently "amorphous and fluid" (Arthur 2001: 133) as well as a contested space. Their struggle over spaces and for social inclusion in a xenophobic South Africa echoes the spatial contestation in Somali. The violence in the former served as preparatory time and time of emboldening (co-existence of temporalities) for the xenophobia in the latter country. He goes on to demonstrate how resilience concurrently implies the risk of endangerment or significant adversity even in the face of great assault and active adaptation to the process of social development. Faced with incessant violence at home, Somali refugees developed survival strategies and the abilities to deal with hostilities in the course of their journeys into exile. The narratives of their fragmented travel/flight into exile connect different places ("spatiality of the journey") and temporalities because each transit point in the course of their journey created a particular migratory experience worth remembering or forgetting.

Ernest uses storytelling to reconstruct the experiences of Somali migrants. He connects disparate places through the spatial and temporal metaphors that express the physical and psychological effects of exile, immigration and displacement. Their journeys into exile are concurrently characterized by memory and imagination as they negotiated between old and new, past and present, self and other, safety and danger. Memories of violence in Somalia are concurrent with memories of displacement. Concurrently, their ability to take a business risk and operate businesses in volatile environments has exposed them to xenophobia from the local South African population who faced with failing and poor delivery of social services, suspect successful migrant business operators of casting a spell on them. Somali refugees constitute a community of forced migrants whose national identities and sense of belonging have been simultaneously shattered by the "destructive insurgency of Al-Qa'ida activities and the counter-terrorism actions of the United States". As accounts of displacement, Somali narratives of home and flight to exile serve as tropes of memory that shape our understanding of their resilience to post-apartheid violence and their strategies to navigate hostile spaces using survival tactics in spaces where they are not wanted. Pineteh demonstrates how by transforming their past traumatic memories into social capital and narratives, they gain a sense of place and time and chart the future. While they make sense of their selves, their collective identity and the events that have shaped their lives, they are concurrently caught up in the logic of ambivalence between remembering and forgetting. They can choose to either talk about the past, suppress it or let the past reside in the past. It is about the realization, textualization, suppression, burial or avoidance of the past. Somali memories serve as stories that attach political agency to their sense of belonging and which help us make sense of their social existence in a new South Africa fraught with anti-foreigner sentiments. The migrant journeys often concurrently involve diversion, repetition and simultaneity. In this description of flight, there is an interesting interconnection of different events, which helps to shape our understanding of this migrant's experiences, exposing us to "complex webs of historical past in the present" (Hautaniemi 2006: 82).

The Latin American and Caribbean scholar Kristian Van Haesendonck addresses the similarity between autobiographical writing concerning "diaspora" or "migration" literature and autofiction—the concurrence of facts and fiction in an author's life. Van Haesendonck argues that as a mode of writing, autofiction is used to create meaning in the post-colony and to give a semblance of truth to the multiple but concurrent voices of different characters that allow an author to express, rather than multiple personalities, the cultural complexity that is involved in diasporic lives. Through autofiction, the autobiography of an individual is written across different characters. The classic first person narrator ("I") is not the only possible voice. There are concurrent characters corresponding to the narrator and author. Real life events are spread out across the lives of very different characters. He compares two novels: Guilherme Mendes da Silva's *De humeuren van meneer Utac* and Junot Díaz's *The Brief Wondrous Life of Oscar Wao* and beside their seamless mix of autobiographical elements with fictional ones, he addresses the themes of displacement, connections between home and abroad through diaspora as well as connected histories that are central to these. Although Diaz grew up as a nerd in the Dominican ghetto, he simultaneously finds himself uprooted because of his love for academic pursuits in particular and Western pop culture in general. Mendes da Silva's transnational autofiction takes root in the United States. He addresses the corflictive relationship between the Dominican Republic's national history and its diaspora.

Van Haesendonck concedes that both authors explore the self (the auto in autofiction) which functions as a lens for examining broader issues of national, regional, and diasporic identities, the construction of an alternative modernity as well as the postcolonial status of the more general regions. In his autofictional account, Junot Díaz reflects on his nomadic life in both the Caribbean and Cape Verde as well as on his feeling of a sense of double belonging and uprootedness. Using his fictionalized name of mister Utac, the latter articulates his sense of loss and uprootedness, which is the result of his migration from Cape Verde to the Netherlands and his decision to return to the latter country. In Junot Díaz's autofictional account, he self-embedded himself into two different characters—Yunior and Oscar without "fitting" into none of them with ease.

Although the autobiography of a person is narrated by himself/herself and is believed to be an objective and a non-fictional account of that individual's life, autofiction, Van Haesendonck argues, is however fraught with ambiguities because of the simultaneity between factual and fictional elements. Though lacking conceptual popularity when compared to an autobiographical account, it is characterized by diversity in the genre. Although autobiographical writing concurrently integrates elements of an individual's history, it fails to privilege the author's biography. Similarly, while autofiction tends to authenticate an autobiography, it carries only a semblance of truth (verisimilitude). Fictional elements can, however, undermine an autobiographical narrative. Despite divergences in cultural contexts, both da Silva and Díaz are preoccupied with profound long-term cultural encounters and connected histories between the Caribbean and Cape Verde and their respective Diasporas. In tracing the cultural and historical links between the Caribbean and Africa, da Silva shows how syncretic forms of cultural expression have taken root in African religions and suffered significant transformations because of contact with the local Caribbean religious and cultural practices. The syncretic cultural productions that constitute the divergent modernities of both the Caribbean and Africa are usually relegated to the realm of primitive practices—that is, as in opposition to what modernity should look like. In reality, these practices have modernized in a way that cannot easily be explained through Western concepts.

Homophobia and the transnationalization of homosexuality

The globalization of human rights activism, which partly speaks to the need to respect the rights of homosexuals has instead tended to endanger same-sex individuals and made them increasingly invisible in most of Africa. They face homophobic reactions and death threats and are obliged to live in a closet. While lesbian, gay, bisexual and transgender (LGBT) individuals are objects of homophobia; gay right activists are accused of violating Africa's cultural codes. Artists who attempt to give the LGBT community visibility and voice play a dual role. They simultaneously call attention to the plight of these sexual minorities while also exposing them to the violence and homophobia of society. Furthermore, they are simultaneously Africans and the queer and are associated with the typically homophobic and discriminatory African context in which LGBT people live in fear. Various international exhibitions, galleries and museums serve as arenas for negotiating queerness by making queer visibility relevant by creating awareness about their daily sufferings and humiliations. On the one hand, the LGBT community is concurrently acknowledged and designated while on the other they face resistance, disrespect and hatred ("oppositional forces") from various sectors of society including the media in Africa. Even in African countries like South Africa where the LGBT community is acknowledged and granted rights, they remain on the margins of society, since these rights are never implemented. The non-implementation of their rights takes place even when queer exists as individuals and as a group, and look like everyone else.

The social anthropologist Ngambouk Vitalis Pemunta combines local level ethnography and auto-ethnography and engages with the concurrent and contentious debates between African and

Western societies over the supposed "UnAfrican" practice of same-sex intimacy, which African countries are coerced into legitimizing by Western nations. Respect for human rights including the rights of same-sex partners is increasingly linked to the disbursement of development aid. Pemunta demonstrates that while same-sex relationships among the elites are intertwined with class and the maintenance of power through supernatural means, they are fiercely opposed by society thereby leading to homophobia. Concurrently, the competing ideals of universal human rights and sexual orientation, which is a protected category of nondiscrimination, are in competition with African tradition/authenticity and presumed ideological colonization from the West. African politicians are expected to display evidence of respect for human rights by being tolerant of homosexuality while as moral entrepreneurs; they should serve as custodians of traditional values that extol biological reproduction to their constituents.

Using the case of Cameroon, and building on the core notions of "heterosexual citizenship" and "heteronormativity", Pemunta demonstrates how the deployment of political homophobia against political activists and the LGBT community and how the competing visions between nation and sexuality are primordial in national identity construction. While Western imposed norms of democratization and good governance have brought to the fore the issue of the status of sexual minorities, it has simultaneously exposed the LGBT community to the homophobic violence of society in Africa. Homophobia is, however, doubly appropriated by disenchanted masses left out of the benefits of the economic growth associated with democracy to question the morality of their rulers and the ruling elites to account for their failure to deliver on the dividends of democracy to their people. Caught up in a situation of role conflict, there is the second appropriation of the concept of privacy and individual autonomy by the political class and ambivalence as a political strategy among the ruling elites who simultaneously have to comply with donor conditionalities as well as to reflect their cultural credentials as moral entrepreneurs in their communities. There is also the simultaneous appropriation of the concept of democracy and respect for human rights including the rights of LGBT people through official discourses while at the same time;

the LGBT community is stigmatized, humiliated and subjected to persecution. Homophobia is paradoxically a strategy that state agents also appropriate to cover up their inability to deliver social services to the masses as well as to blackmail opponents.

Visual art scholar Melanie Klein employs the idea of the "travelling concept" to examine strategies of queering in artistic works from Africa within the context of exhibitions, and their relationship to intersecting political, social and cultural debates around the issue of homosexuality. Relying on the works of various artists, Klein demonstrates how through various exhibitions queerness is negotiated across regional boundaries. The Rotterdam (Netherlands) based artist Ato Malinda, and Igshaan Adams who resides in Cape Town, South Africa, provide a multiplicity of alternative conceptualizations and narrations of homosexuality. Designation, acknowledgement and solidarity as well as resistance, disrespect and hate concurrently surround homosexuality. These issues intersect with categories such as race, ethnicity, class, religion and spatial locations. In the face of the constant conflicts and homophobia that characterize homosexuality, same-sex partners negotiate their identities both as individuals and as a group within a global network of antagonistic forces. These forces include African anti-gay movements, American evangelicals on the one hand and on the other hand, internationally engaged non-governmental organizations promoting gay rights. The extended battlefields of Western or American oppositional contestations on homosexuality and transgender politics are, however, found in African countries. The concurrent representations of "the West as the epitome of modernity and civilized values" as well as the rest as needing to be "civilized" which is evident of hierarchical power relationships inform the politically and discursively conflicting constellation surrounding homosexuality.

Klein argues that in presenting representations of queerness in arts from Africa, artists find themselves in a dilemma in their dual position of marginality: artists are concurrently African and queer. As such, artists are perceived as oppressed LGBTQ protagonists producing 'queer' and thus politically significant art. It emerges from Klein's analysis of discourses, different sources, several relevant exhibitions, and their presentational practice that homosexuality is discursively trapped in the backwardness-progressiveness-dichotomy between African and Western countries. This dichotomy is the result of dominant, interwoven discourses: Africa is reinvented as a heterosexual continent in 'African' debates and stigmatized as homophobic in 'European' debates. The use of the discussion of "sexual minorities in Africa" by Western donors and funding agencies, she argues, present "sexual minorities" as people who are in violation of the cultural codes of their communities. Homosexuality is at the intersection of the battleground between human rights politics and neoliberal dynamics. Simultaneously, the visibility of same-sex intimacy mediated by human rights groups has led to increased vulnerability of the LGBTQ community and their violability that is alleged to violate cultural codes is turned into an acknowledgement of global efforts to fight against discrimination. As a "travelling concept" queerness concurrently refers to both the knowledge to actively engage in theory and discourse formations and the connection to LGBTQ communities as they are circulated, and they travel worldwide through international exhibitions, galleries and museums. Queer visibility simultaneously is politically relevant; it raises awareness and catalyzes the push for social change. The variety and concurrence of the narrations create awareness for the various discriminations but also relations, affirmations and demarcations that LGBTQ people are engaged with.

Drawing on the concepts of queer visibility and visual resistance, art historian Margareta Wallin Wictorin describes and interprets a collection of artworks contesting homophobia. Like Melanie Klein, the collection of artwork she engages with was exhibited at the DAK'Art 2014 in Dakar, Senegal. To give the artworks context, Margareta combines relevant information about them from the exhibition catalogue but also draws on a Peirce-inspired semiotic method that relates iconic, indexical and symbolic signs (Rose, 2012: 119). Differently composed, they could be interpreted differently and have different objectives. Margareta analyzes the works of the artists Ato Malinda, Milumbe Haimbe and Andrew Esiebo. Ato for instance concurrently creates empathy through an interactive performance work meant to draw attention to the everyday torments that homosexual people live through in

Africa. She shared the life stories of LGBT individuals and presented queer visibility and audibility, intimately. She was able to tell the world about their existence in Africa and homosexuality as not the "UnAfrican" practice that political leaders are trying to make people believe. Conspicuous invisibility—represents what can neither be seen nor shown, as well as the censorship of homosexuality and queer ideas. Contrary to Ato, Milumbe used both visual and verbal means to narrate a fictive story and a silent story to promote an antithesis to a stereotypical superhero. This is a way of imagining what possible future role models could look like.

Margareta maintains that LGBT persons as presented through various artistic representations are diverse. They neither are a monolithic group of individuals nor made up of an odd exception. Queer visibility is paradoxical. While it seeks greater space for cultural, economic, political forms of representation, it also mitigates the effects of homophobia. The provision of visual information about the existence of LGBT people and their way of living to resist oppression and exclusion, resist hetero-normativity and give more visibility to the plurality of gender and sexualities. Both artists use visual art to provide visibility to queering for ideas and statements and to serve as a medium for contesting homophobia. On his part, Esiebo demonstrates through art that despite the presumed role-conflict and accompanying homophobia, there is no contradiction between being religious and gay. He concedes that the sexual practices of homosexuality and not issues of love, desire, aspirations, compassion or faith have been the misplaced focus of homophobia. The coexistence of visual resistance by queer visibility and artwork on conspicuous invisibility (South Africa), Margareta concedes, highlights the gap between granting LGBT individuals constitutional rights and failing to uphold same by the South African state. Art is further used not only to create awareness but also to influence politicians to promote the human rights of the LGBT community.

Entanglement and Colonial Encounter

Contradictory and paradoxical entanglements are a prominent feature of colonial encounters. They are often characterized by the lack of any homogenous and unitary voices ("in-between positions"). At the same time, multiple concurrent narratives are embedded in the dominant civilizing trope and the discourse of colonial/missionary benevolence. Capitalist benevolence masks the enduring legacy of resource colonialism and the exploitation of the indigenous population as well as their conquest and the ensuing cultural balkanization, uprootedness, loss of local knowledge and cultural genocide (see Catherine Hoyser's contribution). The relationship between the subaltern and the powerful, the colonizer and the colonized is characterized by a seamlessness of temporality between the past, present and future in both space and time. Colonial encounters also transform the identities of the colonized and the colonizer who come to the encounter with different, and often, competing for perspectives in the light of their worldviews. As seen in the Kongo Kingdom between the missionaries and the indigenous Congolese, these encounters are sometimes characterized by cultural reciprocity/hybridization/creolization. Attempts by missionaries from the Swedish Missionary Society to convert indigenous villagers resulted in the amalgamation/hybridization of Christian and indigenous religious beliefs (see Pia Lundqvist's contribution). In these encounters, neither the missionaries nor the colonialists were a homogenous group. The relationship between colonialism and missionaries was both complex and ambiguous but also dynamic, and characterized by co-operation and conflict. At times, the colonial establishment provided security to the missionaries, but still, complicity and resistance marked their relationship. Similarly, friendship and co-operation initially characterized the relationship between the Chiefs in the Congo and the missionaries but later changed to a missionary offensive and an indigenous resistance. While the Portuguese state in Lunda forwarded labour as a form of "imperial benevolence" that was inevitable for improving local conditions, both the state and the Diamang mining company used the discourse to justify coercive and compulsory labour practices meted out on the natives. Although most of the labour was coercive, labourers were equally able to negotiate longer stays and multiple contracts in the mines as well as incentives for their work. This shows the dynamism of relationships over time and the coexistence of conflict and co-operation (see Cristina Sá Valentim's contribution).

Similarly, Terry Yong addresses the contentious issue of competing knowledge systems and policy imposition/lending between the World Bank and African countries. Through both consent and coercion, African countries are imposed a global one-size-fit-all education solution by the World Bank that fails to take cognizance of their socioeconomic realities and needs. They consent to implement educational policies that prioritize poverty alleviation and that serve their political interests by investing more in primary education whereas to be competitive, and to encourage research and development, they need to jump start the higher educational sector and increase investment as well as participation. Developing African countries were accordingly, forced to enhance their support for primary education over higher education as a way of identification and being in line with the international community.

Literary scholar Catherine E. Hoyser uses a biographical approach to document the relationship between native Hawaiians and a member of the fifth generation of New England missionary descendants Amos Starr Cooke's retrospective look at her family's culpability in cultural genocide and land grabbing. Cooke's descendants had negated every good thing about Hawaiian life and culture including their sophisticated system of sustainable agriculture. In Hoyser's analysis, the descendants of the missionary mask resource exploitation with the use of the discourse of benevolence whereas their ancestors brought chaos, death, poverty and ruined the landscape through the development of capitalism, Christianity and democracy. One of their descendants Cooke is, however, guilty and concurrently willing to make amends for the deeds of her ancestors to avoid the curse of early and premature death on her relatives. Despite the presumed benevolence of the Mission Boys, protest and resistance from the local inhabitants marked the occupation of the native Hawaiian Islands.

Hoyser juxtaposes the entanglement of the concurrent narratives of contemporary life with the past trauma of missionary history localized in one mission descendant's processing of trauma by challenging the historic narrative of missionary benevolence and compensation for the damage that her ancestors helped perpetuate. She simultaneously enacts her own attempts at reparations to native Hawaiians as an effort to break a cycle of loss and grief for Hawaiians and her own family. Missionary benevolence, Hoyser argues, was complicit with colonialist and capitalist agendas. This was despite a vow in the original charter that forbade interference in local politics or culture. Although the alphabet ensured literacy in the Hawaiian language, it was a tool of conquest. The translation of the Bible was a mechanism of governmentality—it was a mechanism for converting Hawaiians into Christianity. By leaving out many sounds in the spoken language, the missionaries distorted the language. They caused violence and Balkanized the culture. Their actions led to the loss of identity, cultural genocide, and loss of local knowledge, world sense, idiosyncrasies, and the orchestration of cultural genocide by missionaries, erasure of collective memory, cultural pride and sense of identity. They controlled the educational system—directed the Chief's children's school where Royal children were taught Western customs and language so that they could interact with representatives and royalty from other countries. The instruction was provided in Western European subjects—a development that contributed to the near annihilation of Hawaiian customs, arts, and beliefs in their charges.

Hoyser looks beyond the purported benevolence of the missionaries and points out that the aim was to ensure the deeply entrenched financial, political, and cultural dominance of missionary descendants in the Islands. Missionary descendants claimed to have developed and transformed the various Islands that constitute Hawaii into functioning Congregationalist, Christian, capitalist democracy with a titular monarchy. The self-serving civilizing narrative mask atrocities including the annexation of Hawaii in 1898. Until date, the long-lasting trauma of colonialism, haunt the psyche of Hawaiians. Hoyser skillfully unpacks the multiple concurrent narratives embedded in the dominant civilizing narrative. She chronicles the impact of one dominant civilizing narrative and one dissenting voice-a missionary descendant who eschews the saviour narrative of her missionary ancestors and regards the legacy as an actual curse still being enacted on her family.

Historian Pia Lundqvist examines the contradictory encounter between the Swedish Missionary Society and the indigenous population in the Congo Free State. Lundqvist concedes that despite the intertwined history of colonialism and missionaries, the latter were not a monolithic group of actors. Furthermore, they stood for different opinions and actions, and even the character and organization of the mission changed over time. A further distinction was made between "God's Whitemen" (the missionaries) from other white people in the Congo. Additionally, despite imbalances in the first encounter between Congolese natives and the missionaries, as the missionary enterprise became institutionalized and formalized, the latter subjected Congolese converts to more detailed, formal regulations. In the analyzed texts, the differences between the missionaries and the indigenous population are explained regarding race, whereas, at an earlier stage, these discrepancies were instead explained by the religious and cultural disparity.

In analyzing the complexity and ambiguity of the relationship between colonialism and missionaries, Lundqvist demonstrates that both the missionary and indigenous culture and identity were dynamic. She examines the multidimensionality, complexity and contradictions of the relations between the SMS and the Congolese natives. One hallmark of colonial relations that emerges in these encounters is that of ambivalent relations orchestrated by the fact that the subjects under colonial rule are never simply and completely against the colonizer "ambivalence suggests that complicity and resistance exist in a fluctuating relation within the colonial subject" (Ashcroft 1998: 12–13). Lundqvist's analyses of the colonial archives show that the missionary position was "in-between" over time. While ambiguities existed within the missionary organization as a whole, it also presumably existed within inside each missionary. The converts concurrently had a dual identity—while they originated from the Congo, they were also socialized within the culture of the missionaries. Their cultural origin from within Congolese culture made their position as ambivalent as that of the missionaries some of whom found themselves in a dilemma by their modest backgrounds and superiority complex vis-à-vis the natives and the promotion of brotherhood.

The encounter was characterized by cultural reciprocity/hybridization/creolization. There was the amalgamation/hybridization of Christian and indigenous religious beliefs in the Kongo Kingdom. For example, the first meeting in Kibunzi between the missionaries and the native Chiefs was characterized by friendship and co-operation. However, as the missionaries attempted to implant Christianity, this interactive encounter later transformed over time into a missionary offensive and indigenous resistance. The latter encounter at the Diadia missionary station sharply contradicts the earlier encounter with local Chiefs and people in Kibunzi. Although some Chiefs in Diadia were against the missionaries, it was, however, not the entire village. The founding of both mission stations, Lundqvist concedes demonstrates that the missionary encounter concurrently, "include[d] the exchange of gifts, negotiations and displays of kindness—and perhaps even friendship—as well as fear and violence". She further highlights the divergent voices of indigenous people through empirical cases and themes. While colonial archives and records tend to exclude vast amounts of information (Stoler 2002) kept by missionaries, archival materials and printed sources also silence the voices of female Swedish missionaries and indigenous women, though not in the same ways or in equal measure. Drawing on the stories of Congolese converts ("converted native teachers") who were supposed to have been re-shaped by Christianity to expose the nature of these encounters, the stories demonstrate that missionary encounters were not monolithic: They were concurrently characterized by "cultural imperialism, missionary offensive and indigenous resistance, as well as mutual exchange, openness and friendship". These encounters were simultaneously characterized by competition and co-operation. A complex relationship also existed between the missionaries, colonial state and the indigenous population. Common interests and conflicts sometimes existed between the government and missionaries, as well as people and missionaries. Missionaries were paradoxically divided between promoting brotherhood and the imperial agenda.

Doctoral researcher in social anthropology Cristina Sá Valentim analyzes songs among which is the *Mwambwambwa* of the Cokwe to explore the hierarchical nature and simultaneous complexities of the colonial encounter between labourers in Lunda, Angola and a Portuguese mining company, Diamang that was involved in voluntary and forced labour conscriptions. Portuguese colonialists through the aegis of the Dundu Museum recorded the songs. The Portuguese colonial labour regime perceived forced labour as a form of "imperial benevolence" and as inevitable for improving local living conditions. The songs explore the ambiguous and complex dimension as well as the new anxieties raised by the new ambitions and social expectations associated with labour in the mines—particularly the fear of returning from forced labour without goods and money. Such a scenario would trigger several processes of violence among contract workers at the mines. Sá Valentim describes the double bind situation that simultaneously entailed physical, emotional and symbolic violence. Being unable to do the hard work was a sign of shame and an individual could lose his wife to the man who completed the job. Escaping from the harsh labour conditions carried the danger of being caught by the Whiteman and taken back to the mines where the vicious cycle of violence would continue.

The natives used musical expressions (a form of covert resistance strategy) to make their voices heard and to expose ambiguous engagements within the context of the new, modern colonial realities. Sá Valentim goes beyond the surface level realities of forced labour recruitment and examines the construction of colonial identities as embedded within different and concurrent constraints, purposes and agendas. The songs that Sá Valentim analyses highlight the core issues of the affirmation of cultural identity, compliance with the colonial rule, dynamics of gender, power as well as resistance. The native population resisted assimilation through their songs, and in the process preserved their cultural values in the face of modernity. Underlying these colonial complexities is a web of relations among persons entangled in high-level hierarchical and asymmetrical power relationships but who were always scratching a bare existence. Sá Valentim conceptualizes colonialism as a set of performative and social practices made up of contradictory or ambiguous meanings where different agencies, times, and places overlap and intersect. The identities of colonized and colonizer is simultaneously constructed through suffering, anxieties, inquietudes, worries, hopes, expectations, dilemmas, desires, unpredictable situations, engagements and different negotiations. Native agency and the ambiguous as well as hidden transcripts of resistance (Scott, 1990) coexists with the oppression that the colonial process constituted. To unpack and foreground understanding of subtle forms of imposition and the contestation of power, issues of power need to be analyzed beyond the balance between domination and resistance.

Both the colonial state and private enterprises including Diamang appropriated the discourse of the "civilizing mission to justify the coercive and compulsory labour practices meted out on the indigenes". They further used both coercion in labour recruitment and incentives for labourers such as allowing them to stay on longer. Confronted with different knowledge systems articulating both Western and traditional/native rationalities, the colonized and the colonizer developed juggled identities, but at the same time got their identities transformed by the encounter. The colonial encounter produced transformation in the Angolan local knowledge system leading to "a poli-rationality logic that was developed as a mechanism for surviving in the new world".

Drawing on institutional and constructivist theory doctoral researcher in higher education Terry Yong examines the hierarchical relationship between the World Bank and African countries. The former's policy discourses have orchestrated transformations in the African institutional environment that fail to reflect the local level circumstances of African countries. The bank's propagation of a global education policy agenda for growth and development is an act of governmentality on African countries that perpetuate their dependency on the bank and other financial institutions. The bank lumps together the economies of developing African countries into one small economic unit and prescribe a one-size-fit-all development template.

In its relationship with African countries, the World Bank uses a combination of imposition through its mandate and legitimacy, politics, subversion or contestation. This hierarchical relationship involves both imposition and collaboration from African countries who lack the financial wherewithal. Yong suggests that the most appropriate policy measures for the growth and development of a country depend on an understanding of the history and culture of the people in line with their experiences, circumstances, needs and priorities. The reality and knowledge shaping growth and development in most African countries are shaped by the concurrent dominance of Eurocentric and World Bank influence. One example of World Bank dominance that Yong cites is the bank's preference of primary over higher education as well as its promotion of the knowledge for development program (K4D) as measures for guaranteeing growth and development in the region. Policy lending in education—the equivalence of policy imposition on developing African countries is characterized by interaction and collaboration between development donor organizations and developing countries. Education policies are mostly enforced through loan conditionality from the World Bank and the International Monetary Fund (IMF). Terry compares and contrasts the government of Cameroon that accepts and implements borrowed policies without giving due consideration to the functional objectives of such policies and Finland where policies reflect local needs and realities. In Finland and most of the Scandinavia on the contrary, policies are designed from the realities and knowledge distinctive of the history, culture, needs and expectations of the concerned society (constructivist paradigm). Finland increased public support for higher education. Yong argues for the need to match economic growth and development policies to the needs, aspirations and priorities of each country, and not the a-one-size-fit-all paradigm.

Towards Global Histories or the History of Connections?

The disparate works brought together in this collection are in dialogue with each other. They link different and diverse places, bring together co-operating and conflicting agents as well as different temporalities. In a sense, all the different works are attempts meant at avoiding us from silencing others since concepts are used for making political claims. Because of the existence of alternative paths to modernity, we need to abstain from debunking concepts such as modernization. We should rather focus on mid-level or intermediate analytical concepts because of our own multiple locations and identities. The multiple webs of reality and entanglements in the social world call for the adoption of what I designate as rigorous theoretical and methodological encyclopaediasm. Borrowed from the holistic vision of anthropology, this is a shorthand for an overarching framework that is relational, simultaneously integrates multiple spatialities and temporalities as well as multiple and competing voices. These can only be captured through transnational ethnography as Cristina Sá Valentim demonstrates in her study of the the encounter between Portuguese colonialists and native Angolans that took her to the colonial archives in both Lunda and Portugal.

In *Europe and the People without History* (1982), Eric Wolf illuminates the fact that human history like the encounter between the Portuguese and colonized subjects in Northeast Angola, the missionaries and native Hawaiians, Swedish Missionary Society and the native Congolese has always been one of the multiple connections on both macro and micro scales. He provides the historical trajectory of so-called modern globalization and the multiple transformations into which this process eventuated. As William Roseberry rightly comments, Wolf's seminal book is about "history written on a global scale, tracing the connections between communities, regions, peoples and nations that are usually treated as discrete subjects" (Roseberry, 1989: 125). Despite this long-standing interrelatedness, it was the buzzword of globalization that pointed to the increasing interconnections that are mediated by technology. Technology has facilitated space-time compression bringing along with it a bevvy of opportunities and myriad problems about culture, history and identity. The omnipresence of long-standing connections across space and time simultaneously suggests the exclusion of subaltern voices including those of refugees who have had to develop resilience as a coping strategy to make themselves visible in a xenophobic, harsh and unwelcoming environment like post-apartheid South Africa (see Ernest Pineteh's contribution).

By providing a laboratory for the development and subsequent testing of theories of modernization, Africa has been foundational and a key site in the global 'knowledge ecosystem' (Burnett, 2014) and in discussions about modernity. In line with the troublesome principle of equivalence (a form of ethnocentrism) that dominated early studies of Africa, the continent was considered as the antithesis of everything European. Today, modernity scholarship is characterized by a theoretical shift away from studies of Africa based on the global imaginings of the continent as mired in "tradition". African scholars are increasingly preoccupied with the subversion of "dehistoricizing and exoticizing representations by situating Africa as connected to and coeval with the rest of the world" (Thomas, 2011: 732). Like the co-existence of the "modern" and the "traditional" in Africa, the study of modernity becomes only an analytical imperative (Ibid) that recognizes the validity of competing claims and the simultaneous appropriation of different knowledge systems and therefore, alternative modernities. In the same light, interlocutors never reveal all that they know because hierarchical power relationships shape encounters. Reminiscent of colonial entanglements, ethnographic encounters are reminiscent of patronage relationships in which competing claims of knowledge come together but may not always concur (see Burnett, 2014: 1277). Wisdom, Chinua Achebe aptly stated "is like a goat-skin bag; every man carries his own" (Achebe, 1995: 16). This implies that every knowledge is situated thereby imposing the need for a clash of epistemic perspectives and concurrent beliefs and narratives to generate epistemological diversity (multiple voices and accounts). For instance, subaltern groups are increasingly challenging statements about themselves, demonstrating the fragmentary nature as well as the partiality of truth claims. The dynamism of the concept of culture and identity suggests that attempts that fail to capture change simply leads to "simplification and exclusion, the selection of a temporal focus, the construction of a particular self-other relationship, and the imposition or negotiation of a power relationship" (Clifford 1986: 10). The co-production of knowledge is a synergistic process involving the participation of myriad actors from all classes of society, what Burnett (2014) eloquently describes using the all-encompassing metaphor of "an ecology of knowledge". Yuh Terry decries the one-size-fit-all growth and development model that is imposed on African countries by the World Bank and other supra national organisations. He demonstrates that the bank's global development templates including its global education policy agenda fail to reflect local needs. It is, therefore, an act of domination that concurrently exposes the competing knowledge regimes underpinning the transmission of particular market values, knowledge regimes and truth claims. Terry Yong's essay extends postcolonial critique into the domain of policy lending between the World Bank and African countries in the domain of education. The imposition of educational policies on African countries constitutes a form of epistemic violence. They are perceived as backward and requiring recolonization via particular policy blueprints that will civilize them thanks to the benevolence of the World Bank and the international financial system.

Culture remains an interplay of multiple voices showing the concurrent nature of human reality as well as the omnipresence of power. This calls for the rendition of a multiple located account of the social phenomenon. And for the need to constantly negotiate a delicate balance between subjectivity and objectivity to avoid silencing and alienation. This means that to avoid complicity, we should resist any final summation. The task is that of articulating the poly-vocality and multi-subjective nature of culture, clarifying the contextual and contingent nature of culture "truths". This is what James Clifford describes as illuminating the way in which ethnography functions as "a hybrid textual activity" that traverses genres and disciplines (Clifford, 1986: 26, see also Klein, 1992: 18).

Postcolonial scholarship is about "writing against culture" (Nayaran, 1983), challenging normative assumptions, or what might be called the vision of the orientalist 'other' which is alien to 'the West'. The recognition of this long-lasting legacy of European colonialism can lead to the decolonization of our methodological framework and lead us to faithfully capture subaltern voices since the culture of a given society is always what the powerful do. "The recognition of multiple voices and multiple locations will serve a counter-hegemonic function which will, in turn, enhance the emancipation and self-reclamation of subaltern voices and permit us to move beyond "third-worldiest" representations of the "other" (Thomas, 2011). Statism has a long-lasting legacy whereas societies and cultures are in reality dynamic and characterized by contestation of the very concept of culture. Insofar as "culture is dynamic- generalization and abstraction, explanation, description and interpretation, there is no place of overview...from which to map human ways of life" (Clifford, 1986: 12). There is no neutral space from which to talk about other cultures because human life ways tend to contaminate each other: cultural analysis is always enmeshed in global movements of difference and power...a world system now links the planet's societies in a common historical process" (Ibid). Cultures are not bounded spaces. Rather, cultures are permeable, and events in one part of the globe affect other places. Staggering numbers of refugees have flooded the shores of Europe, and barbed-wired fences have not deterred them. The Ebola virus that ravaged West Africa (Liberia, Sierra Leone and Guinea) spread to the West within a very short time-span thanks to space-time compression and the humanitarian ethos. The challenge is for us to capture the impact of extra-local forces because the world has always been one of connections and connectivity, which makes a mockery of the presumed rootedness of peoples and tribes. Even the task of verification is not easy: who should undertake verification, how are truths of cultural accounts to be evaluated when "Ethnography is a hybrid textual activity: [that] traverses genres and disciplines" (Ibid: 26). The pasts of other societies were constrained by normative imaginations from outside, calling for the need to go beyond these normative imaginations to forge futures and potential trajectories because these pasts are dynamic and unconstrained by ahistorical caricatures imposed upon them. The past and present are entangled in ways that defy conventional temporalities (see contributions by Nicklas Hållén, Ernest A. Pineteh, Cristina Sá Valentim, Pia Lundqvist and Catherine E. Hoyser). Pasts and futures, as well as the wider world, remain powerful engines of real cultural, political and economic change. This implies that we should consider our "informants" as co-authors, and ourselves as scribes and archivists as well as interpreting observers. We can ask new, critical questions of all ethnographies. To effectively do this, we need to be cautious of generalizations. If we are examining, for instance, the gendered dimension of a social practice such as female circumcision; we need an intersectional perspective, not just the voices of men or women since culture is contestation and concurrent perspectives are always required to fruitfully understand the cultural whole.

In like manner, "rapid shifts in people, objects and ideas" which is encapsulated by the heuristic notion of multi-locale ethnography for studying "new tribes"- refugees, migrants, displaced and nomadic communities (Gupta and Ferguson, 1997: 4) necessitate the deterritorialization of "locality and space" (Appadurai, 1991: 191) and the need to factor in our analysis multiple locations, temporalities, the intersection of macro and micro, local, regional and global and to take note of the wider politico-economic context as well as to ground lived experiences within its extra-local determinations. Indigenous people like all "new tribes" for instance are multiply located within the countries and regions where they are found as well as in the international system. To faithfully study and represent their views, concerns and the various daily constrains on their lifeworlds; we need a multiscalar perspective that capture the implications of various fields of power on their lives as well as how they are appropriating or subverting these power fields for their own agency.

Cautious and real methodological rigour implies the need to challenge modernization theories and to focus on specificity both in place and in time, while simultaneously factoring in connections, and avoiding statism and dichotomies. European cultures and peoples, as Eric Wolf (1982) ably demonstrates, were never isolated and static entities before the advent of European colonialism and imperialism. The complex, ambiguous and multifaceted encounter between the Swedish Missionary Society and the indigenous population of the Congo Free State and the transformative dynamics of this encounter on each party that eventually led to the formation of a hybrid identity is Pia Lindquist's preoccupation.

She attempts to provide voice and agency to both local women and to the natives whose voices have been erased or muted in missionary accounts of the colonial encounter. Her analysis is about the co-production of identity between the indigenous Congolese people and the missionaries as well as history and entanglement.

In the same light, the rural-urban dichotomy, for instance, is fake: rural people are multiply located, and urban forces affect their lifeworlds thereby bringing them into symbiosis with the urban sphere. Places and peoples have historically never been isolated, but rather entangled in webs of multiple relationships (Wolf, 1982, Pemunta & Bosire). The same is true for nations and implies the need to move beyond "methodological nationalism" (Nayaran, 2013) and to see the world as a world of connections and interactions. History remains important to the process of tracing various multilayered and complex connections. Wolf is right to affirm the universality of history: "Ethnohistory" and 'real history' are intertwined, and the former illuminates the latter (Wolf 1982: 19). Alongside factoring into our analysis multiple spatialities, and avoiding falling into binaries (the contrast between the West and Others), I am in line with Lynn Thomas' view to the effect that social scientists should go for mid-level or intermediate analytical concepts by relating research on issues such as modernity and alternative modernities on "the ideological and institutional formations" that are constitutive of modernity by using such "formations to inspire more intermediate concepts". Such an approach, she maintains, calls for the comparative examination of formations and concepts that countless social theorists including Jean-Jacques Rousseau and Foucault have considered as constitutive elements of modernity. We should also factor into such examinations of formations and concepts, even locations that those theorists considered to be away from the modern. A endosemic perspective does not yield any good results—we have to walk a fine line between an emic and etic (insider/outsider) perspective because we could be both insiders and outsiders at the same time. We have multiple identities and statuses (see Narayan, 2013) which necessitate a high degree of self-reflexivity so that we do not end up silencing our interlocutors.

When I implemented ethnographic fieldwork on female circumcision among the Ejaghams of Southwest Cameroon, I played on various dimensions of my multiple identities as an insider/outsider. I am Cameroonian by nationality but originate from a different region of the country. As a Western educated African anthropologist, I was seen as a "friend of the Whiteman" and therefore an agent of neocolonialism because of my association with a Western institution (Central European University). On the other hand, being a mature male provided me with the latitude to ask both men and women sensitive questions around issues of sexuality to produce a nuanced picture about the institution of female circumcision and various transformations over time. I had to maintain a juggled identity because each aspect of my multiple identity and locations posed its own unique set of problems as well as opportunities (see Pemunta, 2009, Pemunta, 2010). I had to mediate between the biomedicalization of and the cultural context within which female circumcision is practised in the wake of the HIV/AIDS pandemic and the Western moral discourse surrounding the ritual procedures as the abuse of women and young girls. Our preoccupation is to mediate in a rather neutral manner, competing and current positions on issues of identity, culture and heritage and neither to oppress or to connive with oppressors in silencing others. The complexity and multifaceted nature of reality call for theoretical and methodological encyclopaediasm. In a sense, concurrences are about real methodological and theoretical encyclopaediasm.

This collection of articles draws attention to the simultaneity of human action in both space and time—concurrent operations, issues of power and subaltern agency as well as the multiple forms of power and contestations of reality. Power is always fragmentary offering affordances and agency to subaltern groups and social actors. It is about the recovery of subaltern voices, colonial encounters and heterogeneous interactions. The volume pays attention to alternative voices, to subaltern voices to come up with a much more nuanced and complex picture of social reality both in place and in time. It further challenges dichotomies and binaries: "tradition" and "modernity" and accepts the existence of "divergent/alternative modernities", of one thing as encapsulating the other rather than as being contrary to the other. It recognizes the plurality of action in any given situation. It exposes the heterogeneity that characterized colonial encounters, which simultaneously, displayed an amount of contradictory, convergent, complementary, ambiguous or conflicting meanings and narratives. The collection takes an interdisciplinary perspective drawing from the arts, the humanities and the social sciences and myriad sources—including oral history, ethnographic data, songs, colonial archives, textual analysis, discourse analysis, museums, artistic works, exhibitions, and their presentational practice.

Methodologically and theoretically, each of these interdisciplinary articles examines the simultaneity of issues of power, identity, agency between subaltern and dominant groups in society and in space and time. In this collection of essays, the authors articulate the fact among others that: The concurrence of theoretical and methodological perspective is empowering. It factors into analysis both the voice of the voiceless as well as those of the powerful. It is about recovering the voices of the subaltern and presenting a nuanced and balanced perspective of reality. It challenges dominating statements of the past and present by making relevant the Sociology of Absences (Santos 2002). Need to factor in our analysis other contextual voices (narratives, knowledge, cultures), and plurality in the narratives of official history and to go beyond its Eurocentric premises because it is a form of violence and a legacy of the colonial past.

Conclusion

The effects of colonialism and imperialism on encounters in various contact zones across the world often involved hierarchical power relationships. Concurrences research is about deepening our grasp of the conflicting and simultaneous claims concerning culture, history and identity. In line with Mary Loise Pratt, contact zones "are social spaces where cultures meet, clash and grapple with each other, often in contexts of highly asymmetrical relations of power, such as colonialism, slavery, or their aftermaths as they lived out in many parts of the world today" (1991: 34). They are sites for linguistic and cultural encounters, wherein power is negotiated, and struggle occurs. Although this term was first introduced in the context of literacy and literary theories, the term has been appropriated to conversations across the humanities and has been used in the context of feminist theory, critical race theory, postcolonial theory and in discussions of teaching and pedagogy. The contact zone is similar to other concepts that address relation–

ality and contiguity such as positionality, standpoint theory, perspectivism, intersectionality, and relationality (Edelstein, 2005: 14).

In attempting to come up with theoretical perspectives, we realize there are no models from which to draw upon and that it requires an interdisciplinary approach as well as the cross fertilization of ideas (Fur et al. 2014: 1253). Are there any models that can simultaneously capture entangled times, multiple temporalities, diverse voices or juggled identities within a given culture? We need to address relationality and contiguity using mid-level and "travelling concepts" (see Bachmann-Medick 2014: 130–131) that can also be used for explaining and "communicat[ing] multimodal and multivocal forms of concurrences without trivializing the contested power relations that influence who is heard, where and in what way" (Fur et al. 2014: 1253). This speaks to the inadequacy of methodological and theoretical nationalism and the relevance of "travelling concepts" (see Bachmann-Medick 2014: 130–131).

Colonialism affected and continues to affect different places, connect different times and remains omnipresent (spans the past, present and future as coeval). It also involves multiple disciplines showing that colonialism affected different settings to which it bestowed its legacy. The chapters in this collection grapple with diverse and multifaceted processes and depict the inadequacy of binary terms or easily delineated categories for interpreting diverse, contradictory and paradoxical encounters (Ibid). As a result, they present different, interdisciplinary, conceptual and methodological approaches showing the value of "travelling concepts" for studying cultural encounters shaped by colonialism and imperialism in different places and times. Different temporalities are coeval; encounters are dynamic and concomitantly characterized by elements of collaboration and co-operation but also conflict and disagreement. They demonstrate multiple interpretations of various encounters and of colonial systems of interaction that are open to multiple interpretations.

The works brought together in this collection highlight the need for rethinking the concurrent spatio-temporal relations among local, global, and universal ideas and practices, that to do justice to different ways of knowing that have previously been obscured "by narrowly conceived conceptions of a Eurocentrically-based universal" we should see concepts as travelling and as infused with different meanings in place and over time (Fur 2014: 1256, Nicholas, 1994, Spivak, 1998). Such a recognition is illustrative of the multifacetedness, "versatility and resilience of the concept of concurrences for enabling new readings of cultural production within and beyond the binding structures of discursive, geopolitical, and historical power structures" (Fur 2014: 1256) and the necessity to revise history (Fur et al. 2017). The concept of concurrences opens up endless possibilities for intellectual collaboration.

References

Achebe, Chinua. 1995. *Things Fall Apart*. Knopf Doubleday Publishing Group.

Andersson, Burnett L. 2014. "An Eighteenth-Century Ecology of Knowledge", *Culture Unbound*, Vol. 6: 1275–1297.

Arthur, John A. 2010. *African diaspora identities: negotiating culture in transnational migration*. New York: Lexington Books.

Ashcroft, Bill. 1998. *Key concepts in post-colonial studies*. London: Routledge.

Clifford, James. 1986. Introduction: Partial Truths. In: Clifford, James and Marcus, George, E. (Eds). *Writing Culture. The Poetics and Politics of Ethnography*. Pp. 1–26. Berkeley: University of California Press.

Donna McCormack. 2014. *Queer Postcolonial Narratives and the Ethics of Witnessing*. Blomberg: Blomberg Academic.

Edelstein, Marilyn. 2005. "Multiculturalisms Past, Present, and Future". *College English*. 68 (1): 14–41.

Foucault, Michel. 1979. Discipline and Punish The Birth of the Prison. New York: Vintage.

Fur, Gunlög; Diana Brydon; & Peter Forsberg. "Culture Bound and Unbound: Concurrent Voices and Claims in Postcolonial Places" *Culture Unbound* 6: 7 2014: 1253–1257.

Fur, Gunlög; Brydon; Diana & Forsberg, Peter. 2017. Concurrent Imaginaries, Postcolonial Worlds. Amsterdam: Brill/Rodopi.

Geertz, Clifford. 1973. Thick Description: Toward an Interpretive Theory of Culture. In *The Interpretation of Cultures*. Pp. 3–30. New York: Basic Books.

Gilroy, Paul. 1993. *The Black Atlantic: Modernity and Double Consciousness*. London: Verso.

Goebel, Walter and Schabio, Saskia. (2013). *Locating Postcolonial Narrative Genres (Routledge Research in Postcolonial Literatures)* 1st Edition.

Hartman, Saidiya. 2007. *Lose Your Mother: A Journey Along the Atlantic Slave Route*. New York: Farrar, Straus and Giroux.

Hautaniemi, Petri. 2006. Fugitive memories. Howyounf Somali men recall displacement and emplacement in their childhood. *Anthropological Yearbook of European Cultures* 15: 77–91.

Klein, Thompson, J. 1992. "Text/Context: The Rhetoric of the Social Science", Richard Brown (ed). *Writing the Social Text: Poetics and Politics in Social Science Discourse*. New York: Walter de Gruyter, Inc.

Mbembe, Achille. 2001. *On the Postcolony*. Berkely: University of California Press.

Narayan, Kirin. 2013. "How Native Is a Native Anthropologist?" pp. 23–41, In Lamphere, Louise and Ragoné, Helena. (Eds.). *Situated Lives: Culture in Everyday Life*. London: Routledge.

Peirce, Charles. S., 1982, The Writings of Charles S. Peirce: A Chronological Edition, volume 1, edited by the Peirce Edition Project, Bloomington, IN, Indiana University Press.

Pemunta, Ngambouk V. 2010. Intersubjectivity and Power in Ethnographic Research. *Qualitative Research Journal*. Vol. 10 (2): 38–54.

Pemunta, Ngambouk V. 2009. Multiple Identities: Gender, Power and the Production of Anthropological knowledge. *Anthropology Matters*. Spring, Vol. 11 (1) http://www.anthropologymatters.com/journal/2009-1/index.html

Pemunta, Ngambouk V & Obara, Bosire, T. 2012. Rethinking the urban-rural concept in the social sciences. *Aston Journal of Arts and Social Sciences*. Available http://www.omicsonline.com/open-access/toward-a-reconceptualization-of-the-urban-and-rural-as-conceptual-and-analytical-categories-in-the-social-sciences-2151-6200.1000035.pdf

Pratt, Louis M.1991. *Imperial Eyes, Travel Writing and Transculturation*. London.

Thomas, Lynn M. 2011. AHR Roundtable: Historians and the Question of "Modernity" Modernity's Failings, Political Claims, and Intermediate Concepts. *American Historical Review*, Vol. 116 (3): 727–740. doi:10.1086/ahr.116.3.727.

Rose, Gillian. 2012. *Visual Methodologies*. London: SAGE.

Roseberry, William. 1989. "European History and the Construction of Anthropological Subjects" in Anthropologies and Histories: essay in culture, history and political economy. New Brunswick, NJ: Rutgers University Press.

Said, Edward W. 1993. *Orientalism*. Stockholm: Ordfront.

Santos, Boaventura de Sousa. 2002. "Para uma sociologia das ausências e uma sociologia das emergências", *Revista Crítica de Ciências Sociais*, 63 outubro: 237–280.

Scott, James C. 1990. *Domination and the Arts of Resistance: Hidden Transcripts*. Yale: Yale University Press.

Stoler, Ann Laura. 2009. *Along the Archival Grain: Epistemic Anxieties and Colonial Common Sense*. Princeton: Princeton University Press.

Stoler, Ann. 2002. "Colonial Archives and the Arts of Governance", *Archival Science* 2: 87–109.

Vansina, Jan. 2010. *Being Colonized. The Kuba Experience in Rural Congo, 1880–1960*. Wisconsin: The University of Wisconsin Press.

Wolf, Eric. 1982. *Europe and the People without History*. California: University of California Press.

Concurrent Subjectivities and Coevalness in Saidiya Hartman's *Lose Your Mother*[1]

Nicklas Hållén
Centre for Concurrences in Colonial
and Postcolonial Studies,
Linnaeus University, Växjö, Sweden

This chapter is the result of an attempt to think about coevalness through the concept of concurrences. Coevalness is an implicit element in the concept of concurrences, a theoretical and methodological concept outlined and developed by historian and indigenous studies scholar Gunlög Fur and members of the research centre Concurrences in Colonial and Postcolonial Studies. The concept of concurrences refers to contexts where "multiple and concurring claims of reality, experience and meaning" come into contact with each other (Fur et al 1253). For two events to be concurrent, they must exist in the same moment, at a distance from each other or in the same geographical space. Furthermore, for it to be meaningful to speak of concurrent reality claims and experiences, these must arguably be comparable on a discursive level. It would make little sense to talk of concurrent views if there is not at least some minimal correspondence and translatability between them.

The element of translatability and comparability is a key difference between concurrences, as the members of the Concurrences centre use the term, and the concept of coevalness as first theorised by Johannes Fabian and developed by later generations of scholars in postcolonial studies. Whereas Fabian and other have demonstrated and studied how the "denial of coevalness" has been used as a strategy of colonial discursive dominance, the concept of

---

[1] This article was written as part of a project funded by the Swedish Research Council (proj. 2012–6712).

concurrences assumes a methodological perspective that takes into account the epistemological position of those who the hegemonic discourse deny coevalness.

In this chapter I will explore the concepts of coevalness and concurrences as products of a creative process, of aesthetically explorative travel writing, by reading Saidiya Hartman's book about her travels in Ghana, *Lose Your Mother* (2007). A professor of African American literature and history, Hartman travels to Ghana as a Fulbright scholar to study and write about the history of the slave trade, and how one could approach this past ethically and politically in a present marked by racism and exclusion. The over-arching problem that Hartman sets out to negotiate, if not solve, is the fact that the strategies employed by diasporic travellers to narrow the gap between the present and the past are at best inadequate and at worst problematic. She explores the entangled problems involved in attempting to stage an encounter between the self and a past that keeps shaping the present, but always remains distant and unreachable. In this explorative project, she uses the travelogue as literary form, with its dynamic of introspection and description, to unpack and rethink the problem of time in diaspora literature and thought. She discusses the possibilities and impossibilities inscribed in what Yogita Goyal has described as the "axiom that racial injustice in the present can only be understood by recovering the slave past" (ix). Thus the implicit question at the heart of the text is how one can approach a past that has been severed from the present not by the normal passing of time, but by the rupture of the Middle passage and forced amnesia under slavery. Hartman in other words seeks to reverse the mechanics of the anthropological discourse that places its referents, or Other, "in a Time other than that of the producer" of this discourse (Fabian 31).

In literature about the African diaspora in the West, the slave trade and its violence on a people's sense of rootedness and belonging in the world typically figures as an event that brings about a "the shattering of genealogical temporality" (Samuelsen 38). This shattering of histories of generations following generations is what defines what Goyal and others have referred to as diaspora time, a temporality and history that is "discontinuous and fractured" and "shot through with the memory of the Middle Passage" (Goyal x). It contrasts to nation time, which is exclusionary and only accessible to those who have a privileged and largely uncontested position within the narrative of the Western nation. If "diaspora time emphasizes ... breaks and continuities," nation time "links past, present and future in a march toward progress" (x). Because of ruptures and shifts, the temporal structure that Hartman describes shape it and the way it shapes the subject may seem to have much in common with what Achille Mbembe refers to as the "time of entanglement" that characterises the postcolony, with its "pattern of ebbs and flows" and "sharp breaks" (16). However, while Mbembe describes a sometimes chaotic entanglement of temporal flows and histories that shape the immensely complex and multifaceted "field where individuals' existence unfolds in practice," diaspora time or what Hartman refers to as the time of slavery is comparatively structured. It is created by one monumental and disastrous event—the middle passage—which constitutes an irreversible "passing from one stage (before) and another (after)," while the temporal entanglement of the postcolony involves reversals of linear time, according to Mbembe (Mbembe 15, 16).

However, diaspora time is also characterised by "various kinds of imagined or projected simultaneities" and this imagination is at the heart of Hartman's book (Goyal x). Though Hartman does not offer any simple answers to the questions she asks, there is a dialectic relation between the content and form of her book that can be read as part of an answer. She acknowledges the insufficiency of archival research in attempts to bridge the divide between the present and the pre-slavery past and instead brings "personal narrative into scholarship" in order to use the "affective dynamics of cultural memory" to imagine an encounter with a pre-slavery subjectivity (Cvetkovich 132). She explores her own reactions and feelings when visiting the Elmina slave castle, and when talking to Ghanaians and fellow African Americans in Ghana, in order to think about how the past can and cannot be made accessible, coeval and concurrent, through affect and imagination. Ann Cvetkovic writes in an article about Hartman's book, which Cvetkovic reads as a form of academic research text, that Hartman's quest for understanding "leads her out of the archive ... to the material landscape of Africa", but also back to the archive again "to explain what she has seen and felt" (140). In other words, Hartman establishes a circular relationship between the archive, Ghana and its material and immaterial memories of the slave trade, and her inner, emotional landscape. However, Hartman's "unusual methods of research and writing risk the seemingly incommensurate connections between one's own feelings and public histories and between despair and hope in order to both remember the dead and provide a way forward" (143). What she is really searching for in Ghana, thus, is a method of writing that can imagine a future that is not burdened by the weight of history.

Hartman's book includes a fictional narrative about a group of refugees fleeing slave raiders, in which a distant, otherwise unreachable past is imagined. These passages afford another way out of the cycle of archival work and emotional, often pessimistic responses to that work. They are the result not (only) of Hartman's research, introspection and travels, but of a creative and imaginative process that does not recreate the past as the past as much as it creates a form of coevalness by imagining a past that unfolds in the present. At the same time, the focus of the implicit questions that Hartman asks change from what a historian can do to recover and reinterpret the past to what the creative writer can do to imagine a new future. The passages about the refugees erase the difference that divide pre-slavery subjectivity and Hartman as the narrating voice of the text by portraying the group of refugees as, at the same time, the ancestors of contemporary Ghanaian, as American pilgrims and as diasporic subjects who have been freed from the corrosive effects of the history of slavery. As will be shown below, in these passages the past and present merge and become coeval and concurrent, since they achieve a kind of encounter between the two subjectivities. It is however an encounter that is marked by its fictitiousness, because in this textual moment more than one past and one present intersect.

I. Travel and the distance of the past

In the works by famous black Western travellers before Hartman, like Richard Wright, Maya Angelou and Caryl Phillips, there is typically a sudden or gradual realisation that Ghana as a symbolical place and the material traces of the slave trade will neither allow the traveller to redefine his or her identity, nor trigger a radical inner transformation. Hartman, however, travelling to Ghana decades after Wright and Angelou, is already aware of these facts when she arrives. She writes that as a young adult, she projected onto Ghana her hopes for a future in which it would be possible to identify with an African heritage without at the same time being weighed down by the history of the slave trade, of loss, cruelty and oppression: "I had dreamed about living in Ghana since I was in college. I had imagined a world less racist than the one from which I came. I had longed for a country in which my inheritance would amount to more than dispossession and in which I would no longer be a problem" (57). The point of departure in the book, however, is a feeling that has emerged since then, that "no matter how far from home I traveled, I would never be able to leave my past behind. I would never be able to imagine being the kind of person who had not been made and marked by slavery" (40). She writes that there is nothing to discover in Ghana that will make her feel like she belongs there and that she knows in her heart that her "losses were irreparable" (54). Her rejection of the possibility of a "return" to Ghana, as "a symbolical racial homeland" has led some of her critics to read *Lose your Mother* as a fundamentally pessimistic text (Wood 7).

Hartman cannot see her arrival in Ghana as a homecoming, since she cannot ignore the distance that her Otherness there puts between her and the people around her. This distance is not too different from the difference she feels exists between her and white America. In Ghana she is an *obruni*, she writes on the very first page—a "stranger. A foreigner from across the sea" (3). Hurled at her by a group of children when she steps off the bus in Cape Coast, the word immediately forces her to "acknowledge that [she does not] belong anywhere" (3). This sets the tone of the rest of the book: Hartman portrays herself as a "wandering seed bereft of the possibility of taking root" (4). Referencing James Baldwin's essay by the same name, she refers to herself as "a stranger in the village" (4). This village happens to be in Africa rather than high up in the Swiss alps, where Baldwin had occasion to meditate on what it is like to be the only black person for miles around. When she observes that in Ghana, her "black face" does not make her "kin", it is not primarily to underscore the dehumanising effects of racial compartmentalisation, but to state the fact that hers is not a narrative of a wayward daughter's return to the homeland. It is a search for a method of renegotiating the relations between past and present, history and identity.

Hartman portrays herself as a member of a generation of travellers who unlike the travellers of an earlier generation, who went to Africa to reclaim a lost homeland, inspired by Alex Haley's novel *Roots*, is there on the "quixotic mission" to "find the remnants of those who [have] vanished" (17). *Lose your Mother* has been described as an example of "footsteps" travel writing, since she "positions her own [journey] as an implicit reworking, repetition" and refraction of an "earlier, more horrific, [journey]" (Nayar 82, 84). However, Hartman signals that she is there to explore and make sense of a personal sense of loss. In an article published before *Lose Your Mother*, she explains that to the extent that black American travellers identify with Africa, it is an identification that is always already preceded by a break between the present and the past, since it is through the Middle Passage and slavery that Africa becomes a symbolical, lost homeland (2002: 764).

> The journey 'home' is always a journey back, that is, back in time, since the identification with Africa as an originary site occurs by way of experience of enslavement. And, above all else, it is a belated return. One has come too late to recuperate an authentic identity or to establish one's kinship with a place or people. Ultimately these encounters or journeys occur too late, far too long after the event, to be considered a return. (2002: 762)

Coevalness, according to Hartman, cannot be achieved through the narrative of returning home, because the symbolical home will always remain attached to a past in which the black diasporic subject, as such, did not yet exist. This subject is born on the forced journey from the homeland to the Americas. The journey back in time is a journey back in the time of slavery. This regression is in other words not the same kind of backwards time travel that is common in colonial literature, where travellers from the West find themselves going back to what is perceived as a "prehistoric" point in time when they travel through Africa (Conrad 43). This colonial temporal model, after all, consists of a shared, temporal line where Africa and the west are separated only in terms of the points to which they have progressed. In Ghana, as will be further discussed below, Hartman realises that she is stuck in the time of slavery, whereas the African is not. Therefore, it is "in the routes of the slaves rather than in the communities and families in Ghana that she would, she believes, find her own identity", as Pramod Nayar has pointed out (84).

Because of the complexity involved in the relations between past and present, Africa and the black Western subject, Hartman avoids using concepts that are based on a certain theoretical view of these relations, such as *African-American* and *diaspora*. Another reason for their relative scarcity in the text is the fact that many of her African colleagues do not use such concepts or use them to signal distance and difference rather than closeness and sameness. When she travels with a group of African scholars she has trouble feeling that she is part of the group. One member of the group insists on calling her his "friend from the diaspora," she writes, while he refers to the rest of the members of the group as his brothers and sisters. She feels that "diaspora was really just a euphemism for stranger," since for the most part none of my colleagues, with the exceptions of Prof and Hannington, gave much thought to the way their history was enmeshed with mine, nor did they entertain the idea that the Africa in my hyphenated African-American identity had anything to do with their Africa" (215). The way in which this attitude undermines the logic of these concepts in the text creates a rupture between the past and Hartman's present. It reverses the work that the concept of diaspora performs, according to Paul Gilroy, who describes it as an "eruption of space into the linear temporal order of modern black politics which enforces the obligation that space and time must be considered relationally in their interarticulation with racialised being" (198). To Gilroy, the concept and its impact on the lived experience of the diaspora create connections between "past and present, living and dead, traditional and modern" (197). To Hartman, in contrast, the concept drives a wedge between the past and the present, and between the black African and the black American, and racial solidarity is not enough to mend the resulting fractures.

Since a true return is not possible in Hartman's eyes, she discusses the implications of the impossibility of coming home and to feel a real connection to the people who were captured and shipped across the sea. For her, the "rupture was the story. Whatever bridges I might build were as much the reminder of my separation as my connection. The holding cell had supplanted the ancestral village. The slave loomed larger for me than any memory of a glorious African past or sense of belonging in the present" (2007: 42). "The slave" in other words, does not exist entirely in the past, but is an absence in the present. The slave exists in what Hartman refers as "the time of slavery," which "negates the common-sense intuition of time as continuity or progression, then and now coexist; we are coeval with the dead" (2002: 759). The absent slave coexists with the living, because as Hartman writes, "I, too, live in the time of slavery, by which I mean I am living in the future created by it" (2007: 133). This future is defined by "the relation between the past and present, the horizon of loss, the extant legacy of slavery, the antinomies of redemption (a salvational principle that will help us overcome the injury of slavery and the long history of defeat) and irreparability" (2002: 759). Coeval with the living, the slave shapes the present and how it is conceived. Hartman's present is therefore a "future that [has] been created by men and women in chains, by human commodities, by chattel persons" (233).

The time of slavery does not make the slave's world concurrent with that of the American who travels to Ghana to search for those who are gone, because the coevalness of Hartman and the slave does not automatically bring the two together so that there can be some kind reciprocity between them. This is not because they exist in two different times, but because they are separated by the forces of history. Hartman therefore deploys a host of images and words related to the physical proximity of bodies to represent her longing for the slave. When she visits the slave castles along the Ghanaian coast, one of which is depicted on the cover of the book, the slave is nowhere to be found. She has come to the castle to "reach through time and touch the prisoners" (119), but the only thing left of the absent slave is the "filth" that covers the floor of the dungeon where the slaves were held before they were shipped off to the Americas (115). She explains that the human waste that covered the floor when the last captives had been taken to the last slave ships to depart from the coast was not removed, but simply covered by sand and lime to make the stench bearable. When archaeologists excavated the dungeon in 1972, they found layers of compressed "feces, blood and exfoliated skin" and these base matters are now all that remains that she can "put [her] hands on" (115). The dungeon, lined with "layers of skin and shit," Cvetkovic writes in her article about Hartman's book, ultimately embodies a "missed encounter since rather than a sense of connection with the slaves who inhabited the space, she feels only a sense of loss" (139). Pramod Nayar points out that this sense of loss takes the form of physical sensations in Hartman's text. She "somatises" the past, he argues, by describing how her visit affects her body (91). She describes how the sight of the dungeons makes her lightheaded, how her skin feels prickly and she begins to sweat (118). Nayar reads Hartman's physical discomfort as something that amounts to "a materiality of memory" that records "the memories of a suffering from long ago" in the "present body" (91). This physical discomfort contrasts to the impossibility of feeling spatially close to the slave. Hartman revisits the slave castle in search of something more than compacted organic matter, from which she "recoils," but finds nothing tangible that can ease her mind and bring her closer to the slave: "Each time it was the same. I failed to discover anything. No revenants lurked in the dungeon. The hold was stark. No hands embraced mine" (118). As imposing as the slave castle is as a physical manifestation of the pain of the past, as overwhelming is the sense of loss and absence to the traveller who has come there to seek those who are gone.

Hartman keeps coming back to the relation between different forms of absence and presence throughout the text. In the tourist guide for Cape Coast castle, a stone's throw from the Elmina castle, she sees a picture in which local school children sit in the cells, chained to the walls. It triggers a flood of questions about how the children understand the history that they are made to reenact. She asks herself what their relation is to the people they represent, in this failed "effort to invoke the dead" (135). It is a failure, Hartman concludes, because the photo can "only express the loss, not repair it" (135). The "proxies and surrogates" in the photo do not "mend the wound or bridge the distance between the living and dead" (135). Rather than an image of the slave, the picture represents the absence of the slave. Likewise, the materiality of the slave fort is of no help in the traveller's search for closeness to the people who were once interred there and shipped off across the sea. It instead attains the form of an ironic symbol of the absence and emptiness that accompanies the metaphor of touch and physical contact in Hartman's text. The castle is "picturesque in a way that made you cringe" and makes Hartman aware that it is "easy to forget the slaves crushed under the weight of all that monumentality" (69). In the slave dungeons, Hartman lets her hands glide "over the walls, as though the rough surfaces were a script that [she can] read through [her] dull fingers" (119). The monumentality of the fort, the robustness of its walls and the absence and invisibility of the bodies that were shackled and mutilated there combine into a symbol of the time of slavery, in which the past unremittingly creates a present in which the living is burdened by loss.

The title of Hartman's book includes another metaphor for loss that is central in the book. To lose one's mother, Hartman explains, is to "forget your past" and to "lose your kin, county and identity" (85). She points out that "the most universal definition of the slave is a stranger" (5), an observation that Nayar sees as the starting point of "a re-reading of the entire archive of slavery as a history of making-foreigners" (93). At the heart of Hartman's understanding of the slave trade is the complicity of those Africans who sold their neighbours into slavery and made them strangers to themselves and to their homelands. It is with this forced estrangement that the time of slavery begins. However, Hartman also discusses the fact that the metaphor of the motherless child was prevalent in the vocabulary of slavery in West Africa during and after the slave trade. In order to protect their children from being taken away by death, mothers referred to their offspring as slaves, *odonkor*, and by so doing signaled to death that the child was not only chained to their parents and to life, but also that their lives were not worth taking, Hartman explains (86). In the literal sense, the word was used for someone who was "bought and sold at the market, a commodity" (86). However, the semantic components of *odonkor* are "love" and "don't go," Hartman continues: "Odo nti nka: because of my love to you, don't go" (87). Thus the language of love and kinship and that of domination and ownership of property are intertwined in the discursive history of the slave trade. It is a language of relationships in which the temporal and spatial concepts of coevalness and closeness are central. They are central because the relationship is threatened by the slave's and child's departure and estrangement from their people.

Hartman explains that this language of time, space and death and the dialectics of presence/absence and life/death also surrounded narratives of slave revolts in the Caribbean. She discusses the slave revolt at St. John in 1733 and explains that the slaves that led it had been powerful and rich before they were enslaved. Some formerly powerful men and women had starved themselves to death and refused to work for their masters. Others rebelled, killed their masters and sacked a fort, after which they waged a guerilla war for six months before they were attacked by French soldiers from Martinique (91–95). One group of rebels took to the woods, pursued by the soldiers, where they committed suicide in order to avoid having to surrender, vowing that "when I die, I shall return to my homeland" (95). Hartman points out Hanna Arendt's observation that it was not before the French revolution in 1789 that the concept of revolution lost its connotations to a backwards revolting motion, a reversal of the progression of history (91). Predating the French revolution by half a century, the slave revolt at St John was a way to return to a time before they were enslaved and when they themselves were slave owners, Hartman argues. The place the slaves longed for, she writes, "promised first and foremost a radical break with the present" (96). By committing mass suicide, they acknowledged that their present had nothing to offer them and that "the past was the only country left, the only horizon visible, the only world inhabitable" (95). The rebels, like the "odonkor"-child and Hartman herself, are returnees, she writes, "circling back to times past, revisiting the routes that might have led to alternative presents" (100). The return the rebels and Hartman dream of is impossible, however, and as an idea it has as much to do with the world "in which you have yet to make a home" than it has to do with "the world to which you no longer belong" (100). To Hartman, therefore, the tragedy is not so much the insurmountable obstacles to returning home, but that the loss of belief in the idea of a return to the past entails another loss. She ends the chapter about the return and the slave revolt thus:

> *I shall return to my native land.* Those disbelieving in the promise and refusing to make the pledge have no choice but to avow the loss that inaugurates one's existence. It is to be bound to other promises. It is to lose your mother, always. (100)

To ultimately not believe that there is a way to reach across history to the people whose uprooting created the ruptures of diasporic time is to become tethered to a present shaped by the past. Stuck in the present, one experiences the loss of the past over and over again, since this experience of loss is the present that history has created. In her article about the time of slavery, Hartman writes that "loss affixes our gaze to the past, determines the present, and perhaps even eclipses a vision of the future" (2002: 759). The way out of this circle of loss is either death, as the rebels realized, or to go forward and to try to imagine a future that is no longer shaped by the moment in which one lost one's mother.

The purpose of Hartman's journey and of her writing is to try to "envision a future in which this past [has] ended" (233). She admits that this endeavor "most often" fails, but it is nevertheless the act of envisioning a future that like the past is severed from the present that is the only viable way forward. Though Hartman sees little value in the tourist economy that surrounds the slave castles or the absence and loss that the castles represent, she sees in diasporic travellers' engagement with the material remains of the slave trade a secondary, perhaps unexpected value, because "essentially, these belated encounters illuminate the disparate temporalities of unfreedom" (2002: 763). If they do not bring the traveller closer to the departed, then at least "the encounter with the seemingly remote anteriority of the past—slavery and the transatlantic slave trade—provides a vehicle for articulating the disfigured promises of the present, that is, equality, freedom from discrimination, the abolition of the badges of slavery, and so on" (2002: 763). The castles and travellers' staged returns in other words do not so much embody the ungraspable tragedy of the slave trade as they are reminders of the fact that the present is continually shaped by the past. The very fact that it is not possible to return, or to "encounter" Ghana "in its contemporaneity" creates the diaspora, which consists of those to whom the homeland is "always already lost" (2002: 763). The traveller who visits Elmina and Cape Coast castle, thus, engages with the injustice of the present and embraces the time of slavery, which they share with the absent and dead.

II. Writing the slave into presence

Hartman refers to the photograph of the school children posing as slaves in the Cape Coast guide pamphlet as a "fiction of love" that permits the viewer "to believe that we could coexist with the captives, witness their suffering, and remedy their defacement" (135). Her attempt "to remedy the slave's oblivion" is ultimately unsuccessful and makes her feel that "missing the dead was as close to them as I would come" (135). However, in the chapters about her visits to the slave castles and the emotions triggered by the presences and absences she senses there, Hartman's text begins to become less analytical. Her writing relies less and less on the careful handling of archival sources, on dates and historical records, and a different kind of writing begins to enter the text. Being unable to reach through to the slave, "Hartman's only source of hope in this text is to explore the psychological landscape of the imagination: an interior, atemporal terrain as yet unscarred and unfettered by forces of enslavement," as Celeste-Marie Bernier writes in a comment on Hartman's book (4). The methodological questions that the text seems to try to answer—how can the archive of written sources, records and material culture be used to mend and bridge the ruptures and fissures of diasporic time?—are replaced by an aesthetic exploration of fiction and imagination.

This shift is gradual, however. Hartman uses fictional techniques to fill out the gaps and silences in the archival material she refers to and studies. Discussing the establishment of the Elmina castle in the late 1400s, she imagines the historical meeting between Portuguese nobleman Diego de Azambuja and King Caramansa (Kwamin Ansah) on the beach where the castle now stands. The passages about Azambuja and Ansah are dense with historical detail. The reader learns how big the numbers of Portuguese soldiers and sailors were, and what the nobleman and king said to each other, according to archival sources. When these sources are vague on the method by which the former convinced the latter to let him build a storehouse on the coast, however, Hartman writes that whether it was by "threats or a flurry of sweet words is anyone's guess" (62). She neatly lists her sources in the book's endnotes, but recreates this moment as a narrative, in which she imagines Azambuja surveying the coast from the deck of his ship, looking for a strategic spot to claim for his king. Hartman imagines that he must have "cut a striking figure" when he stood on the beach, clothed as he was "in a jerkin of silk brocade with a golden collar of precious stones" that he had put on to impress Ansah who met him there (61).

Hartman does not only employ narrative to present historical facts and figures and make forgotten fates vivid to the reader, but also mobilises other forms of aesthetic and rhetorical techniques to explore the ironies of the semiotics of the slave trade. She describes how the Portuguese bestowed the storehouse that Azambuja had built on the beach in Elmina to their country's patron saint Sao Jorge, or Saint George. Perhaps more than other saints, he embodied the fortitude of the servant of Christ, because unlike other saints who were tortured in the hands of barbaric non-believers, he was tortured in a myriad of ways and died countless times according to apocryphal accounts (67). He died in Palestine. He was tortured in Persia. He was tortured for seven years in "Nubia," died and was resurrected three times, just to be killed again. Hartman lists the horrible plights that Saint George had to suffer all over the world and the ways in which he died, and then offers a reinterpretation of the saint, whose battle against the dragon offered early European slave traders a metaphor for their own war on those they saw as members of "monstrous races" (65).

Hartman suddenly reinterprets the image of the saint. She asks if Saint George provided "an emblem for the suffering of slaves or a vision of life resurrected," and proceeds to evoke the many deaths that Saint George, as a slave, dies around the Atlantic world. In this gruesome passage, that which Saint George's tormentors are unable or unwilling to see is not his holiness and closeness to God, but his humanness.

> In Georgia he was covered with sugar and buried in an anthill. In Curaçao, his face was scorched and his head cut off and placed on a pole for the amusement of the vultures. In Surinam, they cut off his hands and crushed his head with a sledgehammer. In Trinidad, he was dismembered and his body parts were thrown into the Atlantic. (66–67)

In Christian hagiography Saint George restores order by slaying the dragon, the symbol of disorder and barbarism. However, it is not before he dies at the hands of his tormentors that he becomes a saint. By being tortured and murdered by his enemies and the enemies of God he becomes *victor quia victim,* victor because victim (Morabito 151). In *Lose Your Mother,* as in the original story of Saint George, his martyrdom is an image of the barbarism of his tormentors. However, by taking the place of those who suffered and died under slavery Hartman's Saint George does not give the tormented a final victory. He is caught in the endless time of slavery in which the pain lingers.

In the passage about Saint George, Hartman creates a powerful image that restores the slave's disavowed humanity and also reverses the erasure of the slave. In other parts of the book, Hartman deploys techniques that are closer to fiction than the passage in which she transforms the symbolism of the Christian martyr: she begins a chapter in which she describes her visit in Salaga not by describing the place as it looks to her when she arrives but by describing what a traveller might have seen there some hundred years before. The first short section in the chapter explains that the town is a place that the southern Ghanaians Hartman has talked to describe as inhabited by savage people and that it was once the first stop on many slaves' forced journey to and across the sea. In the beginning of the second section, the style changes with every sentence. "Seven roads radiated from the hub of Salaga," Hartman informs the reader (179). "Had you been travelling along this road in the eighteenth or nineteenth century," she speculates, "no doubt you would have seen a band of strangers, whose chains were the clear sign that they would never pass this way again, heading toward the market." The next sentences read as fiction: "A fleeting horseman with a young girl tied across the back of his steed reminded everyone they passed that life was at the mercy of men with guns and horses—*kambonga*. The hefty bags of cowries saddling the pack animals of mercenary soldiers sauntering home at dusk were the only remnants of the hamlet upon which they had descended, the houses they had burned, the men they had slaughtered, and the women and children they had sold at the market" (179–180). Hartman lists plenty of sources that she bases her description of historical Salaga on. However, Hartman invites the reader to imagine seeing what she describes first hand, as a moment that unfolds in the present. In other words, the phrase "had you been travelling" invites Hartman's readers to "project themselves" into a fictional world "by playing games of make-believe with themselves" and the following sentences "as props" (Lamarque 41).

Hartman's invitation to the reader to imagine and participate in the "game" of fiction continues later in the book, when she interlaces the travel narrative with a fiction narrative that is not directly based on historical sources. In this narrative, informed by the stories imprinted on the landscape she travels through, she imagines a past and a story of a people who escapes slavery and therefore never fully enters the time of slavery. "The desolate landscape and the great plain of uninhabited territory told the story of rout and pillage," she writes, "and also the story of the people who ran for safety" (219). However, like the slave castles on the coast, the landscape at the same time tells a story of violence and, paradoxically, serves as a reminder of the futility of searching for those who were killed or sent across the sea. Hartman writes that "it is said that when you spot a cluster of baobab trees it's the sign that a village once existed in that spot" (219). On her journey through northern Ghana, she at one time counts more than a dozen such clusters, which preserve "the memory of the stateless" — "an archive of the defeated" (219). The villages that once stood here were sacked and burned by their neighbours and by European slavers, and their inhabitants either killed or marched to the European castles at the coast. Hartman writes that the architecture of the West African village changed as a response to the frequent raids. Even today, a traveller can see the crumbling walls that once surrounded the dwellings of people under constant threat of being captured by slave raiders.

Thinking about the will of the people who erected these walls to stay free, Hartman imagines a group of people travelling inland, over the plain, in search for a new home. This group of refugees enters the text in a section that begins thus: "on foot they had fled from the slave raiders and traders from Asante, Gonja, Dagomba, and Mossi. The fugitives traveled for weeks not knowing where they were headed or what they'd find or how far away was safe" (222). She imagines that while wandering across the plain "they dreamed of farms and watching their children grow up rather than disappear, they dreamed of toiling for themselves, and they dreamed of a place without royals and where they would never again hear the words 'barbarian,' 'savage,' or 'slave'" (223). When she writes this group of pregnant mothers, worrying fathers and oblivious children into the text, she begins to imagine a world without the absence of the slave. It does not in itself make the slave present, of course, but it portrays the slave as something more than an absence at the centre of the text.

Though the people that Hartman writes about have more in common with the contemporary Ghanaian, since they escape slavery, there is a marked similarity between them and Hartman. This similarity, curiously, is also partly due to the similarities between their story and narratives of American mythology that Hartman as an African American are excluded from. Like an African version of the pilgrims, the group of travellers set out to escape persecution and oppression, and find a new home where there are no kings and where they are no longer under the watchful eye of their neighbours. Wandering north, the women, men and children travel so far away from the "old world" that the gap becomes "unbridgeable" (224). They thus leave slavery behind by creating a rupture between the old and the new that is like the ruptures of diasporic time, but that is as a safeguard against rather than a cause of the pain. When they at long last settle in their new home on the savanna in the north they take comfort in the fact that they have successfully "fled slave raiders, predatory states, drought and exhausted land" even though they have little among them apart from "the rift" between now and then (225). The group is ultimately identified as members of the ethnic group Sisala, who live in northern Ghana. Hartman's story about the travellers thus become an origin story of a people who, "knowing that you don't ever regain what you've lost" embrace the process of "becoming something other than who they had been" and who therefore give themselves a name that means "to come together" (225). The group thereby enters a new national time that does not create a now that is weighed down by the pain of the past, but that is a form of national time that begins with and is shaped by a break from the past.

The group of travellers are at the same time American pilgrims, the ancestors of contemporary Ghanaians, and African Americans who escape slavery. Like Hartman, they exist in the time of slavery insofar as it shapes their world and their identity as a people of refugees, but they are at the same time free from the constraints of this horizon-less temporality. It is, paradoxically, this layering of temporalities—nation time, diasporic time and the time of slavery—that makes them coeval with Hartman and the reader and that makes possible the encounter between concurrent subjectivities. Hartman manipulates the relation between temporalities in her story about the Sisala and thereby make them concurrent with herself. The layering of temporalities makes it possible to reimagine the world through the "interior, atemporal terrain" that she invents and which is the home of the people who "came together" and made a home outside the history and landscapes of slavery.

Works Cited

Bernier, Celeste-Marie. 2010. "Lose Your Mother: A Journey along the Atlantic Slave Route" *Journal of American Studies* 44: 1: 3–6.

Conrad, Joseph. [1899]. 2011. Heart of Darkness. Cambridge: Penguin,

Cvetkovic, Ann. 2012. "Depression is Ordinary: Public Feelings and Saidiya Hartman's *Lose Your Mother*." *Feminist Theory* 13: 2: 131–146.

Fabian, Johannes. *Time and the Other: How Anthropology Makes Its Object*. New York: Columbia, 1983.

Fur, Gunlög; Diana Brydon; Peter Forsberg. "Culture Bound and Unbound: Concurrent Voices and Claims in Postcolonial Places" *Culture Unbound* 6:7 2014: 1253–1257.

Gilroy, Paul. 1993. *The Black Atlantic: Modernity and Double Consciousness*. London: Verso.

Goyal, Yogita. 2004. "Africa and the Black Atlantic" *Research in African Literatures* 45:3: v–xxv.

Hartman, Saidiya. *Lose Your Mother: A Journey Along the Atlantic Slave Route*. New York: Farrar, Straus and Giroux, 2007.

Hartman, Saidiya. 2002. "The Time of Slavery." *South Atlantic Quarterly* 101:4: 757–777.

Lamarque, Peter. 2015. "Thought, Make-Believe and the Opacity of Narrative" *How to Make Believe*, edited by J. Alexander Bareis, and Lene Nordrum (Eds). Berlin: De Gruyter.

Mbembe, Achille. 2001. *On the Postcolony*. Berkely: University of California Press.

Morabito, Pasquale Maria. 2011. "Saint George and the Dragon: Cult, Culture, and Foundation of the City" *Contagion: Journal of Violence, Mimesis, and Culture*, 18: 135–153

Nayar, Parmod. 2013. "Mobility, migrant mnemonics and memory citizenship: Saidiya Hartman's *Lose Your Mother*" *Nordic Journal of English Studies* 12:2: 81–101.

Samuelsen, Meg. 2008. "'Lose your Mother, Kill your Child': The Passage of Slavery and its Afterlife in Narratives of Yvette Christiansë and Saiydia Hartman" *English Studies in Africa* 51:2: 38–48.

Wood, Marcus. 2010. "Lose Your Mother: A Journey along the Atlantic Slave Route" *Journal of American Studies* 44:1: 6–11.

Autofiction as a Postcolonial Strategy:
Guilherme Mendes da Silva's *The Moods of Mister Utac* (De humeuren van meneer Utac) and Junot Díaz' *The Brief Wondrous Life of Oscar Wao*

Kristian Van Haesendonck,
Department of Literature,
University of Antwerp, Belgium

Introduction:
From autobiography to autofiction

While scholars have acknowledged the importance of autobiographical writing in postcolonial literatures (e.g. Moore-Gilbert 2009, Lebdai 2015), especially with reference to so-called "diaspora" or "migration" literature, rarely autobiographical narratives are defined as *autofictional*.[1] Coined by French writer Serge Doubrovsky in the late seventies, the term "autofiction" is mostly used by scholars but often mixed up with the more common (non academic) term "autobiography".[2] The term did not lead immediately to a positive critical response among French scholars, but Doubrovsky, himself a specialist in Corneille, endeavored to theorizing autofiction through a particularly productive (but arguably narcissistic) move, rarely seen in the world of writers: by taking his own work as a conceptual laboratorium and showcase for his theory, in order to challenge the self-sufficiency surrounding the autobiographical genre. Doubrovsky, in an attempt to clarify his concept, usually

---

[1] The study of autofictional novels from the Francophone Caribbean by Larrier (2006) is a rare exception to the rule.
[2] Doubrovsky's novel *Fils* (1977) counts as the first (conscious) attempt to write autofiction. For a comprehensive updated work on the (still ongoing) theoretical debate on autofiction, see Gasparini (2008) and Grell (2014).

proceeded by commenting his own fictional work as an "autocritic"; Instead of downplaying Doubrovsky's reflections as a form of critical and creative narcissism, scholars have engaged in a productive debate about the specificities of autofiction, and its difference with related notions such as autobiography and autobiographical novel. As the term suggests, autofiction is close to autobiography, however it is not a synonym of the latter. Autobiography is usually defined, quite simply, as the biography of a person narrated by him/herself. It is, in addition to a retrospective narrative, a literary genre: a type of non-fictional narrative which aims to retell one's life in the most objective way possible. As famously argued by Doubrovsky's French colleague Philippe Lejeune, author of *Le pacte autobiographique* (1975), an autobiography implies that a few conditions are being fulfilled, in the form of a (symbolical) contract or "pact" between the author and the reader, which consists, for the author, in exposing him/herself as he/she is, in a "spirit of truth" (["esprit de vérité"] Lejeune 31). As any concept, however, this one does not come flawlessly: autofiction is ridden with ambiguities, and it could not be otherwise given its inherent conflict between the factual and the fictional. It goes without saying that its undecided status in between fiction and non-fiction has not helped to make it as popular and conceptually strong as its relative, the autobiography. These flaws have even led one critic to call autofiction "un genre pas sérieux" (Darrieussecq 1996), but such bold, derogatory statements miss the point: the most common mistake indeed consists in approaching autofiction as a *genre*, which it is not.

Rather, autofiction is a *mode* of writing, one which deserves more attention in the field of postcolonial literatures and (visual) cultures, as it is, because of the diversity of autofictional forms, a particularly productive one. As Anneleen Maschelein points out, the term is nowadays being used in the (visual) arts as much as in literature:

"Autofiction" as a modus rather than a literary genre is a widespread phenomenon at the end of the 20th and early 21st century in various national and linguistic traditions. It borrows its forms from formalism, modernism, postmodernism or other avant-garde literary traditions: autobiographical narratives are cunningly undermined by fictional elements, memoirs are presented as fragments (often arranged by the alphabet or keywords, i.e. *Roland Barthes by Roland Barthes*). Most importantly, the boundaries of different media are conflated, especially by mixing narrative and images (photographs, comics or cinema). Finally, the phenomenon also oscillates on the verge of art and popular culture—television and the internet—where public confession, reality TV, docudrama, "true fictions" and avatars are extremely popular. (Masschelein 2007)

Autofiction can best be defined, I believe, as autobiographical fiction, even though I am fully aware of this *contradictio in terminis*. The difference is fairly clear, though: contrary to autobiography, which schews any kind of fictionality, or even any reference to any other characters than the narrative persona (self) who writes (usually the first person narrator) autofiction creatively integrates—with a fair dose of freedom—autobiographical elements, without explicitly claiming any form of empirical objectivity, authenticity or verisimilitude. Instead of a genre, then, autofiction, which can be written in the third person, is quite literally a mix of fiction and (tied within the fictional framework) autobiographical elements, without privileging the author's biography. Autofiction's underlying philosophy is to give autobiography a more authentic character than "reality". What I mean by that is the more commonly accepted idea that the power of fiction resides in being more efficient in reaching an effect of verisimilitude than non-fictional narratives who claim to render objectively the "truth". How does postcolonial fiction proceed to reach its goal of verisimilitude? What strategical tools does it use within the text?

While postcolonial narratives differ widely, they usually deal with issues of self (identity), migration, and cultural—often traumatic—memories. These issues are usually related to specific autobiographical "elements" embedded in the textual tissue. Although the importance of autobiography and autobiographical forms in postcolonial literatures has been acknowledged, little critical attention has gone to this important mode in postcolonial writing. Many postcolonial narratives are rooted in the individual experiences of displacement and diaspora, of a writer who typically moved away (or was forced to leave) from his or her home island, usually (but not always) at a young age.³ What is less known is that postcolonial texts are a particularly good testing ground for studying the ways autobiographical narratives can be "cunningly undermined by fictional elements. The two authors I will comment upon here engage in different ways with autofictional writing. Although I will analyze two novels from a comparative perspective, I will mainly focus on the one that has not received any critical attention as of today: *De humeuren van meneer Utac* [*The moods of mister Utac*], published in 2012 by Guilherme Mendes da Silva, a Cape Verdean author based in the Netherlands. Critics, in the Netherlands as elsewhere, have so far surprisingly ignored this voluminous novel. In turn, the second novel *The Brief Wondrous Life of Oscar Wao* won Junot Díaz a Pulitzer and has been studied by quite a few scholars; only months after its publication in 2007 the book already became an internationally acclaimed best seller.⁴ However, the autofictional aspects of his work have not been scrutinized yet. I argue that in both authors, the exploration of "self" (the *auto* in autofiction) functions as a gateway to discuss broader issues of national, regional and diasporic identities and the construction of an alternative modernity, as well as the postcolonial status of the broader regions. Moreover, I argue that, in spite of obvious divergences between the cultural contexts (the Caribbean and Cape Verde and their respective diasporas), there are reasons why it is worth exploring the autofictional aspects of their work.

Utac or the changing moods of a return migrant

Very few books, in fact almost none, have first been published in translation, instead of originally having appeared in the author's native language. This uncommon fact—that of being published exclusively in translation—applies to *De humeuren van meneer*

---

[3] This is emblematically the case in a novel such as *When I was Puerto Rican*, by Puerto Rican writerEsmeralda Santiago where the young Esmeralda is torn away from her Island of Enchantment and dropped in the whole new, cold environment of New York.

[4] For convenience, I will use the following abbreviations: MU (= De humeuren van meneer Utac) and OW (= *The Brief Wondrous Life of Oscar Wao*). All translations of quotes are my own.

Utac ["The humors of Mister Utac"], the first novel by Guilherme Mendes da Silva, a hitherto unknown Cape Verdean writer. The book was published entirely in Dutch, while the native languages of the writer are Portuguese and Cape Verdean Creole (*crioulo*) as it is spoken on the island of Santiago. Born in 1935, Mendes da Silva wrote the novel as a way to look back and reflect upon his nomadic life. Rather than classical "memoires", which one usually writes as a way of autobiographical reflection, Mendes da Silva's book is clearly, like Junot Díaz', an example of autofiction. Published in the Netherlands in a translation from Portuguese to Dutch by Arie Pos, a well-known translator, the lack of a Portuguese version already gives the book a curious place in the literary landscape: that of a medium which is a result of a life of travelling, yet whose writing does not—to put it with Césaire—make a round trip to his "native land", the archipelago of Cape Verde. It is significant that the book was first published in the Netherlands, place of residence of an important Verdean diaspora (especially in the port city of Rotterdam) and the place of residence of Guilherme Mendes da Silva. The publication in the Netherlands (instead of Cape Verde or a Lusophone country) can be seen as a statement by itself, for it suggests the readership is in the first place proficient in Dutch.

The novel has a fairly traditional, chronologic storyline, but events happen in a rather random fashion. Mendes da Silva takes us to colonial Cape Verde, in the early sixties of past century, when he worked as a *kapitein op de grote vaart*, a captain of the seas on a large carrier. In the novel, the protagonist, a certain "mister Utac",[5] returns to his home-island of Santiago after fifteen years of having traveled the world, like Mendes da Silva, as a captain of a carrier operating from its home base, the Dutch city of Rotterdam.[6] The story centers on Utac's reencounter with his home is-

---

[5] In a filmed interview (Bos and Van der Wel 2013), the author argues the protagonist's name ("Utac") is purely fictional and does not exist in the real world.

[6] For an anthropological approach to the Cape Verdean diaspora in the Netherlands, see Jørgen Carling's chapter in Batalha and Carling (2008). In the sixties, many Cape Verdeans came to Rotterdam as seafarers. Nowadays, almost one-third of them still lives in the city's central borough of Delfshaven. However, the first generation of migrants (like Guilherme Mendes da Silva), unlike

land, as well as the existential doubts and anxieties that this "return to the native land" triggers in him. The book, four hundred and eighty pages is, in spite of its dimensions, well structured, divided in nothing less than eighty nine chapters spread out over four hundred twenty nine pages. Furthermore, we find a table of contents, a foreword, and some informative annexes targeted specifically at the Dutch reader: a descriptive list featuring the main characters, a glossary, a *personalia* list explaining the historical characters mentioned in the novel (such as key politicians under the Salazar dictatorship) and, finally, some geographical maps of Cape Verde, including a detailed map of Praia, Santiago's capital city. The eighty nine chapters are albeit short ones, as the subtitles reflect small events that happen during his wanderings on Cape Verde from the moment of arrival to his return to the Netherlands. Another Cape Verdean writer, Germano Almeida, wittingly refers to such stories as *estórias*,[7] a mixture of historical facts, chronicles and fictional stories.

The novel thus inverts the general *leitmotiv* we find in migration literature: the usual pattern one encounters in the genre "migration literature" is indeed the prioritizing of either *e*migration or *im*migration; both terms are nowadays often conflated with the term "diaspora", which is more in tune with the global migration fluxes. While the reader is lured into the less common narrative of a returnmigrant, it is important to point out that what we have here is a *failed* attempt to return to the home-island, i.e. the opposite of the common pattern in diaspora literature: the island as idealized locus, as paradise lost, where one eventually travels back to, usually in order to stay in spite of newly encountered problems of identity and/or social acceptance. Although initially he has the

---

their descendants, did not yet envision transnational connections with the Archipelago: "While first-generation migrants emphasised emotional ties to Cape Verde, the descendants made more explicit references to the different ways of life in the two countries. The vast majority of the pre-independence migrants came with the intention of returning. For many, this has been replaced by a desire for a transnational existence" (Carling 98).

[7] Some random examples: chapter 24 is titled "Mister Utac digresses about democracy" (112); chapter 30 "Pastor Nogueira's speech"; chapter 65 "a visit to the penal colony"; chapter 70 "Simplício predicts mister Utac's future", etcetera.

firm purpose to show his home community how he has succeeded abroad, Utac's re-encounter with family, acquaintances and other locals causes lots of frictions, both in Santiago as well as during his visits to the neighboring islands. Utac eventually concludes that he does not fit well in Verdean society and finally, after a long period of hesitation, he decides to return to the Netherlands.

The characterization of Utac as a moody character par excellence is already announced in the title, which could hardly be more explicit: Utac is projected as a subject whose humors determine his acts, a man incapable of controlling his emotional excesses. What he finds in Santiago after fifteen years of traveling does not quite please him and any insignificant event adds fuel to the emotional fire. While Utac boasts about his accomplishments as a well-traveled, self-made man, who is keen on his individualism, a value he acquired in the West, he does not excel in something the Dutch (among other nations from Western and Northern Europe) are almost stereotypically known for: controlling one's personal emotions and seeking consensus to serve the common good; especially the repression of feelings of anger is perceived as a typically Dutch trait, usually at the cost of personal interests. About everyone in Utac's social circles knows that he is not particularly good in managing his emotions, on the contrary: especially his explosions of anger get him in trouble more than once. In addition, he is also very opinionated about everything, ranging from politics, religion, to history, as we learn from his conversations with Taninho, the local head of police in his community of Achada Grande, and also his best friend. Utac's emotional excesses often extend to his affective life: he maintains simultaneously multiple relationships and is a self-declared womanizer; however, his passion for women is a trait he is rather discrete about when speaking to his close friends; to make things worse, his love for the local liquor (*grogue*), is not very helpful in controlling his emotions. In addition, he is also extremely undecided; for instance, he often visits his friend Bia and seeks her advice on his troubled love life: should he settle in Cape Verde or return to the Netherlands to get married to Trudy, his soon to be pregnant Dutch fiancé? Any doubt or futility could potentially make Utac angry. At one point he simply gets mad for some flies circling around him, depriving him from a good night's sleep and causing him to curse and generalize about Cape Verdean society as a whole: "only uncivilized people can live in a country like this one. I do not believe that I would be a civilized person if from the day I was born until now I would have lived [here] among this vermin" (*MU* 53).[8] On another occasion Utac in a sarcastic tone criticizes his fellow Verdeans for lacking a basic awareness and understanding of democracy and of democratic values, turning them in his view into an easy target for political manipulation by the Portuguese metropolis and its colonization of the Verdean psyche. Addressing another friend, one of the local taxi drivers, he complains:

> My dear Friend Arthur! They say that democracy is a system of government whereby the people possess sovereignty. I hope that you, no matter how uneducated you are, do not fall into that trap. Okay, I know that my words are falling on deaf ears, because you ignore what democracy is and I do not blame you. The one to be blamed is mister Salazar, who closes everyone's eyes, as much here as in his own country, in order for nobody to see the sun and let everybody dwell in darkness. I am sorry to say so but I am only repeating that mister's philosophy. (*MU* 113–114)[9]

In spite of blaming him, Utac's position towards António de Oliveira Salazar (who was Portugal's dictator for over forty years) remains highly ambiguous; on the one hand he blames the Verdean population's ignorance towards their colonial regime, on the other he feels an emotional attachment to Portugal, his "fatherland" (*MU* 332); he even expresses an honest admiration for its dictator, praising him without ironies as "the most intelligent politician of the whole world and of all times" (ibid). The narrator, in various significant meta-fictional comments, addresses the reader

---

[8] "Alleen onbeschaafde mensen kunnen leven in een land als dit. Ik geloof niet dat ik beschaafd zou zijn als ik vanaf mijn geboorte tot nu tussen al dat ongedierte had geleefd. " (*MU*53; my translation).

[9] "Beste vriend Artur! Ze zeggen dat de democratie een regeringssysteem is waarin het volk de soevereiniteit bezit. Ik hoop dat je, hoe achterlijk je ook bent, het daar niet mee eens bent. Goed, ik weet dat ik tegen de muur praat, want je zult wel niet weten wat democratie is en ik verwijt je niets. De grote schuldige is Salazar, die de ogen van iedereen hier en in zijn land laat sluiten zodat niemand de zon ziet en alle blinden in duisternis ronddolen. Neem me niet kwalijk maar ik herhaal hier alleen maar de filosofie van die meneer. " (*MU* 114; my translation).

directly, anticipating the latter's perplexity and need for an explanation after hearing such praise. He clarifies that Utac's highly ambiguous attitude towards Portugal's dictator is subject to change according to his particular mood of the day: "Perhaps the reader finds it strange that mister Utac was such an admirer of Prof. Dr. António de Oliveira Salazar. But perhaps even stranger is the fact that the reader finds that strange. Salazar was since 1928 minister of Finance and saved Portugal from a very difficult situation, and, thanks to his diplomatic skills, managed to keep the country out of the second World War" (*MU* 332).[10] Reflecting on Portugal's colonial politics, the narrator suddenly turns our attention to the fact that we are reading a fictional work, relativizing the historical weight of his words: "Let's stop here because this is a work of fiction and not a political dissertation" (ibid.).[11]

While Utac's return to Cape Verde is situated in the sixties, the narrator (or, more specifically the narrator's moment of enunciation) is clearly situated in the post-Salazar era; the anonymous narrator suggests that he is the fictional (textual) equivalent of the author narrating Utac's story in the third person, thus reinforcing our thesis of autofiction. At first sight this third person narrator seems to be omniscient and extradiegetic (located outside of the story), but the reader quickly realizes that his voice is all except authoritarian; possibly he is an intradiegetic narrator,[12] but the text does not provide sufficient clues to confirm that hypothesis. In spite of being situated outside of the narrative plot, the narrator's narrative perspective (focalization) comes closest to the viewpoint of an anonymous character, a non-identified companion who travels around with Utac. Even though the narrator is neither reliable

---

[10] "De lezer vindt het misschien vreemd dat meneer Utac zo'n bewonderaar was van prof. Dr. António de Oliveira Salazar. Maar misschien is het vreemder dat de lezer dat vreemd vindt. Salazar was vanaf 1928 minister van Financiën en redde Portugal uit een heel moeilijke situatie en dankzij zijn diplomatieke optreden wist hij het land buiten de Tweede Wereldoorlog te houden. " (*MU* 332; my translation).

[11] "Laten we het hierbij laten want dit is een werk van fictie en geen politieke verhandeling" (*MU* 332; my translation).

[12] An intradiegetic narrator is usually (but not always) one of the known characters in a story, which can have many narrators (i.e. so called "polyphony" of narrative voices).

nor omniscient, he is often empathic to the protagonist and rarely refutes Utac's visions as hallucinations or madness. As a matter of fact, Utac does not escape—at least not any more than the local habitants on the island of Santiago—his own belief in superstition which is as strong as his fellow countrymen's.

Significantly, among Utac's wanderings and small incidents and stories, there is a constant reference to superstition and witchcraft. When nhu Maninho, a local paria who used to be a respected tailor is unexpectedly killed during a *batuque*[13], organized to celebrate Utac's return to Santiago, the story quite abruptly turns fantastic or magic, up to such a degree that it is hard to differentiate what is actually "magic" and what is "real". A dramatic incident occurs when one of the local invited VIP's, Augusto Pele, becomes envious of nhu Maninho as soon as he starts dancing with Bía, whom Pele considers to be his personal concubine: nhu Maninho faints and is brought to hospital but dies soon afterwards. A few days later Utac is struck when he sees the ghost of nhu Maninho, sitting a few benches behind him in his local church. Utac coincides with him once more in Achada Grande Frente, a nearby neighborhood, and runs away as soon as he perceives his appearance. Utac still beliefs that what he had seen was not a product of his imagination but truly Maninho's ghost. He informs policeman Taninho about the ghost haunting the neighborhood. When nhu Maninho is finally found alive by authorities, Taninho orders him to return home, accusing him that his sudden death was not Pele's but his own fault. At this point, however, the narrator reflects how these events led to a major injustice: because of the common belief that nhu Maninho possesses some strange kind of supernatural power, common people effectively turned him into an outcast:

---

[13] In Cape Verdean culture, a *batuque* can refer either to a celebration in honor of a special person (as is the case here), or to a form of dance. Due to its supposedly "profane" character, under colonial rule all forms of *batuque* were condemned by the Portuguese Catholic church, and temporarily prohibited by Salazar.

If everybody tells you: "Get out of here and go to the place you belong to because this is the place of the living!", then why would that person [nhu Maninho] not believe that he is dead, if he has become a living death who everyone rejects and isolates? (172)[14]

In a similar episode, the protagonist re-encounters Bitézio, a practitioner of witchcraft whom he has known since his youth, and who is feared by the habitants of Santiago as he is deemed dangerous. However, as with nhu Maninho, Utac's encounters with Bitézio take hilarious proportions, without ever jeopardizing Utac's safety. Most importantly, such encounters reveal Utac's deep and often unconscious attachment to local beliefs, in spite of presenting himself to his peers as an educated, well-traveled man. Finally, in another, rather dramatic episode towards the end of the novel, Mister Utac collapses while on a boat trip with the local fishermen. In the wake of nhu Maninho, he believes it is now his turn to die, as confirmed by his fiancé Trudy (who accompanies him on the trip) and the crew. However, next day they witness Utac's wondrous resurrection, and the fishermen speak of an unprecedented miracle. Suddenly a shoal of flying fish surrounds the boat, and they have the best catch in years. This "food miracle" which accompanies Utac's resurrection clearly has biblical connotations, most obviously the reference to the miracle of draught of fish in the gospels of Luke and John.

It would be tempting to interpret the above mentioned events as "magical realist", an often used—and abused—term by scholars especially in discussions on Latin American and Caribbean literatures. While echoing the fantastic or marvelous events found in the work of, for instance, Alejo Carpentier or Gabriel García Márquez, in Mendes da Silva they are radically different in at least two ways: firstly, they have an explicit religious (biblical) connotation and, secondly, they deal with the dialectics of life and death. Moreover, from an autofictional point of view, we witness how in Mendes da Silva's novel wondrous or magic events are tied up with autobiographical events, as well as with the collective religious or supersti-

---

[14] "Als iedereen tegen iemand zegt: 'Ga weg van hier en ga naar je bestemming want dit is de plaats van de levenden!', waarom zou zo iemand dan niet geloven dat hij dood is als hij een levende dode is geworden die wordt geweerd en geïsoleerd?" (*MU* 172; my translation).

tious beliefs of a larger community. What is peculiar in the novel is that biblical phenomena appear as natural events, and, seamlessly mix with traditional African beliefs in witchcraft, thus emphasizing the syncretism of Cape Verdean culture, a historical hotspot of processes of cultural mixing.[15] In the work of authors from across the Caribbean, where cultural and religious creolization have always appeared as natural processes since the early days of slavery, we also find a fusion of religious elements, for instance in the work of Boeli Van Leeuwen from Curaçao, whose novel *The sign of Jonah* (originally written in Dutch: *Het teken van Jona*, 1988) is imbued with biblical references and quotations.[16] Beyond the specific phenomenon of Caribbean syncretism, one should not forget about the many historical and cultural links between Africa and the Caribbean. Before the heydays of the Latin American literary *boom* of the sixties, Cuban author Alejo Carpentier was inspired by the Caribbean traditions of vodou and Santería (until today also practiced in the Caribbean diaspora), which he used to formulate his theory of *lo real maravilloso*, for many the predecessor of magical realism. These syncretic forms of cultural expression take root in African religions, but suffered important transformations in contact with local Caribbean cultures. Nowadays, magical events, superstition, healing practices, belief in the supernatural and reference to Afro-Caribbean (religious) practice are classical themes of both Caribbean and African literatures. What is less known is that they function as a binding force to local communities both in the Caribbean and Africa. Instead of simple expressions of folk culture, these expressions are rarely seen as part of the divergent modernities of both the Caribbean and Africa, usually relegated to the realm of primitive practices, i.e. the opposite of what "modernity" should look like. Nevertheless, they are fully part of how Africa and the Caribbean "work"—to use Daloz and Chabal's term (1990)—and how they modernize in a fashion which cannot simply be explained through Western concepts.

---

[15] *Crioulo* is the main spoken, creole language in the archipelago in many varieties, itself the result of an intense process of linguistic creolisation).
[16] The gospels of Luke and John tell the story of the disobedient prophet Jonah who is swallowed by a blue whale who spits him out again.

Cape Verde: lusotropicalism and changing colonial tides

It is significant that the novel is set in the sixties, the decade of important changes in Cape Verde due to the weakening of late Portuguese colonialism in Africa. The topic announced in the title and central to the novel is, as we have said, emotional excess: the ever-changing moods of a Cape Verdean return migrant. However, I argue that these emotional tides are not merely the expression of an individual's dissatisfaction with Cape Verde's perceived "primitiveness" or lack of "modernity" as compared to Western countries. On a deeper level, Utac's hyper-sensitivity and anger—his predominant mood—stems from a preoccupation not so much with Portugal's dictator as with the Cape Verdean nation's *reaction* to the colonial stronghold: above all he is frustrated by the way people submit in a docile way to Portuguese rule. Looking beyond colonialism, he proves to be even more skeptical about the Cape Verdean's lack of action, vocality and sense of belonging, as the archipelago peacefully floats between Europe, Africa, and the Americas. Speaking to his friend Taninho, Utac rationalizes that Cape Verde is simultaneously perceived as nowhere and everywhere, both Atlantic and a-continental:

> If it [Cape Verde] isn't located in any of these [continents], it can only be located in the Atlantic Ocean. I've read and heard so many things that I don't understand. Some call us Africans without giving any explanation. Others refuse without any explanation to be called Africans, as if to be African means to be inferior. I am proud to be an African and I am proud of that continent. I believe that it is our luck that our Archipelago is being accepted as the African continent's most Western and not its most arbitrary islands (236).[17]

---

[17] "Als het [Kaapverdië] daar allemaal niet ligt kan het alleen nog maar in de Atlantische Oceaan liggen. Ik heb al zoveel gelezen en gehoord wat ik niet begrijp. Sommigen noemen ons zonder enige uitleg Afrikanen. Anderen willen geen Afrikanen zijn zonder redden of uitleg, alsof Afrikaan zijn wil zeggen dat je inferieur bent. Ik ben er trots op een Afrikaan te zijn en ben trots op dat continent. Ik geloof dat het een geluk is dat onze archipel door het Afrikaanse continent als zijn meest westelijke en niet als zijn meest willekeurige eilanden wordt aanvaard" (*MU* 236; my translation).

In spite of the sincere pride Utac takes in being African, how is his harshness towards Cape Verdeans to be explained? Underneath the rejection of the nation's docility and passivity we find a highly ambiguous attitude towards the ideology that for decades galvanized and justified Portuguese colonialism: lusotropicalism, which was a convenient justifying banner for Salazar in allowing it to continue his colonial project in times where most European imperial forces (e.g. France, Great Britain, Belgium, Spain) had long granted independence to their African territories. The Brazilian writer and intellectual Gilberto Freyre saw luso-tropicalism as an "inclination, on the part of the Portuguese, to an adaptation to the tropics that is not just based on interest, but is also voluptuous..." (Freyre 1955: 134; cited in Vale de Almeida 48). Lusotropicalism was the perfect alibi to continue colonialism for it smoothly integrated the idea of multiculturalism and multiracialism with African occupation instead of decolonization. While Freyre formulated his key ideas of lusotropicalism almost a century ago, the ideology was progressively implemented under Salazar's regime, but not without any changes—Salazar was cautious, for instance, to make crucial adaptations to Freyre's original formulations, in order to match lusotropicalism with his own ultra-nationalist agenda, something that went against Freyre's ideological viewpoints.

Mendes da Silva's novel does explicitly refer to the many ambiguities involved under Portuguese colonial rule, whereby Cape Verdeans were being integrated as fully Portuguese "white" citizens, in the line of Freyre's ideas on lusotropicalism, which saw Portugal and its colonies romantically as a "tropical" multicultural and multiracial nation, and thus a more "civilized" colonizer than the repressive politics practiced by other European imperial powers at the time. In other words Salazar's lusotropical project installed ambiguity—in various degrees of intensity—at the heart of Lusophone Africa. Likewise, Utac's attitude towards colonialism itself is highly ambiguous: on the one hand he is conscious about his Portuguese citizenship, on the other he remains critical of the abuses and violent repression commited by colonialism. At times colonial authority indeed went into areas where it was less obvious, such as language. In one of his many conversations with Taninho, Utac suggests authority is unconsciously being imposed through the colonizer's language. From a Caribbean perspective, this is a clear allusion to Caliban's submission and resistance to Prospero: in order to curse Prospero, Caliban does not have any option but recur to his Master's language.[18] Utac complains to his friend about the lack of "democratic" value of the Portuguese language:

> Our [Portuguese] grammar is more dictatorial than [the dictatorship of] mister Prof. Dr. António de Oliveira Salazar and has more rules than all the police in the world together. Also, our grammar is not at all democratic. [...] Those grammaticians only make these little rules for themselves and for their friends! That's why this country does not make one inch of progress, because they are egocentric people who want to be the only ones to be able to talk and write correctly. Maybe you've never thought about it, but those folks talk and write in such a manner that only they can understand themselves. (*MU* 213)[19]

Beyond the question whether he is right or wrong, Utac engages time and again in a monologue: he behaves towards his relatives and friends, in spite of his often good intentions, as narcissistic and obsessed with democratic and moral values. Interestingly, he does not mention at any time in the text that the first spoken (yet as of today still unofficial) language of Cape Verde is not Portuguese but Creole (*crioulo*), a creole language with many varieties across the archipelago. Instead, Portuguese is downplayed as a marginal and unnecessarily complex language from a global perspective: "Why don't they [the Portuguese] make a simple language, like the English did? English is spoken anywhere in this world; on the seas and in the air, in commerce and in transporta-

---

[18] In an influential essay, Boaventura de Sousa Santos (2003) located Portugal's colonial situation as a particular one wedged in between Próspero and Caliban, i.e. while it was doubtlessly a colonizer the country was itself being colonized by Great Britain; therefore, Portugal would not have been comparable to other colonizing empires because of the country's semi-colonial status. The loss of its colonies, while applauded by most, also would have created a strong sense of insecurity for the fear of being Caliban within the European context.

[19] "Die grammatica van ons is ook dictatorialer dan meneer prof. Dr. António de Oliveira Salazar en heeft meer regeltjes dan alle polities ter wereld. Ze is ook helemaal niet democratisch. [...] Die grammaticamensen maken die regeltjes alleen maar voor henzelf en hun vrienden! Daarom gaat dit land geen steek vooruit, omdat het egoisten zijn die willen dat zij de enigen zijn die correct praten en schrijven. " (*MU* 213; my translation).

tion. It is the most frequently spoken and most respected language in the world." (*MU* 213).[20] Instead of addressing a (predictable) one-way, moralistic critique to the colonizer and the politics of language, Utac once again blames his fellow citizens for its lack of self-consciousness and willingness to take action in order to change the colonial stronghold.

Although no mention is made to other Lusophone African countries, the broader colonial context matters to situate Cape Verde's apparently passive political attitude: the sixties saw Portuguese colonialism enter its final phase in Africa through clashes and violent wars. While in Cape Verde no significant rebellion took place, the colonial wars had already started on the mainland African colonies, as was the case in Guiné-Bissau, under the command of Amilcar Cabral (Guiné-Bissau born of Cape Verdean parents). Although Cape Verde was united with Guiné-Bissau when it obtained independence, and even though Verdeans fought for independence in Guiné-Bissau under Cabral's leadership, in fact Cape Verde under Portuguese rule already enjoyed more autonomy than Angola, Guiné-Buissau and Mozambique. The narrator in the novel, clearly situated in a postcolonial moment, recognizes Cabral's merit in the wars for independence, but downplays the importance of the national hero in Cape Verde's contemporary context. He reflects: "If Amilcar Cabral would have fought in his own country for the independence of Cape Verde, he would not have been forgotten but neither would he have been adored, as is the case now. Maybe he would have been admired as much, or just a little bit more, as the great heroes that did not participate in the armed battle" (*MU* 309).[21] Instead, the narrator favors the foregrounding of forgotten, historically much less visible "great heroes"; persons which played a major role in the history of Cape Verde, such as

---

[20] "Waarom maken ze geen simpele taal zoals de Engelsen? Overal en op de hele wereld wordt Engels gesproken; in de scheepvaart en de luchtvaart, in de handel en het transport. Het is de meest gesproken en meest gerespecteerde taal ter wereld" (*MU* 213; my translation).

[21] "Als Amilcar Cabral in eigen land had gevochten voor de onafhankelijkheid van Kaapverdië, dan zou hij niet zijn vergeten maar zou hij nooit zo zijn vereerd als nu het geval is. Misschien zou hij net zo of iets meer worden bewonderd als de grote voorvechters die niet hadden deelgenomen aan de gewapende strijd" (*MU* 309; my translation).

Joaquim Ribeiro, governor of the municipality (*concelho*) of Santa Catarina, but unknown to most Cape Verdeans. Ribeiro, known as "Quimquim" (written "Kimkim" in the novel)[22] while not related in any way to supporting Cabral's struggle for independence, was a highly successful businessman. Among other achievements Ribeiro was the founder of an aeroclub which rapidly evolved into TACV, a successful airline company that is nowadays Cape Verde's national airline). By making reference to Ribeiro's life in a chapter titled "Kimkim Ribeiro and Amilcar Cabral" (*MU* 307–310), the narrator seeks to emphasize and recycle the historical legacy of such unknown civilian (not military) heroes. Other references to important cultural personalities include Nha Guida Mendi, the archipelago's most famous "batucadeira" (*MU* 162), who is said to have made such a deep impression on Portuguese general Craveiro Lopes during his visit to the island, that the *batuque* parties, which initially were forbidden by Salazar (because of its "profane" character), became institutionalized as one of Cape Verde's traditional dance forms.[23]

Multiplying the Autofictional Self: The Brief Wondrous Life of Oscar Wao

Postcolonial autofiction, however, can take various forms. Due to this diversity and frequency among postcolonial narratives, it has become one of the major literary strategies authors recur to. Like Mendes da Silva, Junot Díaz is a so called "diaspora writer" born in the Dominican Republic, albeit one with a very different history of displacement, as his transnational autofiction takes root in the early experience of migration to the US. In approaching Díaz' work, most critics have focused on aspects such as genre, gender, and cultural memory (the conflictive relation between Dominican

---

[22] One blogger, for instance, suggests that Praia's International airport should be renamed *Aeroporto Joaquim Ribeiro* in praise of the governor of Santa Catarina. "Desconcerto ou atávica preguiça histórica?", http://coral-vermelho. blogspot. be/2012/01/. While the Portuguese spelling is "Quimquim", the novel uses "Kimkim", as this corresponds phonetically with the Portuguese phonetic form.

[23] General Francisco Craveiro Lopes was president of Portugal from 1951 to 1958.

Republic's national history and its diaspora). However, the autofictional aspect of the novel remains unexplored. Yet this is a crucial one: Junot Díaz creates an original and innovative concept of autofiction. Instead of the classical identification of author and character, I argue the author proceeds to unfold his persona over two characters: Yunior and Oscar. In other words, the proper autobiographical elements are embedded in the text by attributing specific traits to each character.

Díaz' first novel, *The Brief Wondrous Life of Oscar Wao*, tells the story of Oscar, described as a Dominican ghetto nerd growing up in Paterson, New Jersey. Oscar Wao, the protagonist does not escape the all-encompassing curse that has affected Dominicans home and abroad, and which he mysteriously refers to as "the *fukú*". The *fukú* turns out to be not a personal curse, but one that set foot on *Hispaniola* (now the Dominican Republic and Haiti) as soon as Columbus discovered the New World:

> *Fukú americanus*, or more colloquially, *fukú*—generally a curse or a doom of some kind; specifically the Curse and the Doom of the New World. [...] No matter what its name or provenance, it is believed that the arrival of Europeans on Hispaniola unleashed the *fukú* on the world, and we've all been in the shit ever since. Santo Domingo might be *fukú's* Kilometer Zero, its port of entry, but we are all of us its children, whether we know it or not. (*OW* 15–16)

The spell referred to as "fukú" affects the different characters in *Oscar Wao*: rather than a *fait-divers* in the plot, the spell becomes the final diasporic character of the novel, present in its ghostly form, deeply penetrating the narrative system of the text, what I would like to call the "deep structure" of the autofictional text, as it links with the existentialist theme of the novel: the diasporic subject is paradoxically most present in its absence, as a ghost, i.e. as an invisible subject in between the real and the imaginary world. Moreover, the novel emphasizes the popular (Dominican and broader Caribbean) belief in the supernatural and tragic destiny as the deeper (unconscious) dynamic to dictatorship and repression.

On a superficial level, the novel can be read in the tradition of other writing about the Caribbean diaspora and migration: we learn about the difficulties and obstacles encountered by the protagonist as he grows up in the Dominican ghetto as a self-declared nerd. He perceives he does not quite fit in the ghetto due to his love for books, ranging from classical literature to sci-fi to comic books, and more broadly anything pop culture. Oscar even succeeds in escaping the ghetto by obtaining a University degree and dedicating himself (like Díaz and Mendes da Silva in a later stage of life) to his passion of writing. The art of writing is also an activity his best friend Yunior engages in, before eventually writing a novel about Oscar's life. Having been unsuccessful with women since he was at College, Oscar eventually falls in love with a Dominican prostitute, and he eventually travels to the Dominican Republic to meet up with her. He discovers important details about his family's past and about himself, but also, tied in with his mother's obscure past, about the traumatic cultural memory of the Dominican Republic and the broader Caribbean. He learns, among other obscured facts, that his grandfather Abelard was tortured under dictator Rafael Trujillo's regime, and he seeks to shed light on the mystery that surrounds his family's traumatic and silenced past.

While the novel is narrated by various voices, the predominant voice is Yunior's, Oscar's best friend, who stands for the traditional Dominican macho. Moreover, Yunior is also the main narrator in the book, performing as an authoritarian—for indeed dictatorial—voice that narrates Oscar's and the Dominican diaspora's (hi)story. As a narrative voice, the authority of Yunior leading the narration is not a coincidence and, clearly, has a specific function in the text. If Dominicans are all unconsciously "deeply attached" to authority, even to dictatorship, the novel suggests, it is because it could not be otherwise, for they have *a priori* been cursed by a major force against which any battle is vain. Moreover, Díaz suggests that not only Dominicans but humanity as a whole is conditioned by blinding forms of authority. Not by coincidence, the name Yunior is also the name of the protagonists in different short stories in *Drown*, Díaz' first collection of short stories. As Machado Saéz (531) argues, the book provides too few clues to determine which of the different Yunior-narrators of the different short stories in *Drown* coincides with the narrator of the novel.

There is no doubt, however, that Díaz himself identified not only with "ghetto nerd" (Oscar) but also with Yunior when writing the novel, as confirmed in an interview:

> I know that the work transforms utterly any attempt I make at subtle autobiography. By the time the work gets done with it, it's unrecognizable. In fact, the book that is completely *fiction, Oscar Wao*, I would argue is *more autobiographical* [...] If a rumor is going to give my work more verisimilitude, I won't discourage it. Sometimes you get a lot simply *by giving your protagonist your same nickname* [Yunior]. (my emphasis)

Even though he does not use the term autofiction, Junot Díaz describes his whole novel as an attempt to writing autobiography through his *alter ego* Yunior. I argue, however, that Junot Díaz codes his autofictional *döppelganger* in the DNA of two characters: Yunior *and* Oscar, both writers who in many ways complement each other, in spite of their radical differences. Through Yunior's words we learn that he feels it is his mission to accomplish the task of making an end to the fukú, as Oscar, lost in his sci-fi fantasies, "strangely enough didn't think it worth incorporating [the fukú] into his fiction" (*OW* 32). Like Oscar, his novel's main character, the author also grew up in New Jersey. He moved from the Dominican Republic to the US in his early childhood, growing up as a simple "kid from New Jersey" (Irvine 2008), a Dominican nerd who escaped the ghetto. And like Oscar in the novel, the young Junot graduated from Rutgers University in the Garden state.

The act of writing itself is thus an autobiographical gesture for the Dominican author. Autofiction fulfills a therapeutic function, even though it does not escape the ghost of authority. Significantly, the novel combines the unavoidably authoritarian way of telling with postmodern techniques and genres that tend, in their own way, to obscure any authoritarianism. The narration is arguably a combination of traditional beliefs, modes of writing and (post)modern techniques, including the way it combines fictionality and factuality. A good example is the presence of social media as a popular (yet often historically inaccurate) source of information. Not by coincidence, *Oscar Wao*, written at the dawn of the "facebook-era", from the outset recognizes the anti-hero's hedonism and links it with traditional Caribbean beliefs. Indeed, Yunior confesses from the outset that after finishing the novel he wrote about Oscar he created a special thread about the "fukú" on an online forum about the Dominican Republic ("DR1"):

> A couple weeks ago, *while I was finishing this book*, I posted the thread *fukú* on the DR1 forum, just out of curiosity. These days I'm nerdy like that. The talkback blew the fuck up. You should see how many responses I've gotten. They just keep coming in. And not just from Domos. The Puertorocks want to talk about fufus, and the Haitians have some shit just like it. There are a zillion of these fukú stories. Even my mother, who almost never talks about Santo Domingo, has started sharing hers with me. (*OW* 6; my emphasis)

Autofiction as a mode of writing indeed has been absorbing the effects of new technologies on writing; as Gasparini (2007) rightly points out, autofiction has also fallen prey to postmodernism's hedonistic search and idolatry of the Self, transfixing the subject in virtual worlds. Yunior, who became a writer after Oscar taught his friend how to tell stories, focuses on exorcising the "fukú" through the act of writing. Autofiction here becomes a "zafa", a term he uses to refer to his "very own counterspell" (*OW* 7), the opposite of and only possible remedy against the omnipresent and all-condemning fukú.

Contrary to what Díaz suggests in the interview—that his novel follows the rule of onomastic identity whereby he assigns his nickname to Yunior and makes him the intradiegetic narrator—Yunior is not the only alter ego for Junot Díaz. In another interview with his peer, the Haitian American writer Edwidge Danticat, Díaz refers to the analogy between Oscar's life and his own:

> But the character himself, this supernerd. *I was a ghetto nerd supreme:* a smart kid in a poor-ass-community. The thing with me was that I was a nerd embedded in a dictatorial military family (. . .) Oscar was *a composite of all the nerds that I grew up with* who didn't have that special reservoir of masculine privilege. *Oscar was who I would have been* if it had not been for my father or my brother or my own willingness to fight or *my owninability to fit into any category easily*. ("Interview with Junot Díaz", Danticat 2007; my emphasis)

Díaz proceeds in his novel not only to resurrect Oscar as the "composite of all the nerds" he grew up with and came to be part of his identity, the narrative itself is an autofictional composite of Díaz' self embedded in two different characters without "fitting" into none of them with ease. Two characters who ambitioned to be, like Junot, writers, as a natural consequence of their voracity of literature and pop culture. I argue that autofiction can thus be written across different characters, instead of privileging the classical "I" (first person narrator) as the only possible voice and character corresponding to the narrator and author. Real life events, i.e. events happened during an author's life can be strategically spread across the lives of very different characters, while they are all part of the author's repertoire of biographical facts. As these events get tied into the fiction, the autofictional narrative exposes the multiplicity of the author's self, arguably creating an effect of verisimilitude and authenticity. Through these characters, Díaz writes about those diasporic lives that he has experienced, and those of others he has witnessed or imagined, to the point that the writing itself becomes a maze of autobiographical elements that seamlessly mix with fictional ones.

Conclusion

Autofiction as a mode of writing thus allows, I argue, to create meaning in the postcolony and, as stated above, an effect of verisimilitude through the polyphonic voicing of different characters, allowing for the author to express, rather than multiple personalities, the cultural complexity itself involved in diasporic lives. Díaz uses autofiction to question the authority of the narrative voice itself; Díaz's rejection of an authoritarian Voice, which represents false "dreams of unity, of purity" (O'Rourke 2008) cannot be seen isolated from his belief that the classical genre of autobiography and autobiographical writing must be in some ways transformed, made "impure", "Caribbeanized", i.e. transformed into a new kind of writing adapted to the diasporic experience of the Caribbean. Such a preoccupation with the very way how the author should interweave autobiographical elements in the fictional tissue is absent in the Cape Verdean's work. Mendes da Silva, from a technical perspective, is more conservative in his use of autofiction as a mode of writing: autofiction is used to narrate a story which mixes autobiographical elements with fictional ones, including the fictional name of the protagonist. In Mendes da Silva's novel, autofiction serves as an indirect strategy to show how the ideology of lusotropicalism has permeated Cape Verdean culture under colonialism, and—as rendered through the narrator's scope—extends into the postcolonial era. Lusotropicalism was a form of justifying colonialism through the promotion of multiracialism and multiculturalism along Salazar's slogan that *Portugal não é um país pequeno*.[24] Indeed, the protagonist of Mendes da Silva's novel to a certain extent embodies the lusotropicalist ideals, as a contradictory conjugation of multicultural conviviality and authoritarian patriarchy.

By using autofiction as a *mode* of writing, authors can give verisimilitude to postcolonial lives through the eyes of different characters. This is the case in *Oscar Wao*, where Junot Díaz draws on both Yunior and Oscar to tell his experience and the existential implications of growing up as a Dominican kid in diaspora. However, as with Mendes da Silva's autofictional narrative, the analysis of all the parallels running between the author's and the characters' lives have not been our main concern here. Rather, we have focused on the question how and why autofiction is the preferred mode of writing in these texts, and why it is an important mode in postcolonial writing which conjugates the poetical and political; hence the importance of situating these novels in their context of emergence.

As in Mendes da Silva, belief in the supernatural (in witchcraft, ghosts, "fukú", "zafa", etcetera) in Díaz takes root in local popular traditions, which are entirely part of the Caribbean's modernity. Even though traditional beliefs in the supranatural are so often packaged with the label *magical realism*, I believe applying such a used and abused label would do these works injustice. Not by coincidence, Yunior makes a reference to García Márquez' *Macondo* and the parody of the latter by a younger generation of Latin American writers as *McOndo*: "It used to be more popular in the old days, bigger, so to speak, in Macondo than in McOndo" (*OW* 7). Caribbean literature, both the texts written in the Caribbean basin as well as those in diaspora, share some transnational features with African narratives: both insist on what we may call the "informalisation of writing", much in the way can be observed in

---

[24] "Portugal is not a small country": slogan used by Salazar as propaganda for reinforcing the argument that the Portugal is a great Empire. The sentence was visually represented by a map of Lusophone African countries superposed over the map of Europe, in order to show the empire's geographical dimensions.

contemporary African societies. Political scientists Patrick Chabal and Jean-Pascal Daloz insist on the importance to take serious the "informalisation of politics" in Africa, as opposed to Western modes of rational thinking in boxes and classifications. They claim "it is not possible to understand what might constitute the 'modern' and the 'formal' in Africa without paying proper attention to the 'traditional' and the 'informal'" (Chabal and Daloz 155). Modernity in their view is not the opposite of the traditional but a "dynamic process rather than a state of equilibrium" (ibid). In cultural terms, the informal is represented by phenomena such as witchcraft, usually approached through a Western scope as folk culture or, worse, as a sign of backwardness, of the exact opposite of the "modern". The juxtaposition of "modern" and "tradition" is also true, I believe, in the postcolonial Caribbean and its diaspora where cultural forms so often escape Western rationality and categorization. While Chabal and Daloz claim that nowhere like in Africa the juxtaposition of the 'traditional' with the 'modern' is more striking, we should not forget the Caribbean's deep historical and cultural entanglements with the African continent. The view that societies could modernize *without* becoming Westernized is one which most scholars in the social sciences and Humanities do not subscribe to, as they usually speak *from* a position that sees modernization as a mirror image of the Western state and democracy.

Likewise, the appropriation and informalisation of the autobiographical and autofictional norms as defined by French theorists is but one example of the creativity of both Caribbean and African postcolonial writers. The autofictional narratives briefly analyzed in this article are witness of how postcolonial autofiction questions established ideas of (post)modernity versus tradition, as well as of the potential to rethink and expand the category of autofiction itself as multiplicity. I have not subscribed here to autofiction's criteria of onomastic identity ("identité onomastique"), as a defining trait of autofiction (e.g. Doubrovsky, Vilain, Gasparini, Colonna) who state that, in order to be able to speak of autofiction, there must be absolute homonymous identity between protagonist, narrator, and author (Gasparini 209). Indeed, an author and narrator could well use different names, while maintaining autofictional verosimilitude with his or her character. These novels go beyond the norm of identity between author, narrator, and character; the postcolonial writer reinvents his/her self beyond the textual and aesthetic boundaries imposed on autobiography, recognizing him/herself in the multiple characters and excesses that the legacy of colonialism and the experience of displacement inscribed in the colonized subject and continues to reproduce itself—albeit in different and more complex ways than before—in the postcolony. We have insisted on the importance of traditional elements, not as a nostalgic recycling of national folklore or myths, but rather as a way of asserting what Julio Ramos (2001) calls "divergent modernities" not one that is opposed to, but rather challenges the notion that there is only one model of modernity, represented by the nations of northern Europe and defined exclusively in terms of capitalist development.[25]

References

Clifford, James. 1986. Introduction: Partial Truths. In: Clifford, James and Marcus, George, E. (Eds). *Writing Culture. The Poetics and Politics of Ethnography*. Pp. 1–26. Berkeley: University of California Press.

Bos, Ronald and Cees van der Wel. 2013. "UTAC tussen Kaapverdie en Rotterdam". Documentary. Stichting Interakt. Rotterdam: TV Rijnmond. Broadcasted 9 February, 2013.

Carling, Jørgen. 2008. "Cape Verdeans in the Netherlands", in *Transnational Archipelago. Perspectives on Cape Verdean Migration and Diaspora*, in Luís Batalha and Jørgen Carling, eds., Amsterdam University Press.

Chabal, Patrick, & Daloz, Jean-Pascal. 1999. *Africa Works: Disorder as political instrument*. African issues. Oxford: James Currey; Bloomington: Indiana University Press.

Colonna, Vincent. 2004. *Autofiction & autres mythomanies littéraires*. Auch: Tristram.

Danticat, Edwidge. 2007. "Interview with Junot Díaz". *Bomb Magazine* 101, 89–95.

---

[25] As an alternative to the definition of modernity as a homogeneous form of Western capitalist development, Jo Labanye (2007) proposes, in the line of Chabal and Daloz, a definition "in terms not of capitalist modernization but of attitudes toward the relation of present to past" (Labanye 91).

De Almeida, Miguel Vale. 2004. *An Earth-colored Sea: "Race", Culture, and the Politics of Identity in the Postcolonial Portuguese-speaking World* (Vol. 22). New York: Berghahn Books.

Díaz, Junot. 2007. *The brief wondrous life of Oscar Wao*. New York: Penguin.

Doubrovsky, Serge. 2001 [1977]. *Fils*. Paris: Gallimard.

Gasparini, Philippe. 2008. *Autofiction: une aventure du langage*. Paris : Seuil.

Grell, Isabelle. *L'autofiction*. Paris: Armand Colin, 2014.

Irvine, Lindesay. 2008. "Junot Díaz wins Pulitzer". *The guardian*, 8 April, http://www.theguardian.com/books/2008/apr/08/news.pulitzerprize. Consulted 16 March 2015.

Kiper, Dmitry. 2012. "Junot Diaz on Heartbreak, Love and his Latest Book, This is How You Lose Her", *NBC New York*, http://www.nbcnewyork.com/the-scene/events/Junot-Diaz-Talks-about-His-New-Book-Heartbreak-Poetry-and-The-Craft-of-Writing-169354486.html. Accessed March 16, 2015.

Labanyi, Jo. 2007. "Memory and Modernity in Democratic Spain: The Difficulty of Coming to Terms with the Spanish Civil War." *Poetics Today* 28. Spring 2007 (2007): 89–116.

Larrier, Renée. 2006. *Autofiction and Advocacy in the Francophone Caribbean*. Gainesville: UP of Florida.

Lebdai, Benaouda, ed. 2015. *Autobiography as a Writing Strategy in Postcolonial Literature*. Newcastle, Cambridge Scholars Publishing.

Lejeune, Philippe. 2015. *Le pacte autobiographique*. Paris: Seuil.

Elena Machado Sáez. 2011. "Dictating Desire, Dictating Diaspora: Junot Díaz's The Brief Wondrous Life of Oscar Wao as Foundational Romance". *Contemporary Literature* 52, 3. 522–555.

Masschelein, Anneleen. 2007. "Foreword". Autofiction and/in Image - Autofiction visuelle. *Image and Narrative* 19. http://www.imageandnarrative.be/inarchive/autofiction/foreword.htm. Accessed 21 May 2015.

Mendes da Silva, Guilherme. 2012. *De humeuren van meneer Utac*, tr. Arie Pos, Amsterdam: Nieuw Amsterdam.

Mendes da Silva, Guilherme. 2016. *Os humores do senhor Utac*. Luxemburg: Editora Brial.

Moore-Gilbert, Bart. 2009. *Postcolonial life-writing: culture, politics, and self-representation*. Routledge

Santiago, Esmeralda. 2006. *When I Was Puerto Rican*. Boston: Da Capo Press.

O'Rourke, Megan. 2008. "Questions for Junot Díaz. An interview with the Pulitzer Prize-winning author". *Slate Magazine*, April 8, http://www.slate.com/articles/news_and_politics/recycled/2008/04/questions_for_junot_daz.html. Accessed 14 April, 2015.

Ramos, Julio. 2001. *Divergent Modernities: Culture and Politics in Nineteenth-Century Latin America*. Durham [N.C.]: Duke University Press.

Santos, Boaventura de Sousa. 2003. "Entre Próspero e Caliban. Colonialismo, Pós-colonialismo e interidentidade". *Novos Estudos CEBRAP* 66, July 2003. 24–29.

Van Leeuwen, Boeli. 2007. Het teken van Jona. Amsterdam: In de knipscheer [translated as *The Sign of Jonah*, Amsterdam: In de knipscheer]

Vilain, Philippe. 2009. *L'autofiction en théorie. Suivi de deux entretiens avec Philippe Sollers & Philippe Lejeune*. Chatou: Les éditions de la transparence.

Moments of Suffering, Pain and Resilience:
Somali Refugees' Memories of Home and Journeys to Exile

Ernest Angu Pineteh
Faculty of Humanities, University of Pretoria,
South Africa

Introduction

Somali migrants in South Africa are mostly asylum seekers and refugees and their memories of displacement may begin with remembering experiences of homelessness at home and the psychological and physical pain of flight to exile. To write about Somalia is to write about its state of statelessness and the archetypal collapse of a sense of nationhood and ethnic solidarity (Sadouni 2009; Menkhaus 2004). It is a grand narrative of tribal disputes, armed conflicts, piracy and foreign incursions as well as countless attempts to broker long-lasting peace. The stories told by Somali migrants are fraught with disconcerting and traumatic images of savagery, banditry, human rights abuse and forced displacement (Ingiriis 2016; Bakonyi 2010; Ibrahim 2010; Besteman 1996). These are captured in a corpus of literature, which has for many years focused on Somalia's unprecedented history of armed insurgency, an "epidemic of piracy, massive displacement, and a humanitarian crisis deemed as the most dangerous in the world" (Menkhaus 2010, 320). Today, Somalia is an exemplar of a mutilated postcolonial state, which "reveals itself in the guise of arbitrariness and absolute power to give death anytime, anywhere, by any means, and for any reason" (Mbembe 2001, 13). The collapse of political and economic institutions in Somalia has led to the massive forced displacement and influx of Somali asylum-seekers into Kenya, Tanzania and South Africa.

This article emerges out of a broader project on the experiences of xenophobia of Somali migrants in Cape Town, South Africa. It is based on a collection of stories about victimization, resistance and resilience during xenophobic attacks, told by thirty Somali migrants. The article seeks to understand how this group of displaced persons remember their experiences of homelessness in their ancestral home and their tumultuous journeys to exile. Using excerpts from their stories, this article analyses the multiple meanings of home and flight and how they shape our understanding of the xenophobic experiences of Cape Town-based Somali migrants.

The article argues that although the modes of violence in Somalia are different from xenophobic violence in South Africa, their survival in a mutilated state like Somali emboldened and prepared Somali refugees for the hostilities associated with forced migration. From the narratives, the participants tended to attribute their resistance and resilience to social violence to their experiences of political and social violence in Somalia, the development of survival strategies and their abilities to deal with hostilities during their journeys to exile. To explain this argument, firstly I position Somali experiences within a historical and political context, and I provide a theoretical lens for analysing Somali memories of displacement. Secondly, I describe my research journey and the data collection procedures and finally I analyse the meanings embedded in Somali memories of home and flight.

Brief historical context and theoretical framework

The population of Somali migrants in South African has grown exponentially since the collapse of apartheid. This is because Somalia is a politically unstable state plagued by armed incursions and piracy, and also because South Africa is a relatively stable political economy, with economic opportunities for migrants (Charman and Piper 2012; Anderson 2010; Crush 2008). Today, there are approximately 50, 000 Somalis living as refugees and asylum seekers in South Africa and many of them have appropriated spaces and set up businesses in several major cities and townships in South Africa despite recurring violent attacks on African migrants (Crush & al 2015).

In Cape Town as elsewhere in South Africa, most Somali migrants operate a network of businesses involving wholesale, retail and spaza shops. In fact this community is made up of migrants who are willing to risk everything for business success, "willing to run the risk of robbery" or even being murdered (Charman and Piper 2012, 96). For example Somalis' appropriation of business spaces and the outsmarting of local competitors in peri-urban and urban areas have been attributed to *muthi* or black magic. Consequently, their business tactics have made them prime targets during xenophobic violence, as locals associate their "economic misfortunes like poverty, joblessness, and the consequent inability to marry…" to a spiritual spell cast on them by successful foreign business owners (Hickel 2014, 108). However, Somalis' business success is one but several factors responsible for the violent attacks of Africans by South Africans. The narrative of criminality links South Africa's high crime statistics to the presence of Africans while some political discourses blame xenophobic violence to an outburst of frustration because of poor delivery of social services (see Nyamnjoh 2006; Landau 2008; Hassim et al 2008). Despite the multiple causes of xenophobic violence and the effects on the livelihoods of Somali refugees, the Somali community still live and operate businesses in volatile localities such as Nyanga, Khayelitsha, and Mitchell's Plain, peri-urban areas in Cape Town.

From this study, it was clear that we cannot possibly understand Somalis' suffering, pain and resilience to victimization during the xenophobic attacks in South Africa without making sense of their social histories of home, dislocation from family, and their journeys through and to hostile and unfamiliar spaces (see Mwangi 2012; Sadouni 2009; Collyer 2007). In fact, Somalia's history of civil wars and piracy has "structured Somali modes of socialisation into the new South Africa" (Sadouni 2009, 235). The Cape Town-based Somali community is unquestionably a community of forced migrants whose national identities and sense of belonging have been shattered by "destructive insurgency and counter-insurgency campaigns, intensification of Al-Qa'ida activities and counter-terrorism actions by the United States" (Menkhaus

2010, 320). Life for Somali migrants is about learning how to survive in hostile spaces and the violent images during the xenophobic attacks in South Africa are indeed familiar scenes. It is not surprising, then, that they operate businesses in crime-ridden and anti-African spaces dreaded by other African migrants.

In this article, I examine Somali narratives of home and flight to exile as accounts of displacement or as tropes of memory which can help to shape our understanding of Somali migrants' resilience to post-apartheid violence and their strategies to belong in spaces where they are not wanted (Landau 2011; Gibson 2011; Neocosmos 2010; Hassim et al. 2008). Given that war, famine and humanitarian crises are prime causes of human displacement in Somalia, I am particularly interested in the reconstruction of memories of these postcolonial pathologies and how they mediate trajectories of xenophobic experiences (Arthur 2010; Landau and Freemantle 2010). This includes exploring how Somali migrants remember navigating hostile spaces using survival tactics, and how these experiences provide them with the mental and physical capacities to cope in South Africa (Sadouni 2009; Baynham and De Fina 2005; Malkki 1992).

To understand how Somali refugees reconstruct memories of home and journey, I turned to the politics of memory. The representation of exile in narratives is in a way a process of recollection of specific moments in the lives of migrants. This process is expected to show some "consistency of consciousness and a sense of continuity between the actions and events of the past, and the experiences of the present…" (King 2000, 2). The narratives evince Somalis sense of personal identity and connection to space and time because; the process is a "journey into the memory and imagination that negotiates between old and new, past and present, self and other, safety and danger" (Henderson 1995, 4). The need to engage in memory work usually emerges from a major rupture in the life of an individual, which needs to be remembered or forgotten. In the case of Somali migrants, this rupture is the conflict and violence at home. Memory work therefore involves painful journeys into the past to help us to make sense of the present and the future. When an experience is remembered, "it assumes the form of narrative of the past that charts the trajectory of how one's self came to be" (Freeman 1993, 33). The meanings of our lives are buried in our memories and the transformation of memories into narratives gives us a sense of place and time (Pineteh 2005). Here, I examine the contents of Somali memories of home and flight as "their ways of defining who [they] are in the present, of framing choices for the future, of finding solace from immediate troubles..." (Thelen 1994, 119).

The process of remembering enhances the ability to challenge tragic happenings in life while establishing links between members of communities and nations (Eckardt 1993). In the context of Somali refugees, memory work provides a prism through which they make sense of their individual selves, their collective identity and the events that have shaped their lives. However, the politics of memory is also understood through the logic of ambivalence between remembering and forgetting. Memory work is considered a therapeutic or healing process, which can work in two directions (Freeman 1993; Pineteh 2005). While some people prefer to deal with key moments in their lives by talking about them, some prefer to suppress them and let the past reside in the past. The process of remembrance is therefore structured around the way memory is realized, textualized, ruptured or suppressed, buried or avoided (Pineteh 2005; Thelen 1995).

Since the politics of memory is about the way individuals remember and retell episodes of their social experiences, this article has also drawn on conventions of storytelling to analyse Somali memories of displacement. For example, Labov (2013), Schiffrin, De Fina and Nylund (2010), Bal (2009) and Jackson (2002) argue that human beings make meaning of their worlds through storytelling. For Jackson (2002, 13), the stories that human beings tell about their experiences involve "an ongoing struggle to negotiate, reconcile, balance or mediate...antithetical potentialities of being". This implies that human lives are storied lives because "telling the story of the life we have lived thoroughly and deeply shows us the powerful presence of archetypes, those common elements of being human than others, through time and across all cultures" (Atkinson 2011, 41). From this standpoint, this article attempts to analyze Somali memories as stories that attach political agency to their sense of belonging and which help us make sense of their social existence in a new South Africa fraught with anti-foreigner sentiments (Nyamnjoh 2006; Landau and Freemantle 2010).

Research journey and data collection

Although Somali refugees operate businesses in Cape Town, they struggle to communicate fluently in English, thus participating in a thirty to sixty-minute interview in English was a major challenge for most participants. To collect rich qualitative data for a project of this nature, I had to find ways to conduct many of the interviews in their home language. I therefore recruited a postgraduate Somali student at the University of the Western Cape as a research assistant, as he had relevant research experience and was familiar with the Somali community. His primary responsibilities included scheduling interview appointments, conducting/translating some of the interviews, and transcribing the data.

The interviews were arranged during a time and a place convenient to each participant. Some of the interviews were conducted after business hours and the venues were the participants' business premises, my car or their homes. Timing of interviews was crucial because we had to make sure that we did not interfere with participants' dinner and/or prayer routines. These were some of the challenges that research assistant and I had to overcome in order to collect their stories. Fortunately, after each successful interview; the interviewees referred us to other possible participants. Despite the difficulties, there was a general willingness to participate in the project because for participants, it was an opportunity to add their voices to the discussions about xenophobia. Prior to each interview, I explained the purpose of the research and the research assistant explained the consent form that participants were expected to sign. This consent form granted us permission to conduct and audio-record all the interviews and it assured participants that they would be cited anonymously in the project. For this reason, the interviewees are represented as 'participant' plus a suffix number between one and thirty.

The interviews were conducted in the frame of narrative research understood as interconnectedness between the narrator, the story and the meaning associated with the story (Henning et al

2004; Maree 2007). With this in mind, the interview took the form of a storytelling event or a conversation about the participants and how they remembered different events or experiences at home and during exile (Andrews, Squire and Tamboukou 2013; Maree 2007). After setting up appointments with possible participants, I met my first participant on 20 July 2015 at 8: 00pm and the interview lasted for about one hour. The questions were framed around his life before exile and the journey to exile. The interviewee eloquently narrated a somewhat logical story about his experiences from home to exile. Although he was not fluent in English, he remembered key events through intermittent code switching with his mother tongue, thus creating an intricate and rich narrative. His story helped me to "fully understand the phenomenon [of memory] by grappling with people's particular representations of otherness" (Hickel 2014, 104).

After this interview, we proceeded to conduct the other twenty-nine interviews between July and September 2015. At the end of this process, we had met with thirty Somali refugees and asylum seekers in our journeys to shops, homes and from one township to another, at different times of the day. As the interviewees recounted their experiences at home, during flight and in exile, we began to uncover the intricacies of these spaces and the characteristics of xenophobia in post-apartheid South Africa. The narrative of selfhood and belonging as well as the images of pain, suffering and disillusionment began to emerge as the stories unfolded.

Nostalgic memories of home and the meaning of belonging

I began the interview by asking participants about their families and why they decided to flee from Somali. The intention was to establish how their memories connected their lives at home with a historical context and with their lives in South Africa through different temporal and spatial trajectories (Sadouni 2009; Agnew 2005). Somali oral accounts of the experiences of xenophobia began with nostalgic memories of a fractured homeland, the painful dislocation from family and an imaginary sense of reunion with family. In re-storying episodes of their lives in Somalia, the participants constructed contesting narratives framed around their personal identity, their family histories and a political discourse characterized by military incursions. These narratives tended to focus on civil conflicts in Somalia and the contributions of Al-Shabaab insurgents to destabilise the state. One participant testified:

> I left Somalia because of the civil war which broke up 1990 and I am looking for a peaceful place to live the way I lived in Somalia. It is a long story. I came to South Africa in 2001 because of the massive killing which was taking place so I decided to leave in order not to become a victim... The situation at that time was quite complex and everywhere there were gun sounds and the citizens were running away. I personally was not willing to die. (Participant 15)

The narrator paints a graphic image of a Somalia dismembered by indiscriminate killing of civilians, the "history and identity of a [postcolonial state] shattered under the weight of unmourned violence" (Watkins and Shulman 2008, 51). This Somali migrant uses "gun sounds" and the frantic image of people running for their lives to capture the state of lawlessness and insecurity in Somali that precipitated his departure. It is a narrative about victimization which seems to fluctuate between "taking stock, bearing witness, shaping new forms of social identification or composing coherent versions of self and social experiences against a turbulent past and uncertain future" (Adams 2009, 161).

Somali narratives of home and a sense of belonging were constructed as a political discourse, illustrating how Al-Shabaab, the Islamic fundamentalist movement that has for years used arbitrary and coercive force as well as tactical violence to terrorize civilians, has legitimized its existence in Somalia (Mwangi 2012; Bakonyi 2010; Ibrahim 2010). Here, memories of war, murders and forced displacement represent Al-Shabaab as "a political ideology and not a theological construct" whose rationale for the violence is framed around the Islamic notion of war as jihad (Mwangi 2012, 514).

> It was chaos, it was chaos, there was no peace. Al-Shabaab had taken over the country and was forcing us to work with them and if you didn't cooperate with them they would kill you...they were killing men and children, raping women... I wasn't ready to join them so l left. I didn't want to become a rebel; I didn't want to carry a gun and to kill other Somalis. I wanted a better a bright future for myself, so decided to leave to look for a different life in another country... (Participant 3)

This narrative is constructed against the backdrop of bestial images such as killing and rape showing the fragility of Somalia as a state incapable of protecting its own citizens. It also uses imagery of worst lived experiences they remember, to illustrate the morbidity of state which has not only "created opportunities for Al-Shabaab to adopt strategies aimed at seeking community support and legitimising itself" but has also forced many Somalis to seek refuge in other countries (Mwangi 2012, 520). This narrative reconstruction provides an opportunity to reread painful human experiences that connect the past to the present and future, while conveying displaced communities' premigration myth that exile is a safe haven, especially in conditions of war (Pineteh 2005; Malkki 1995). This was particularly evident when I asked participants why they decided to migrate to South Africa and in narratives about their early days in South Africa.

This autobiographical narrative about homelessness and Somalis' construction of the self during Al-Shabaab's insurgency recurred prominently in memories about home, providing a multilayered interpretation of a social history fraught with images of terror, fear and pain, stemming from Al-Shabaab's "destructive power of perpetrating violence on others [and] the pernicious wounds occasioned by inequity [and] injustice" (Watkins and Shulman 2008, 51). This is evident in the following narrative:

> The central government of Somalia was destroyed and civil war broke out in the country, War lords had destroyed all facilities in our country. They attacked us at our homes, they killed my father, looted all our properties and they threatened to kill me. So I fled because of these terrible things that were happening. When they killed my father and raped my sister, looted our property I fled away from Kismayo to Mozambique and then to South Africa... (Participant 27)

In this excerpt, I began to make sense of Somalis' determination to implant themselves in South Africa despite the merciless attacks on foreigners and the locals' rhetoric of "go home or die here" (Hassim et al. 2008, 1). One can argue that "given the personal, familial and cultural tragedies that had befallen them" back home; they are likely to be more resilient to xenophobia (Watkins and Shulman 2008, 57). The narrative symbolizes "the interplay of violence, banditry and systemic looting together with the violent displacement of thousands of people" disrupting Somalis' patterns of life in their homeland (Bakonyi 2010, 240). Again the stark images of rape, killing and looting illustrate a withering Somalia state whereby violence is used by Al-Shabaab to claim legitimacy (Mwangi 2012; Bakonyi 2010). These memories of an atrocious social history do not only justify Somalis' struggle for inclusion in South Africa but they also reconstruct xenophobic violence as a form of déjà vu for many Somali migrants.

Although the modes of violence in Somalia and South Africa are different, participants tended to narrate their experiences of xenophobic violence as a familiar way of life. There is a sense of déjà vu, which seems to normalise xenophobia.

> There is no difference between xenophobia and the war in Somalia. When I was leaving Somalia I thought I would live in peace and be free from all sorts of problems if I reached South Africa, But I just found out this country is not different from Somalia I am saying this because all the things that made me to escape from Somalia have happened to me here. I have been robbed, my shop has been burnt and I have been shot. It is bad here but this violence is nothing new to many of us (Participant 5)

> I left Somalia because there was no stable government and the civil war in my country very bad. Hence I came here to look for a better life. I also left my country because of drought, hunger and lack of stability. I came to live with my fellow African brothers but now South Africa is like my home country. I live in fear every day (Participant 20).

These Somalis' reconstruction of home as resembling post-apartheid South Africa is somewhat exaggerated, but it renders the concept of home as "amorphous and fluid" (Arthur 2010, 133). These interviewees see the xenophobic violence in post-apartheid South Africa and clan-like military insurgency in Somali as their normal "lived experiences" and as "the spaces of everyday life" (Niemann 2003, 118). As a result, when I inquired whether they had any plans to return home, many of the participants tended to imagine South Africa as their home away from home. For them home is always a "contested space characterized by the mystification of a hegemonic system and the struggle to overcome it" (Niemann 2003, 117). Their struggle over spaces and for social inclusion in a xenophobic South Africa is seen as the same spatial contestation in Somali. This mode of diasporic memory shed light on Somalis' sense of belonging and the forms of citizenship they claim, especially in post-apartheid South Africa.

Their journeys to exile and the development of survival strategies

After narrating their experiences of not belonging in their homeland, Somalis' memory of displacement shifted towards their flight experiences through other volatile spaces. Given the horrific stories about the Al-Shabaab insurgency in Somalia, their journeys were usually unplanned flights—the "destination is [often] not determined when they leave home; it may change many times during the course of the journeys" (Collyer 2007, 668). The narratives therefore paid attention to the temporality and "spatiality of the journey" because each transit point in the course of their journey created a particular migratory experience worth remembering or forgetting (Collyer 2007, 668).

For example, Collyer's and Arnone's seminal papers on migrant journeys examine the way migrant experiences are constructed in spatial and temporal metaphors that express "the physical and psychological effects of exile, immigration and displacement" (Loshitzky 2006, 745). Collyer's (2009) discussion of the trepidations and dangers of flight in 'Stranded migrants and the fragmented journey' exposes the complex realities of Moroccan refugees' journeys across the Sahara into Europe. Reading the journey to exile as fragmented, his article affirms the contention that "migration journeys rarely conform to expectations of sequential trajectory, instead involving diversion, repetition and simultaneity". Arnone (2008: 328), on Eritreans' journeys to exile, discusses the whole experience of flight through space and time, the interplay between sordid memories of home and imaginations of exile as well as the construction of new transnational identities. In this case, the multiple trajectories of understanding migrant journeys shed light on "the dynamics of inclusion and exclusion within the collectivity of Eritreans in Milan" (325).

Somalis' narratives of flight were a continuation of episodes of pain and trauma as they escaped from the insurgency in pursuit of a safe haven. These journeys captured "the experience of movement through place and hint[ed] at how identity is shaped through movement" (Arnone 2008, 326). The journeys did not usually follow a careful premigration plan but were involuntary and clandestine escapes. One participant testifies:

> No, I had no idea where I was going. I just wanted to find a country where I could be safe. I didn't want to go too far from Somalia because my family was still at home. Initially I thought of maybe Tanzania because it is not too far from home. I had never heard of Mozambique or South Africa and I had no information about the two countries but I ended staying in these countries (Participant 15).

The narrator remembers the experience of flight as an unplanned decision triggered by killings and increasing political uncertainty. The notion of time is critical as it is "perceived ... as a measure of the distance between events" such as the frequency of political murders and the flight to exile (Sanadjian 1995, 4). Here, the narration represents home not in characteristic metaphors of kinship and motherland because home has become a danger zone to escape from (Pineteh 2005; Malkki 1992). Not knowing the destination implies that forced migration is a perilous adventure, which requires extreme courage and conviction. For Collyer (2007), the journey of forced migrants like the Somali cited above is in fact a fragmented one in that "their destination is not determined when they leave home, it may change many times during the course of the journey..." (668). This dangerous and somewhat adventurist behaviour resembles what Charman and Piper (2012) refer to as a unique kind of violent entrepreneurism which has pitted Somalis against locals and led to the eruption of violence in commercial spaces in townships all over South Africa (also see Abdi 2011; Dodson 2010; Crush 2008). Traversing unfamiliar and hostile spaces in the pursuit of safety is a common pattern of diasporization and

Somali journeys to unknown destinations had prepared them for a hostile reception in South African townships.

Escaping from a derelict homeland was remembered as a shared memory which tended to create a sense of group identity among Cape Town based Somali migrants. This was influenced by the unpredictability of their social existence and the dream of a safe haven beyond the borders of Somalia (Arnone 2008; Collyer 2007; Pineteh 2005). Although their journeys to exile were undertaken spontaneously, they claimed that they were usually mentally and physical prepared to confront the challenges. Their memories of journey unfolded "in some sense [as] an often frightening and painful ritual through which one becomes part of the [Somali] diaspora" (Arnone 2008, 330). One participant remembers their journey:

> The journey was very horrible; it was very horrific. You know... it was a situation whereby you didn't even know where you were going, you only knew where you were coming from. I had to leave because others who had crossed the border survived the war. Yes, sometimes you got into trouble with border guards, the migration officials, especially in Somalia but you were still determined to leave. When we were traveling from the border of Kiswayo to Kenya, it was very a risky journey, we were stopped at various border controls, searched and arrested or we were attacked by the people of Kenya but we kept going [sic]. (Participant 1)

This particular interviewee claimed to be a victim of several violent attacks and robberies all connected to xenophobia. During the interview he showed me scars of wounds from the attacks and for him living in South Africa is as dangerous as home and the arduous journey, in his word was "nothing I have not seen before". The construction of experiences of flight in "time and space, indexes the shifts in [Somali] social identities, and the processes and characteristic of displacement", especially when he compares those experiences to xenophobic violence in South Africa (Baynham and De Fina 2005, 5). Here, Participant 1 fashions his personal experiences of flight and xenophobia against the backdrop of a history of fear and Somalis' survival instincts. This narrative pattern continues in the following quotes:

> The main thing that forced me to leave was insecurity and uncertainty. As a young man, I needed to think about my future life. I left the country because of the war that had been going on for several years. You can imagine, we couldn't go to school, that was the first thing we needed to secure a better future. Secondly, we couldn't do business because we would be risking our lives. So when I saw that I couldn't do anything that made sense then I decided to leave. When I left, I was ready to face anything on the way because I did not want to come back to Somalia [sic]. (Participant 14)

> I didn't know where I was going. I just heard about South Africa, but at that time I didn't intend to come to South Africa. I was just looking for a better life, where I could live at least peacefully. When I passed through other countries like Kenya, the people didn't like us and I didn't get what I wanted. I just stayed at the Kenyan border refugee camp for some months and the conditions were very bad, so decided to continue my journey to look for a better life. The worst thing was that we had to travel through the sea and I had never travelled by sea but I was ready to take the risk. (Participant 12)

By remembering home against the background of experiences of xenophobia in South Africa, these Somali migrants were able to recreate the hopelessness of existence in their homeland. In the above testimonies, the flight to exile is constructed as the pursuit of a good life and the respondent "struggles to maintain a secure sense of [their] capacities in the face of an unknowable future" (Mar 2005, 366). What becomes very apparent in this case is the "dialectical relationship between home and exile" storied through contrasting images of fear and hopelessness and an imaginary good life in an unknown safe haven (Pineteh 2005, 391).

Crossing Somali borders into countries such as Ethiopia, Kenya or Tanzania marked the beginning of a long and tumultuous journey to unknown destinations. In the case of the Somalis I interviewed, this journey has increasingly become a trope of memory which is not only necessary for excavating their exilic experiences but also for building their sense of collective consciousness in the wake of xenophobic violence (Steinberg 2014; Pineteh 2005). As the participants narrated their journey experiences, they focused on individual and collective tactics for survival, similar tactics plotted during xenophobic attacks.

In Jonny Steinberg's non-fictional text about a Somali refugee's diasporic experiences, entitled *A Man of Good Hope*, the author captures in an extraordinary manner the eccentricities of global transnational human mobility as well as the temporalities and the dominant discourses about spatiality and belonging especially when people are forcefully uprooted from home (see also Neocosmos 2010; Nyamnjoh 2004, 2006). Through young Somali migrant Asad Abdullah's memories this fictionalized biography unearths "the subjective construction of these movements of human beings, rather than their objectivist othering in nationalist or racist mainstream discourses" (Baynham and De Fina 2005, 2). As Asad Abdullah tries to hem together fragmented episodes of his stories of leaving home at a tender of 8, his journey to and life in Cape Town as well as the rites of passage through childhood to adulthood, the readers are shown "the unhealable rift forced between a human being and a native place, between the self and its true home..." (Said 2001, 173). These stories also capture the difficulties of crossing borders, the hostile receptions in unfamiliar exotic spaces and the generalised social sufferings of a displaced person (Collyer 2007; Fisiy 1998; Besteman 1996).

Somalis' journeys to exile were therefore remembered as " the process of passage from one state or identity into another, the freedom or right to pass through; passage in a temporal sense-the passage of time and the effects on the individual" (Munro 2006, 35).

> I left Somali in 2000 with other Somalis who were also escaping from the war. I came through a vehicle from Kismayo up to the border of Kenya. From the border, we managed to find our way into Kenya. We didn't enter directly through the border post because we thought they might arrest us. We came in through other means, we were smuggled into the country by special smugglers. We paid them and they smuggled us into the next country. I stayed in Kenya for quite some time, I think three years and then, I left for South Africa in 2004 with the help of the smugglers. (Participant 1)

> I started my journey at night by foot while hiding from Al-Shabaab because they were looking for me. Immediately five minutes after I left, they came and searched my house. They tied up my family and hit them badly, while I was footing up to Kenya and that was how I left Somalia. I went to a place called Mombasa in Kenya and there I boarded a boat to Mozambique. In Mozambique I was arrested, beaten and jailed for fifteen days with other Somalis but we were freed later and then I came to South Africa [sic]. (Participant 5)

These two Somalis' descriptions of their journeys epitomize the precariousness of the passage from one space to another, represented here in images of silencing and victimization through incarceration and "existential alienation and physical separation" from Somalia (Munro 2006, 35). Again, we see an uncanny relationship between Somali experiences during flight and the different forms of physical and mental resistance to xenophobic violence. There is a strong sense of resilience, the kind of resilience at the epicentre of Somali existence in South Africa. These experiences resulted in "the development of a particular historical consciousness and heightened a sense of group identity" (Besteman 1996, 580) often displayed during the violent attacks in South Africa.

Although fleeing from home was constructed as the pursuit of happiness or better lives, the journeys to exile prepared Somalis for a more tactical approach to finding happiness or a better life. Their memories of their difficult and violent lives in Somali and the complexities of the journeys to freedom engendered the development and application of tactics for circumventing hostilities in different places. In the following quotations, we experience how one Somali migrant negotiated a passage to freedom:

> Coming to South Africa was a long way from home and it was the worst experience of my life. Coming out from Somalia itself to Kenya I used 4 vehicles, and from Kenya to the border of Tanzania, 3 vehicles. I came through sea by boat to Dares-Salaam. From there I came through a bus straight to a Malawian refugee camp, via the Mozambique border, and I jumped onto another car travelled the longest journey through Mozambique. After weeks, we reached the border of Mozambique and South Africa. I jumped over the fence and handed myself over to the government of South Africa [sic]. (Participant 20)

One distinct aspect of narrating border crossing experiences was the reconstruction of the influx of refugees and asylum-seekers from Somalia into neighbouring countries. In this narrative there is an underlying imagery of a refugee crisis in countries like Kenya, Ethiopia and Tanzania similar to that in South Africa (Kaiser 2006; Hautaniemi 2006). The journeys are storied as episodes of a never-ending struggle because as in South Africa, Somali refugees were blamed and victimized for economic and social misfortunes in countries that they fled to. For example, in 1999 the Kenyan government tightened its borders to regulate the entry of Somali asylum-seekers following the President's public statement "linking refugees to crime and illicit arms proliferation…" as well as security threats (Mogire 2009, 21). By linking crimes to refugees, this political rhetoric spurred xenophobic violence in Kenya. Through Somalis' ethnographic accounts of flight, we are able witness the same patterns of social violence experienced in South Africa.

As they are victimized and ostracized everywhere they go, Somalis' narratives tended to employ "kinds of narratological and dramaturgical tools for describing and communicating related memories and specific events" (Hautaniemi 2006, 81). In the following testimony, one interviewee remembers a personal experience of incarceration during flight, to explain a strong sense of collective identity, which has strengthened during their struggles to belong in South Africa.

> Indeed, the journey to South Africa was very long, and the reason was that I was looking for a place that I could get an education and a better life. So I escaped to Tanzania, via the Kenya-Tanzania border, known as Namanga, and later I came to Arusha where I was arrested and imprisoned for six months. Later some Somali guys released me from the jail and I stayed with them in Arusha for twenty-one days and after that I went to Dar-es-salaam, where I met a lot of Somali guys, around twenty-one of them living in a room, owned by one of the people who was helping immigrants to come to South Africa. That was when those guys told me about South Africa and that South Africa is a good country where I could get a good education and a better life. This is how I ended up in South Africa. (Participant 17)

In this description of flight there is an interesting interconnection of different events, which helps to shape our understanding of this migrant's experiences, exposing us to "complex webs of historical past in the present" (Hautaniemi 2006, 82). His personal memory is marked by the tragic loss of dignity when he is jailed and by images of hope as he imagines South Africa as a "good country". Through different events of flight and spatial practices, we experience a narrative trajectory, which constructs the past as the present and the present as the past through the contradictions of lived spaces (Bakonyi 2010; Agnew 2005; Fisiy 1998).

Memories of perilous journeys through countries where Somali refugees were victimized and incarcerated help us to make sense of the complexities of forced displacement within Sub-Saharan Africa and how migrant journeys "are seen as important rites of passage" (Collyer 2010, 278). This interpretation connects to the spectacle of social violence against Somali migrants and their uncharacteristic resilience to different forms of social suffering. As they traverse hostile spaces they develop mechanisms for self-reliance and collective consciousness (Collyer 2010; Kaiser 2006). Below, we see how crossing the South African border is negotiated.

> I heard that South Africa was peaceful and that if one worked hard, they could make a good living, so decided to come to this country. After several attempts, I finally arrived at the Musina border and the police arrested us, transferred us to Johannesburg, where other police officers took us to Home Affairs. We were given 3 month permits. We met some other Somali people in Johannesburg who welcomed us but we were not very happy with the way they treated us. (Participant 23)

> We crossed the border and the bus stopped somewhere. I didn't even know that we were near a border, the border of Swaziland. We crossed the border and we walked like half an hour through the bushes and then we came back to the road, same road. The bus was waiting for us there. We took the bus again and came to the border of South Africa. The driver dropped us and left. We paid someone to take us through the border and we walked for three hours, before taking another vehicle to Johannesburg. (Participant 10)

Through the interactions between the police officers, intermediaries and Somalis, these migrants' experiences of flight expose us to "all sorts of social, geographic, generic and linguistic boundaries that need to be crossed" (Baynham and De Fina 2005, 178). Here, the image of a safe haven is juxtaposed with images of a cold reception from fellow Somali migrants in South Africa creating the impression that survival in South Africa is more about individual actions than about community participation.

Conclusion

To understand Somali experiences of xenophobia in post-apartheid South Africa we have to trace their lives from home and their experiences in different spaces during the process of flight to

South Africa. From Somali memories of home, I have argued that despite the pain and suffering caused by xenophobia, Somalis are still resilient to xenophobic violence because they experienced similar violence in Somalia. Before migration, they lived through the devastating effects of the Al-Shabaab insurgency, which exposed them to extreme violence and fear. As Somali migrants narrated their experiences, they tended to use phraseology indicating their immunity to social violence and their ability to survive in hostile spaces and under adverse conditions. Moreover, they are ready to defend themselves as they have done for years under the Al-Shabaab insurgency. Most importantly, they do not have a home to return to. Post-apartheid violence triggered memories of a similar history of political and social instability at home (Kaiser 2006; King 2000; Malkki 1992), positioning home as both a trope of memory and a metaphor of displacement which helps us to make sense of the Somali diasporic community.

As victims of a fractured state, they had to flee into exile precipitating a humanitarian crisis in neighbouring countries such as Ethiopia, Kenya and Tanzania. In the memories of flight, they described episodes of similar violence and hostilities in spaces where they sought asylum. Through individual stories, we see a community of forced migrants being blamed for the host countries' social problems and being victimized for seeking safety. The narratives constructed their journeys as being as perilous as their lives at home and yet again forcing struggles for survival. During the journeys they developed critical skills and tactics, which they have deployed during xenophobic violence in South Africa. For them, xenophobic violence is similar to the violence and victimization experienced during Al-Shabaab insurgency and during flight through countries like Kenya and Tanzania. The journey is not just a metaphor of displacement but also an outlet for meaning making as we try to unlock Somali xenophobia experiences.

Acknowledgements

This article is part of a broader project on Cape Town-based Somali victims of xenophobia, funded by the American Council of Learned Societies through its African Humanities Program. I would like to sincerely thank this organization for its financial generosity.

The article was written during a one month visiting research fellowship at the Centre for Concurrences in Colonial and Postcolonial Studies at Linnaeus University in Sweden. During the fellowship, I received financial support and I was provided with office space, internet and library access. I would like to express my deepest gratitude to the Centre for hosting me.

References

Abdi, Cawo M. 2011. Moving beyond xenophobia: structural violence, conflict and encounters with the 'other' Africans. *Development Southern African* 28 (5): 691–704.

Adams, Mary. 2009. Stories of fracture and claims for belonging: young migrant narratives of arrival in Britain. *Children's Geographies* 7 (2): 159–171.

Anderson, Elliot A. 2010. It's a Pirate's Life for Some: The Development of an Illegal Industry in Response to an Unjust Global Power Dynamic. *Indiana Journal of Global Legal Studies* 17 (2): 319–339.

Agnew, Vijay. 2005. *Diaspora, memory, and identity; A search for home.* Toronto: University of Toronto Press.

Andrews, Molly., Squire, Corrine & Tamboukou, Maria (eds.). 2013. *Doing narrative research*, 2nd ed. London: Sage.

Arnone, Anna. 2008. Journeys to exile: the construction of Eritrean identity through narratives and experiences. *Journal of Ethnic and Migration Studies* 34 (2): 325–340.

Arthur, John A. 2010. *African diaspora identities: negotiating culture in transnational migration.* New York: Lexington Books.

Bal, Mieke. 2009. *Narratology: Introduction to the theory of narrative.* Toronto: University of Toronto Press.

Bakonyi, Juta. 2010. Between protest, revenge and material interests. A phenomenological analysis of looting in the Somali war. *Disasters* 34 (2): 238–255.

Baynham, Mike & De Fina, Anna. (eds.). 2005. *Dislocations/relocations: Narratives of displacement.* Manchester: St Jerome Publishing.

Besteman, Catherine. 1996. Violent politics and the politics of violence: The dissolution of the Somali nation-state. *American Ethnologist* 23 (3): 579–596.

Charman, Andrew & Piper, Laurence. 2012. Xenophobia, criminality and violent entrepreneurship: violence against Somali shopkeepers in Delft South, Cape Town, South Africa. *South African Review of Sociology* 43 (3): 81–105.

Collyer, Michael. 2007. In-between places: Trans-Saharan transit migrants in Morocco and the fragmented journey to Europe. *Antipode* 668–690.

Crush, Jonathan (ed.). 2008. The perfect storm: Xenophobia in contemporary South Africa. *South African Migration Project*. Cape Town: Institute for Democracy in South Africa.

Dodson, Belinda. 2010. Locating xenophobia; Debate, Discourse, and everyday experience in Cape Town, South Africa. *Africa Today* 56 (3): 2–22.

Eckardt, Alice L. 1993. *Burning Memory, Times of Testing and Reckoning*. New York: Pergamon Press.

Fadlalla, Amal H. 2009. Contested borders of (In)humanity: Sudanese Refugees and the mediation of suffering and subaltern visibilities. *Urban Anthropology* 38 (1): 79–120.

Fisiy, Cyprian F. 1998. Of journeys and border crossings: Return of refugees, identity and reconstruction in Rwanda. *African Studies Review* 41 (1): 17–28.

Freeman, Mark. 1993. *Rewriting the Self: History, Memory, Narrative*. London: Routledge.

Gibson, Nigel C. 2011. *Fanonian Practices in South Africa*. Durban: University of KwaZulu-Natal Press.

Griffiths, Melanie, Rogers, Ali &Anderson, Bridget. 2013. Migration, time and temporalities: Review and prospect. COMPASS Research Resources Paper.

Hassim, Shireen., Kupe, Tawana & Worby, Eric (eds.). 2008. *Go home or die here: violence, xenophobia and the reinvention of difference in South Africa*. Johannesburg: Wits University Press.

Hautaniemi, Petri. 2006. Fugitive memories. Howyounf Somali men recall displacement and emplacement in their childhood. *Anthropological Yearbook of European Cultures* 15: 77–91.

Henderson, Mae G. 1995. *Borders, Boundaries and Frames*. New York: Routledge.

Hickel, Jason. 2014. 'Xenophobia' in South Africa: Order, chaos, and the moral economy of witchcraft. *Cultural Anthropology* 29 (1): 103–127.

Ibrahim, Mohamed. 2010. Somali and global terrorism: A growing connection? *Journal of Contemporary African Studies* 28 (3): 283–293.

Ingiriis, Mohamed H. 2016. Many Somalia(s), multiple memories: remembrances as present politics, past politics as remembrances in war-torn Somali discourses. *African Identities* 14 (4): 348–369.

Jackson, Michael. 2002. *The politics of storytelling. Violence, transgression and intersubjectivity*. Chicago: University of Chicago Press.

Kaiser, Tania. 2006. Between a camp and a hard place: Rights, livelihood and experiences of the local settlement system for long-term refugees in Uganda. *The Journal of Modern African Studies* 44 (4): 597–621.

King, Nicola. 2000. *Memory, narrative, identity. Remembering the self*. Edinburgh: Edinburgh University Press.

Labov, William. 2013. *The language of life and death: The transformation of experience in oral narratives*. Cambridge: Cambridge University Press.

Landau, Loren B. & Freemantle, Iriann. 2010. Tactical cosmopolitanism and idioms of belonging: insertion and self-exclusion in Johannesburg. *Journal of Ethnic and Migration Studies* 36 (3): 375–390.

Landau, Loren B., (ed.). 2011. *Exorcising the demons within: xenophobia, violence and statecraft in contemporary South Africa*. Johannesburg: Wits University Press.

Loshitzky, Yosefa. 2006. Journeys of hope to fortress Europe. *Third Text* 20 (6): 745–754.

Mbembe, Achille. 2001. *On the postcolony*. Los Angeles: University of California Press.

Malkki, Liisa. 1992. National Geographic: The rooting of peoples and the territorialisation of national identity among scholars and refugees. *Cultural Anthropology* 7 (1): 24–44.

Maree, Kobus. (ed.). 2007. *First steps in research*. Pretoria: Van Schaik Books.

Mar, Phillip. 2005. Unsettling Potentialities: Topographies of Hope in Transnational Migration. *Journal of Intercultural Studies* 26 (4): 361–378.

Menkhaus, Ken. 2004. *Somali: State collapse and the threat of terrorism*. London and New York: Routledge.

Menkhaus, Ken. 2010. Stabilisation and humanitarian access in a collapsed state: the Somali case. *Disasters* 34 (3): 320–341.

Mogire, Edward. 2009. Refugee realities: Refugee rights versus state security in Kenya and Tanzania. *Transformations: An International Journal of Holistic Mission Studies* 26 (1): 15–29.

Munro, Martin. 2006. Unfinished journeys: exile, Africanity and intertextuality in Emile Ollivier's Passages. *Journal of Modern Literature* 29 (2): 33–49.

Mwangi, Oscar G. 2012. State collapse, Al-Shabaab, Islamism, and legitimacy in Somali. *Politics, Religion and Ideology* 13 (4): 513–527.

Neocosmos, Micahel. 2010. *From 'foreign natives' to 'native foreigners': Explaining xenophobia in post-apartheid South Africa. Citizenship and nationalism, identity and politics*. Dakar: Codesria.

Niemann, Michael. 2003. Migration and the lived spaces of Southern Africa. *Alternatives: Global, Local, Political* 28 (1): 115–140

Nyamnjoh, Francis B. 2004. Globalisation, Boundaries, Livelihoods: Perspectives on Africa. *Identity, Culture and Politics* 5 (1and2): 37–59.

Nyamnjoh, Francis B. 2006. *Insiders and outsiders: citizenship and xenophobia in contemporary Southern Africa*. Dakar: Codesria.

Pineteh, Ernest. 2005. Memories of home and exile: Narratives of Cameroonian asylum seekers in Johannesburg. *Journal of Intercultural Studies* 26 (4): 379–400.

Rousseau, Cécile, Said, Taher M., Gagné, Marie-Josée, Bibeau, Gilles. 1998. Between myth and madness: The premigration dreams of living among young Somali refugees. *Cult. Med. Psychiatry* 22 (4), 385–411.

Sadouni, Samadia. 2009. God is not unemployed: Journeys of Somali refugees in Johannesburg. *African Studies* 68 (2): 235- 249.

Said, Edward W. 2001. *Reflections on Exile and Other Literary and Cultural Essays*. London: Granta Books.

Sanadjian, Manuchehr. 1995. Temporality of home and spatiality of market in exile: Iranians in Germany. *New German Critique* 64: 2–6.

Schiffrin, Deborah., De Fina, Anna & Nylund, Anastasia (eds.). 2010. *Telling stories: Language narrative and social life*. Washington: Georgetown University Press.

Steinberg, J. 2014. *A man of hope*. Cape Town: Jonathan Ball Publishers.

Thelen, David. 1995. The Postmodern Challenge of Introducing Past to Present: Teaching about Memories and Monuments. *Perspectives in Education* 14 (2): 117–138.

Thelen, David. 1994. Memory and American History. *Journal of American History* 7 (4): 1117–1129.

Watkins, Mary & Shulman, Helene. 2008. *Toward psychologies of liberation*. New York: Palgrave Macmillan.

Homosexuality as "UnAfrican":
Heteronormativity, Power, and Ambivalence in Cameroon

Ngambouk Vitalis Pemunta
Centre for Concurrences in Colonial
and Postcolonial Studies,
Linnaeus University, Växjö, Sweden

Introduction

In 2006, Cameroon was rocked by an anti-gay crusade when some tabloids beamed their searchlight on more than 50 of the country's prominent figures for homosexuality. The denunciation campaign against homosexuality set in motion a furious national debate on gay rights in the country. This chapter examines the Cameroon government's ambivalence to lesbian, gay, bisexual and transgender (LGBT) relationships and the simultaneous entanglement of same-sex relationships with power and social mobility. Same-sex relationships involving the powerful, is part of human rights—"the right to a private life". However, when it involves the poor, it is criminalized, and considered as a threat to national identity and sovereignty. Homosexual relationships by the former are reportedly intertwined with occultic powers and serve as a gateway to social mobility in the country's sociopolitical landscape. Framed in terms of African nationalism—a national identity inscribed on women's bodies since they are charged with biological reproduction, the public resistance of Cameroon's leaders to same-sex relationships is a veil to produce a counter hegemonic discourse against the perceived intrusion of Western values as well as to deflect Western attention from profligacy, human rights violations, long stays in power, and unbridled corruption. Cast against the anti-democracy discourse of the 1990s, the anti-same-sex discourse feeds into larger narratives about resistance to perceived

Western values and the double appropriation of political homophobia by various social actors.

> Men making love to other men . . . is filthy. It may be normal in the west, but in Africa and Cameroon in particular, it is unthinkable. We could not remain silent. We had to ring the alarm bell. We don't regret it and we have to do it again . . . in spite of numerous death threats that me and my fellow journalists have had (L'Anecdote publisher, Jean Pierre Amougou Belinga).

President Barack Obama's visit to Kenya (25–26 July, 2015) was almost overshadowed by the contentious debate between African and Western (American and European) societies over the supposed"unAfrican" practice of homosexuality. Homosexuality is being allegedly imposed by the West on African countries by being linked to development aid in the same way that Western-styled democracy ("donor democracy") was imposed on African countries (Pemunta, 2011). Timothy Geithner, the US treasury secretary, stated that his Treasury Department "will continue to instruct the US executive directors at each of the [multilateral development banks] (MDBs) to seek to channel MDB resources away from those countries whose governments engage in a pattern of gross violations of human rights"[1],[2]. In the same light, the European Union (EU) reaffirmed its democratic credentials. Without mincing words, the European parliament passed a resolution in December 2011 "reminding" Africa that "the EU is responsible for more than half of development aid and remains Africa's most important trading partner" and that "in all actions conducted under the terms of various partnerships" sexual orientation is a protected category of non-discrimination[3] (see also Geschiere, 2010). In February 2014, when Uganda's government passed a law that threatened gay people with life imprisonment, the World Bank withheld a $90m

---

[1] http://www.theguardian.com/commentisfree/cifamerica/2011/apr/20/anti-gay-laws-africa-uganda-ssempa

[2] http://crin2.crin.org/en/library/news-archive/africa-international-pressure-anti-gay-laws-must-not-stop?&session-id=8c0fca29d046fa6f9b29fd8d71873491.

[3] http://crin2.crin.org/en/library/news-archive/africa-international-pressure-anti-gay-laws-must-not-stop?&session-id=8c0fca29d046fa6f9b29fd8d71873491.

loan that was going to be spent on the country's health service on grounds that the bank wanted to ensure that "development objectives would not be adversely affected by the enactment of this new law"[4]. The Norwegian, Danish and Swedish governments also suspended aid to Uganda because of the country's hardline stance against LGBT individuals (Ibid). In Cameroon where anti-EU support for LGBT rights is framed in terms of national identity and sovereignty and therefore in heteronormative terms, the country's one time (2007 to 2011) foreign minister, Henri Eyebe Ayissi, summoned the head of the EU delegation to protest against the EU's support for people who "violate the laws of Cameroon" (Pemunta, 2011: 4). Like other activists in Africa, Cameroonian activists have received death threats. Bodies such as Amnesty International and the Global Fund to Fight Aids, Tuberculosis and Malaria are increasingly questioning the criminalization of homosexuality in countries including Cameroon. However, health promotion activities targeting HIV/AIDS among LGBT people which governments are being required to tolerate, has triggered a flurry of community developments in many countries worldwide and especially in Africa[5] where the deployment of political homophobia against political opponents and LGBT activists has excluded and led to the invisibility of the LGBT community in the implementation of state backed HIV/AIDS prevention, education, and treatment campaigns (Lorway, 2008, cf Currier 2010, Reid, 2015). What is the influence of Western-driven democratization and human rights norms on the rights of sexual minorities (LGBT individuals) in Cameroon? In a bid to attempt an answer to this question, this chapter argues that while the competing visions between nation and sexuality has been primordial in national identity construction, Western imposed norms of democratization and good governance have brought to the fore the issue of the status of sexual minorities.

---

[4] Talkpoint: should aid be withdrawn from countries violating LGBT rights? http://www.theguardian.com/global-development-professionals-network/2014/jul/09/lgbt-aid-development-rights

[5] http://www.theguardian.com/commentisfree/cifamerica/2011/apr/20/anti-gay-laws-africa-uganda-ssempa

The essay speaks to a growing body of scholarly works that examine the entanglement of power and occultic practices in Africa (see e.g Geschiere 2010, 1997, Lado, 2011, Mbembe, 2000, Abega, 2007, Nyamsi, 2007, Ellis & Teer, 2004) and on the double appropriation of political homophobia by the disenchanted masses left out of the benefits of the economic growth associated with democracy to question the morality of their rulers and the ruling elites to account for their failure to deliver on the dividends of democracy to their people (Murray, 1998, Currier, 2010, Geschiere 2010, Epprecht, 2004).

The remainder of this essay is structured into three main parts and a conclusion. First, I articulate the methodological, theoretical, and analytical position regarding the notion of sexual citizenship, the interplay between symbolic processes through which national communities are imagined with reference to the citizenship status of sexual minorities in Cameroon. The second section examines the dynamic religious context of Cameroon which has witnessed the mushrooming of an unprecedented number of revivalist movements preaching the gospel of material riches and salvation. These movements are fiercely in competition with the mainstream Catholic and protestant churches for converts. Despite schism and intolerance among various denominations, they are united against homosexual practices which are part of initiation procedures into some sects. The third part deals with the unending debate about homosexuality as an "UnAfrican practice", explores varied reactions to the homosexuality "epidemic", the double appropriation of the concept of privacy and individual autonomy by the political class and ambivalence as a political strategy among the political elites who simultaneously have to comply with donor conditionalities as well as to reflect their cultural credentials as moral entrepreneurs in their communities. Lastly follows the conclusion.

Methodological, Theoretical and Analytical Framework

This chapter combines a review of existing literature on LGBT issues in Cameroon and other African countries with informal discussion sessions involving rights activists and participant observation to explore the class dimension of homosexuality. During HIV/AIDS related ethnographic fieldwork conducted between 2006–2007 and in 2010, the lack of access to counselling and antiretroviral drugs by LGBT individuals constantly cropped up in conversations with rights activists. Additionally, I draw heavily from my insider knowledge/personal experience of Cameroon's sociopolitical scene as well as extensive fieldwork spanning over 20 years in the country. The chapter is therefore partly a conscious form of autoethnography: "an approach to research and writing that seeks to describe and systematically analyze personal experience in order to understand cultural experience" (Ellis et al. 2010: 1). Such an approach is contrary to standard research methods because it "treats research as a political, socially-just and socially-conscious act" (Ibid). This methodological approach recognizes and accommodates [my own] "subjective, emotionality, [and] influence on research, rather than hiding from these matters or assuming they do not exist" (Ellis, 2010: 2, see also Besio & Butz, 2004).

From a dispassionate third space, and while being simultaneously cautious, I will refrain from presenting Western societies (European and American)—including their values and practices—as liberators of LGBT people from the jaws of heteronationalism and homophobia in Africa in general and Cameroon in particular. Rather, I will regard Western and particularly EU pressure as opening up a space for political mobilization not only for sexual rights activists who draw on different normative assumptions about sexuality in order to contest the heteronormative vision of national identity and desired future but also for greater freedoms through the currencies of democracy and good governance. The use of the term 'sexual minorities' captures the marginal voices of different groups of social actors who are in the margins of mainstream society on the basis of their 'abnormal' sexuality. The notion of minority is used to capture existing, hierarchical power relations that differentially construct and position groups on the scale of power (Alcoff and Mohanty, 2006: 7–8, cf. Kahlina, 2013: 5). The quantitative approach—relationship between different social groups, naturalizes ethnic and national differences as given, closed, indivisible and unified, thus re/producing the existing relations of power (Yuval-Davis, 1997, cf. Kahlina, 2013: 5). I use minority here to refer to "unequal relations to the dominant group" (Alcoff and Mohanty, 2006: 7–8, cf. Kahlina, 2013: 5), that is to stress how unequal citizenship based on sexuality is reproduced in the media and in official discourses in Cameroon. I conceptualize sexual minority like other minorities who often live on the margins of mainstream society as an all-encompassing category injected in Cameroon's social policy arena by donors—particularly through EU and World Bank policies in the forestry sector.

This chapter draws on the concept of class (Wright, 2005, Bourdieu, 1979, 1986) as an analytical lens for foregrounding understanding of elite's involvement in homosexual practices as a mechanism for conserving political power with all its associated socio-economic and political advantages. Class serves as the main determinant of an individual's economic prospects and life chances as well as granting access "to economically valuable assets of various sorts" (Wright, 2005: 2). According to Pierre Bourdieu, class is a multidimensional and all-encompassing concept that is associated with myriad forms of "capital". Socio-economic capital is made up of several components—it is a multidimensional space of power that brings together and confers several types of symbolic, social, economic and political resources that shape both the opportunities and the dispositions of actors (Wright, 2005: 3). The privileged position of the political class simultaneously exposes its members to accusations of witchcraft and political homophobia (Mbembe 2000, Abega 2007, Geschier 2010, 1997, Lado 2011) from the impoverished masses who use accusations of, and the stigma of homosexuality to demonize its members (Lado, 2011: 922, see also Currier 2010, Reid 2015). Like the simultaneous appropriation of the concept of democracy and respect for human rights including the rights of LGBT people, homophobia is a paradoxical strategy that is also appropriated by state agents to cover up their inability to deliver social services to the masses as well as to blackmail opponents (Lado, 2011, Currier 2010, Reid 2015). In the next section I examine the dynamic religious context of Cameroon within which same-sex relationships that are usually intertwined with class and power but fiercely opposed thereby leading to homophobia take place.

The Religious Context of Homosexuality in Cameroon

Cameroon's religious landscape has remained dynamic and characterized by an exponential jump in the number of revivalist movements as well as schism and intolerance among and even within various religious denominations. Like in other African countries, religions of all denominations and the state are fiercely opposed to homosexuality. Both converge around several of the arguments underpinning opposition to homosexuality as being against culture and national law (legal argument), the demonization of the West (anticolonialism argument), and the demographic argument according to which humans need to procreate so as to perpetuate the existence of human society(see also Lado, 2011). In Burundi, the Church and state even organized joined marches against homosexuality (Currier, 2010). Ironically, not even half of the estimated 1000 denominations that Cameroon counts are legalized (International Crisis Group, 2015, Heunggroup 2015). Some 63% of the population claim to be nominally Christian, 22% Muslim, 14% adhere to traditional faiths and 1% agnostic (International Crisis Group 2015: 1). The mainstream Catholic and Protestant congregations are facing stiff religious competition and losing ground, mostly to Revivalist Churches (Heunggroup 2015) the plank of whose preaching is the gospel of material wealth and prosperity. These movements often preach religious intolerance, avoid interreligious dialogue "and are kept out of official religious spheres, although they mostly support the regime" (International Crisis Group, 2015: i) during electoral contests.

Among the mosaic of a thousand Christian, Muslim and traditional religious organizations, only 47 are registered. Cameroon's

1996 Constitution and the law of 19 December 1990 guarantee religious freedom and secularism. The enactment of the law on religious freedom shattered the monopoly of the Catholic Church and led to an upsurge in the number of revivalist churches in the country. Between 1992 and 2003, 471 churches applied for registration with the Ministry of Territorial Administration and Decentralisation (International Crisis Group 2015: 1, Tanku, 2013, Pemunta et al. 2013). "These neo-Pentecostal Churches" constituted the second wave of the Cameroon Pentecostal Movement. "Their discourse focuses on material prosperity and miracles, and they borrow, theologically and culturally, from Pentecostalism, American evangelism and Baptist movement" (International Crisis Group, 2015: 11). While they are radically opposed to mainstream Catholicism they are also "in fierce competition with each other" (Ibid).

A complex web of political, economic and theological factors has contributed to the rise of revivalist churches. Apart from the law on religious freedom, the economic crisis of 1986–1994 worked in favour of these revivalist movements. They forward "God as a source of wealth and miracles capable of providing a solution to unemployment, sorcery, infertility, celibacy, and educational failure" (Ibid). Those disappointed by the Catholic Church and the poor flock to these churches. "The Catholic Church has remained a victim of its own institutional rigidity, the neo-Pentecostal churches offered lively acts of worship and a close relationship between believers and pastors" (Ibid). Revivalist churches maintain a system of mutual recognition and indebtedness to politicians of the ruling Cameroon People's Democratic Movement (CPDM) party and regime. Contrary to the Catholic Church which through its episcopal council has been vigorously critical of the regime, the revivalist churches preach respect for authority and often appeal to their followers to vote incumbent president Paul Biya during electoral contests. They consistently pay homage to the president, rather than criticizing him. The legally registered churches are often full of praise for the president's "initiatives to promote peace, while illegal churches thank him for the administration's tolerance" (International Crisis Group, 2015: 11, Tanku, 2013, Pemunta et al. 2013). The government's laissez-faire approach to the disorderly proliferation of revivalist chapels worked in their favour. In 2013 when prefects suspended about 50 illegal revivalist churches in the cities of Bafoussam, Yaounde, Douala, and Bamenda for allegedly disturbing public order, president Biya ordered the ministry of territorial administration (MINTAD) to lift the suspensions. He subsequently signed a decree empowering the MINTAD to decide on the closure of religious organizations that were deemed to be involved in unorthodox practices (International Crisis Group, 2015: 11, Tanku, 2013).

Some members of government maintain a cosy relationship with some well-known pastors, such as Tsala Essomba and Achille Mendongo. The Pastor of one Church quipped about his relationship thus:

> We regularly work with politicians and members of the government. They consult us. They often visit us and we help them. Politicians admit consulting revivalist pastors soliciting electoral support and also protection from sorcery. These pastors have in effect become the Christian marabouts of some politicians (International Crisis Group, 2015: 12).

Apart from serving as a source of hope to church members through the theology of wealth, revivalist churches serve the interests of the regime. In the face of the government's inability to alleviate unemployment or poverty, "the churches play the role of social stabilizers and purveyors of dreams for the part of the population". "By inviting their followers to trust Jesus Christ to resolve their problems and protect them from the cause of those problems, that is, the Devil, they deflect grievances against the government, which is further legitimized by their belief that there is no authority except from God" (International Crisis Group, 2015: 11, Geschiere, 2010, Tanku, 2013, Mbuy, 1994). In fact, most pastors are grateful for the way they are tolerated and for the private assistance they sometimes receive from politicians. The result is a system of mutual recognition and indebtedness (Geschiere, 2010, Tanku, 2013, International Crisis Group, 2011, Lado, 2011). Despite this mutual recognition and indebtedness, Cameroonian authorities often clamp down on churches for alleged unorthodox practices. They sometimes maintain ambivalence with some Pentecostal churches that criticize them. When Biya ordered the closure of some 100 Pentecostal churches which had allegedly outstretched their liberty, the pastors conceded that the real reason was "insecurity about the churches' criticism of the government". They marched against the government's decision. The government accuses some Pentecostal pastors of misusing "the name of Jesus Christ to fake miracles and kill citizens in their churches" (Tanku, 2013, see also International Crisis Group, 2015). Apart from displaying the president's photo in places of worship, support for the regime is more explicit during electoral contests. In 2011 pastors called on their followers to vote for Paul Biya. The most vocal figures were Tsala Essomba of International Go Tell Ministry and Achille Mendongo of the Christian Pentecostal Church of Cameroon (EPCC). The former openly campaigned for Biya during his sermons (International Crisis Group, 2015: 11).

Apart from the unprecedented jump in the number of protestant churches, there is also the proliferation of sects run by people close to power in Cameroon. Some of the rituals associated with membership of these sects involve the use of body parts (ritual killing for power), sexual perversion, homosexual practices (the practice of sexual magic) and child sacrifice during midnight rites as mechanisms of acquiring supernatural powers. On August 21, 2006 Djomo Pokam was mysteriously murdered in cold blood in one of the suites of Hilton Hotel and his corpse thrown out from an eighth floor window. His body was littered with burns and injuries in intimate areas. Two top brass of the Yaounde regime were allegedly in the suites of the hotel at the time. One was the former chief of protocol to the president and the Cameroonian ambassador to the United Nations, while the other was the president of the Cameroon Chamber of Commerce, Industry and Crafts. Investigating police officers confided that they needed clearance from the president, who at the time was on an official visit to China before they could make any arrests of the untouchable suspects. What became dubbed as the Djomo Pokam Affair was alleged to be a ritual murder linked to homosexual practices (see Lado, 2011). The African elites are often accused of the antisocial use of mystical powers (marabouts or exorcists) for achieving political ends. Merit has been sacrificed for membership in an esoteric organization which is associated with supposedly abominable acts including homosexuality so as to gain access at the trough (Bokande, 2007: 10 cited in Lado, 2011, Nyamsi, 2007). This alleged use of mystical powers has led to the stigmatization of the elites because of their actions of bad governance and corruption as a semblance to witchcraft in Africa (Lado, 2011, Geschierre, 1997). According to Stephen Ellis and Gerrie Teer Haar "African politicians, for example, typically pay great regard to the spirit world as a source of power" (Ellis and Teer, 2004: 3). In Cameroon sects such as Freemasonry, Rose cross, their different branches and recruitment poles including the Rotary club and the Lions club recruit adherents from among Catholics, Protestants, and Muslims. They have infiltrated these congregations (see Mbuy, 1994, Geschiere, 1997, 2010, http://africanrevolution.org/Sect-influence.html). Membership of one of these cults or the backing of a follower/lobby has gradually become the *conditio sine qua non* for upward social mobility. Initiation is perceived as a form of class practice that grants access to class interest which is comprised of the material interests of people accruing from their location-within-relations including standards of living, working conditions, material security. The opportunities and tradeoffs enjoyed in pursuing these interests "are structured by their class locations" (Wright, 2005: 20). Cultural capital is partly acquired through socialization and therefore incorporated in the habitus—the internalization of the objective structures of the environment in the form of practices. The lessons (social practices) learned through the process of socialization are internalized and constantly reproduced over time (Bourdieu, 1977). The various dimensions of capital accruing from initiation resonates with the socio-economic argument according to which young African men practice homosexuality for purely economic reasons by offering their sexual services to powerful men—a result of poverty and destitution (Lado, 2011). These sects wield a lot of power, "has a diversified operating field. They are at the heart of spy ring, money laundering and feymania. They mainly invest in activities like gambling, sex commerce, drugs and alcohol, everything which causes addiction in a country where misery and despair do not offer many alternatives" (http://africanrevolution.org/Sect-influence.html). Power is conceptualized as flowing between visible material world and invisible spiritual world…"power seen as unitary by politicians and indivisible into separate boxes" (Ellis and Teer, 2004: 3). Most of the members of these cults who are politicians and prominent businessmen are blamed by the masses and the Catholic Church for the country's socioeconomic woes—staggering youth unemployment, deeply entrenched and generalized poverty, hopelessness and despair. Desperate young men are lured into same-sex relationships. These relationships with men in authority at various echelons of the state are perceived as offering a form of symbolic authority. This symbolic authority might be converted and used to achieve other things (see Bourdieu, 1986: 47, 1989: 18–19) including the building and sustenance of a network that might lead to economic gain and forms of political influence. Homophobia has actually become a double edged sword: It is appropriated by the masses (popular opinion) against those in power"to question their morality" as well as to account for "Cameroon's multidimensional crisis" (Lado, 2011: 923, Abega, 2007: 95). It is simultaneously appropriated by those in power who use the crackdown on homosexuals to cover up their failure to deliver on the dividends of the donor darling pseudo-democracy they hastily put in place under Western pressure(see also Currier, 2010: 110–111). Homosexuality, Nyamsi (2007: 62) underlines, serves as a form of moral condemnation and is used by the citizenry to jettison the elites. It serves as a form of sociological commentary against social inequality, which is sometimes, explained in terms of witchcraft (Pemunta et al., 2013) a mechanism for oppressing the wealthy who being accused of inordinate and greedy accumulation without any redistribution amidst deeply entrenched poverty. As Colin Spencer (1998: 467) rightly concedes"A society in crisis exacerbates homophobia" (cf. Lado, 2011: 923). According to Ferree (2004: 88) homosexuality is a form of soft repression for eradicating "oppositional ideas" and for containing political opponents. It was successfully used in Namibia against LGBTS activists and "generally to silence political opponents" by clamping down on "dissent and to preempt criticism of their leadership...as a gendered strategy...utilized to maintain and defend their masculinist control of the state" (Currier, 2010: 110–111). Despite deep divisions even within the same denomination, all religious denominations condemn same-sex relationships. Like most of the masses, they accuse those in authority of bad governance because of their alleged membership in various sects, magico-religious rituals involving same-sex relationships and ritual murder (Djomo, 2013) for the achievement and maintenance of upward social mobility.

While the United States and other Western powers stand for the adoption of wholesale democracy including the rights of sexual minorities, African states vigorously opposed to same-sex relationships invoke such practices as "unAfrican". They have a ready ally in religions of all denominations and creed who maintain that same-sex relationships are antithetical to the teachings of the scriptures/teachings of God—even when God created man as an autonomous social agent. There seems to be a further double standard in the Church's position. For instance, the Vatican dismissed Monsignor Krzysztof Charamsa, "an evil Polish priest" from his Holy See job after he came out as gay and called for changes in Catholic teachings against homosexual activity sequel to the 2015 Synod on the family, (Oct. 4–25) under the theme of "The vocation and mission of the family in the Church and the modern world". His dismissal was justified on grounds that while "the Church teaches that homosexuality is not a sin but homosexual activity is, and priests, whether heterosexual or gay, take vows of celibacy" (Cameroon Concord, October 16, 2015). At the Synod, heavy criticism of the West imposing secular values on Africa in exchange for aid almost overshadowed debates among African bishops. They vehemently condemned what Pope Francis terms "ideological colonization," in which Western nations have made the acceptance of legislature favouring gay rights and "marriage" contingent on receiving financial aid. As Cardinal Wilfred Napier of South Africa eloquently stated while alluding to "the danger of "political colonization" being replaced "by a different kind of colonization", "What we are talking about is when countries are told unless you pass certain legislation, you're not going to get aid from the governments or aid agencies,". Cardinal Napier held up the example of the Obama administration, specifically the President's visit to Kenya in July 2015 during which despite the unwillingness of Kenya's political class that he not address the issue, Obama spoke out about the importance of gay rights. Church leaders including Archbishop John Baptist Odama of Gulu and president of the Ugandan Episcopal Conference called the act "criminal," concede that

> ideologies must never be attached to receiving aid, which is meant to save lives. "The issue of homosexuality should not be linked with saying 'if you don't accept this we won't help you[6]". "Aid should not be linked with ideological acceptance or rejection. Aid is to save human life. If you link it to ideology it becomes contradictory. . . it is self-defeating (Population Research Institute, 2015, unpaginated).

According to Bishop Odama, "the family exists precisely to promote human life" (Cameroon Concord, online, October 11 October 2015). While both African and Western communities trade concurrent arguments and counterarguments, the human rights of sexual minorities is violated with impunity. Sexual minorities are victims of punitive rape, police harassment, violence, and stigma. In fact, the persecution of same-sex partners has become the order of the day. The alleged undemocratic threats of Western nations to cut aid are perceived as a deliberate mechanism of killing homosexuality bills. Political leaders, the most radical of which is Robert Mugabe of Zimbabwe have taken a hardline stance against LGBT. According to Mugabe, "a smelling vagina is better than a well cleaned anus", "We reject attempts to prescribe new rights that are contrary to our values, norms, traditions and beliefs. We are not gays"[7]. When the US Supreme Court legalized gay marriage across all 50 states, Mugabe jokingly vowed to travel to the White House to propose to Barack Obama. In Cameroon, masses have been sponsored in churches by some overzealous members of the Yaoundé regime to pray against same-sex relationships.

This chapter examines the state of Cameroon's ambivalence and opposition to LGBT practices. Same-sex sexual activity involving the powerful are considered as part of human rights: "the right to a private life". However, when the poor engage in consensual same-sex relationships, it is criminalized. Why this double standard and institutionalized inequality? Homosexual practices per-

---

[6] http://www.catholicnewsagency.com/news/african-bishops-throw-swift-punch-at-ideological-colonization-68745/

[7] http://www.sowetanlive.co.za/news/africa/2015/09/30/we-are-not-gays-robert-mugabe-tells-un.

formed by the rich and powerful are reportedly intertwined with power and the occult in Cameroon. Any allusion to ritual and cosmology, Peter Geschiere (1997) argues, can have both critical and conservative aspects. The alleged exploitation of same-sex relationships by the rich and powerful for the acquisition of magical power/ritual fortification is believed to make the privileges available to these social actors appears unassailable. Ritual tends to fortify and invigorate the individual and as Emile Durkheim claimed, "There is no religion that is not both a cosmology and a speculation about the divine" (Durkheim 1915: 8). In line with the essence of the discourse that ritual fortifies, the only way to become a powerful leader is to acquire membership of secret societies as well as to constantly participate in re-invigorating the relationship between the individual and the supernatural realm through ritual practices that partly involve gay practices that are believed to imbue the individual with ritual blessings and to improve their chances for upward social mobility and dominance. Rituals whether sacred or profane are often regular and their regularity creates social cohesion, and the calendar and the need for re-invigoration often ensures the regularity of rites, festivals and public ceremonies at precise intervals or periods of the year (Durkheim 1915: 8). Homosexual practices and at times ritual human sacrifices meant to ensure best effect are perceived as granting access to symbolic and social capital (Bourdieu, 1977, 1986) which in turn gives participants dominance, political leverage and success in every sphere of life (see also Obara, 2012). Simultaneously, same-sex relationships may be said to mystify power and certainly allows politicians to maintain power. As Pierre Bourdieu rightly concedes (1986, 1989: 19), ritual practice constitutes a form of symbolic authority, which is used to achieve ulterior political and socio-economic aims/gains. Their positions will be seen as inaccessible to anybody apart from those ritually sanctioned through homosexual acts. These ritual accounts and beliefs constitute a kind of societal idiom about contemporary social and political life in Cameroon. The mystification embedded in ritual knowledge acquired through same-sex relationships thus positions such acts as integral in the acquisition and consolidation of power. The Catholic Church's condemnation of homosexuality should be read within the broader context of the Church's concern about the influence of secret societies from European origin—mostly Freemasons, but also Rosicrucian among top Cameroonian elite, including the president, Paul Biya. Both secret societies are intimately associated with homosexuality (Geschiere, 2010: 127). While the resistance of African leaders to the decriminalization of homosexuality is framed in terms of African nationalism, the forwarding of the practice as a Western importation is simultaneously used as a veil to produce a counter hegemonic discourse against the perceived intrusion of Western values as well as to detract Western attention from societal ills—gross human rights violations, long stays in power, corruption and opaque management.

Pronatalism, Homosexuality and Christianity

The argument that homosexuality is an unAfrican sexual practice suggests the existence of a monolithic African culture as well as "a timeless, singular African sexuality", sexual orientation and that homosexuals are deviants. In other words, African societies are heteronormal and pronatalism—sexual intercourse as not for pleasure but rather for procreation is the norm. The public framing and subsequent rejection of "same-sex relationships as a Western import antithetical to African culture" by political and religious leaders is because, it is considered as…self-serving (and perhaps belittling [of the] sperm) which, because of the spiritual link of childbearing, was symbolic of cultural identity and purpose. Ultimately, the denial of homosexuality among Africans [as well as its attribution] to colonialism is a desperate attempt to define morality through sexual practices" (Lopang 2014: 83). This section will demonstrate that this is not the case: there is no monolithic African culture. Those masking homophobia with anti-imperialist rhetoric often argue that homosexuality was not a part of "traditional" African societies, and has been introduced to the continent through the corrupting influence of Western imperialism. Criticisms of and resistance to homosexuality provides a postcolonial critique of Western societies—Western moral values: "homosexuality [as] as a western creation" (Lodo 2011: 110).

In Africa, homosexuality predates the colonial encounter (see Ndzomo, 2013, Geschiere, 2010, Murray, 1998, Epprecht, 2008, Tamale, 2011). According to Sylvia Tamale, within Africa, sexuality is still viewed through the lens of a superficial myth purportedly created by colonizers to establish control and power over black Africans. She cites Frantz Fanon: "The myth of black sexuality was simply a myth of excessive sexuality [hypersexuality]: it held that 'with the Negro everything takes place at the genital level." (quoted in Vaughan, 1991: 131, see also Tamale, 2011: 6). Tamale believes that if this is truly only a myth and not reality, sexuality within Africa should be seen differently. In line with Fanon, sexuality goes beyond the actual sexual relation (act) and beyond emphasis on the genital organs. In attempting to demonstrate better understanding of human sexual attitudes and behaviors; Tamale presents different sexual orientations encompassed by the concept of African sexualities. Tamale, I argue, captures the complexity of the often, popularly contested concept of homosexuality in Africa. According to her, heterosexuality has led to the male gaze on women and their subsequent objectification on the basis of their dress code: "First, the senator assumes that women's sole motivation in dressing is to please, impress or attract men as well as to stimulate male desire... (Tamale, 2011: 124)". She establishes a connection between the perception of women exposing as well as those who do not expose their bodies and the possible impact of the former on the male gaze and the incidence of harassment, rape or physical beating. Since in Fanon's view black sexuality revolved around the genital organ, the Negro woman, has been objectified. All impulses and attractions lead to one thing: the urge to have sex. Marc Epprecht (2008) provides evidence of the longstanding existence of homosexuality in African culture. European colonial authorities, settlers and scholars, Epprecht concedes, did not introduce homosexual practices to Africa, but did introduce their own homophobia and racism—projecting those ideas onto studies of sexuality in Africa. He concedes that homosexuality was accepted when the ruler was indulging in these practices. In Southern Africa, colonial and apartheid rule quickly led to the creation of new environments—mines, prisons, hostels, work camps, industrial ports, and military barracks—where same-sex sexual contact increased, particularly between men. These institutions were vital to colonial powers and private corporations as they sought to exploit and control the African population. Homosexual practices preceded the arrival of the first German colonialists on the west coast of Cameroon.

During the pre-colonial era the state strengthened same-sex bonds in the believe that such bonds contributed to the cohesiveness, ability and strength of a warrior. As Wazha Lopang concedes,

> homosexuality was consciously omitted from the content of African literature by writers who commented on colonialism and the African identity...The need to project a strong, masculine image of a married male overrode the need to depict an alternative sexuality. Homosexual relationships were presented as alien to the African continent and presented as colonial side effects that corrupted the African personality and in cases, reduced him to a catatonic state. The idea of African sexuality was chiefly that of a man who slept with a woman to provide children and hence continue the important link with his culture and his ancestors (Lopang 2014: 84).

While heterosexuality was simply a cover up, the state is today the leading opponent of the LGBTI community in Africa. The media and religious leaders also encourage anti-gay discrimination. The cultural bias of heterosexuality as normal harboured by the African community blinds most Africans to the other side of the horizon where sexualities other than heterosexuality exist. In their discussion of socialization as the process through which a certain set of normative values are imposed on, and imbibed as being both the standard norm and as a source of the power wielded by leaders in secondary states, John G. Ikenberry and Charles Kupchan concede that "rulers enjoy legitimacy when the values that they espouse correspond with the values of those they rule" (Ikenberry and Kupchan, 1990: 290). Apart from manipulating material incentives, Ikenberry and Kupchan argue that hegemons also significantly shape the beliefs of national elites. They further concede that socialization and normative orientation into new hegemonic forms is most likely to occur during a period of deep social crisis (Fatton, 1986: 63, Ikenberry and Kupchan, 1990: 29) like in the wake of the political homophobia engendered by the homosexuality epidemic. Studies have indicated that in patron/client relationships, political entrepreneurs employ a strategy of "accommodation with and acceptance of the traditional conservative classes" (usually the values of the mainstream society) to legitimize their rule (Fatton, 1986: 63). This is usually the case even when their powers are sometimes based on magico-religious rituals involving gay practices. Peter Geshiere concedes that in Cameroon homosexuality is associated with witchcraft. He argues that homosexuals are associated with witchcraft practices because witches have traditionally been portrayed as wearing the costumes of the opposite gender when they go out to bewitch others (Geschiere, 2010: 128). Despite Cameroon's huge diversity, homosexuality is associated with witchcraft. In the South of the country where most of the ruling political elite come from, the nightly gathering of witches who come together to "eat" their victim (cannibalism) is intertwined with sexual escapades:

> But that central motive of eating and cannibalism is often linked to unnatural forms of sexuality that would equally mark these nocturnal meetings: during such orgies men would do 'it' with men and 'even' women with women. The consequence is that insinuations concerning somebody's gay inclinations are immediately associated with occult practices, which no doubt facilitated the equation with a secret society such as freemasons when this was introduced under colonial rule.... In these societies travesty is also associated with the occult. In practice, many *nganga* (healers) are cross-dressers, especially the healers who mark their healing sessions by ecstatic dancing expressly combine male and female attributes. But this does not mean necessarily that they indulge in gay practices (Ibid).

Geschiere (2010) suggests the presence of homosexuality, albeit in a secret form in these societies. This is analogous to the existence of gay practices among the elites and speaks to the idea of Communication minister, Issa Chiroma for gays to keep a low profile. It also suggests that there is no room for the expression of a gay identity. 'On the contrary, in North Cameroon the intensification of fundamentalist currents causes a sharp formal condemnation of homosexuality as conflicting with the Koran (Ibid: 129). Similarly, Murray Roscoe concedes that homosexuality was a practice embedded in African culture and therefore in pre-colonial African society long before the colonial era (Roscoe, 1987). While homosexuals were not openly accepted, they were concurrently, not strongly condemned as is the case within these societies today (Geschiere, 2010, Murray, 1998). Scholars have conclusively established that homosexuality is not an imperialist legacy. Cameroonian lawyers Alice Nkom and Michel Togue both confided in Jean Cedric Ndzomo that top officials in African countries are appropriating the anti-homosexuality discourse as a colonial legacy to scapegoat and to distract the public from real problems that are hindering their country's development (Ndzomo, 2013: 8–9). Africans, studies have demonstrated were generally not heteronormative. Heteronormativity is the cultural bias in favor of opposite-sex, in contrast to same-sex relationships of a sexual nature, although most communities have been found to be "normatively fluid (here seen as the standard or the norm created by society)" (Bernadette, 2003).

A Heterosexual Cameroon Nation?

Framed around the notion of citizenship, this section will examine the apparent tension between local and global processes with reference to democratization and human rights by highlighting the ambivalent attitude of the African political class.

According to Roger Brubaker (1996) historically the notion of citizenship has been intertwined with the formation of the nation-states in nineteenth century Europe (see also Kahlina, 2013). As a notion, citizenship is a reference to the rules which determine who can belong to a particular geographical entity (polity), as well as the rights and obligations for those who belong. Feminist and sexuality scholars have underscored that rights and duties as well as the meanings of 'good citizenship' significantly differs for different groups of people—categories of gender and sexuality play significant roles in creating and maintaining these differences (Pateman 1994, Lister 2003a, b). In line with gendered division of labour, men and women are entitled to exercise different duties, to have different rights and to be remunerated differently. Once citizenship is linked to the idea of a nation, "it is indirectly implicated in the normalisation of heterosexual reproductive (monogamous) sexuality and, by extension, in discrimination against non-heterosexual practices and subjects" (Kahlina, 2013: 1–2).

The association of citizenship with sexuality facilitated the emergence of the notion of sexual citizenship. This shows how citizenship, although universal, is a source of inequality, based on sexuality. It is broadly defined as "social membership in a nation-state, as a set of rights and responsibilities associated with that membership, and as a set of practices defining membership in the community" (Crossman, 2007: 7, cf. Kahlina, 2013: 2). Sexual citizenship could be defined as membership in a particular nation on the basis of sexuality. "Sexual citizenship", Katja Kahlina (2013: 2) argues "refers to the ways in which sexuality is implicated in the scope of rights that form the basis of citizenship, such as civil, social, and cultural rights and which determine the unequal citizenship status of sexual minorities, i. e of those individuals whose sexual practices do not comply with the heterosexual norm" (Lister, 2003b). While the global LGBTIQ community has pressured public opinion on the status of sexual minorities, the scope of rights determining the citizenship status of sexual minorities differ significantly from state to state and has been a source of tension between global tendencies and dominant socio-political processes going on at the national level (stychin, 2003, Binnie, 2004, Kahlina, 2013: 2). Cultural nationalists in southern Africa allegedly tended to treat "gay rights . . . as a modern-day continuation of a colonial past, which undermines a previously colonized people's right to self-determination" (Stychin [2001, 275] cf Asley, 2010: 119). In Africa, sexual minorities are erased from human rights and have to live in a closet for their own safety.

In Africa, the democratic upsurge of the 1990s reflected the tensions between local and global processes—calls for democratization, the respect of human rights and good governance reforms that swept through the continent. To thwart the democratic tornado, African "strong men" adopted different strategies: they either resisted change or made only cosmetic reforms. In the face of calls for genuine democratic reforms, political authorities have held competitive, multiparty elections that have often not met the minimal democratic criteria of freeness and fairness. In Cameroon, election results are known even before the votes are cast. Exploiting institutional advantages, many incumbent parties have denied the opposition any chance of winning power in the new multi-party regimes. These regimes are best understood as "pseudo-democracies" or what Richard Joseph has termed "virtual democracies." Some opted for what they variously called "African Democracy", "Advanced Democracy" as a strategy of resisting supposedly imposed Western-styled democratic norms. The 1990s, Epprecht reminds us saw the full impact of "structural adjustment programmes" taking its toll on African societies. Imposed by Western financial institutions and countries like the United States for the promotion of their own self-interests, these programmes left many African leaders wealthy, while impoverishing the vast majority. One method of diverting potential anti-government unrest was to identify a scapegoat, whether ethnic, national, or in some cases sexual (Epprecht, 2008). Reminiscent of the anticolonial movement which was forwarded as meant to preserve African values against Western balkanization, anti-homosexuality discourses are a type of sociological commentary against perceived Western intrusion/imperialism. The West has been accused of imposing its political and economic values across the globe with Africa as a prime target. The adoption of Western-styled democracy became the precondition for African countries that sought foreign aid and loans, especially from the International Monetary Fund (IMF) and the World Bank, in order to redress their dire politico-economic crises (Bayart et al. 1999: 2–3, see also Zeleza 1994, Joseph 1997). As Paul Zeleza describes it, this "marriage of economic 'perestroika' and political 'glasnost, '", "seemed so radical, so new" in the emergent world order (Zeleza 1994: 476).

The critical dynamic for democratization, as Richard Joseph points out, involves the "domination of the world economy by the market-oriented economies, the geostrategic hegemony of western industrialized nations, and direct or indirect external pressures for democratization." On the other hand, the end of the Cold War "opened up domestic spaces for democratic politics in many African countries" and the implementation of the "iron fisted structural adjustment" of the donor agencies provoked popular resistance and democratic movements (Zeleza 1994: 476–477). Realizing that regimes they had previously backed were standing on shaky ground, the West and its donor agencies had to make sharp turns in their policies to curry favor with the new democratic movements. Thus, the role of Africans in pushing for democratization based on their local conditions, a phenomenon they referred to as the "second independence," should not be overlooked in any analysis.

Particular normative visions of gender and sexuality often play a preponderant role in the national identity construction process (Yuval-Davis, 1997). For instance, when nationalists invoke a fictive common descent as the basis of defining the frontiers of a community, women's bodies—reproductive capacities and reproductive heterosexuality are often constructed as the obvious and ultimate bearers of national unity and survival (Anthias and Yuval-Davis, 1989, Yuval-Davis, 1997, cf. Kahlina, 2013: 3–4). Women's bodies were for instance, imbricated in the anticolonial movements in both Kenya and Algeria. Against this backdrop, non-heterosexual relationships are perceived as 'immoral', their practitioners are demonized and presented as "possessed by the devil". Same-sex relationships are further framed as "improper proposals" (Geschiere, 2010), same-sex partners represented as "suffering from psychiatric disorder", 'foreign' and as posing a threat to an imagined national tradition and essence (see also Kahlina, 2013: 4). In Cameroon, homosexuality is widely perceived as a malediction or disease that a person might have, causing them to be dishonored, beaten, banned from participation in multiple aspects of society or even killed. Homophobic violence in Cameroon, as well as in many other regions of Africa such as Uganda or Kenya, is often sanctioned or ignored (Ndzomo, 2013: 2) as anathema to the country's religion, roots and culture. In some parts of the country, homosexuality is associated with witchcraft, based on the belief that witches routinely perform same-sex acts with each other (Geschiere, 2010: 129). Homosexuality is viewed as a "disease" or "sin" that was purportedly brought to the African continent by the white colonialists (Ndzomo, 2013, McAllister, 2015, Geschiere, 2010). In some of the most dangerous countries for the LGBTI community in Africa—Sudan, Sierra Leone or Tanzania and Uganda—apart from being stoned or killed, jail sentences of up to 14 years hang over homosexuals (Ndzomo 2010: 10). Homosexuals who evidence their "true self" through actions or physical appearance are either shunned or incarcerated for long periods of time by state officials (Ibid: 2).

Laws and policies—family codes (anti-homosexuality law), citizenship and immigration acts—are replete with dominant conceptions of nation, gender and sexuality. Article 52 (3) of the Civil Status Registration Ordinance of Cameroon (Ordinance No. 81–02 of June 29, 1981) provides that: "no marriage maybe celebrated if the spouses-to-be are of the same sex." Such laws and policies are deployed alongside labour and health insurance acts in the production of particular regimes of gender and sexuality and become the defining feature of the citizenship status of sexual minorities (see also Kahlina, 2013). Law, Brenda Crossman (2007) concedes is embedded in particular socio-cultural context, intertwined with the non-legal socio-cultural domain where the various meanings that participate in the production of sexual citizenship are constituted. According to Crossman, images, norms and narratives of popular culture seep into the legal discourse and conversely, the ways legal discourse casts its shadow over popular culture' (p. 18). Brenda Crossman's argument on the interplay between the law and available cultural repertoire in particular socio-cultural milieu resonate with the situation in Cameroon and most of Africa where pronatalism enforced through heterosexuality is the official norm.

Reactions to the homosexuality "epidemic"

Media reports have instead exacerbated the situation of sexual minorities by fueling hostility towards these minorities for allegedly not conforming to heterosexual norms. Their lives are on the line. The heterosexual mindset has also come to underlie studies of HIV/AIDS: "researchers have studied HIV/AIDS as a heterosexual disease in Africa because they have been told and have read that there is no homosexuality in Africa.... the assumption that Africa is a continent of heterosexual sex has been deadly for too many people for too long." Often characterized as "unnatural carnal acts" (Ibid: 75) or "acts against the order of nature" (Ibid), homosexuality is a crime in 31 countries in sub-Saharan Africa. Cameroon, like most African countries, is a conservative society in which homosexuality is frowned upon and attracts stiff prison sentences. In Cameroon, although the law does not explicitly forbid discrimination based on race, language, or social status, it however prohibits discrimination based on gender and mandates that "everyone has equal rights and obligations" (Preamble of Cameroon Constitution, 2006). Although the constitution prohibits all forms of discrimination, the government of Cameroon does not normally enforce these provisions effectively, and violence and discrimination against women and girls, trafficked persons, ethnic minorities, and members of the LGBT community pose problems (Country Reports on Human Rights Practices, 2013). Cameroonian law provides for sentences of up to five years for homosexual activity. While the usual maximum for same-sex relations is a five-year sentence, the penalty is doubled for sex with someone between ages 16 and 21. Under Cameroonian law same-sex intercourse carries a penalty of six months to five years in prison and fines of up to $370 (£210). Section 347 of Cameroon's Penal Code states that "whoever has sexual relations with a person of the same sex shall be punished with imprisonment for six months to five years and a fine of 20.000 to 200.000 CFA Francs". Ironically, "In too many cases (homophobic) attacks on individuals and groups are being fueled by key politicians and religious leaders who should be using their position to fight discrimination and promote equality" (Amnesty International 2013: 1). In most of Africa, LGBTI are an unwanted social group who face homophobic attacks and harassment. In Cameroon, the anti-homosexual media campaign that began with the publication of a list of 50 highly placed members of society presumed to be homosexuals by the tabloid *La Meteo* launched the campaign with the aim of "exorcizing" gays from Cameroon.

Catholic Archbishop Andre Bakot vigorously criticized the EU for giving legitimacy to homosexuality under the banner of human and minority rights. In his sermons, he consistently lashed out at those calling for the legalization of same-sex marriages. He further derided gay people who wanted to adopt children. According to the archbishop, Cameroonians had "resorted" to homosexuality in order to advance their careers and earn more money. The archbishop's arguments were largely re-echoed by the newspapers. It was in sequel to monsignor Victor Tonye Bakot's Christmas sermon decrying homosexuality among Cameroon's elite while also taking a very uncompromising stance against the EU's requirement prohibiting member states from any form of discrimination based on sexual orientation (see also Geschiere, 2010: 126).

Reactions to the list of alleged homosexuals varied. One of the suspects, Cameroon's communications minister at the time, Pierre Moukoko Mbonjo, threatened legal action and warned that the newspapers risked breaking up families. He re-echoed the government's position on the right to privacy thus: "Whether heterosexual or homosexual, sexual intercourse takes place in an intimate environment between two persons". His utterance has resonance with what Peter Geschiere presents as the defence of "a more modern approach which emphasizes that sexuality is a private affair and by implication, there is no reason to portray homosexuality as immoral" (2010: 128). Others who were named in the list said they were consulting their lawyers—meaning they were contemplating court action, some sought publicity by denying the 'terrible accusations'. While "most of them just kept their heads low", a few filed libel complaints (Geschiere, 2010: 127, Ndzomo, 2013). A Cameroon court jailed Jean Pierre Amougou Belinga for four months for allegedly defaming Gregoire Owona—a government minister named in the list of 50 supposed homosexuals. Two others wrote letters to the editors of various newspapers denying the reports. Cameroon's president, Paul Biya waded in and chided the newspapers for "violating the privacy of individuals". In Cameroon, homophobic laws against LGBTI individuals have been enforced. Many suspected LGBT individuals and same-sex partners have been arrested, tried, jailed, and beaten. Security forces actively target alleged LGBT individuals and cooperated with vigilante groups to entrap and arrest them. In 2013, at least 200 individuals were allegedly incarcerated in the country on charges of same-sex sexual relations. Most of the evidence proffered against some alleged homosexuals may not hold up to legal scrutiny elsewhere in the world. Behaviours that "deviates from traditional marked ideas about masculinity: hairstyles that are similar to those of women's, elegant ways of moving" (Geschiere, 2010: 129) are some of the evidences constantly used against alleged same-sex partners. LGBT individuals regularly face social stigmatization, mob violence and a witch hunt—which sometimes result in their deaths. Even those defending their human rights are targeted for elimination. Human rights lawyer, Alice Kom can no longer remember how many threats and physical abuses she has received (Pemunta, 2011). In July 2013, for example, Eric Ohena Lembembe—a journalist, LGBT activist, and the executive director of the Cameroonian Foundation against AIDS—was found strangled to death at his home in Yaounde. Lembembe had been bound, beaten, and burned with an iron. Civil society members and human rights organizations credibly claimed that the killing was linked to Lembembe's activism and sexual orientation, a contention that Cameroon's communication minister publicly questioned in the days following the crime. Human rights groups consider the official investigation into Lembembe's death as uniformly unprofessional. No suspects were ever identified[8]. Over the years, an anti-gay movement—The Movement of Cameroonian Youth—has constantly organized anti-homosexual brigades to locate and harass LGBT individuals in nightclubs. In August 2013, the movement organized a public march to fan antigay sentiments and to urge a more heavy-handed government crackdown on homosexuality[9]. Suspected members of the LGBT community and their lawyers including Kom have constantly received anonymous threats by telephone, text message, and e-mail. LGBT individuals who were bold enough to seek services or protection from the authorities have been regularly rebuffed, extorted, or arrested. LGBT organizations also were targeted. Gay right NGO activists are regularly targeted, while their institutions are vandalized[10]. In July 2014, arsonists set fire to the NGO Alternatives Cameroon Access Center in Douala. This resulted in significant damage to the center's HIV testing and counseling records and equipment. Although the police ruled the fire a criminal act, no suspects were identified (Stewart, 2013).

During his first homily in August 2016, Jean Mbarga, the newly appointed administrator of the Catholic Archdiocese of Yaounde and the archbishop of Ebolowa, condemned and derided homosexuality as a foreign practice and called on Africans to "resist

---

[8] https://www.hrw.org/news/2013/07/16/cameroon-lgbti-rights-activist-found-dead-tortured
[9] https://76crimes.com/2012/08/15/organizing-opposition-to-african-gay-hate-day/
[10] http://allocameroon.unblog.fr/tag/homosexuality/page/2/

what will destroy their culture and family." Despite the hostile environment (state and church hostility), various human rights and health organizations continue to advocate for the LGBT community by defending LGBT individuals being prosecuted, promoting HIV/AIDS initiatives, and working to change laws prohibiting consensual same-sex activity. In Africa, church and state leaders "generally share common interests and sentiments, forming together with other well-positioned individuals such as businesspeople an informal coalition of elites who seek to exercise hegemonic control over society" (Gifford, 1995: 197, See also Bayart, 1989). In the wake of the democratic tornado, the church departed from traditional areas of education and health to direct political involvement: "challenging political structures, urging reform, advocating political change and even presiding over change itself" (Gifford, 1995: 3). In Francophone Africa, the Church played a preponderant role in preventing democratic deadlock by stepping in to organize national conferences and by overseeing the transition process. In Benin for instance, Mgr Isidore de Sousa, archbishop of Cotonou presided over the country's national conference (see Gifford, 1995: 1–2). In Cameroon, the church however played an ambiguous political role in political restructuring. The mainstream churches, particularly the Catholic Church were manipulated by politicians into organizing masses against multipartism as divisive and a threat to national unity. President Paul Biya was presented as "a God-fearing leader/appointed/given wisdom by God to steer the affairs of Cameroon". In the same light, multipartism was forwarded as divisive and a foreign import that threatened national unity and turned brothers and sisters into enemies. Christians were constantly urged to pray for the government and for Paul Biya as a God sent leader.

It might be argued that the emphasize on "African traditions" as capable of ensuring proper moral conduct through the condemnation of same-sex relationships signify the need to shift politics from an economic-political arena to an arena of morals and traditions (Pemunta, 2011). According to Graeme Reid (2015) homophobia is deployed as "a tool to bolster legitimacy, increase popularity and distract from pressing social ills" (Reid, 2015: online). African states use attack on LGBT including scapegoating to create a moral panic: "a perceived threat to the social order which can easily escalate into a witch hunt. They are a convenient change of subject for political leaders facing rampant unemployment, political unrest and spiraling economies" (Reid, 2015: online). Through this shift, politicians are able to assert their influence and compliance with cultural norms by policing the sexual behaviour of their population. This seems to be the case as some people often debate the issue of condoms as a Western import meant to discourage people from enjoying sex. Those against the use of condom point out that its use leads to immorality. Similarly, they maintain that the different types and prices imply the sentencing of the poor to death since they cannot afford expensive condoms which are perceived as being more protective. The hardline stance against homosexuality might thus be an attempt to re-assert African independence and for African leaders to attempt to distance themselves from the unwarranted influence of foreign donors. Like other African countries, Cameroon overwhelming relies on foreign aid that often comes with ideological strings (Pemunta, 2011).

For instance, in the wake of the HIV/AIDS pandemic, an incessant standoff has been brewing between the government of Cameroon and the EU over the latter's perceived "unacceptable funding" for the promotion of gay rights. The controversy began with a grant of circa 305, 000€ issued by the EU in early January, 2011 to a group of three local associations- including a gay rights association (*Association de Défense des Homosexuels – Adhefo*) founded by a lawyer, Alice Nkom. The funding was to help buttress the association's project to bring "assistance" to homosexual minorities. For accepting the EU grant, Alice Nkom was accused of being guilty of "crimes against the laws ... and of compromising the sovereignty and independence of Cameroon." (Pemunta, 2011: 5, quoting *Agence France-Presse*, News, of 5th January, 2011). Henri Eyebe Ayissi, then Foreign Affairs Minister allegedly stated to *Cameroon Tribune*, a state-controlled newspaper that "Cameroonians are not ready or willing to go in this direction" concerning the "development of these [homosexual] practices on its territory". He allegedly "summoned" the head of the EU delegation in Cameroon, Raoul Mateus Paula, to inform him of "the government's disapproval of funding groups which violate Cameroonian laws". He expressly called for the funding to be rescinded. The Minister's statement risks being considered as an official position which may encourage violent anti-homosexual groups or individuals to take matters into their own hands. This is especially the case as an anti-gay group, *Rassemblement de la Jeunesse Camerounaise* reportedly issued a *fatwa* against homosexuals- admonishing people to "hunt down and condemn [homosexuals] without any mercy." *Agence France-Presse* holds that 10 local NGOs asked the government to "protect human rights workers and actors in the fight against HIV/AIDS among homosexuals," arguing that "lives are now being endangered by threats perpetrated through the media in Cameroon" (*Agence France-Presse*, News, 5th January, 2011, cf. Pemunta, 2011: 5).

Although the row between the government of Cameroon and the EU over homosexuality reflects the former's pronatalist policy and ability to protect national sovereignty, this policy is fraught with contradictions. For instance, the Cameroon government's endorsement of the Maputo Protocol led to countrywide debate pitting traditionalists and religious groups against the government. The bone of contention is Article 14, which forbids all forms of gender-based discrimination. This is clearly a challenge to the dominant patriarchal mindset that justifies women's oppression. While the protocol guarantees women's fundamental rights in matters of sexual and reproductive health, including the right to choose any method of contraception- detractors, particularly Church groups and ardent traditionalists- see it as a dangerous blueprint that will overturn traditional values that promote life and encourage specific gender roles in which boys are raised as breadwinners, and women stay within the private sphere of the home and bear children. Moreover, they argue that it will endanger "tradition" by encouraging respect for gay men and lesbians and by promoting same-sex marriages (Pemunta, 2011: 4–6).

The claims of politicians who maintain that homosexuality is a recent Western import have been countered by anthropologists who argue that it has a long history in the continent. However, two significant elements in the debate over homosexuality in Africa are of Western provenance—first, colonial-era laws against homosexual activities (sodomy) and, more recently, the establishment of groups opposing discrimination against gays, lesbians and transgender people. Eric O. Lembembe (2010) concede, "Homosexuality has always existed, but some of the current forms of gay self-identification and gay activism originated elsewhere" (cf. Ndzomo 2010, Geschiere 2010). Historical records attests to homosexual practices in Africa—Cameroon, Zimbabwe, Burkina Faso and Benin. Mossi kings' allegedly had sexual relations with their pages while in Dahomey women got married to other women. In Cameroon, same-sex relationships existed among the Beti, through pre-colonial traditions such as the "mevungu" ritual of a secret society for women. Analysis of "indigenous" speech, first collected by ethnologists, shed light on what homosexuality represented in those cultures, along with their discussions about it, indicates that both homosexuality and debate about it have always existed.

Contributors to the edited volume by Stephen Murray and Will Roscoe (1998) have provided perceptive insights from anthropologists and explorers about homosexual relationships throughout the African continent. Homosexual practices had different meanings depending on class, age, and other social characteristics. Evans-Pritchard reported that Azande warriors "routinely married boys who functioned as temporary wives". He called this homoerotic practice "age-stratified homosexuality" (Murray& Roscoe, 1998: xiii). African homosexuality is not a monolithic practice—not the same for a king, as among the Mossi of Burkina Faso, and for a page in the king's service in the same region and in the same group. Pages—including young men sometimes disguised as women, (cross-dressing) could play the role of a woman for the king in certain ritual circumstances where it was forbidden to touch women. When the king had homosexual relations with his pages, it was more or less recognized and "institutionalized". Melville Herkovits also described "marriages" between women in the ancient kingdom of Dahomey, now Benin. In this case women—often wealthy older women—sometimes married women in the absence of men. These wives could have lovers, and their children were recognized as those of the "husband-wife." There are all sorts of configurations on the continent (see also Geschiere 2010).

The reasons for the recent wave of homophobia against same-sex partners seem to include the recent history of colonization of the African continent, and the heterosexual norm of human societies. Additionally, new meanings are being placed on old practices—for example, what went on in ancient rituals is now considered to be something that contributes to modern homosexual identity. One set of causes can be summarized as "postcolonial tensions". These tensions arise between the former colonial powers like France and African countries (Françafrique) including Cameroon. Some of these former colonial powers are now seen as "moral leaders" in defense of sexual minorities, even though that is debatable. Ongoing advocacy by these "moral leaders" in favour of universal decriminalization of homosexuality causes conservative reactions in many countries. For example, increased funding from the EU to Cameroonian groups fighting for the rights of homosexuals provoked outrage from the authorities and led to a standoff in 2011 (Pemunta, 2011). The situation revived memories of colonialism, thereby putting homosexuality at the heart of a postcolonial controversy. Africans are led to regard homosexuality as an expression of the alleged decadence of the West.

The other current issue on the African continent is political leaders' reliance on criticizing society in order to build public support. The anthropologist Saskia Weiringa called this politicians' "moral sexual strategy" which consists of "othering" nonpatriarchal sexual practices and the creation of moral panics (see also Pemunta, 2011, Merton 1976). Two seemingly intertwined, but contradictory processes are at play: on the one hand, there is a postcolonial amnesia of particular sexual practices, politics and relations in relation to women's sexual autonomy and homoerotic practices in general. On the other hand, there is a striking resonance to the sexual politics of postcolonial rulers compared to their colonial predecessors (Wieringa, 2009: 204–5). A variety of political actors use the "moral sexual strategy" to make themselves known. This is true of all groups of young people on the continent that publish texts "against homosexuality" even though, in reality, they are trying to make their voices heard on other issues, like corruption, nepotism, incompetent leadership, etc. Besides all this, heterosexism is a universal fact, even though some analyses of

"African homophobia" depict it as applying to Africa alone. The effects of the "norm of heterosexuality" and its macho partner—"phallocracy"—must also be considered seriously. All these facts and others may explain the negative perception of homosexuality on the continent which has led to state and church-sanctioned homophobia. Ironically, the labelling of homosexuality as "UnAfrican" and a Western import, that is antithetical to authentic African values and cultures—in a situation where labels invoke values and conventions—is itself an imported attitude. Pre-colonial African societies accommodated sexual and gender non-conformity (Epprecht, 2008, McAllister, 2015). In the same light, the criminalization of sodomy was a colonial innovation. As John McAllister maintains "The roots of contemporary African homophobia are nineteen-century European prudery and racist fantasies of 'primitive' black sexuality, yet, despite this irony, the power of the 'unAfrican' argument seems undiminished" (McAllister, 2015: 43).

Homosexuality is largely perceived as being antithetical to African traditional values that extol heterosexual relationships including marriage which is considered as the perpetuation of the family, society and future generations (Pemunta, 2011, McAllister, 2015: 43, Tamale, 2011). While public opinion against homosexuality is hardened, the media sensationalizes anything that has to do with sexuality. In Africa, gay rights activists are appropriating the discourse of universal human rights by presenting sexual minorities as an oppressed social category, entitled to equal citizenship, but whose rights are trampled upon with impunity. The resilience of the unAfrican argument has stifled gay activism, and exposed defenders of gay rights to the mayhem of the majority population. Since the human rights discourse originates from a Western constituency, it is perceived as a self-interested discourse that propagates the hegemony of Western values—including gay rights. Apart from failing to address the issue of gay rights in a context of state-church sanctioned homophobia and heteronormativity, "the concept of human rights is vulnerable to the same reactionary nationalism" (McAllister, 2015: 43). The wholesale condemnation of gayism as a Western imposition through homophobic appropriations of "tradition", "African culture" and the rights of communities speak to well-founded resentment of a long, and continuing, history of Western cultural imperialism". There has been the transformation of the LGBT issue in Africa, from a private matter, in which case, "don't-ask-don't-tell" (in the style of Issa Chiroma Bakary) into a significant political issue (Cole, 2012) associated "with intense post-colonial anxieties about social cohesion and public morality" (McAllister, 2015: 43).

While African political and moral entrepreneurs (religious denominations) are promoting political and religious demagogy by appropriating "the protection of traditional African values"—to their own advantage, Western governments, human rights groups and celebrities apart from angry public communiques, are threatening to cut aid from countries adopting laws against same-sex relationships. During the independence movement and early years of nation-building, the ruling elites made strong claims to cultural authenticity by disparaging Western values as antithetical to African traditional values (one man, one wife was countered with polygyny). The Western threat of cutting development aid constitutes one element in the complex Western arsenal (comprised of material and immaterial/discursive dimensions) that might be called "the White Saviour Industrial Complex" (Cole, 2012): no matter the sincerity or good intention of Western indignation and threats, such threats convey an idea of the superiority of Western moral values ("civilisational superiority"). This bears close semblance to Western efforts to "introduce" democracy to Africa to the concept of the "civilizing mission" trumpeted by Europeans during the colonial encounter in the nineteenth century. Even the legal scholar Sylvia Tamale (2011) concedes that while the Western enlightenment about LGBT is still recent; the concepts of sexual identity and social self-understandings on which these strategies are based have been slammed. There is clearly a schism between Western gay activists who are increasingly questioning the Western approach as they increasingly reject Western interventionism and Western strategies of activism. While Western outrage is often considered as tinged with neo-colonial or racist talk, it has played into the hands of the African political establishment with gross human rights, extended tenures and seem to be a replication of the "civilized" versus "primitive" dichotomy and to give many Africans the believe that 'gay rights are a Western pet project especially when other human rights abuses in Africa fail "to capture the western imagination" (McAllister, 2015: 44). The overall effect has been the reinforcement of the perception that LGBT identities are foreign intrusions and that LGBT activism is a new form of neo-colonial bullying. African activists feel the counter-productive effects on their work and, in many cases, their own security" (Ibid). Human rights may be universal, but the sexual identities constructed in the West over the past century or so are not, and the popular misconception that 'gayism' is a neocolonial Western phenomenon is probably the single most formidable barrier to the acceptance of sexual difference in Africa (Ibid: 46) and in Cameroon where there is a self-serving concept of individual autonomy.

Double Appropriation of the Concept of Privacy and Individual Autonomy?

The Cameroon government's double appropriation of the modern Western concepts of privacy and individual autonomy on which the human rights system has been built are at odds with botho's[11] emphasis on the centrality of the community and one's obligations to it. From this emphasis, proponents of botho typically extrapolate a duty for the individual to conform to community standards in order to be entitled to protection, respect and acceptance (Ibid: 46). The Western human rights discourse preaches the ideology of 'universal', 'inalienable rights' and 'autonomous individuals' whereas in Africa, the society/community supersedes the individual: "I am because we are". This statement highlights the complex interplay between individual autonomy and community obligations. It is the collectivity that matters and the individual depends on the collective for his identity and wellbeing (see Pemunta, 2011, Pemunta et al. 2013). The prohibition of same-sex relationships implies that sexual minorities are excluded from the realm of citizenship and the nation—rights that are intertwined with heterosexuality. The community accordingly has a legitimate interest, as

---

[11] Literally means 'human-ness'—'an indigenous African philosophy of what it means to be a social being'. Its emphasis is on the individual's social obligations to the community and vice versa" (McAllister, 2015: 45).

well as a 'right' to interfere, in matters that in the Western human rights discourse will be considered as a violation of the individual's right to privacy. This is where the Cameroon government's ambivalence becomes evident: when homosexual acts are practiced by members of upper society, they are interpreted as exercises of the right to privacy. In Canada in 1968, Pierre Trudeau "declared that the state had no business in people's bedrooms". This is unlike in botho where "the community, and by extension the state, arguably have precisely that right" (McAllister, 2015: 47, see also Epprecht, 2013).

African leaders are capitalizing on anti-gay sentiments and using 'gayism' as a whipping horse if LGBT rights were not opposed by most citizens. Politicians know very well that they can rely on the issue to create politically convenient moral panics to detract attention from pressing social issues: galloping rate of youth unemployment, widening gap between rich and poor, generalized poverty and insecurity as well as acute lack of social services. Most of those on the list of fifty prominent homosexuals were alleged to have forced job applicants into homosexual acts. This speaks to the inordinate and deeply entrenched corruption among the elite and their "willingness to take advantage of the unwillingness of unemployed youths to do anything for a job, including accepting a homosexual initiation" (Geschiere, 2010: 126). This is why Western denunciations and threats are counter-productive and Western-style activism invites a dangerous backlash. An approach that builds public support incrementally by leveraging and reinterpreting locally meaningful cultural values may be the way to make progress for the time being" (McAllister, 2015: 47). A middle ground to fierce opposition and extreme reaction to LGBT individuals (self-assertion) may be achieved through the reconciliation of the Western adopted concepts of personal identity, individual autonomy, and innate sexual orientations with indigenous ways of thinking about personhood and community (Ibid: 47). Postcolonial modernity has created anxieties about nationality, citizenship and gender as well as contradictions between individual and collective self-understandings and between individual and collective rights (Ibid: 47–48).

The concept of culture is invoked as constitutive of national identity: "...national identity [is] constituted out of a huge cultural matrix which provides innumerable points of connection, nodal points where authorities try to fix meaning, and constellations around which cultural elements cohere" (Edensor, 2002: vii). One dimension of national identity in most of Africa is heterosexuality. Despite globalization and the dynamism, contested nature, multiplicity and fluidity of national identity, the nation remains at the heart of identity formation (Edensor, 2002: vi, Kahlina, 2013, Yuval-Davis, 1997, Brubaker, 1996). Popular culture including heterosexuality is often invoked as a defining claim in nationalist discourses. In their analyses of Korean beliefs about healing powers and modernity, Linda H Connor, and Geoffrey Connor Samuel (2001: 32) have argued that "the politics of culture as defined by new middle-class intellectuals merged with early nationalist agendas in the belief that the defining essence of a "people" was to be found in their folk traditions" (see also Edensor, 2002, Bauman and Sawin, 1991). Connor and Samuel further note that in Korea, "ancient shamanic practices were infused, retrospectively with nationalistic spirituality, a theme revived by Korean Folklore" (2001: 33). In Cameroon like in most African countries, nationalism is similarly conflated with culture. Accordingly, politicians who are not perceived as custodians of the people's culture, especially anti-homosexuality, may put their own careers at stake. Supporting culture constitutes a form of cultural capital (see Bourdieu 1977) which can be readily deployed in the game of politics as obtains in Sierra Leone among members of the Bondo and Sande secret societies (see also Obara 2012, Pemunta and Obara 2011).

Western attempts to impose homosexuality as part and parcel of "donor democracy" through threats to cut aid (Pemunta, 2011), and Cameroon's simultaneous resistance evident in its persecution of same-sex partners as well as its ratification of international conventions like the Maputo Protocol lends credence to Robertson's (1992: 400) assertion that the market economy constitutes a likely medium for the perception of universal world images. Similarly, Kabiru Ibrahim Yankuzo has observed that the increasing compression of the world into 'a global village' implies that less developed countries are being compelled "to take account of an ever expanding interconnection of sociocultural issues and economies in the management of their national affairs" (Yakunzo, 2014: 1). The capacity of these states to govern and to regulate has been withered down in this "increasingly borderless world; with an increasing homogenization and domination of traditional African cultures" (Ibid). According to Robertson despite the semblance of a "universalistic, potentially global social interaction and exchange" network that the market economy epitomizes, it may represent a "dangerous intrusion on traditional forms of sociality and solidarity" (Robertson, 1992: 400). The dilemma inherent in this situation resonates with the case of Cameroon. While nationalistic discourses against same-sex relationships are a counterpoint, world images of tolerance towards same-sex partners endeavours to "restructure global change" by insisting that anti-homosexual states including Cameroon live up to the expectations of "normative" (international treaties) and "material dimensions"—by decriminalizing same-sex relationships as a precondition for the continuous reception of donor aid. Conversely, the depenalization or toleration of same-sex relationships will affect "traditional forms of sociality and solidarity" constituted by heterosexuality and put 'soft' states like Cameroon in a more contradictory position. Both state actors and political entrepreneurs find themselves in a dilemma given that they are still beholden to the interests of their local level supporters and are thus hampered in steering the state to "global modernity". Political entrepreneurs may thus be said to have resorted to "traditional modernity" by banning same-sex relationships. This is a strategy that is propagated through ambivalent tendencies. In order to keep the balance between appeasing traditional actors for whom they want to present themselves as moral entrepreneurs, as well as not outrightly (but covertly) opposing the West, they are therefore placed in a situation where they are required to behave in an ambivalent manner (see also Obara, 2012, Pemunta and Obara, 2011). It is this ambivalence which I consider next.

Ambivalence as a Political Practice

In most of Africa ethnic or national identities significantly influence political behaviour. Faced with this ethnic reality, ambivalence is often used as a significant political strategy by political and social actors to protect the advantages that accrue to themselves and to forestall social upheavals that can threaten these advantages. They pretend to espouse the values of society or to conform to international norms of democracy and human rights including the rights of gays and other sexual minorities. Ambivalence has been variously defined (Merton 1976, Nuckolls 1996, Lüscher 1998). According to Kurt Lüscher,

> we speak of ambivalence in a social science perspective when dilemmas and polarisation of feelings, thoughts, actions and, furthermore, contradictions in social relations and social structures, which are relevant for personal and societal development, are interpreted as in the West.

Following Merton (1976: 18), ambivalence serves as a social device, "for helping people in designated statuses to cope with the contingencies that they face in trying to fulfil their functions." In Cameroon, politicians routinely use ambivalence as one of several strategies in their attempt to retain power and to divert attention to contemporary issues of massive unemployment, corruption, clientelism and bad governance. When African political entrepreneurs were pressurized to democratize, they hookwinked the West and adopted democracies with various designations—"virtual democracy", "African Democracy", "pseudodemocracy" (see Bayart et al. 1999, Joseph 1997, Zeleza 1994) which are all forms of personal rule. The "role-relations" (Nuckolls 1996: 117–118), politicians operate in, are such that they have to appease the public and also assuage themselves to the demands of international and multilateral donors who have placed conditions in relation to the decriminalization and therefore an end to the oppression of sexual minorities. Some scholars have suggested that the predominant 'dualistic solidarity-versus-conflict' framework (Lüscher and Pillemer, 1997: 17, cf Lorenz-Meyer, 2001: 4), a type of role conflict, which perceives "solidarity and conflict" as opposing ends of a continuum, should be replaced by a focus on ambivalence that can account for countervailing positive and negative forces simultaneously inherent in and generated by (political) relationships. The 'logic of ambivalence' serves as a useful framework for 'understanding, analyzing, and explaining . . . (that goes) beyond the scope of rational-choice explanations' in contexts of interdependence where actors feel 'locked in' by personal or institutional commitments and constraints like between politicians and their constituents (Smelser, 1998: 5, cf. Lorenz-Meyer, 2001: 4).

By "role-relations" which is evident in the relationship between politicians and their communities, Nuckolls conceptualizes a situation where one reconciles contradictory beliefs in a particular subject position in order to perform a given task effectively within a particular cultural context (Nuckolls, 1996: 117–118). The context here is that of generalized homophobia against perceived homosexuals who are seen as a danger to the heterosexual and pronatalist mindset as well as politicians and members of upper society who appropriate these practices for their upward social mobility and to maintain themselves in power. Nuckolls specifically discusses a situation in which people have different conceptions of values depending on their worldviews, some of which are opposed to each other. The result of these inconsistencies, he argues (following Weber) is a paradox that is resolved by compromises which eventually leads to new knowledge systems sustained by the tensions inherent in attaining a cultural goal. Stated differently, no culture is an "open and shut case" (1996: 30). This neatly describes the situation of government authorities in Cameroon who are supposed to extol the values of society (See Obara, 2012, Pemunta and Obara, 2011). Even within the political class, there are vested and contending interests. This "conditions" the strategies employed by politicians in the quest to legitimate their rule in order to govern effectively. The result is a resort to ambivalence. In their search for legitimacy, politicians and moral entrepreneurs weep up sentiments of homophobia against LGBT community. Such a situation, of course, creates ambiguities because the same actors also need to also recognize and respond to globalized discourses of human rights and modernity (Scott, 2007, Robertson, 1992; Gill and Law 1989: 478). It has been argued that Westernization which is being imposed and diffused poses a serious threat to African cultural values, knowledge systems and societies. The growing homogeneity of cultures that underpins globalization is leading to "a form of global assimilation in the direction of dominant groups and societies" (Scott, 2007: 3). The government of Cameroon depends on international aid to sustain government operations. It also depends on remittances which serve as a type of opium to maintain its stranglehold on the largely poor and impoverished population which could become a time bomb. Most of the aid from Western governments and multilateral and bilateral institutions comes with conditionalities attached by the donor (see also Obara, 2012, Pemunta and Obara, 2011). Moreover, Cameroon has ratified the Maputo convention treaty which is in favour of homosexuality. This convention in itself has been problematic on politicians who often invoke "culture" to justify their being in power, but at the same time resort to occultic practices to keep power (Pemunta, 2011).

In his study of global culture and images of the world, Robertson (1992: 398) has argued that in the quest for "modernity" there is an increasing homogeneity (sameness) in terms of values and practices (see also Scott, 2007). I will rather argue that in this increasingly homogenizing world, Euro-American societies represent globalized images of an ideal society. That is one with the same set of cultural beliefs, practices, values and norms and the benchmark for the implied patterns that a society should follow in order to be seen as part of globalized modernity is to be like them. This is expressed through what Roland Robertson calls metaphors of the appropriate structure of the world: "the legitimacy of societal actions, attributes and trends has increasingly become an issue that is cast in global terms like 'global public' and 'world citizenry' which have become part of contemporary public discourse" (Robertson, 1992: 398). It is precisely in relation to such shifts that homosexual practices have elicited homophobic reactions and their plight has come under scrutiny from both international and local actors culminating in a powerful anti-homophobic discourse and the need for the decriminalization of homosexuality. With anti-homophobic rhetoric increasingly intertwined with the continuous provision of development aid, the government of Cameroon has to showcase evidence that it is doing something in regard to upholding of the human rights of sexual minorities. The politicians in addition to employing a kind of "double speak"—double appropriation of the discourse of human rights/individual autonomy being propagated by both the international community and the government of Cameroon. is simultaneously also pretending to be with their constituents by condemning homosexuality in public.

Conclusion

The witch hunt against the homosexuality epidemic and the ambivalence and negation of the torture of homosexuals by African governments has led to an influx of refugees asking for asylum in Europe on the well-founded grounds of persecution. While they risk being arrested and persecuted, they also suffer from witch hunting and violent aggression in the wider society. In the case of Cameroon, both government officials and some foreign country officials share the view that "homosexuality is not actively persecuted" (Geschiere, 2010: 130) even when this contrasts with reality on the ground. As often stated by Issa Chiroma, as long as same-sex partners keep a low profile, they will not be harmed: they should remain in the closet. He has consistently argued that in Cameroon "There is no judicial harassment of homosexuals"[12]. In a similar manner, Uhuru Kenyatta responded to Barack Obama's observation that the oppression of gays was a "wrong, full stop" by making it clear that gay rights are a "non-issue" in his country[13] because homosexual practices are diametrically opposed to the values of Kenyan society.

According to Ashley Currier (Currie 2010: 115–6) the three uses of political homophobia include: first to crack down on dissent (Conway, 2008 cited in Currie 2010) from both gender and sexual-diversity activists as well as the silencing of political opponents. State authorities deploy political homophobia to clamp down on political opponents. For example, it was used in South Africa to

---

[12] https://76crimes.com/2016/01/01/91-anti-lgbt-attacks-and-violations-cameroons-2015-tally/.
[13] http://www.theguardian.com/commentisfree/cifamerica/2011/apr/20/anti-gay-laws-africa-uganda-ssempa

crack down on antiapartheid dissent in the 1980s. Those who opposed the compulsory military conscription and associated service of the South African Defence Force were blackmailed as "gay" and "lesbian". Further, homosexuality has allegedly been used to divert attention from issues considered as sensitive by state leaders (Bhana et al. 2007, Lado, 2011: 920) in the Gambia, Malaysia, Egypt, Russia, Nigeria and Zimbabwe among others. Goodluck Jonathan allegedly used "same-sex marriages as a ruse to shore up his flagging political fortunes" (Reid, 2015) in the face of the serious security threats from Boko Haram, unbridled corruption scandals and internal division within his party, he signed and promulgated into law the Same-sex Marriage (Prohibition) Bill. Similarly, Robert Mugabe's acerbic criticism of the West is perceived as a mechanism for deflecting Western criticism of his authoritarian rule and the socioeconomic quagmire in which Zimbabwe is mired (Hoad 1999: 555 cf., see also Epprecht 2004). As Bhana et al. (2007: 133) maintain "Sex has been a convenient issue to deflect attention away from far more pressing concerns". The labelling of homosexuality as Western is a negation of historical subjectivity to gender and sexual dissenters. Thirdly, it is used by powerful social actors to distort and rewrite history and to simultaneously silence the voices of less powerful actors. For example, the former national liberation movement in South Africa is associated with "patriotic history" (Ranger 2004: 19 cited in Currie 2010) while their opponents are excluded from official history because of their lack of "liberation credentials" (cf Currie 2010: 116).

Homosexuality is not inseparable from other practices. Therefore to evaluate a country's stance on the issue in isolation is out of place. The emancipation of gays and the centrality of gay rights within the larger framework of human rights policies-components of the idea of global modernity— are push factors for the growing turmoil about homosexuality in Africa and other continents. Judith Butler has come to the "challenging conclusion that 'the promiscuous gay' is becoming the pinnacle of modernity. She argues that to many people in Europe—including people who used to be quite homophobic— acceptation of homosexuality has become the litmus test of being modern. The people who have to be tested on this are, of course, especially immigrants from various parts of Africa or Turkey" (cited in Geschiere, 2010: 129–130). The witch hunt against homosexuals is intertwined with popular unease about a model of modernity so powerfully presented by the West. This should be read as part of larger contestations about a presumed "all-encompassing Westernization...that threatens to take over the developing countries of Africa: the complete and total disregard for traditional culture, customs, natural environment and socioeconomic status of the place..." (Scott, 2007: 11, Yankuuzo, 2014). This all-encompassing Westernization borders on cultural colonization which usually involves among others the imposition of sociocultural, religious and linguistic structures on an indigenous population (Scott, 2007: 11, cf. Yankuzo, 2014). Cultural colonization is perceived as one of several negative Western influences presumably diffused through the mass media—one of the effects of "globalisation of cultural industries and mass consumption" which have definitely impacted on "local practices and identities", and "brings the question of culture's orientation roles into sharp focus" (Warnier 2004: 52, cf. Lado 2011: 921, Yankuzo, 2014, Scott, 2007). The growing homogeneity of cultures of the world has led to a form of "global assimilation" from the dominant Western and American cultures. This trend has been dubbed as "cultural imperialism, Westernization and Americanization of weaker societies" (Yankuzo, 2014: 3) which has generated intense resistance. There is a clash between those who subscribe to cultural differentialism—to the view that between and among cultures there are incompatible differences that have remained unaffected by globalizing trends. This includes the view of the nation state as having a heterosexual identity and the individuals within it as heterosexual beings (Pemunta, 2011). Stated otherwise, globalization does not affect every structure/institution of a society. On the contrary, those who adopt cultural convergence argue that globalization leads to "increasing sameness throughout the world" (Yankuzo, 2014: 2). This suggests that globalization might lead to deep transformation of cultural values. Those who advocate cultural hybridization concede that globalization leads to the mixing of cultures, the integration and interpenetration of the global and the local. This mixing has resulted in the "production of a new and unique hybrid cultures that can neither be reduced to the local or the global cultures" (Ibid).

While the practice of homosexuality is discursively framed as an "unAfrican" practice, this currency of resistance to Western modernity and its imposition by the West has left some refugees with no option than to exploit this European modernity, yet even some genuine ones are still refused asylum meaning that they are now faced with a double dilemma situation: excluded from citizenship because of their sexuality, yet refused the benefits of global modernity by the same countries that advocate gay rights—but are faced with unease about the same modernity they are forwarding (see also Geschiere, 2010).

A wide range of social actors/stakeholders need to be targeted with sensitization messages—teachers, nurses, public health officials, police and legal officers, ministry of labour officials—about LGBT issues and leveraged for non-discriminatory policies and services.

References

Alcoff, Linda M and Mohanty, Satya P. 2006. Reconsidering Identity Politics: An Introduction. In L. M Alcoff, Linda M, Hames-Garcia, Michael, Mohanty, Satya P and Moya, Paula ML. (Eds.), *Identity Politics Reconsidered* (pp. 1–9). New York: Palgrave Macmillan.

Bayart, Jean-François, Ellis, Stephen and Hibou, Béatrice. 1999. *The Criminalization of the State in Africa*. Bloomington: Indiana University Press.

Bayart, Jean-François. 1989. *L'Etat en Afrique: La Politique du Ventre*. Paris: Fayart.

Bayart, Jean-Francois. 1989. Les Églises Chrétiennes et la politique du ventre: le partage du gâteau ecclesial, *Politique africaine*, Vol. 35, pp. 3–26.

Besio, Kathryn B & Butz, David. 2004. Autoethnography: A Limited Endorsement. The Professional Geographer, Vol. 56(3): 432–438.

Bourdieu, Pierre. 1977. *Outline of a theory of practice*. Cambridge: Cambridge University Press.

Bourdieu, Pierre. 1979. "Symbolic Power." *Critique of Anthropology, 4* (13–14), 77–85.

Bourdieu, Pierre. 1980. *The Logic of Practice*. Stanford: Stanford University Press.

Bourdieu, Pierre. 1986. Forms of Capital. In R. J. G, *Handbook for Theory and Research for the Sociology of Education*. New York: Green Wood Press.

Bourdieu, Pierre. 1989. Social Space and Symbolic Power. *Sociological Theory, 7* (1), 14–25.

Bosire, Obara Tom. 2012. The Bondo secret society: female circumcision and the Sierra Leonean state. PhD thesis, Social and Political Sciences, University of Glasgow. Available: http://theses.gla.ac.uk/3506/1/2012BosirePhD.pdf (accessed March 20, 2017).

Brubaker, Rogers. 1996. *Nationalism Reframed: Nationhood and the national question in the New Europe.* Cambridge: Cambridge University Press.

Cameroon Concord online. (October 2015). African Roman Catholic Bishops throw swift punch at ideological colonization—Available: http://cameroon-concord.com/news/religion/item/4384-african-roman-catholic-bishops-throw-swift-punch-at-ideological-colonization#sthash.iRLSFfuD.dpuf.

Connor, Linda H. & Samuel, Geoffrey. 2001. *Healing powers and modernity: traditional medicine, shamanism, and science in Asian societies.* London: Bergin & Garvey.

Bauman, Richard and Sawin, Patricia. 1991. The Politics of Participation in Folk-life Festivals. In *Exhibiting Cultures*, Karp, Ivan and Lavine, Steven. (Eds). pp. 288–314. London: Smithsonian Institute Press.

Canning, Paul. 2011. International pressure on anti-gay laws in Africa must not stop. Available: http://www.theguardian.com/commentisfree/cifamerica/2011/apr/20/anti-gay-laws-africa-uganda-ssempa.

Cole, Tamale. 2012. The white saviour industrial complex. The Atlantic. 21 March. Retrieved from http://www.theatlantic.com/international/archive/2012/03/the-white-savior-industrial-complex/254843/.

Country Reports on Human Rights Practices for 2013 United States Department of State Bureau of Democracy, Human Rights and Labor.

Crossman, Brenda. 2007. *Sexual citizens: The legal and cultural regulation of sex and belonging.* Stanford: Stanford University Press.

Crossman, Brenda. 1997. Turning the gaze back on itself: Comparative Law, feminist legal studies, and the postcolonial project. *Utah Law Review*, 525, 525–543.

Durkheim, Emile. 1915. *The elementary forms of religious life.* in Fields, K (ed.), The Free Press, 1995.

Edensor, Tim. 2002. *National Identity, Popular Culture and Everyday Life.* Oxford: Berg.

Epprecht, Marc. 2008. *Heterosexual Africa? The History of an Idea from the Age of Exploration to the Age of AIDS.* Columbus OH: Ohio University Press.

Eppretch, Marc. 2013. *Sexuality and Social Justice in Africa.* London: Zed Books.

Ellis, Carolyn; Adams, Tony E. & Bochner, Arthur P. 2010. Autoethnography: An Overview [40 paragraphs]. *Forum Qualitative Sozialforschung /Forum: Qualitative Social Research*, 12(1), Art. 10, http://nbn-re solving.de/urn:nbn:de:0114-fqs1101108.

Geschiere, Peter. 2010. Homosexuality in Cameroon: identity and persecution In Dubel, Ireen and Hielkema, Andre, (Eds), *Urgency required: gay and lesbian rights are human rights*, pp. 126–131. Amsterdam: Amsterdam Institute for Social Science Research (AISSR).

Geschiere, Peter. 1997. *The Modernity of Witchcraft: Politics and the Occult in Postcolonial Africa*. Charlottesville and London: University of Virginia Press.

Gifford, Paul. (Ed.). 1995. *The Christian Churches and the Democratization of Africa*. Leiden: E. J Brill: The Netherlands.

Heunggroup, Hans de Marie. 2015. African Arguments. Cameroon's Rising Religious Tensions. Available: http://africanarguments.org/2015/09/08/cameroons-rising-religious-tensions/.

Ikenberry, John G and Kupchan, Charles. A. 1990. Socialization and Hegemonic Power. *International Organisation*, Vol. 44(3): 283–315.

International Crisis Group. 2015. Cameroon. The Threat of Religious Radicalism. Africa Report No. 229. Nairobi/Brussels.

Joseph, Richard. 1997. "Democratization in Africa after 1989: Comparative and Theoretical Perspectives," *Comparative Politics* 29, no. 3: 373.

Kahlina, Katja. 2013. Contested terrain of sexual citizenship: EU accession and the changing position of sexual minorities in the post-Yugoslav context. Working Paper 2013/33. Available: www.citseee.ed.ac.uk/workingpapers.

Kahlina, Katja. 2012. Sexual politics of belonging: sexual identities, nationalism, and citizenship in post-Yugoslav Croatia (Unpublished Ph. D Dissertation). Central European University, Budapest.

Lado, Ludovic. 2011. Popular Homophobia in Cameroon. *Les Cahiers d'Études africaines*, No 4: 921–944.

Lister, Ruth. 2003a. Citizenship, *Feminist Perspectives*. London: Palgrave Macmillan.

Lister, Ruth. 2003b. Sexual Citizenship In Isin, Engin F and Turner, Bryan S (Eds), *Handbook of Citizenship Studies*. London: Sage Publications Ltd, pp. 191–209.

Lopang, Wazha. 2014. No place for Gays: Colonialism and the African Homosexual in African Literature. *International Journal of Humanities and Social Science*, Vol. 4, No. 9(1): 77–83.

Lüscher, Kurt. 1998. A heuristic model for the study of intergenerational ambivalence, Arbeitspapier 29, Sozialwissenschaftliche Fakultät, Universität Konstanz.

Lorenz-Meyer, Dagmar. 2001. The Politics of ambivalence: Towards A Conceptualisation Of Structural Ambivalence In Intergenerational Relations, Gender Institute New Working Paper Series, Issue 2, February 2001. Available: http://www.lse.ac.uk/genderInstitute/pdf/thePoliticsOfAmbivalence.pdf (accessed December 27, 2016).

Mbuy, Tatah H. 1994. *Sects, secret societies, and new religious movements in modern Cameroon: A pastoral challenge, an obstacle, and to national unity*. Bamenda: Muma House Ntarikon.

McAllister, John. 2015. LGBT Activism and 'Traditional Values': Promoting Dialogue through Indigenous Cultural Values in Botswana. Available: https://hivos.org/sites/default/files/7._lgbt_activism_and_traditional_values_by_john_mcallister.pdf.

Murray, Steven O. 1998. "Homosexuality in 'Traditional' Sub-Saharan Africa and contemporary South Africa: an overview," in *Boy-wives and Female-husbands. Studies on African Homosexualities*, pp. 1–18, ed. Murray, Steven O and Roscoe, Will. New York: St Martin's Press.

Muthien, Bernedette. 2003. "Heteronormativity in the African Women's movement", Women's global reproductive rights, newsletter, 79, #2.

Ndzomo, Jean Cedric. 2013. Re-Visiting Homosexuality in Cameroon: Effective Advocacy on the Path from Homophobia to Dignity and Equality. Master's Theses. Paper 75. University of San Francisco.

Pateman, Carole. 1994. 1988. *The Sexual Contract*. Oxford: Polity Press.

Pemunta, Ngambouk. V, Tabenyang, Tabi-Chama, & Fubah, Alubafi, M. 2013. "Communitarianism and the Obasinjom mask performance in ritual healing among the Bayang and Ejagham of Southwest Cameroon", 1–39, Smith, Johnson. B. (ed.). *Rituals, Practices, Ethnic and cultural aspects and role in Emotional Healing*. Georgia, United States: Nova Science Publishers.

Pemunta, Ngambouk V and Obara, Tom Bosire. 2011. War, Social dislocation and the double appropriation of women's human security in Sierra Leone. *Journal of Human Security*. Vol. 8(2): 105–124.

Pemunta, Ngambouk V. 2011. *Culture, Human rights and Socio-legal resistance against Female Genital Cutting practices: An anthropological Perspective*. VDM Publishers.

Population Research Institute. 2015. PRI Review Podcast—African Bishops Speak Out To Defend The Family, With Support From Pope Francis. https://www.pop.org/content/pri-review-podcast-african-bishops-speak-out-defend-family-support-pope-francis.

Reid, Graeme. 2015. Homophobia as a Political Strategy. Published in CNN. Available: https://www.hrw.org/news/2015/06/29/homophobia-political-strategy (accessed 20 August, 2016).

Robertson, Roland. 1992. Globality, Global Culture and Images of World order. In Haferkamp, Hans & Smelser, Neil. *J Social change and modernity* (pp 394–409). Berkeley: University of California Press.

Roscoe, Will. 1987. The Mamlukes, in Cultural Diversity and Homosexualities, ed. Murray, Stephen O. New York: Irvington, pp. 213–219.

Scott, Meghan, M. 2007. Westernization in Sub-Saharan Africa: Facing Loss of Culture, Knowledge, and Environment. A thesis submitted in partial fulfilment of the requirements for the degree of Master of Architecture. Montana State University, Bozeman, Montana.

Stewart, Colin. 2013. Arsonists, burglars attack LGBT advocates in Cameroon. https://76crimes.com/2013/07/01/arsonists-burglars-attack-lgbt-advocates-in-cameroon/.

Stychin, Carl. F. 1998. *A nation by rights: National cultures, sexual identity politics, and the discourse of rights.* Philadelphia: Temple University Press.

Stychin, Carl F. 2003. *Governing sexuality: The changing politics of citizenship and law reform.* Oxford and Portland: Hart.

Tamale, Sylvia. 2011. Researching and theorizing sexualities in Africa. In Tamale, Sylva (Ed.). *African Sexualities: A Reader.* (pp. 11–36). Nairobi: Pambazuka Press.

Tamale, Sylvia. 2011. "Nudity and Morality: Legislating women's bodies and dress in Nigeria", pp. 199–210 in *African Sexuality: A reader.* Cape Town: Pambazuka Press.

Tanku, Tapang Ivo. 2013. Cameroon's president orders Pentecostal churches closed. Available: http://edition.cnn.com/2013/08/14/world/africa/cameroon-churches/

United States Department of State Bureau of Democracy, Human Rights and Labor. 2013. Country Reports on Human Rights Practices for 2013.

Wieringa, Saskia E. 2009. 'Moral Panics, Memory, Postcolonial Amnesia: Sexual and imperial Power', 205–233 in Herdt, Gilbert. (Ed.) *Moral Fear and Panics: The Fight over Sexual Rights.* New York: New York University Press.

Yuval-Davis, Nira, and Anthias, Floya. (Eds.). 1989. *Woman-national-state.* London: Macmillan.

Yuval-Davis, Nira. 1997. *Gender and Nation.* London: Sage.

Zeleza, Paul Tiyambe. 1994. "The Democratic Transition in Africa and the Anglophone Writer," *Canadian Journal of African Studies* Vol. 28, no. 3: 476.

Yankuzo, Kabiru Ibrahim. 2014. Impact of Globalization on the Traditional African Cultures. *International Letters of Social and Humanistic Sciences Online*: 2013-10-31, ISSN: 2300-2697, Vol. 15, pp 1–8, doi:10.18 052/www.scipress.com/ILSHS.15.1.

Concurrent Contestations: Framing, and Naming the 'Queer' in Art from Africa

Melanie Klein
Freie Universität Berlin

Introduction

In this essay, I will examine strategies of queering in exemplary works of artists from Africa, and I will ask about how these works are presented in exhibition contexts as well as how they relate to political, social and cultural debates surrounding them. To frame these debates, I will first turn to attributive terms of same-sex intimacies to show their precarious position in African contexts. Furthermore, I will have a look at how queerness as a concept that is travelling across regional boundaries is negotiated especially in various exhibitions. The above will deliver brief insight into the discourses on issues of homosexuality, queer as political yet also cultural marker and the power relations or rather interpretive authority that is underway. Eventually, I will ask about the potential of queer strategies as a movement of thinking (Paul and Schaffer 2009: 8) that works against fixations or unambiguous distinctions and continually analyses different axes of power.

In particular, I will ask what kind of alternative conceptualizations and narrations of homosexuality are provided by artists Ato Malinda, who currently works and lives in Rotterdam, and Igshaan Adams in Cape Town and secondly, how these narratives relate to the travelling concept of queerness in discourses of normative, reactionary or liberal attitudes. I would thus like to set a starting point for an ample taxonomy of different forms of artistic queering in African contexts. It indicates a research agenda, which still is a desideratum, and the more so as the complexity of creative comments on homosexuality and its representations as well as compulsory heterosexuality is rarely dealt with in detail.

Queerness in the Global Contemporary[1]

The reluctance to normalize homosexuality can be found in every single society. Correspondent legislative attempts trigger off conflicting processes of designation, acknowledgement and solidarity as well as resistance, disrespect and hate. These processes take different routes and turn in different sociocultural surroundings that cut across national boundaries, but also intersect with categorizations of race, ethnicity, class, religion and spatial locations. Individuals in Africa engaging in same-sex practices are part of a social milieu in which homosexuality is an increasingly visible and highly contested political and activist parameter. At the same time, homosexuality is negotiated within a global network of antagonistic parties such as African anti-gay movements as well as American evangelical Christians on the one side and internationally engaged non-governmental organizations that promote gay rights on the other.[2] In some instances, African countries serve as effectively extended battlefields of Western or especially American oppositional contestations on homosexuality as well as what the Time Magazine entitled "America's next civil rights frontier" in 2014 referring to transgender politics. And corresponding representations of "the West and the rest"[3] inform this politically and discursively conflicting constellation. It seems that both anti-gay polemics and the rhetoric of civilized values fall on fertile ground here, yet often fail to translate appropriately into specific African contexts.[4]

---

[1] For a conceptualization of the *Global Contemporary* see Hans Belting, Andrea Buddensieg and Peter Weibel (2013): *The global contemporary and the rise of the new art worlds*, Cambridge, MIT Press.

[2] Conflicting situations and emancipatory strategies within the framework of gay rights and LGBTQ activist work in Africa adopt, in fact, diverse trajectories, implementations and activities in specific local contexts with distinct histories.

[3] Stuart Hall (1992): "The West and the rest. Discourse and power", in: Stuart Hall and Bram Gieben (Eds.), *Formations of modernity*, Cambridge, Polity Press, pp. 276–320.

[4] See, for example, the conflicting forces of evangelical groups and their influence on Uganda's Anti-Homosexuality Bill of 2009 and supportive gay activists from the U. S. involved in "American culture wars" on the continent (Jeffrey Gettleman (2010): "Americans' role seen in Uganda anti-gay push", in:

In the realm of global art or specifically, the Global Contemporary such abiding dichotomies seem to be surmounted progressively in favour of a more differentiated view on visual cultures worldwide. Power asymmetries and limited scopes of agency within cultural infrastructures are still evident. Here, representations of queerness in the art from Africa seem to be confiscated as a new and updated aesthetic currency which in turn results in the capitalization of the twofold marginal, the African and the queer. The artist who is addressing homosexuality is constructed as a critical, trailblazing mind connected to both, her or his African surrounding—typically presented as the discriminatory site—as well as an international gay community, i.e. ambassador of the 'West'[5] pointing the way to legal security and, more loftily, freedom. Apart from—or actually because of—being African, artists become oppressed LGBTQ protagonists producing 'queer' and thus politically significant art; however, the handy catchword seldom refers to the actual artistic strategies of queering that artists employ to question the ideological facets of identity formations and privileges of normative heterosexuality with its close connections to ethnicity and religion. "Queer can be understood as playing with the professionalization of representation" (Müller 1998)[6] and, furthermore, as an engagement with the dynamics of power that impact such professionalization or naturalization. And this is exactly what artists

---

The New York Times, http://www.nytimes.com/2010/01/04/world/africa/04uganda.html, accessed 09.12.2015). In the meantime, the Ugandan gay rights group *Sexual Minorities Uganda* sues an American evangelist for actions that resulted in the persecution, torture and murder of gay men and women. Think as well of the backlashes in many African countries on Hillary Clinton's speech at the *UN Human Rights Council* in Geneva in 2011 and Barack Obama's concurrent memorandum to elevate foreign policy of decriminalizing homosexuality as well as on his recent speech in Kenya on July 25th 2015.

[5] I use inverted commas for terms that I believe are rather used simplistically to imply sets of common discourses and experiences but have at least to some extent been transformed and rendered obsolete.

[6] My own translation of „queer kann verstanden werden als Spiel mit der [...] Professionalisierung der Darstellung" in Birgit Müller (1998): "Queer handeln. Performanz und Veränderung", in: *Psychologie und Postmoderne*, Freie Universität Berlin, http://web.fu-berlin.de/postmoderne-psych/berichte1/mueller.htm, accessed 23.03.2016.

from Africa—like any other artist addressing the politics of identity and representation—are interested in.

I certainly do not attempt to criticize an exhibition practice that unveils examples of discrimination and legal violation. Artists who address homosexuality in Africa and elsewhere contribute to a necessary visibility and debate around such violations. The question is what kind of audiences can and should be reached by specific works and—art historically speaking—if we should give away complex and differentiated aesthetic articulations to politically and ideologically charged familiar places?

For this paper, I consulted and analyzed studies of scholars working on LGBTQ issues in Africa from a sociological and political perspective. I utilized discourses in newspapers, magazines and online platforms, and I had an attentive look at several relevant exhibitions and their presentational practice. Finally, the analysis of works of the Ato Malinda and Igshaan Adams completed the data.

Discursive dichotomies: Framing and naming same-sex intimacies in Africa

In a case study on meanings of homosexuality in South African townships historians, Marc Epprecht and Veronica Sigamoney (2013) point to the fact of different degrees of stigmatization of deviant sexualities in Africa but also acknowledge their broad acceptance. Their connection to immoral behaviour had instead been introduced by missionaries and travellers. "Indeed", they write, "other studies and memoirs by African LGBTQ individuals have argued that cultures of qualified acceptance are manifest in Africa, discursively coded in silence, discretion, not naming, identity blurring, connections between same-sex sexuality and spirit possession, and so on" (Epprecht and Sigamoney 2013: 87). The term homosexuality was rarely and ambivalently used in the township surrounding they investigated. The notion of queer was nonexistent. Nevertheless, regional descriptions were used pejoratively as well as to name certain behaviours. It seems as if it is not so much about the act of naming as such that constitutes the problem of the vulnerability of LGBTQ people but rather their increased visibility through the establishment of new identity categories that exacerbate the complicated matrix of colonial legacies and neo-colonialist tendencies of playing an alleged 'African' homophobia against more liberal countries.

"Sexual minorities in Africa", notes literary scholar Ayo Coly, "have the burden of making themselves intelligible and legible to Western donors and audiences, and Western NGOs, in fact, often fund gender and sexual identity workshops to familiarize African sexual minorities with Western terminology" (Coly 2013: 24). She claims that the adoption of such categories to mobilize LGBTQ people and claim their rights had "positioned sexual minorities in violation of the cultural codes of their communities" (Coly 2013: 26). In Zimbabwe, homophobia had thus not been provoked through issues of same-sex desire as such but rather through an enforcement of public discourses about them. Non-African identity markers are thus "exported as a value" to recall Édouard Glissant's (1990) thoughts on the relationship between colonizers and colonized that bear analogy to current discursive constellations. Coly's effort to write against an equalization of Africa with homophobia is necessary and commendable. Her denunciation of politically potent terminologies most probably applicable to activist endeavours worldwide—albeit modified and questioned—denies the incessant dynamics of change but also the agency and self-positioning of African protagonists. It reminds me of an urban legend I heard from a boda boda[7] driver in Kampala on one of my research tours about straight men identifying themselves as gay to get money from the West. Human rights politics meet neo-liberal dynamics.

Sylvia Rosila Tamale, a lawyer, feminist academic and editor of the *African Sexualities reader*, rightly criticizes the ahistoricity which homophobia in Africa is associated with and diagnoses a tendency towards yet another kind of backwardness-progressiveness-dichotomy between African and Western countries which is established by dominant, interwoven discourses:

---

[7] Motorcycle taxis in East Africa. The term as such, though, is most often used in Uganda.

Africa is reinvented as a heterosexual continent in 'African' debates and stigmatized as homophobic in 'European' debates. "Europe is being reconstructed concerning sexual democracy" (Tamale 2013: 36). "The more important point to note", she writes, "is that antihomosexuality rhetoric serves to strengthen the standing of its proponents in mainstream thought and maintains their social relevance—whether in the West or Africa" (Tamale 2013: 34). Literary scholar Keguro Macharia claims a thorough contextualization of anti-homosexual statements in Africa to avoid their simple classification and a straightening approach to shared experiences and minority statuses. "Homophobia in Africa is a problem", he concedes, "but not as African homophobia, a special class that requires special interventions" (Macharia 2010). A similar tendency is criticized by cultural scientist Henriette Gunkel who notes that "[…] gay rights are being increasingly associated with the West while Islam [and African countries in general as I would like to add] is constituted as homophobic and thus outside the discourse of 'human rights'" (Gunkel 2010: 9). Macharia also states that human rights groups' "increased visibility has led to increased vulnerability, a trajectory shared by progressive organizations across the world" (Macharia 2010). The violability of queer people that Coly diagnosed primarily for African contexts, in which gay rights would violate cultural codes, is shifted towards an acknowledgement of efforts worldwide to fight against discrimination by Macharia. In a period of increasing exchange of knowledge, of far-reaching networks and indeed the sharing of experiences, worries and successes, yet also of still existing asymmetrical power relations and financial dependencies, of tensions between alleged 'authentic' identities or modes of life that have to be 'rescued', the awkward position of LGBTQ communities in Africa constitutes their participation in the continuing game of national and cultural alignments.

Far beyond their stigmatization and victimization queers in Africa and queers of colour are actively engaged in negotiating their identity, position and partake in local communities and 'traditions'. It is important to analyze and differentiate historical complexity and to acknowledge the fact that homosexuality was historically not criminalized in Africa but in the 'West'. It is important to distinguish the contexts and forms in which same-sex intimacy was lived out. Nevertheless, the merits of and desire for great activist stances and queering acts relating to normative and discriminating representations cannot be underestimated even if they implicate increased violability. In the end, historical incidences of tolerated same-sex sexuality may indeed be acknowledged structurally as practices of queering. Gunkel aptly argues that even if "the term queer has not been used widely throughout the history of and scholarship on homosexuality and non-normative sexualities" (Gunkel 2010: 15) in Africa, Queer Theory can be a useful instrument and that its point of emergence does not reveal anything about its analyzing potential. And queer theorist Jack Halberstam notes referring to everyday and artistic practices of queer life in South Africa that "the criticality of queerness in the context of Black South Africa, indeed, depends absolutely upon its refutation of a temporality that places Euro-American sexual politics in the center of modernity; and it locates queerness, here and now, as simultaneously a postcolonial critique of normative historiographies of queer worlds and a futuristic summons for a new world-making endeavour that joins queer of colour critique in the U. S. to critical queerness in South Africa" (Halberstam 2014: 12).

In this sense, I suggest to differentiate between queer as an attribution—used politically, socially but also relating to attention values and expectations in a global art world—and queer as a methodological approach, analytical tool and artistic strategy. In the realm of art, this differentiation translates as attributions and artists' self-positioning within an asymmetrically regulated set of exhibitions and art markets as well as their presence in art journals, online platforms or the media in general and the act of artistic queering with separate analyses of these practices.

'Sexuality marketing'.
Appropriating queerness in activism and art

One of the most relevant and recurring scepticism towards LGBTQ and queer labelling has to do with the fact that it has its roots in 'Western' political activism and does not encompass different forms of same-sex intimacies in many African regions. It is indeed true that homosexual practices and non-normative sexuality or gender adopt different formulations throughout the world. Especially colonialism's standardizations of such phenomena have to be and are increasingly questioned. And the debates around issues of homo-normative and racist structures of LGBTQ politics are necessary and hopefully persistent[8] It is also true that the human rights debate as such—with gay rights as part of it—has been criticized for its Western-oriented logic[9] and more so that it is difficult "to discuss sexualities as sources of empowerment" (Bennett 2011: 78) in political contexts in Africa. Curator Koyo Kouoh explicates this circumstance in referring to her conversations with linguist Ibrahima Ndiaye in preparation for the exhibition "Precarious imaging. Visibility surrounding African queerness" at the Raw Material Company in Dakar 2014: "He taught us something that is quite striking. According to him, the difference between Western and African ways of dealing with the subject is in the naming. As long as there is a practice and nobody knows about it, and nobody speaks about it, it is fine. Homosexuality is indeed present in [...] any [...] society. The problem is that people don't want to name it, they don't want to discuss it, and they don't want it to be visible."[10] Concerning political and activist movements in Africa, feminist theorist Jane Bennett provides an insight into these dynamisms of naming. She writes: "There is a long history of [...] activism, and whether one names the diverse threads of voice, movement, organisation and policy work as feminist [or queer as I would like to add], or not, has a great deal to do with the local and strategic

---

[8] See Jasbir Puhar (2007): *Terrorist assemblages. Homonationalism in queer times*, Durham, Duke University Press, as one of the most prominent examples.

[9] See, for example, Bachmann-Medick (2012) and also more specifically literary scholar Neville Hoad who writes that "tolerance for homosexuality becomes an indicator of civilised modernity, but in the African context, and perhaps also in a more generalised postcolonial one, the bourgeois nuclear family is often seen as the proper intimate form of modernity" (Hoad 2005: 15).

[10] Koyo Kouoh cited in Moses Serubiri (2014): "'The police told me I shouldn't put on a show like that'. Conversation with Koyo Kouoh on the contested issues of homosexuality, media and religious power in Africa", in: *Manifesta Journal*, pp. 129–134.

politics of a particular time and place. [...] suffice to say that though the term feminist has, at times, carried overtones of western women's dominance over the expression of African-based discourses on injustice (and hence been roundly rejected), many contemporary struggles about gender justice on the continent embrace the term feminist" (Bennett 2011: 85). This passage illustrates the potential of travelling concepts, such as queerness, to explain the very conditions of global circulations[11] as well as concomitant occurrences of appropriation, demarcation and refusal.

It is not possible to discuss in detail, here, the historical genealogy of the concept of queerness which was initially applied in the United States since the 1980s as a political and later theoretical tool. It should be mentioned, though, that the concept was attacking the White middle-class heterosexual mainstream (Voss 2005: 1108) and was thus able to thematize different experiences of socalled queers of colour. In Africa, historical formations of same-sex intimacies are only recently researched. Often, definitions that were developed and produced in Western contexts—such as gay, lesbian, transgender or indeed queer—cannot adequately grasp such intimate relationships and are only ambiguously used or not employed at all in actual daily situations. In the activist environment of gay rights organizations, though, the term queer stands for political effectiveness and international attention and unfolds, once again, the dichotomy between a backward and—in an updated form—homophobic African continent and a progressive liberality of Western layout. These organizations are often part of an international network and funded accordingly. In this respect, supposedly 'civilized' sexual values are associated with Western

---

[11] For a comprehensive elaboration of travelling concepts see Doris Bachmann-Medick (2014): "From hybridity to translation. Reflections on travelling concepts", in: Bachmann-Medick, Doris (Ed.), *The trans/national study of culture. A translational perspective*, Berlin und Boston, De Gruyter, S. 119–136. Referring to research perspectives, she explicates that "here we should look more carefully at the differences between cultural semantics, knowledge traditions, and knowledge gaps. But we should also concentrate on smaller units of social interaction, on misunderstandings, or even battles over interpretation" (Bachmann-Medick 2014: 130–131).

donors; and pioneering political tasks, as well as cultural contemporaneity, are being authenticated.[12]

These somewhat attributing dynamics, in turn, become noticeable in African artists' trajectories. As an attribution gay, lesbian, queer or LGBTQ become markers of subversive, contemporary artistic practices almost exclusively related to activist art from Africa. Others trade these practices as highly topical and currently relevant counterbalances to constructions of a homogeneous Africanity. Paradoxically, visibilities of homosexuality obtain the status of a new and entirely 'authentic' African experience within the global art system at the same time. The kind of visibilities that circulate internationally can be found mostly in connection with borrowings from documentary and activist repertoires. Other forms of queering as an artistic strategy are often marginalized in favour of an alignment to a more stringent, urgent and obvious making visible of gay, lesbian and transgender everyday lives. When looking at examples of exhibiting works of art related to homosexuality in Africa within an international art world, it is striking that the dynamics of categorizing and labelling art from Africa disclose similar structures as those that have been characterized by, for example, Olu Oguibe. Oguibe and others have repeatedly pointed to the fiction of Africanity and the West's appetite for the other in a seemingly democratic yet still highly hierarchized global art world.[13] In his collection of essays The culture game in 2003 Oguibe wrote: "It speaks to a discourse of power and confinement in current Western appreciation of modern African art, a discourse of speech and utterative regulation, which, by

---

[12] Interestingly, anachronistic phenomena in the 'West', such as the work of evangelical churches from the U. S. or the continuing blocking of equal same-sex marriage laws by German conservative parties, are not part of the liberal and human rights narrative within global discourses.

[13] See, for example, Harris who writes about the art market's mechanisms as still dominated by Western gatekeeper organizations. He states that "the international markets for contemporary art have been created and cornered by Western institutions—auction houses, dealing galleries, museums and broadly what might be called, in Althusserian fashion, 'the art discourse' apparatus. Taken together, this global art world power nexus needs art still come 'from' China or Korea—that is, to exhibit signs of authentic difference that help brand it at the international marketplace" (Harris 2013: 440–441).

denying African artists the right to language and self-articulation, incarcerates them in the policed colonies of Western desire" (Oguibe 2004: 13). The right to the self-articulation of artists from Africa is in fact no longer denied these days as Oguibe was able to appositely diagnose by reference to an interview that was conducted by Thomas McEvilley with artist Ouattara Watts twenty years previously; however, the hierarchy of interpretive authority, or Deutungshoheit, and expectations does not seem to be leveled at last, but rather shifted or elegantly circumnavigated at times. On the other hand, though, artists from Africa and elsewhere are increasingly intervening in and channelling global discourses and image productions. They take part in the creation and modification of categories and position themselves beyond any essentialist attributions.

The visibility of issues of same-sex intimacies and its implications for art from Africa has increased in the past years, prominently spearheaded by South African photographer Zanele Muholi who has already achieved an exceptional international career. Muholi calls herself a queer activist and thus uses a term that is rarely employed in the African context. Most NGOs, for example, refer to LGBTQ rights or bear the labels of distinct sexual identities.[14] In South Africa, however, the term queer is used proficiently to coin the visibility of predominantly gays, lesbians and transgender people in political and activist frameworks. The online human rights platform *Iranti*, for example, is denominated as "queer vernacular visual narratives".[15] It offers archival storage of personal stories, and its makers are also engaged in several political projects. On *Inkanyiso*, another archival platform founded by Zanele Muholi, it says that "the first thing that every reader should think of when entering this platform is Queer Activism = Queer Media. A flexible and unique source of information for art advoca-

---

[14] For example, *Sexual Minorities Uganda* - SMUG, *Gays and Lesbians of Zimbabwe*, *Sappho Mambo*, a group for lesbians in Kenya, *The Inner Circle* or *The Lesbian and Gay Equality Project* in South Africa or the *Coalition of African Lesbians* - CAL, a formation of more than 30 organizations in 19 African countries and many others.

[15] See website of Iranti: http://www.iranti-org.co.za/, accessed 10.11.2015.

cy".[16] The application of the concept of queerness refers to both, the knowledge to actively engage in theory and discourse formations and the connection to LGBTQ communities worldwide. In Inkanyiso's case, queer alludes to an inclusive approach even though Muholi's activism mainly addresses lesbians. And the organizers of the exhibition Critically Queer that Iranti coordinated in 2013 invited a local audience "to come observe and interpret various forms of queerness, and to bring into question our present state of sexual and gender expressions."[17]. At the same time, curator Jabu Pereira pointed to the general significance of this rather regional event to understand homophobic structures. The most prominent utilization of the term queer together with other associative titles, though, can be witnessed when visual representations of LGBTQ people travel to international exhibitions, galleries and museums. There is a leitmotif, in this context, to clearly mark queer visibility as politically relevant, as raising awareness and pushing social change.[18]

---

[16] See the website of *Inkanyiso*: http://inkanyiso.org/about/, accessed 10.11.2015.
[17] See *Iranti* (2013): "'Critically Queer' celebrates sexuality, gender identity in Africa", in: http://www.iranti-org.co.za/content/Events/2013/2013-Exhibition-Critically-Queer/2013-Critically-Queer.html, accessed 10.12.2015.
[18] Some examples of such exhibitions are "Going south. Queer cartographies in post-apartheid South Africa" at the *Institute of Contemporary Arts* in London in 2013, "Queer and trans art-iculations. Collaborative art for social change" with works by Zanele Muholi and Gabrielle Le Roux at the *Wits Art Museum* in Johannesburg in 2014, "Precarious imaging. Visibility and media surrounding African queerness" at the *Raw Material Company* in Dakar in 2014 or "Transitions. In search of an authentic queer" at the *Goethe Institute* in Johannesburg in 2014 to 2015.

Zanele Muholi, *Sizile Rongo-Nkosi, Glenwood, Durban*, 2012, silver gelatine print, 76, 5 x 50, 5 cm, Michael Stevenson Gallery.

The exhibitory presentation of activist and photographer Zanele Muholi illustrates this phenomenon. In several exhibitions, she was represented with her work "Faces and phases", an ongoing series of black-and-white portraits of lesbians and transgender women and men mainly from South Africa.[19] The photographs of highly aesthetic appeal yet also conventional layout, reminiscent of African studio photography, were commonly linked to incidences of so-called 'corrective rape'[20] in the country. The potential of Muholi's vast overall oeuvre to visually queer images and perceptions of especially lesbians was never really addressed or exhibited. Instead, "Faces and phases" as only representative part of her artistic as well as activist[21] work seemed and still seems to become a fast-selling item in its global circulation. Through "Faces and phases" the issue of 'corrective rape' was mediated to an international art audience as an artistic mode to save homosexual women's dignity from victimization and as a translation of their always clearly indicated suffering and discrimination into an aesthetically digestible language. Through the way of presenting this particular section of Muholi's work the dreadful facts of rape and homicide of women could easily be associated with the community as a whole, even if the series rather exemplifies the diversity of lesbians and transgender people, their transformative phases in life as well as their sheer existence that has to be—according to Muholi—documented and archived. Muholi herself writes in this respect: "Whatever I have captured and still capture is for the world to see that we exist as black lesbians, women, trans men, intersexed,

---

[19] "Faces and phases" was shown, for example, in *Deutsches Historisches Museum* in Berlin 2015, *Schwules Museum* in Berlin 2014, *Einsteinhaus* in Ulm 2014, the *Ryerson Image Centre* in Toronto 2014, *Massimadi Festival* in Montreal 2014), *Galerie Wentrup* in Berlin 2014, the Pride in Venice and Trento 2014, *Palazzo S. Agostino* in Modena 2013, the *Yancey Richardson Gallery* in New York 2013, the *Documenta 13* in Kassel 2012, the *Goethe Institut* in Johannesburg 2012, *Fred Gallery* in London 2010 and *Brodie & Stevenson* in Johannesburg 2009.

[20] See, for example, the extensive coverage in the *Mail & Guardian* and especially the article "Changing the language of prejudice" by activist Melanie Judge from 2011 for a critical view on the term 'corrective rape': http://mg.co.za/article/2011-06-12-changing-the-language-of-prejudice, accessed 05.04.2016.

[21] See, again, *Inkanyiso*: http://inkanyiso.org/about/, accessed 10.11.2015.

bisexuals, trans women—as queer Africans" (Muholi 2011: 11). Muholi's primarily activist endeavor, that also yields various visual and collectively produced documents and works against unilateral representations in the South African media, is—if at all—mentioned in international exhibition contexts in a sole informative manner but seems to be unwelcomed as aesthetic evidence. Paradoxically, the 'African' form of queerness in Muholi's work as topical, political and thus contemporary element[22] is sanitized and emphasized at the same time in this series—partly by Muholi herself—when shown separately and detached from its social and political origins. In the recent exhibition "Homosexualität_en" in *Deutsches Historisches Museum* in Berlin 2015 "Faces and phases" was exhibited in the section "Shame and disgrace" together with audio documents on discrimination against homosexuality in Nazi Germany as the second and non-German example of homophobia, i.e. as *the* representative of worldwide discrimination against LGBTQ groups *and* as artistic contribution in an otherwise mostly historical exposition. A shortage of space and this extensive show might have been a simple reason for, once again, hanging up Muholi's well-known portraits. As elucidation of the complexities of homophobia in a continent such as Africa or as a comprehensive demonstration of the artistic strategies of an artist like Muholi the images failed.

---

[22] The "political urgency, outside the trappings of counter-cultural cool" of Muholi's work is also addressed in the film screening "Going South. Queer cartographies in post-apartheid South Africa" curated by art historians Tamar Garb and Liese van der Watt at the *Institute of Contemporary Arts* in London 2013. Garb and van der Watt coupled the political urgency of broaching the issue of queerness in South Africa with Muholi's filmic documentary work and the footage of a performance by Steven Cohen. With this, they blurred the lines between art and activism and put emphasis on the "sole dialogue" around queerness and concomitant narrative strategies; a small but effective and enlightening event. For citations see https://www.ica.org.uk/whats-on/going-south-queer-cartographies-post-apartheid-south-africa, accessed 15.02.2016.

Artistic strategies and their (global) circulation

Acts of queering in the art from Africa and elsewhere work tentatively and negotiate precarious identities within highly sensitive societal situations. When looking at specific case studies throughout the African continent, the question is how artistic enunciations confront issues of homosexuality.

In the global art world the term queer seems to be, first of all, a common denominator for same-sex related and transgender issues in general and secondly suggests a criticality that meets today's desire for socially and politically relevant artistic comments. In this respect, artists who work with same-sex phenomena in African contexts do fathom not only creative strategies and activist agendas but also the question of how and where their results can be presented. Attributions and meanings of same-sex and gender related artworks constantly shift in this semantic merry-go-round of (self-)positioning, regionally specific receptions and sociocultural and political struggles. And this is exactly where queerness reaches it's limitations—when the concept is only unknown in regions other than the 'West'- yet is also discovered as a refreshed version of grazed political and theoretical terrain.[23] What kind of alliances are imposed, offered and accepted here one might ask? How then can the politically charged and still widely unfamiliar term queer be adequately implemented in the context of art exhibitions in Africa and elsewhere without merely reiterating exactly those institutional structures that the idea and concomitant theory was developed in? Or we might ask with art historian Charlotte Bydler: "In an all-over world, who represents what? Anything that lacks relevance to the mechanisms of Empire disappears from its representational index" (Bydler 2013). Yet, queerness made in Africa does certainly not have a shadowy existence within the

---

[23] Gender and queer theorist Jack Halberstam, for example, writes in the exhibition catalogue *Reclaiming Afrikan. Queer perspectives on sexual and gender identities*: "While the fantasies, aspirations and trajectories of queer politics grind sadly and slowly to a halt in the US and Europe, stalled by the mediocre and complacent politics of marriage and the neo-liberal desire for inclusion, the stakes in queer politics and queer aesthetics become critically important in other sites, for other groups with wilder and more ambitious political goals. And so, we might look [...] to South Africa [...]." (Halberstam 2014: 12)

Global Contemporary; the application of the concept simply seems to adjust those mechanisms.

Artists dealing with issues of same-sex intimacies are both part of the conflicting environment—described in the previous paragraphs—as individuals with particular experiences *and* cultural agents and mediators who offer visual epistemological and semantic alternatives to normative categories of sexuality and gender. These social roles often intersect. Artists work as cultural as well as activist protagonists at times while others turn towards aesthetic approaches exclusively. Common to all these endeavors are strategies of making visible the lives and stories of LGBTQ people and strategies of queering normative images. Yet, these strategies have to be differentiated from processes of attribution and thus matters of applicability of same-sex related terms. I hope to approximate the discrepancy between actual artistic enunciations and the attributive concepts they are escorted with when travelling to different frames of reference.

It is inevitable to consider political conditions when working on artistic strategies that address issues of same-sex intimacies in Africa. And this is because each artist is crucially embedded in networks of political and social discourses that label, influence and inform her or his approach. Some artists respond directly to mostly stereotyping forms of (in)visibilities of people that identify as gay, lesbian, bisexual, transgender or queer, such as photographer and visual activist Zanele Muholi or artist and activist Gabrielle Le Roux to just name two prominent examples from South Africa; or they negotiate same-sex practices with an explicit emphasis on artistic solutions and interventions. In any case, attributions of queer more so than the actual aesthetic practices of queering have become a semantic currency that applies especially to the global realm of contemporary art. In other words, more emphasis is put on the actual phenomenon of 'queer' art from Africa than on the artistic strategies subjacent to it.

In utilizing visual queering as an artistic method artists produce and claim identities and indeed spaces that reside in the ambivalent structures of both an African and a global past and present. Reflecting on such a method communication scholar Bryant Keith Alexander writes: "I claim a tensive comfort in postcolonialism and queer theory, knowing that I am both placed and displaced in both, yet I move forth boldly voicing experience, engaged in 'the production of identity' by narrating the past and resisting the treachery of invisibility and exclusion that each promotes" (Alexander 2008: 103). To be more precise, queering as an artistic strategy not only requests the visibility of marginalized experiences but also reappraises dominant as well as displaced imageries.

Ato Malinda

Ato Malinda was born in Kenya in 1981. She grew up in the Netherlands, returned to Kenya as a teenager and moved to the U. S. to study art history and molecular biology at the University of Texas. Malinda eventually moved back to Kenya where she worked in various art disciplines such as performance, painting, drawing or video art. She now lives and works in Rotterdam.

In her performance piece Mshoga Mpya, or the new homosexual that Malinda presented at Dak'Art 2014 she built an opaque cube made of found wood with space for only her and one person from the audience. The cubicle was painted in blackboard paint and inscribed in white chalk with personal narrations of LGBTQ individuals in both English and French and with some of the words garbled. In a later version of the work, the audience was invited to erase part of the text and add new comments. The ephemeral and fluid nature of the writings was thus emphasized. In Dakar, the box could only be entered after having answered the question whether one would support the anti-homosexuality act in Uganda which had then just been signed by president Museveni and later, after the biennale, was ruled invalid by the Ugandan Constitutional Court. The agreement with Nigeria's anti-gay laws was also requested.[24] Supportive persons to these laws were denied an entry, an effective way to indicate the complex yet also strikingly plain patterns of inclusion, exclusion, the hiding, disclosing and protecting of LGBTQ people.

---

[24] See also Julia Defabo (2014): "Ato Malinda and Raw Material Company addressing homosexuality at Dak'Art 2014", in: *AADAT. African & Afro-Diasporan Art Talks*, http://aadatart.com/ato-malinda-raw-material-company-addressing-homosexuality-dakart-2014/, accessed 24.06.2015.

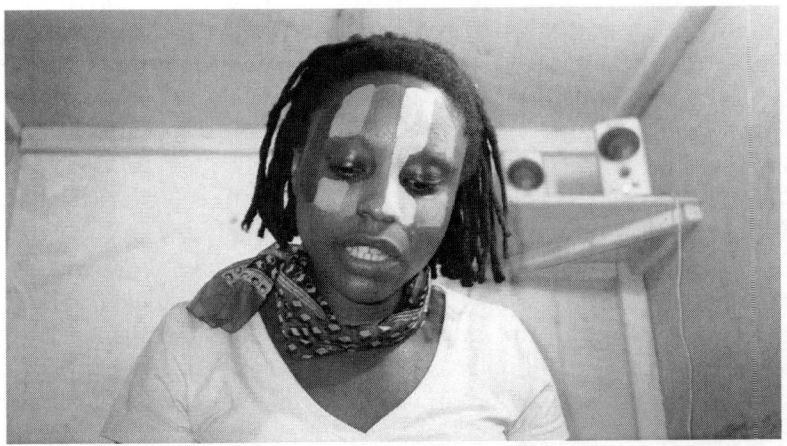

Ato Malinda, *Mshoga Mpya or the new homosexual*, 2014, performance, property of the artist.

While in the cube Malinda was sitting on the floor. I sat down on a stool. The artist's face was painted in rainbow colours.[25] She told me one of the stories of queer people in Nairobi that she had collected over the period of almost a year. Her performance was accompanied by gestures of silencing and interrupting the accounts. Malinda commented on her approach: "I didn't want the risk of having a complacent audience, so I decided to do it one-on-one where people had to enter a tiny cubicle and sit in front of me, and I would do the performance. These performances were taken from the interviews, but my mouth was obstructed so I would release little by little pieces of information to the audience. I didn't want to give it all away at once because there was so much power in it."[26] It was a very personal and evocative encounter. Malinda's way of serving as some attentive medium for shared and highly intimate experiences was, for me, more intensive than any documentary on LGBTQ people I have seen so far. I would thus like to suggest that the effective motivation of Malinda's secondary narra-

---

[25] For images of the perfomances s. http://alexmawimbi.com/mshoga%20mpya.html.

[26] Anjana Varma (2014): „Ato Malinda on sexuality, African feminism and performance as art", in: *Art Radar*, http://artradarjournal.com/2014/08/01/ato-malinda-on-sexuality-african-feminism-and-performance-as-art-interview/, accessed 04.06.2015.

tion was increased through her physical presence and the face-to-face encounter. This subjective implementation of issues of homosexuality also shifted general discourses and the theoretical baggage—that most of Dak'Art's visitors presumably carried with them—towards a critical examination of clear-cut attributions and identifications. The queering potential in Malinda's work can be described regarding the locations and eventually the dynamics of discourses: in establishing not only an imaginary but concrete threshold between audience and the utterances of LGBTQ people the latter's need for protection yet also their potential agency within defined spaces are made physically comprehensible. Secondly, the variety and concurrence of the narrations create awareness for the various discriminations yet also relations, affirmations and demarcations that LGBTQ people are engaged with. It is precisely these specific occurrences and the acknowledgement of small-scale narrative knowledge that queer theorists send a reminder about when referring to historical and local concretions in Africa. In this respect, political scientist Isabell Lorey (1996) states that shifts and contradictions in identifications are not only conjured up by deliberate misinterpretation—in Judith Butler's sense—but also through the sheer diversity of demands and alignments in according discourses. Butler's theorizing of the capacity to act through repeated performance is extended, in Lorey's investigation, towards a heterogeneous network of multifaceted and local effects of (discursive) power. Malinda offers both a spatial understanding of the limits of visibility and audibility of LGBTQ people as well as a differentiated account of their stories and identities.

Igshaan Adams

Igshaan Adams was born in Cape Town in 1982 where he still works and lives. He graduated from the Ruth Prowse School of Art and was a resident artist in Cape Town, Basel and Bern in Switzerland. He had several solo and group exhibitions, most of them in Cape Town. He exhibited at Wanås Konst gallery in the exhibition "Barriers: Artists based in South Africa" in 2015. Here, he has also had a permanent work commissioned for the sculpture park.

Adams was born to Muslim parents, raised by a Christian grandmother and "in a community racially classified [...] as 'coloured'"[27] in the apartheid era. He therefore never felt associated to any particular community, wavered between Sufism as a young student and being openly gay since the age of nineteen. One of his role models used to be the homosexual Imam Muhsin Hendricks, well-known in South Africa and beyond for his mediation between Islam and LGBTQ modes of life. In his work Adams regularly negotiates his process oriented search for identity and the interaction between external attributions and the inner freedom for ambivalence. Authenticity, for him, is thus not related to subordination to apparently fixed religious or social laws but rather to an 'authentic', i.e. personal yet dangerous working with them. It is a continuing attempt of reconciliation with different identity parameters and not a reference to the atrocities usually connected to 'homophobic' African societies. This intimate process of self-positioning, I would like to suggest, might be the reason why Adams oeuvre is only tentatively shown outside the South African art scene.

Igshaan Adams, *In between*, 2011, Islamic prayer mats, blankets, cotton, canvas, incense, 520 x 314 x 2 cm, Michael Stevenson Gallery.

---

[27] See: http://www.blankprojects.com/cv-and-bio/igshaan-adams/, accessed 25.06.2015.

Homosexuality is not as clearly addressed in Adams' artworks and installations as it is in Malinda's performance. He rather examines issues of identification with an intersectional approach of visually confronting and intertwining religious, racial and sexual ciphers. In his self-portraits, for example, Adams stitches the image of his face into Islamic prayer mats. In his installations, these carpets are usually lying on the ground facing Mecca such as his work *In between*.

In this case, the snake that is sewed across the mats refers to its ambivalent meaning within different cultures and religions: "In Islam as in Christianity and Judaism", Adams states, "the snake is a symbol of deceit and treachery. Yet, historical records from cultures across the world reference the snake as a symbol of knowledge, and of the energy of transformation within needed to reach spiritual enlightenment."[28] This visual as well as material interference of a sacred environment questions and negotiates both the meaning of this environment without destroying or entirely negating it and forms of historically developed knowledge and values. The material Adams uses is soft in most of his works: lace, cotton thread or fabric. The sewing can be associated with activities traditionally done by women. Adams inscribes himself, alternative knowledge and interrupting cyphers into the known and seemingly unchangeable cyphers that he was socialized with and that are part of performing conventions. Adams acts of interference are not oppositional. His delicate inscriptions seem to merge into the already existing. They disrupt the familiar but at the same time create something new, something that is hidden—in the work Ba for example—or something that layered or inserted. They do not destroy, they transform. Adams practice recalls Butler's (1993) theorizing of performance as affirmation: the constant quoting of norms and ascriptions constitutes identity but also provides the possibility for displacements and deviations. And herein lies the queering potential.

Malinda and Adams employ different artistic agendas of queering. Whereas Malinda investigates the positions and identifica-

---

[28] See: http://www.stevenson.info/exhibitions/sidegallery/adams/index.html, accessed 25.06.2015.

tions of LGBTQ people in Nairobi, Adams negotiates the dynamics of inside and outside, inscription and ascription. Both contextualize their visual and audible narrations within specific locations. They both examine possibilities of queer visibility as part of societal structures, and they both discuss these options at the very intimate level of personal experiences. "Queer moments happen when things fail to cohere", writes feminist and postcolonial theorist, Sara Ahmed (2006: 17). And it is precisely this failure in coherence that opens up both hetero- as well as homonormative spaces in which the personal resists political appropriation or in which the fragmentary becomes something 'authentic'.

Links

Ato Malinda: https://vimeo.com/124501466, accessed 05.04.2016.
Igshaan Adams: http://vimeo.com/107594441, accessed 05.04.2016.

Bibliography

Ahmed, Sara. 2006. *Queer phenomenology. Orientation, objects, others*, Durham, Duke University Press.

Alexander, Bryant Keith. 2008. "Queer(y)ing the postcolonial through the West(ern)", in: Norman K. Denzin, Yvonna S. Lincoln and Linda Tuhiwai Smith (Eds.), *Handbook of critical and indigenous methodologies*, Los Angeles, Sage Publications, pp. 101–133.

Bachmann-Medick (2012): "Menschenrechte als Übersetzungsproblem", in: *Geschichte und Gesellschaft*, Volume 38, No. 2, pp. 331–359.

Bennett, Jane (2011): "Subversion and resistance. Activist initiatives", in: Sylvia Tamale, *African sexualities. A reader*, Oxford, Pambazuka Press, pp. 77–100.

Butler, Judith. 1993. *Bodies that matter. On the discursive limits of 'sex'*, New York and London, Routledge.

Bydler, Charlotte (2013). "Forget the art world", in: *Kunstkritikk*, 02.09.2013, http://www.kunstkritikk.no/kritikk/forget-the-art-world/, accessed 06.03.2015.

Coly, Ayo A. (2013): "ASR forum - Homophobic Africa? Introduction", in: *African Studies Review*, Volume 56, No. 2, pp. 21–30.

Epprecht, Marc & Sigamoney, Veronica. 2013. "Meanings of homosexuality, same-sex sexuality, and Africanness in two South African townships. An evidence-based approach for rethinking same-sex prejudice", in: *African Studies Review*, Volume 56, No. 2, pp. 83–107.

Glissant, Édouard. 1990. *Poétique de la relation*, Paris, Éditions Gallimard.

Green, Adam. 2002. "Gay but not queer. Toward a post-queer study of sexuality", in: *Theory and Society*, Volume 31, No. 4, pp. 521–545.

Gunkel, Henriette. 2010. *The cultural politics of female sexuality in South Africa*, New York and London, Routledge.

Halberstam, Jack. 2014. "Introduction", in: Zethu Matebeni, *Reclaiming Afrikan. Queer perspectives on sexual and gender identities*, Cape Town, Modjaji Books, pp. 12–15.

Harris, Jonathan. 2013. "Introduction. The ABC of globalization and contemporary art", in: *Third Text*, Volume 27, No. 4, pp. 439–441.

Hoad, Neville. 2005. "Introduction", in: Neville Hoad, Karen Martin and Graeme Reid, *Sex and politics in South Africa*, Cape Town, Double Storey Books, pp. 14–25.

Lorenz, Renate. 2012. *Queer art. A freak theory*, Bielefeld, Transcript Verlag.

Lorey, Isabell. 1996. *Immer Ärger mit dem Subjekt. Theoretische und politische Konsequenzen eines juridischen Machtmodells*, Tübingen, Edition Diskord.

Macharia, Keguro. 2010. "Homophobia in Africa is not a single story", in: *The Guardian*, 26.05.2010, http://www.theguardian.com/commentisfree/2010/may/26/homophobia-africa-not-single-story, accessed 06.03.2015.

Muholi, Zanele. 2011. "I have truly lost a woman I loved", in: Alleyn Diesel (Ed.), *Reclaiming the L-word. Sappho's daughters out in Africa*, Athlone, Modjaji Books, pp. 11–25.

Oguibe, Olu. 2004. *The culture game*, Minneapolis, University of Minnesota Press.

Paul, Barbara and Schaffer, Johanne. 2009. "Einleitung. Queer als visuelle politische Praxis", in: Barbara Paul and Johanna Schaffer (Eds.), *Mehr(wert) queer. Visuelle Kultur, Kunst und Gender-Politiken*, Bielefeld, Transcript, pp. 7–33.

Tamale, Sylvia. 2013. "Confronting the politics of nonconforming sexualities in Africa", in: *African Studies Review*, Volume 56, No. 2, pp. 31–45.

Queer Visibility and Visual Resistance against Homophobia at Dak'Art,
The Biennial Exhibition of Contemporary African Art in Dakar 2014

Margareta Wallin Wictorin
Faculty of Arts and Humanities,
Karlstad University, Sweden

1. Introduction

At one of the Off-exhibitions at Dak'Art 2014, the Biennial exhibition of contemporary African Art in Dakar, Senegal, one could take part of an interactive work, called *Etherée*. It was performed in the garden of the private gallery Atiss, between May 11 and June 8, 2014.

Fig. 1. *Etherée,* performance by Mame-Diarra Niang, Dakar May 2014. Photo: Margareta Wallin Wictorin.

The work consisted of a grave dug out of the ground, and clad with mirrors. The audience was invited, by the artist Mame-Diarra Niang, to take part of the performance. She suggested for people to come close, and pretended to give the person a little booklet, but then she threw it into the grave. The person was invited to pick it up, and when doing so, had to look into the grave and see him- or herself reflected. In the little booklet one could see a drawing of a heart and some photos of bunkers outside Dakar. It was an invitation to look for imaginary paths to the grave of the lost. Beside the grave individuals could lay down as if to take the place of the man who was exhumed. The work was a reminder of something that had happened in the city of Thiès in Senegal in 2009.

On 4 May 2009 local and international press reported that the corpse of a man reputed to be homosexual had twice been disinterred from a Muslim cemetery in the city of Thiès in Senegal. The first time, the body was left near the grave. His family then reburied him, but he was once more exhumed. His body was dumped outside the family house. The body was eventually buried away from the cemetery, within the grounds of the family home (*BBC News – Africa*, 4 May 2009). This tragic event triggered the artist Mame-Diarra Niang to create the artwork described above.

At another independent gallery in Dakar, the Raw Material Company, there was another Off-exhibition connected to Dak'Art 2014. It was called *Precarious Imaging: Visibility and Media Surrounding African Queerness*. This exhibition was closed for security reasons, after having been attacked, on May 12, by an Islamic group. The leader of a bigger Senegal-based Islamic organization went on TV to demand the closure of all exhibitions related to homosexuality. A politically sensitive situation occurred since c. 95 % of the population in Senegal are followers of Islam, and it has always been important for the political leaders in the country to have good relations with Islamic groups such as the different brotherhoods, as well as with French and Christian people with influential positions (Cooper 2009: 168–169). At the same time the president, political leader of the state, which is the most important funder of Dak'Art (Wallin Wictorin, 2013: 565), probably didn't want to disturb the international exhibition. The other artworks contesting homophobia at Dak'Art, were left in peace.

This article aims at describing and interpreting artworks contesting homophobia, shown at Dak'Art 2014, the Biennial Exhibition of Contemporary African art in Dakar 2014, where queer visibility was present for the first time in Dak'Art's history. To give an idea of the context in which the artworks were produced, a background text about homosexuality and homophobia in Africa is included, but there is no ambition to give a full explanation of the phenomenon of homophobia in Africa.

The theoretical perspective of the article is based on the concepts *queer visibility* and *visual resistance*. For the interpretations of the artworks a Peirce-inspired semiotic method is used, relating iconic, indexical and symbolic signs to the context (Rose 2012: 119). The works are also related to what is written about them in the Dak'Art catalogue if possible. I compare and discuss the different kinds of queer visibility and visual resistance that I have found in the artworks.

2. Queer visibility

Queer is a broad notion that can be used for describing an approach or a movement that criticizes norms regarding sex and sexualities, especially the heterosexual norm. Queer can also be used as an expression of identification, but according to Andrew Tucker (2009: 15–16), to be queer is to abrade classification, to sit athwart conventional categories. The term can imply the action of disrupting, destabilizing and problematizing "facts" held dear by heteronormative societies, and it has strong emancipatory dimensions. Visibility in terms of sexual identity and sexual politics is not a neutral term. For more than 30 years, gay and lesbian political and intellectual struggle around the world has spent a lot of time, energy and resources on the politics of visibility. The goal for this has been to achieve greater access to and presence within cultural, economic and political forms of representation, and mitigate the effects of homophobia (Tucker 2009: 17).

3. Homophobia in Africa

According to historian Babacar M'Baye, homophobia rather than homosexuality came to Africa from the West through colonisation (M'Baye 2013: 110). Same-sex relationships and practices have for long time been present in many parts of the continent, even if they cannot be understood and catogorized as identities in the same way as in many western countries. In the globalized world of today, however, also Africans sometimes speak of themselves as gay, lesbians and transgender (Iehl 2015: 9, 25).

African states have different attitudes to homosexuality, but in general, lesbian, gay, bisexual, and transgender (LGBT) rights in Africa are very limited. In some nations, such as South Africa, it is accepted, at least *de jure,* and couples of the same sex have the ability to marry, but *de facto* it is problematic (Tucker 2009: 2). In other countries, such as Senegal, homosexuality is now prohibited. In the Senegalese society homosexuality and transgenderism existed during colonial time. In the capital Dakar, homosexuals and transgender persons cohabited with the rest of a society that was predominantly Muslim. These people were called *gor-djigens* (men-women), and they showed their identity through their clothes and hair dress. They didn't suffer much socially—they were even sought after for their good dancing abilities—but the Muslims refused them religious burial. *Gor-djigens* participated in traditional religious ceremonies, such as baptizing and weddings (Mbaye, 2013: 121–123). The pathologizing in France of homosexuality was transferred to their colonies through their "civilizing mission". (M'Baye 2013: 119). Today, in contemporary Senegal both Muslim and political leaders describes homosexuality as an immoral practice that is not indigenous to Senegal, but prohibited by law. So called "improper or "unnatural" acts can be punished with up to five years in prison. (Genschel, 2015: 1).

Today the word *gor-djigens* is used as a derogatory term, and most men who identify themselves as gender nonconforming use other terms, such as *ibbis* (or *oubis)* and *yoos* (or *yauss*). *Ibbis* is used for men who adopt feminine mannierisms, while *yoos* are generally used for the dominant and insertive partner, who doesn't consider himself homosexual. The researcher, Cheik Niang's relates a man in 2003 saying that "When someone says *gor-djigens* in our presence, it makes us shiver. The term is like a siren sound that we expect to be followed by insults, blows, or stones thrown at us by out-of-control mobs" (Cheik Niang 2003 cited in Mbaye 2013: 113).

In Senegal and several other African countries, the amount of expressions of homophobia has increased in recent years. Some researchers allege that there are political leaders throughout the African continent who use the figure of the homosexual as a scapegoat and opportune diversion from problems such as high unemployment, rampant poverty and bad governance. There is also a neo conservative trend that fosters patriarchy. Homophobia is said to be used by the patriarchal states to support the institution of patriarchy and the subjugation of women (Sylvia Tamale 2013 and 2007 cited in Coly 2013: 25). Similarly, according to Genschel (2015: 9), the attack on the exhibition *Precarious imaging. Visibility surrounding African queerness* that took place at the art gallery Raw Material Company in Dakar, in May 2014, might have served for a political agenda related to the elections that were to take place in Senegal in June 2014.

4. Visual resistance against homophobia in Africa

There are several individuals and organisations in Senegal and the rest of Africa that call for civil rights for LGBT-community members, and contest the notion that homosexuality is "Un-African". One way of doing that is to provide visual information about the existence of LGBT people and about their ways of living. The idea and strategy is to resist oppression and exclusion by becoming visual, and to resist heteronormativity as a framed category of gender and sexual identity, giving more visibility to the plurality of gender and sexualities (Iehl 2015: 6). This kind of ideas about queer visibility is applied for example by internet based organisations such as *Inkanyiso*, founded by the South African visual artist and photographer Zanele Muholy in 2009, and *Iranti.org*, founded by the South African human rights activist, curator and photographer Jabu Pereira, in 2012. They seek to document the lives of "queer" Africans and Africa-based individuals with the aim of showing visual narrative evidence of "queer" ways of living, create awareness and influence politicians to promote human rights. (Iehl, 2015: 32–33). Visual art can be used for giving visibility to queering ideas and statements, and be a medium for contesting homophobia. This has also been done in many places around the world. One of these is the main exhibition at Dak'Art 2014.

5. Dak'Art, the Biennial Exhibition of Contpemorary African Art

Dak'Art, the Biennial Exhibition of Contemporary African Art in Dakar, is one of the most important art events in Africa. Since 1992 art exhibitions arranged in Dakar every second year, under the name "Dak'Art", have focused on African contemporary art including art made by artists from Africa and the African diaspora. The event includes several exhibitions, but the main exhibition consists of art made by artists that are selected, by curators appointed by the general secretary, from artist applications. The curators also have the right to include some artists they find interesting for the exhibition (Wallin Wictorin, 2013: 565). There are also exhibitions that show art made by invited guest artists and tribute exhibitions, and a lot of Off-exhibitions in Dakar and other places in Senegal. In 2014 there was also an exhibition of cultural diversity with artists from around the world (African, European, American and Asian), a show presenting the results from the African sculpture symposium that took place in Dakar in October 2013, a Salon of the National Collection (presentation of a selection of artworks owned by the Senegalese government), and meetings and exchanges on the theme "the art professions" including artists, scholars, critics, historians and academics. The university of Dakar was also involved in the program under the heading "Dak'Art into the Campus" (DAK'ART 2014).

The author of this article has been visiting the exhibitions Dak'Art 2008, 2010, 2012 and 2014, and studied the biennial exhibitions since the start in 1992. Artworks dealing with the question of homosexuality in Africa were first seen in 2014. The title and overall theme of the exhibition that year was *Produire le commun/Producing the common,* which has been read as a sign for the organisers trying to be inclusive. In the exhibition catalogue the Algerian/French curator Abdelkader Damani wrote: "It is from this position, of one who speaks, that this biennial attempts to produce the common and to define the idea that art's singular objective is to bring together the human community." (DAK'ART 2014: 38). At the main exhibition works giving visibility to queer ideas or ways of living were presented by the artists Andrew Esiebo from Nigeria, Milumbe Haimbe from Zambia and Ato Malinda from Kenya. Invited artist Jean-Ulrick Désert from Haïti presented queer invisibility, and even "conspicious invisibility" which will also be described, interpreted and discussed below.

Andrew Esiebo

The Photographer Andrew Esiebo, from Nigeria, practiced queer visibility at Dak'Art by exhibiting his work *Who we are*. It consists of a series of photographic images showing men of varying ages in everyday environments. In one photo a young man is sitting in a comfortable chair in an ordinary livingroom, and in another photo a middle aged man with a clerical collar and holding a bible, is standing outside a window with a rainbow flag as curtain, the flag that is a symbol of lesbian, gay, bisexual and transgender (LGBT) pride. The men are looking straight into the camera, meeting the beholder's glance in a calm but cautious way, which might point to possible aggression and discomfort in the public space. There are often signs of different religions, such as the bible, around the portrayed persons to show that there is no contradiction between being religious and gay.

In the Dak'Art exhibition catalogue one can read that Esiebo thinks that attention is too often focused on sexual practices of homosexuality, and not on issues of love, desires, aspirations, compassion or faith. His reaction to that is his photographing of men in their daily lives to reflect on their private identities in everyday spaces. In his work Esiebo suggests that homosexual and heterosexual individuals and couples share many of the same challenges. He questions stereotyped approaches to heteronormativity and addresses the general lack of acceptance when it comes to issues of cultural diversities and sexual complexities. In the catalogue it is also written that "Esiebo's images dually act as intimate stories of individuals and as political commentary of phobias" (DAK'ART 2014: 84).

Milumbe Haimbe

Milumbe Haimbe is an artist from Zambia who is interested in popular culture and how cultural minorities are treated in or excluded from popular media. The artwork that she showed at Dak'Art 2014, *The Revolutionist*, comprises a growing number of digital prints which together form a graphic novel. It tells a dark but optimistic story in science fiction style. Somewhere in the future Ananiya, a 17 year old woman of African origin, works as an agent for the Resistance Army for the Restoration of Womanhood. This army is fighting against a large corporation that has started to introduce sex robots with the intention to replace the need for human women. Although *The Revolutionist* unfolds in a (near) future the work displays stereotypes of women, sexist images of women and the lack of diversity in terms of ethnicity and sexuality found in today's popular culture. Haimbe's work can be seen as a direct response to the lack of female and black heroes in the media. It questions preconceived notions of what women "should" look like, and the story includes people of a variety of ethnicities. When the protagonist Ananiya starts to have feelings for the prototype of the latest generation of female robots this complicates her function within the resistance movement, and a struggle between internal and external conflicts appears. Ananiya grapples with the social conformity in the Army for the Restoration of Womanhood, but also has to confront her own feelings when they do not meet the social expectations of the resistance group. (DAK'ART 2014: 96). This work has not been exhibited in Zambia since the artist hasn't found any organisation interested in presenting it, but it has been shown in South Africa, France and Sweden (Milumbe Haimbe 2015). The work is interesting in many ways, since it discusses an important issue in a future setting, which might make it

Queer Visibility and Visual Resistance against Homophobia 207

less controversial, but also gives an opportunity to show a possible future role model. The protagonist is the antithesis to a stereotypical superhero, since she is a smart woman with brown skin and a cool feminine, but not sexist, dress.

Fig. 2. Milumbe Haimbe, *The Revolutionist*, 2014, first image in the series. Published with permission by Milumbe Haimbe.

Fig. 3. Milumbe Haimbe, *The Revolutionist*, image nr. 6, 2014. Published with permission by Milumbe Haimbe.

Ato Malinda

Ato Malinda is an artist from Kenya who at Dak'Art 2014 staged an interactive performance called *Mshoga Mpya* (New Gay). The work was based on interviews made by Malinda with eight homosexual persons in Nairobi, who were willing to tell "everything" about themselves, about problems connected to how they were treated by heteronormative people. According to Malinda Nairobi is like a hub for queer people in Kenya. At Dak'Art Malinda set up a cube made out of found wood, inside which she received one person at the time, to tell the stories (Malinda 2015).

This work was highly intimate on several levels. Only one person could experience the performance at a time and the single audience member came face-to-face with the artist in the enclosed cubicle. The artist became a vessel through which lived experiences of LGBT individuals were told to the audience one by one. During the talk Malinda's face was painted with the symbolic rainbow flag and she was wearing gender neutral clothes and a small afro wig to convey androgyny. This suggests that the performance was not so much about gender as about the life stories of LGBT individuals being shared. (DAK'ART 2014: 118). Fragments of the stories that were told were also drawn, visualized, on the outside of the wooden hub in which Malinda told the stories orally. One could say that this work showed not only queer visibility but also queer audibility, though in an intimate way. It can be interpreted as an indexical sign showing and telling the world that LGBT exists in Africa, and that it is not Un-African as many political leaders allege.

Jean-Ulrick Désert

The artist who didn't present queer visibility but "conspicious invisibility" at Dak'Art 2014 was Jean-Ulrick Désert. He is a conceptual and visual artist born in Port-au-Prince, Haiti. His art works vary in form: public billboards, actions, paintings, site-specific sculpture, video and art objects, but they can all be regarded as conceptual works engaged with social and cultural practices. Désert has said himself that his practice may be characterized as visualizing "conspicuous invisibility." (*Désert*, "Biography") This is an interesting oxymoron, that speaks about what can not be seen or shown. At Dak'Art 2014 he exhibited a series of handmade wooden placards with strips of fabric. The works was titled *Les battements des ailes des papillons peuvent déclencher des tornades au tour du monde/The Flapping of the Wings of Butterflies Can Generate Violent Storms Around the World*, an idea taken from chaos theory about the interconnectedness of all action and reaction. On the placards blocks/lines of censure were rendered with strips of textiles in varying colors of the rainbow as well as dutch-wax *African* fabrics. The rainbow colors worked as a symbolic sign for the political movements that utilize the rainbow flag as its symbol of diversity, such as the global LGBT communities (*Désert* "Blackout Papillons"). The empty blocs could be interpreted as indexical signs of what usually cannot be shown or said in many African countries. In combination with the rainbow flag, it points to censorship regarding homosexuality and queer ideas.

6. Precarious Imaging: Visibility and Media Surrounding African Queerness

The Off-exhibition to Dak'Art 2014 that took place at the independent gallery Raw Material Company, an exhibition called *Precarious Imaging: Visibility and Media Surrounding African Queerness* was curated by the artist Ato Melinda and the owner of the gallery Koyo Kouoh. The exhibition showed works by several artists. The biggest part consisted of photographic works by the South African artist Zanele Muholi, but photos from Andrew Esiebo's series *Who we are*, were exhibited here, too. The French-Algerian artist Kader Attia showed collages, and Amanda Kerdahi, an artist from Egypt, showed the work *100 conversations*.

The South African artist Zanele Muholi, who is one of the South African artists that since 2009 practice queer visibility on the internet within the organisations *Inkanyiso*, showed a series of photographic images called *Faces and phases*. It is a series of portraits showing people from different cultures and contexts, ages and professions, and it is meant to speak about the experience of living in a country that constitutionally protects the rights of LGBT people but often fails to defend them from targeted violence, South Africa (Genschel 2015: 4–5). It shows people with LGBT-identities, show that they exist, that they are individuals, that they look like anybody else, that they are many. It is another example of queer visibility and resistance by visibility.

Amanda Kerdahi, an artist from Egypt, showed the work *100 conversations*. It consisted of the visual documentation of conversations that Kerdahi had had with a group of woman in Cairo, talking about their sexuality and other intimacies. More mimetic depictions of these women could not be recommended, since it is taboo in Cairo to talk about female sexuality and also women are not supposed to smoke. But here the work was made up of the textile filters of the cigarettes that the women smoked while talking to each other, a kind of indexical sign, and a visual but soundless representation, of the conversations that took place. (Kerdahi 2015)

The French-Algerian artist Kader Attia showed four framed collages entitled *Architecture, transgenre, representation de l'hermaphrodite*. In these collages the artist worked on the relationship between male transvestites and the construction of gender within European architectural history (Genschel 2015: 6). One of the collages showed a picture of a male body, almost naked, but with a female appearance by make-up, pasted on a sheet of architectural design paper with the typical structured grid. In the lower left corner, a picture was pasted showing a man in dark clothes and a male transvestite dressed in a white female dress embracing (hugging) each other. This collage was small in size, but could probably be interpreted as controversial by those who do not recognize everyone's right to marry or have a sexual life according to his or her own desire.

As mentioned above, this exhibition was closed. In the French newspaper *Le Monde*, one could read that it was closed by the Senegalese state after Raw Material Company was attacked, on May 12 2014, by a religious Islamic group (Jardonnet 2014). However, the owner of the Gallery, Koyo Kouo, closed the exhibitions herself, because the mob threatened to come back and continue the destruction (Genschel 2015: 10 and Malinda 2015). The other works contesting homophobia at Dak'Art 2014 were not attacked, even if a leader of a big Senegal-based islamic organisation, went on TV to demand the closure of all exhibitions related to homosexuality. In a further interview, the leader went on to say, "This event is supposed to promote our culture, but proves to be propaganda for unions which are against nature. Undeniably, this edition of Dak'Art has been detrimental to our morality and to our laws." (Jardonnet 2014). Dak'Art's general secretary, Babacar Mbaye Diop skirted association with the controversy-inducing exhibition at Raw Material Company, saying that the biennial was "not responsible for collateral exhibitions," i.e. Off exhibitions, only the works inside Dak'Art itself (Forbes 2014: 1). And the artworks in Dak'Art international exhibition itself were left in peace. Only the Off-exhibition at the gallery Raw Material Company, outside of the international arena, was attacked. The globalized space of Dak'Art seems to have been protected from attacks on queer inspired works. This probably depends on the attention the biennial exhibition gets from its international audience. The private gallery Atiss was also left in peace, which might depend on the organizers not having advertised the work *Ethéré*, and also on its position in a calm part of Dakar, where mostly rich people live in villas surrounded by high walls. The Raw Material Company, on the contrary, is situated in a quite densely populated suburb.

Conclusions

As mentioned earlier, in Senegal open homosexuality can warrant prison time. Also Nigeria, Uganda and many other African nations have strict anti-homosexuality legislation. Dak'Art 2014 was the first Dakar-biennial at which there was art communicating on this subject, where visual resistance by queer visibility was set up and also a work that elaborated on conspicuous invisibility. It is interesting to note how differently the works were composed, could be interpreted and what they seemed to try to achieve. The interactive performance work *Etherée* was set up as a symbolic reproduction of the burial and disinterment of a young homosexual man. The way the spectators were directed to look into the grave and see the reflections of themselves, and also lie down on the ground beside it, can be interpreted as a way of creating empathy with the affected victim and his family. Ato Malinda's work *Mshoga Mpya* (New Gay), also an interactive performance work, was also a way of creating empathy and understanding of what it can be like to live as a homosexual person in Africa, more particularly in Nairobi. Here the media used were oral and written storytelling, with real stories collected from LGBT people living in Nairobi, and the painting of Malinda's face with the symbolic rainbow flag, her gender neutral clothes and a small afro wig to convey androgyny.

Milumbe Haimbe also told a story with both visual and verbal means, though a fictive and silent one. Her work consisted of a graphic novel, promoting a new kind of superhero, an antithesis to a stereotypical superhero, being a smart woman with brown skin and a cool feminine, but not sexist, dress. The work is interesting in many ways, one of them being the fact that it discusses the queer issue in a future setting, which might make it less controversial, but also gives an opportunity to show a possible future role model.

Similar to Malinda and Haimbe, Andrew Esiebo told visual "stories" about LGBT persons, but he aimed at showing them in their everyday setting, as normal human beings, looking and living like anybody. Zanele Muholi did the same thing, and by the high number of photographic portraits, she showed that also in Africa LGBT persons are many and not only odd exceptions. Their images document the lives of "queer" Africans and Africa-based individuals, showing visual evidence of "queer" ways of living that can create awareness and influence politicians to promote human rights.

Finally, while Jean-Ulrick Désert pointed to "conspicuous invisibility" and thereby to (self-) censorship regarding the existence of LGBT persons and their civil rights, censorship by fear was applied against the gallery Raw Material Company that had to close down the exhibition *Precarious Imaging: Visibility and Media Surrounding African Queerness*.

Bibliography

Anonymous. 2009. "Gay man disinterred in Senegal", *BBC News – Africa*, 4 May, http://news.bbc.co.uk/2/hi/africa/8032754.stm, accessed 2014-06-07.

M'Baye, Babacar. 2013. "The Origins of Senegalese Homophobia: Discourses on Homosexuals and Transgender People in Colonial and Postcolonial Senegal." *African Studies Review*, Volume 56, Number 2, September.

Coly, Aya A. 2013. "Introduction", *African Studies Review*. Vol 56: 2, September.

Cooper, Frederick. 2009. *Africa since 1940: The Past of the Present*. Cambridge: Cambridge University Press.

DAK'ART 2014 – 11th Biennial of Contemporary African Art. Exhibition catalogue. Dakar, 2014.

Désert, Jn. Ulrick, "Biography" http://www.jeanulrickdesert.com/accesses, accessed 2015-11-30.

Désert, Jn. Ulrick, "Blackout (Papillons)", http://www.jeanulrickdesert.com/content/blackout-papillons, accessed 2015-11-30.

Forbes, Alexander, "Senegal Censors Homosexual Art", artnet News, 2014-06-04. https://news.artnet.com/art-world/senegal-censors-homosexual-art-33607. Accessed 2014-06-05.

Genschel, Marlene, On the exhibition "Precarious Imaging. Visibility surrounding African Queerness" at Raw material Company, Dak'Art 2014. Wikis.fu-berlin.de/pages,/viewpage.action?pageId=646984871. Accessed 2015-11-24.

Haimbe, Milumbe. 2015. personal communication at the conference *Concurrences in postcolonial research-perspectives, methodologies, engagements,* Linnaeus University, Kalmar, Sweden, 20 August, when Haimbe gave a presentation of her work *The Revolutionist*, and also at the workshop *Present's disjunctive unity. Constructing and deconstructing histories of contemporary cultural and aesthetic practices*. Haus der Kulturen der Welt, Berlin, 27 November 2015.

Iehl, Helene, *About the concept of queerness in the African context*. Wikis.fu-berlin.de/display/queer/About+the+concept+of+queerness+in+theafrican+context, accessed 2015-11-24.

Jardonnet, Emanuelle, Le Sénégal suspend les expositions sur l'homosexualité à la biennale de Dakar. Le Monde Culture, 2014-06-03

Kerdahi, Amanda, personal communication in connection to the exhibition *Precarious Imaging: Visibility and Media Surrounding African Queerness*, at the art gallery Raw Material Company in Dakar, 2014-05-11.

Malinda, Ato. 2015. personal communication at the workshop Present's disjunctive unity. Constructing and deconstructing histories of contemporary cultural and aesthetic practices, Haus der Kulturen der Welt, Berlin, 27 November.

Rose, Gillian, 2012, *Visual Methodologies*. London: SAGE.

Tucker, Andrew, 2009, *Queer visibilities. Space, identity and interaction in Cape Town*. Chichester UK: Wiley-Blackwell.

Wallin Wictorin, Margareta. 2014. "Dak'Art, the Biennial Exhibition of Contemporary African Art in Dakar—a Platform for Critical Global Views", *Third Text: Critical* perspectives *on contemporary Art and Culture,* vol 28, issue 6, December, p. 563–574.

Entangled Voices, Lived Songs.
Mwambwambwa, a Cokwe Song recorded in 1954 at Colonial Lunda, Angola[1]

Cristina Sá Valentim
Centre for Social Studies (CES),
Faculty of Economics
Coimbra University, Portugal

1. Introduction

> In those days they couldn't run away, they couldn't protest with Diamang!
> They could only sing and dance.
> They sang all the time!
> (Soba[2] Domingos Liange Sawlimbo, Bairro Mwangeji, 21 August 2014)[3]

This chapter analyzes the complexities of colonial relations. The hierarchical nature of colonial relationships is expressed in one of several Cokwe songs collected by a diamond enterprise named

---

[1] This chapter arises from an ongoing research project as the basis of my PhD at the University of Coimbra. I have received much needed scientific advising from Dr Catarina Martins (CES-FLUC) and Dr Ricardo Roque (ICS-IUL) for which I am grateful. Some of the considerations in this chapter will form the basis of my doctoral thesis. An early version of this text was presented at the Conference 'Concurrences in postcolonial research-perspectives, methodologies, engagements', 20–23 August 2015 at Kalmar, held by the Centre for Concurrences of Colonial and Postcolonial Studies, Linnaeus University, Sweden. It was profoundly reworked after my stay at that Center in Växjö as Visiting Scholar, from August to September 2015. My doctoral research benefited from 4 years of financial support (2013-2016) from the Foundation for Science and Technology (FCT), (Ref. SFRH/BD/85530/2012), co-financed by the European Social Fund (ESF) through the Operational Program for Human Potential (POPH), and by national funds.

[2] Soba is a Portuguese name given to an Angolan traditional authority that can lead villages or coordinate a neighbourhood. It is derived from the Umbundu name of *soma* that means Chief.

[3] DLS was born in the municipality of Saurimo, South Lunda, in 1927. He was a tailor, a tradesman and a football player. He did clothing to the manpower of Diamang. He is *Regedor-Adjunto* (adjunct head Soba) at *Regedoria* (a head administrative structure) *of Sawlimbo, Bairro* (a kind of neighborhood which can be within the city or in its suburbs) Mwangeji, municipality of Saurimo.

Diamang in the Northeast of Angola during Portuguese colonial rule. Drawing on ethnographic data from Angolan oral history and Portuguese colonial archives, I examine how native musical expressions were vehicles of a plethora of native agencies and ambiguous engagements within the context of new modern colonial realities. And at the same time, how to perceive colonial identities as constructions within different and concurrent constraints, purposes and agendas. Also, I would like to reflect about postcolonial methodologies that could enable for a better understanding of colonial complexities.

1.1. The colonial complexities

During the *cacimbo*[4] of 1954 the Dundo Museum had recorded a particular song at Sobado[5] of Nanjinga, near the Uhamba river, in *Posto Administrativo do Lóvua [Lowua]* at *Circunscrição do Chitato [Citato]*[6], District of Lunda, at the Northeast of the Portuguese colony of Angola. (Fig. 1)

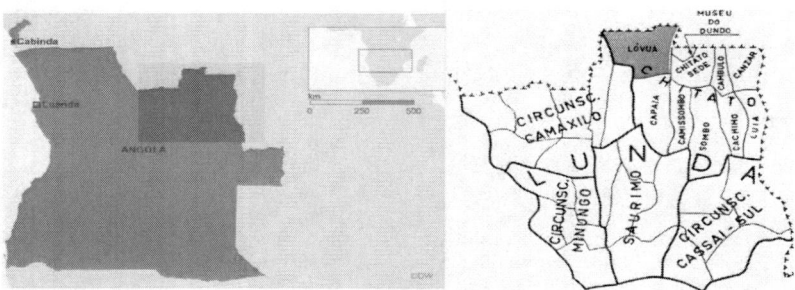

Fig. 1: Map of the colonial District of Lunda located at the Northeast of Angola, and the *Posto Administrativo do Lóvua* [Lovwa] in the North of Lunda near Dundo Museum at *Circunscrição do Chitato* [Citato]. Source: my adaptation from http://www.dw.com/image/0,,15707953_404, 00.jpg and Janmart et al (1961: 16).

The story of the *Mwambwambwa* song registered in the colonial ethnographic reports is about a man named *Mwambwambwa*

---

[4] Cacimbo is the dry season in Angola.
[5] Sobado is a group of villages headed by a Soba.
[6] Colonial administrative divisions.

who escaped from forced labour recruitment and was replaced by another man. Thus my first perception of this song was that of the expression of a collective pride caused by a man who resisted an oppressive colonial regime by fleeing from it. Yet after doing fieldwork in Angola in 2014, through oral testimonies, I realized that the meaning of this song goes beyond that. The song reveals issues of cultural identity affirmation, compliance with colonial rule, dynamics of gender, power and resistance. Underlying these colonial complexities is a web of relations among persons who were entangled in high level hierarchical and asymmetrical power relations and who were always in a struggle for life.

Articulating theoretical and methodological tools from postcolonial studies and critical anthropology, colonialisms are conceptualized here as a set of performative and social practices constituted by contradictory or ambiguous meanings where different agencies, times and places are overlapping and intersecting (Thomas 1994; Dirks 1995; McClintock 1995; Stoler and Cooper 1997; Porto 2009; Fur 2015 and Fur 2017). According to Jan Vansina those need to be inquired not from a top-down perspective but rather from below, namely from the stories that are in the memories embedded in bodies (Vansina 2010: 326), and also available in the interstices of the colonial archives (Porto 2009; Stoler 2011; Roque and Wagner 2012). In doing so it will be easier to understand how identities of colonizer and colonized were constructed upon suffering, anxieties, inquietudes, worries, hopes, expectations, dilemmas, desires, unpredictable situations, engagements, and above all through difficult negotiations. In this regard, the native agency and the ambiguous and veiled mechanisms of resistance to oppression are constitutive of the colonial process, and thus power issues need to be analyzed beyond the balance between domination and resistance in order to understand the subtle forms of imposition and contesting power (Scott, 1990).

Those reflexions draw from an ongoing fieldwork in oral history and on colonial archives in Angola and Portugal. In this paper, I would like to interpret the meanings of the Mwambwambwa song collected in colonial Luanda. The paper will analyze how it was a vehicle of significance and a symbol of knowledge shared by native communities, revealing ambiguous tactics and strategies of transformation of the social world, crucial to regulate and adjust social behaviors, to reach empowerment goals, to manage emotions and desires. Furthermore, it is necessary to reflect about postcolonial and de-colonial methodologies and that could enable us to better understand those colonial complexities. As stated earlier, it is not an easy task to interpret colonial relations, and that is why we need to have some analytical tools for simultaneously uncovering hidden voices and interpreting narratives. Therefore, first, a combination of two postcolonial concepts could enable us to see 'between the lines' of lived experiences and colonial discourses.

1.2. A theoretical and methodological proposal

The relevance of the Sociology of Absences (Santos 2002)[7] can be understood within the theoretical and methodological framework of Epistemologies of the South suggested by Boaventura de Sousa Santos (Santos 2014)[8]. It analyses the diversity of knowledge in the world that was (and still is) silenced by the monoculture logics of modern Western thinking. In particular, it inquires about what was destroyed and/or made invisible by European colonialism as well as about the colonial legacies in the present. It can be understood as a reflexive and political critic to the modern hegemonic model of knowledge of the Global North based on Eurocentric premises that excluded other experiences and knowledges of the world known metaphorical as Global South.

Briefly, the Epistemologies of the South aim at a new balance between knowledge and social practices, epistemology and culture (Santos 2014). To that extent, the Sociology of Absences starts from a critique of the universality of modern western knowledge rooted in dualistic rationalities that make it unique and sovereign (Santos 2002). It recognizes the processes of segregation and ex-

---

[7] For an English reading of this question see Boaventura de Sousa Santos's "A Critique of Lazy Reason: against the Waste of Experience" in I. Wallerstein, ed., The Modern World–System in the Longue Durée. Boulder: Paradigm Publishers, 2004, 157–197.

[8] See also: Boaventura de Sousa Santos and Maria Paula Meneses (Orgs.). 2009. *Epistemologias do Sul*. Coimbra: Almedina.

clusion recreated by 'abyssal lines' that divide the world into dichotomies (civilized and primitive, culture and nature, science and intuition/indigenous knowledge, religion and belief, us and them) (Santos 2007). The author points out a set of monocultures rooted in the Eurocentric logics of thought—the so called Northern Epistemologies—imposed as universal and that consequently overshadow other valid possibilities of engaging in the world: the exclusivity of western scientific knowledge and 'high culture'; the linear time conception made by stages from the primitive to the evolved, the birth to death; the process of social classification which naturalizes social hierarchies through race, class and gender; the dominance of the universal and the global/local scales; the productivity based on capitalism (Santos 2002: 241–248). Together they produce the condition of social, political and ontological nonexistence attributed to certain human beings. The relevance of the Sociology of Absences, then, lies in showing how other lived experiences of the world were wasted, obliterated and transformed in social and political absences, and thus proposing another model of thinking to achieve an ecology of knowledges (Santos 2002: 238, Santos 2007: 65).[9]

Taking into account those other narratives and voices, as well the way they were represented and constructed, to understand them is necessary to use appropriate concepts. The question here is that fieldwork methods seem to reveal even more complexity. In particular, fieldwork revealed to me the tenuous and fragile nature of 'abyssal lines' and all the heterogeneity that characterized colonial encounters which can, at the same time, display an amount of contradictory, convergent, complementary, ambiguous or conflicting meanings and narratives. To that extent, the concept of Concurrences suggested by Günlog Fur (Bryden, Forsgren and Fur 2014; Fur 2015 and Fur 2017), conceived mainly from the colonial experiences in the North of Europe and in the North American continent, is useful in order to understand the complexities of

---

[9] To each 'absence' signalized by the Sociology of Absences there are alternative logics under the idea of 'ecologies' within the Sociology of Emergencies that aims to balance the real and uncovered experiences with social expectations and emancipation action to expand the future (Santos 2002).

colonial relations that can embrace entanglement and concurrent logics.

The basis of the construction of this concept is the recognition that 'absences' or 'unique stories' (silences) are the result of engagements in reality made by historical, specific, asymmetrical and contextual relations. In other words, all knowledge and identities are particular constructions situated in the world. Knowing this, Concurrences means the connections and the cross-cut relations, negotiations between differences and several narratives interrelated, entangled with each other and between different discourses (Fur 2015: 13). Consequently, different discourses on the same reality lead to the interpretation of various layers of meaning that build different realities and different experiences of the same world (idem: 21), evoking the image of a palimpsest. Thus, this poses problems in seeing the official narratives of History as the Truth of one World. In this sense, similarly to the Epistemologies of the South, the notion of Concurrences emerges in conjunction with political concerns intimately connected to the need to look and think the other side of History, and to re-write it, as well as to make visible the experience that was wasted and relegated to silence.

Günlog Fur is referring in particular to the importance of recognizing the absence of other contextual voices (narratives, knowledge, cultures) in the narratives of official History rooted in hegemonic and undeniably Eurocentric premises and in violence that occurred in the colonial past (2015: 16). Precisely, there is a need for recognizing the role of History and western Science in the hierarchization of certain human beings and knowledge through ideas of race, tribe, culture, nation, progress and civilization, which produced ontological, epistemological and political silences that relegated certain voices, and places in the world to a homogenous, ahistorical, distinctive and bounded matter (Wolf 1982: 6). In this regard, there is also the need to understand the formation of western modernity and "the so-called uniqueness of the West" as being produced through the marginalization of the Other upon the discourse of the West and the Rest (Hall 2001: 278), as well as the mutually constructed dichotomy of colonizer and colonized, metropolis and colony (Stoler and Cooper 1997).

Furthermore, there is still lived memory, and post-memory, as well as traumas, embodied violence and consequently claims about those historical pasts (Fur 2017). Basically, the political scope of this concept comes from the need to signal and recognize the confluence of diverse narratives and knowledge about the world, and make them legitimate, as well as the right to claim against the crimes committed during the colonial empires and regimes. That exercise reminds one of the emblematic works for postcolonial studies written by the Kenyan writer Ngũgĩ wa Thiong'o in 1993, *Moving the Centre: The Struggle for Cultural Freedoms*: the disassemble and move of the Center (the hegemonic western and modern thought), and take it reconstruction under diverse polycenters, searching for justice and freedom.

In this sense, Günlog Fur (2015: 14) calls upon the conceptual framework of Epistemologies of the South that states: "there is no global social justice without global cognitive justice." (Santos 2007: 63). It aims at producing a new epistemology that enables to reveal, to remember and to resist the inequalities and the cultural epistemicides caused by a deeply exclusive, unique, "abysmal" thinking (idem). This kind of rationality fed the matrix of modern Western thinking and its relationship with other territories of the Global South, and continues doing so through processes of coloniality sustained by an epistemological ethnocentrism that functions as a strong "structure of colonization" as Valentin Mudimbe points out in *The Invention of Africa* (1988: 2)[10].

Similarly, Günlog Fur questions how those narratives can be listened to, and how its complexities can be communicated and interpreted into a valid and truthful history (Fur 2017). To that extend, the particularity of Concurrences lies in the fact that it helps to recognize the plurality of knowledge in the world and to reach to a certain kind of "postabyssal thinking as a ecological

---

[10] The term of coloniality has been conceived by the Latin American postcolonial studies, and it refers to high hierarchical relations between individuals, societies and places. That process is made by the articulation of issues of power, knowledge and identity through the balance of social classification, economic and human exploitation, and epistemological and ontological practices. Together it relegates those people and cultures to a political and economic margin and social 'absence'. (see Lander 1993; Quijano 2000; Mignolo 2000).

thinking" (Santos 2007: 65), yet considering the hybrid or 'in-between' character of human practices which can be the result of ambivalent, contradictory, concurring, complementary and/or simultaneous logics and goals.

2. Colonial Lunda[11]

2.1. The context

Although the Portuguese influence in Angola dates from the Portuguese imperial expansion beginning in the fifteenth century, the military and administrative Portuguese occupation of Angola began by the late nineteenth century. In response to national economic fragilities and ambitions, alongside the strong political, ideological and strategic interest in African territories uncovered by the Berlin Conference (1884–5) and the British ultimatum in 1890, Portugal began an 'effective colonial' possession in Africa (Alexandre 2004). This renewed Portuguese imperial impulse in Africa, achieved through cultural and scientific explorations, military conquest, *Campanhas de Pacificação* (repression campaigns), administrative decentralization, the establishment of European settlements, infrastructure construction, native taxes, and massive recruitment through forced labour, together reveal the increasing importance of a capitalist attitude (Neto 2012: 88–89, 92).

Precisely in Angola, the discovery of diamond deposits in the basin of the Kasai River in 1912 led to the concession of a part of northeastern Angola[12] to a colonial company engaged in diamond exploitation: Diamang, the *Companhia de Diamantes de Angola* (Diamonds Company of Angola)[13] (Porto 2009).

---

[11] After the independence of Angola on 11th November 1975, the colonial District of Lunda was divided into the Provinces (administrative divisions) of North Lunda and South Lunda.

[12] Originally, the concession area referred almost to all Angolan territory excluding the coastal region. But to prevent illicit exploitation and trafficking, a delimited and protected area was created in the Northeast in 1926.

[13] The Diamang was founded in 1917 with wherewithal from Portugal, Belgium, France and USA. After the independence of Angola, this enterprise gave rise to the present-day Angolan diamond enterprise, the Endiama.

This region was inhabited by several ethnic communities, namely by the Tucokwe[14] and related peoples, all descendents of a large migratory movement that came from the Ruund (or Ruwund) [Lunda] State in Katanga since the XVII century towards the west of central Africa (Fernando 2013: 35).[15] And only after overcoming a long and strong native resistance, Portuguese colonial domination gained ground in the Lunda at the end of the 1920s (Porto 2009: 7–8).

Diamang's engagement with the colonial forced labour regime was achieved largely through forced labour recruitment at the District of Lunda but also in the areas west (Malanje District) and south (Moxiku District). Aside that, to keep the manpower healthy and controlled, but also to endure the Portuguese influence in Africa Diamang created in 1936 an ethnographic museum along with hospitals, churches, schools, bridges and roads. (Fig 2) In a national and international context where colonial science was a part and parcel of political agendas (Roque, 2001), it is from the Dundo Museum [16] that the Diamang organized a set of ethnographic collection campaigns, exhibitions and scientific studies on native material culture and festive performances through which Angola and the Lunda show themselves to the world (Porto 2009).

---

[14] Plural of the Cokwe people.
[15] In that sense, the Tucokwe that had been established as sovereign at the Northeast and East of Angola, and related people (Mbunda, Luvale, Lucazi, Minungu, Xinji, Imbangala and Ngangela people), share with the Aruund [plural of the Ruund people] the same Aruund ancestors. (Fernando 2013: 34) Throughout the text, I write the Angolan vernacular names in *ucokwe* [the Cokwe language], one of the Angolan national languages and the mother tongue most spoken in the North and South Lunda. The spelling adopted took into account the new Cokwe alphabet approved in 1987 by the Council of Ministers of the Republic of Angola.
[16] This Museum reopened in 2012 as *Museu Regional do Dundo* [Regional Dundo Museum] with a permanent exhibition about the history and material culture of the Cokwe people.

Fig. 2: Photo n° 7599. Undated. "Museu do Dundo, fachada norte" [Dundo Museum, north facade]. Box n° 4 *"Exterior e Salas" [Outdoor and Rooms]*
© Universidade de Coimbra, 2018.

For instance, beyond the collection of objects, in 1944, the *Aldeia Nativa do Museu* (native museum village) was completed and it became a site for staging performances of 'traditional rites and festivals' by *Grupos Folclóricos Indígenas* (native folk groups). (Fig. 3) It was also used to receive international visitors at Lunda, and between 1950 and 1963 the Museum regularly organized the *Grande Festa Anual Indígena* (Great Indigenous Annual Festival) to celebrate and honor the colonial labour and western civilization (Porto 2009: 457–498).

All these activities were revealing to the world 'the white man's burden' in order to 'civilize and educate' those who are under the *Estatuto do Indigenato* (Native Status). This social-legal status defined from 1926 to 1961 the *Indígenas* as the non-white people in colonial society who lacked European cultural habits and thus had no access to Portuguese citizenship. In Angola, native people served as manpower for forced labour to state or private agencies. Thus, the designation as *Indígena* means not only someone native or indigenous as well as *não civilizado* (noncivilized person) who does not have citizenship rights.[17]

Fig. 3: Photo n° 18468. 1958. "Visita de Sua Excelência o Embaixador de Inglaterra" [Visit of His Excellency Ambassador of England]. Box n°8, *"Visitas" [Visits]* © Universidade de Coimbra, 2018.

In that context, the Dundo Museum incorporates an ideological, cultural and scientific agenda that articulate diverse discourses: to preserve the traditions facing extinction/annihilation owing to western modernity, to produce scientific knowledge and to control social dissidences and resistances to the colonial regime by keeping local population within traditional values. We can see this in the words of the Museum curator, José Redinha, in 1949 and 1950:

---

[17] This status was applied in 1926 to the African Portuguese colonies of Angola, Mozambique, and in 1927 to Guinea-Bissau, and since 1946 to the non-white populations of Timor and São Tomé e Príncipe, and not to the colonies of Cape Verde, Macau and the Portuguese State of India. (Thomaz, 2001: 61) It was officially abolished owing to the outbreak of the colonial war in the overseas territories of Angola, Guinea-Bissau and Mozambique from 1961 to 1974. Throughout the text I will use the translated term *indigenous* in italics instead of 'native' or simple 'indigenous' to refer to the people under this Status.

> It would be useful a work with a really folk aspect in the broad sense of the term. We wish give a meaning to the native music and their songs, naturally surprised, in their candid and rustic feature if possible casual, open-air, with the sounding board for the forest fund or the scope of the huts. [. . .] (UC. RAMD 1949: 33).

> It is necessary to say that the development of folklore and other traditional, artistic or interesting aspects has considerable importance as normalizing elements of native customs, restraining the modern trend of those "dancing" kind dances and other pernicious diversions to the social balance and discipline. (UC. RAMD 1950: 15)

This kind of discourse is rooted in the European context where the search for a 'popular culture' of rural, traditional and pure matrix named *folklore* was made to preserve the antique ways of life of a people, but also to highlight, by contrast, the values of the paradigm of western modernity visible in ideals of Reason, Civilization, Nation, Progress, Industrialization, Technology and Science (Bendix 1997). In addition, in colonial contexts, particularly in Sub-Saharan Africa from the late nineteenth century, African cultures were transformed into 'native folklore' in line with the same logic. But in those colonial contexts, namely those from the Lunda, those processes were made by the monocultures of western and modern thought that articulated issues of knowledge, time, social classification, scale and modes of productivity in order to highlight the superiority of the West as the civilizing agent and to legitimize colonial rule over African populations as subaltern agents (Santos 2002: 247–248), becoming the "two sides of a single coin" (Hall 2001: 278).

Taking into account international audiences, this Orientalist (or Africanist) representation was made by the Diamang through the use of the image—photography and film—as an agent of social differentiation (Porto 2004; Porto and Valentim 2015). Those colonial practices implied the so called 'invention of traditions' that reinvented native cultures as homogenous, ahistorical and bounded societies, and thus controlled by colonial rule, through a new articulation between the rhetoric of 'authenticity' and primordiality, and the 'exoticism', 'tribalism', 'primitivism' and the practices of economic and human exploitation (Fabian 1978; Wolf 1982; Ranger 1992; Porto 2009; Naithani 2010). These cultural reinventions were produced by a linear conception of time which produced 'abyssal lines' that conceived the two colonial agents as simultaneous but also as non-contemporaneous of the same historical time (Santos 2007: 66).

2.2. Collecting native folk songs

In the international context of decolonization after the Second World War, the Dundo Museum began to collect and study native music within the Mission of Folk Music Collection. Although this activity began in 1949 with the ethnomusicologist Professor Artur Santos[18], the systematic expeditions only began in 1950 and continued until the end of the 1960s.[19] The Mission recorded around fifteen hundred songs through seven campaigns conducted almost during the dry season (*cacimbo*) in villages near Kwandu Kuvangu, and in the Districts of Moxiku and Lunda. (Fig. 4) The materials collected during the expeditions and related to other Diamang activities can be partially accessed at the website 'Diamang Digital' (www.diamangdigital.net) from where I took songs and photos previously digitized to Angola (Fig. 5).[20]

---

[18] From August to November 1949, Professor Artur Santos put together the collection in Lunda and Alto Zambeze (UC. RAMD, 1948, 1949).

[19] In this article I will not talk in detail about the Mission's process. For a further reading see Valentim, 2015.

[20] 'Diamang Digital' Project developed, implemented and made available online a digital archive on the archive materials of the ex-Diamonds Company of Angola (Diamang) held at the University of Coimbra, Portugal. This website contains photographic and sound collections, maps and field reports from several divisions of the enterprise. 'Diamang Digital' is led by Dr Nuno Porto (Museum of Anthropology, University of British Columbia, Canada; CRIA) and together with him and other colleagues I worked on the digitization process and web data updates, and nowadays I am in charge of the 'Diamang Digital' website back office.

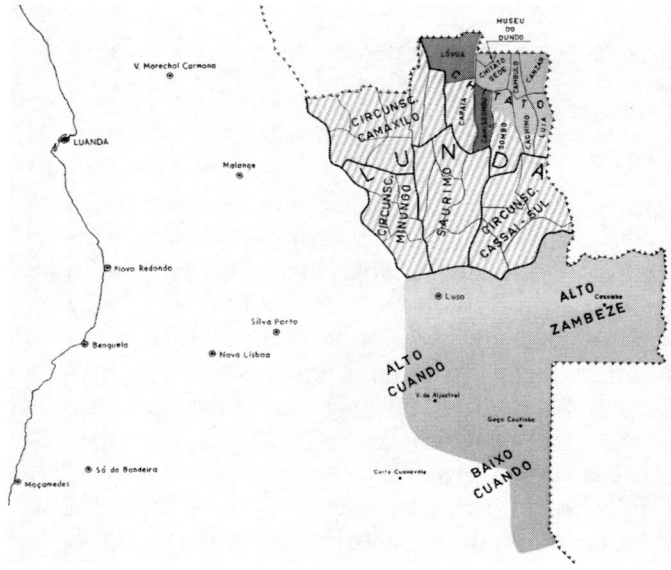

Fig. 4: Map of the Mission of Folk Music Collection from 1960. Source: Janmart et al (1961: 16).

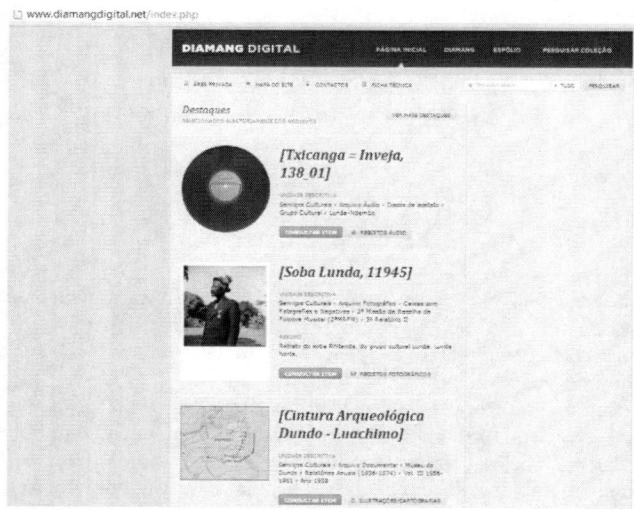

Fig. 5. Website 'Diamang Digital' held at University of Coimbra. Source: www.diamangdigital.net

This Mission was headed by Manuel Pinho da Silva who had previously helped Professor Artur Santos and was working at *Emissora do Dundo* (Broadcast of Dundo, known as *Radio Diamang*) and at the native manpower division. Pinho Silva traveled together with other male employees and *indigenous* staff including cooks and drivers, and with his wife beginning in 1954. (Fig. 6)

The Mission built camps near or in Sobados to receive and audition the best native voices and players brought by their Sobas (Fig. 7). After several rehearsals the sounds ideally more 'primitive', 'authentic' and 'tribal' were recorded, namely those songs whose histories people knew about and that were part of the large festivals where all people danced and men played the strong percussion rhymes with the *cikhuvu* and *ngoma*[21] (Fig. 8). The *indigenous* people were paid with goods like tobacco, clothing, *panos* (cloth used by women as a wrap around garment) textiles, food, and money (UC. 2 R MRFM 1950: 8).

Songs were recorded in acetate discs (lacquer discs) of 78 rpm and since 1954 directly to magnetic tapes. These blank materials were imported from New York and Germany, recorded in Lunda and mastered in Spain (UC. NFM, Vol. I). In the end twenty one music collections from twenty one ethnic groups previously defined and separated were recorded.[22] These songs circulated between Africa (Angola and South Africa), Europe and North and

---

[21] The *cikhuvu* and the *ngoma* are drums. *The cikhuvu* is a large trapezoidal drum made from a unique bloc of wood, with a longitudinal slit at the top and played with two sticks (*mixipho*) covered by rubber (*ulongo*) (Redinha 1938: 128). Traditionally it was also used as an important way to communicate between villages (idem: 31). The *Ngoma* can be of different types but all of them are made by wood and mostly manually played. Each of them is covered on top (or also at the base) by leather (Redinha 1988: 164–167).

[22] The music collections are: Baluba, Baquete, Bângala, Bena Lulua, Bena Mai, Ngoje Bena, Bena Nsapo, Cacangala, Cacongo, Caiauma, Caleutchaje, Caluio, Camacha, Cambunda, Conhengo, Luena, Luena Cassabe, Lunda, Lunda Muatianvua, Lunda Ndembo and Quioco (UC. 1–7 R MRFM, 1950–1963). The last music collection (from the Bângala people, 7° expedition from 1962 to 1963) was lost within the vast archive and not included in the surveys previously made on the sound archive, but it was found during my ongoing research. These names are written with the colonial orthography as appears in the Mission's Reports. The name Quioco is one of the colonial Portuguese names to the Cokwe people.

South America through exhibitions of 'black African art', ethno musicological studies[23], concerts, conferences, radio, and the press.

Fig. 6: Photo n°9400. 1950. "Jangada do Luizavo. Alto-Zambeze" [Pinho Silva and an *indigenous* collaborator crossing the river Luizavo with a raft to reach a village at the Alto Zambeze] (UC. 1R MRFM, 1950: 3). First campaign, Moxiku, Angola. Box n°1 "*1 Rel*". © Universidade de Coimbra, 2018.

---

[23] In 1961, when the Colonial War began, and in 1967, two bilingual studies of ethnomusicology were published, edited by the Dundo Museum based on the cokwe songs collected in 1954 and 1955 (see Janmart et al 1961 and 1967). They were offered, with the magnetic tapes, to Museums and Universities in Europe, Latin America, United States of America, and South Africa and to the main Portuguese cultural Institutes in Angola and Portugal. Despite the ethnographic and political desire to know about native knowledge, these studies conceive Cokwe songs with "high musicality" (Janmart *et al.*, 1961: 56) but through interpretations based on an evolutionist and racial discourse. The representation of Cokwe music is made within the same perception about the western folk songs conceived as naturally authentic, pure and intuitive, but also as mysterious, unreachable and primitive. These studies were an exercise of political propaganda where the cokwe music was interpreted within a romantic, racialized and ethnocentric discourse (Valentim, 2012).

Fig. 7: Photo nº 15009. 1954. "Soba Cangunda, que auxiliou a Missão nos trabalhos de recolha./Chief Cangunda, who helped the Mission in its collecting process" (Janmart et al, 1961: 36). Fifth campaign, Lovwa, Lunda, Angola. Box nº7 "*5 Rel*". © Universidade de Coimbra, 2018.

Drawing from an imaginary that imposed the effort to rescue a native past still immune to colonial presence, the Mission was faced with some difficulties in collecting 'pure' songs that had not been 'contaminated': some of the 'native folk music' reflected a colonial reality experienced and critically commented upon by *indigenous* individuals. We cannot forget that those people were all *indigenous* (in the sense of the Native Status) and most of them (or their relatives) had been *contratados* or *voluntários* at Diamang[24], or involved in building bridges or roads to the Colonial Government. In that sense some of the songs collected talk about the lived colonial reality, namely about violence, hope, native cultural values, advices, anxieties, desires and about the forced labour

---

[24] The *contratados* or 'workers from the exterior' did the excavation mining work and the hard tasks, and they could work in the land fields, roads building and in other infrastructures, while the *voluntários*, or 'workers from the region' made light tasks in mining and various services at the urban centers.

called in *ucokwe* as *cipale*[25]. Some of them were also singing during the forced labour, during the travelling between the *cipale* and the village, or during the large festivals organized within the villages. Alberto Rosa[26] vividly remembers exactly what he heard in the mining camps during the night, when contract workers were allowed to sing after work during the labour days (Monday through Saturday) until 10 pm and on Sundays:

> They were singing to express their pain. Otherwise, it was not possible. It was a way to evade themselves. […] The voices and the words translated that feeling of pain. Basically they sang the impossibility of changing their lives. (Dundo, 27 August 2014)

Due to the song's social criticism, and also owing to ethnographic reasons, the next phase of the Mission was the *recolha escrita* [collection of song lyrics and stories] (Fig. 9) and the revision at Dundo. The aim was to do a final selection on the recorded songs to understand, translate, transcribe and verify the 'authenticity' of the songs' lyrics and stories.

---

[25] Although this word is written as *shibalo* in most of contemporary studies about colonial Angola, it is t*xipale* [*cipale*] that appears in the Cokwe-Portuguese dictionary (see Barbosa 1989: 405). At Lunda its pronunciation depends on the region: in South Lunda it mainly appears like *cipale*, but in North Lunda it mostly appears like *cibale*.

[26] AR is Capeverdian and was born in 1929. He migrated to Angola in 1949 to work at Diamang. He worked on the services of native manpower, as adjunct-foreman in mining and manager at the Diamang's Storage. He is a technical-assistant at the Provincial Government of North Lunda, in Dundo.

Fig. 8: Photo nº 11822. 1951–1952. "Tocador de Chingufo" [At the center, two men playing *cikhuvu*, and on the right two men playing *ngoma*] (UC 3R MRFM, 1952: 322). Third campaign, Lunda, Angola. Source: Box nº4 "*3 Rel II*". © Universidade de Coimbra, 2018.

Fig. 9. Photo nº15567. 1955. "Pesquisa de folclore no sobado de Satanda em Camissombo" [Research on folklore at Satanda, Kamissombo] (UC 6R MRFM, 1955: 209). (Sixth campaign, Kamisombo, Lunda, Angola. Source: Box nº8 "6 Rel". © Universidade de Coimbra, 2018.

3. Mwambwambwa song

The *"Muambuâmbua"* song was collected during the fifth expedition of the Mission. This song belongs to the QUI collection (that means Quioco or Cokwe) with the number 185, disc nº 633 track 2 and it was classified as a "festive and danced song, of txianda" (UC. 5R MRFM 1954: 173).[27] *Ciyanda* is a popular Cokwe rhythm that

---

[27] UC. *Colecção Povo Quioco/Série QUI, nº 185, Disco nº 633, faixa 2*. For a further reading about other songs collected by the Mission, see Valentim,

used to be played with drums and danced during large festivals in villages where everybody is allowed to dance and sing several songs (*myaso*[28]).[29] In those kinds of dances, people usually make huge rounds dancing while the men play drums at the centre.[30] (Fig. 10)

Fig. 10. Photo n°13729. 1952. "Grupo Chianda" [Round dancing exhibition by the Native Folk Group named Chianda [*Ciyanda*] of the Dundo Museum performed at the Folk Yard of the Dundo Museum's Native Village. It can be a performance of *ciyanda* rhythm, but there is no data to confirm it]. Source: Box n° 8, *Folclore do Museu* [Museum Folklore]. © Universidade de Coimbra, 2018.

2015a and, particularly, Valentim, 2016 where parts of the same empirical data that I'm discussion here are presented.

[28] Plural of *mwaso*.

[29] The *ciyanda* rhythm is played with five different types of *ngoma* (drums): *ngoma wa xina*, *ngoma wa mukhundvu*, *ngoma wa kasasulwilo*, *ngoma wa kasumbi* and *ngoma wa mukupela* also known as *ngoma wa mukwanzo* (ou *mukwazo*), and sometimes it can be played the *cikhuvu* (Guerra-Marques 2006: 134, 149).

[30] Those Cokwe round dances (*Wino wa Tucokwe*) could be of different rhythms such as of *kapaka*, *kashinga*, *kateko*, *ciyanda* and *cisela* (Bastin 1992: 39) danced with particular songs to each kind of situation: in initiatic rituals or in masquerade performances (*akixi kuhangana*) (idem: 33).

In general, and like the music of Bantu societies in sub-Saharan Africa, these songs from the Cokwe community often combine dance, song, poetry and orature (oral history, tales, proverbs, myths, rumors); its cultural production is recreated by the context and the meanings are transmitted through storytelling, labour tasks, ritual, masquerade, divination, magico-therapeutic rites, festival celebrations and religious and witchcraft practices; and it is characterized by the predominance of percussion rhythm and melodies (Janmart et al 1961 and 1967; Redinha 1988; Bender 1991; Bastin 1992; Jordán 1998; Guerra-Marques 2006, 2012; Kubik 2010). Therefore, those musical expressions are often enacted as part of everyday practices or on special occasions and thus actively participate in vast social dynamics (at individual, family, communal, economic and political levels). In addition, they can have meanings and hidden messages that are expressed by the rhythms, melodies and by the lyrics. As Mateus Segunda Chicumba[31] told me: "Cokwe people never sing without a specific purpose. They call it *misende*." (Lisbon, 15 April 2015). The word *misende*[32] signifies something that is said to someone to intentionally target a third person, a kind of insinuation or suggestion (Barbosa 1989: 511). It also means saying incisive and important things through an ironic, obscure, covert, discreet, unclear, indirect and metaphorically way.

As we can read in the report (Table 1), this song is about a man who fled from forced labour recruitment. The 'civilizing mission' inherent to the Portuguese colonial labour regime introduced in the colonies since the end of the XIX century perceived native labour as a moral obligation and a duty of the Portuguese Colonial Government—a kind of imperial "benevolence" and "inevitability"—and as a social requirement to improve local living conditions (Jerónimo 2010: 57, 68, 75). Despite the rhetorical dimension, the 'civilization mission' was also used as an argument by state or private enterprises to legitimize the coercive and compulsory practic-

---

[31] MSC was born at the municipality of Lwau, Moxiku, in 1965. His uncle worked in the Diamang mines during the decades of 1950 and 1960. He is a Lecturer in Angola and a PhD candidate/researcher in Applied Linguistics at University of Lisbon, Portugal.
[32] Plural of *musende*.

es of *indigenous* labour (Cruz 2005: 155). Specifically in the colonial District of Lunda, the recruitment for *contratados* was made by Diamang in villages far away from the mining areas, namely from the actual South Lunda or from the Southwest, South or Northwest of the actual North Lunda. All workers recruited compulsorily did at least one period of contract labour which legally could last eighteen months but workers could stay until twenty four months or more doing multiple contracts willingly or by coercion (Cleveland 2008: 52, 230–231). At the end of that contract period they could become local residents by working in others services of the Diamang, or return to their villages after a resting period, and eventually go back for another period of labour contract.

That labour regime had the help of *Chefes do Posto, Sobas, cipaios* and *capitas*[33]. The Diamang asked for convoys of workers from the colonial authorities of the *Circunscrição or Posto Administrativo*; then the colonial officials would demand a few men from each village from the Sobas of several Sobados, who had to offer them to the *cipaios* when they arrived in the villages accompanied by *capitas*.[34] They could bring with them their wives who would also be working under the forced labour regime at cafeterias and mine camps as cleaners and cooks, but also as field laborers on

---

[33] *Cipaio* [or *Sipaio*] is the colonial police force held by African men. *Capita* [*Kapita* in *ucokwe*] is a cokwe word that used to designate the owners of the people who were enslaved, and the name given by native populations to the African man overseer of native labour force and recruitment at Portuguese colonialism.

[34] With colonial war since February 1961, in 1962 the colonial state abolished the *Estatuto do Indigenato* and created the *Código do Trabalho Rural* which replaced the previous legislation on *indigenous* labour and legally abolished compulsory labour by masking it as 'volunteer contract labour' (Cruz 2005: 265–266). As previous measure, since 28 August 1961 the intervention of colonial officials in private recruitments was no longer tolerated. To deal with this new situation, Diamang continued doing coercive recruitment and 'recruitment offices' were created at *Circunscrições*. It used *Angariadores* (travelling labour recruiters) who talked directly with Sobas. (UC. Folder 86B, 6a, 1º. *Mão-de-obra Indígena - Recrutamento, 25/08/61–31/12/61*, "Esboço do plano de trabalhos apresentado a Sua Excelência o Governador da Lunda" 13/10/1961 and "Instalação de escritórios de recrutamento, Nota de informação nº 2" (21/10/61), J. M. de Noronha Feyo)

lavras (plantations) and farms of the Diamang in order to feed all the population under Diamang's colonial rule. Then the journey began by foot from their villages to the *Posto* including several stops in other villages to collect more men, and from the Posto they would take a long and dangerous march to the Dundo and then to the mine camps. During this recruitment process—that could take a week or months—and despite the truck transport since 1948, many of them died or fled. The mining work is remembered as the most violent of all, and according to conversations held in the field, and also realized by the Diamang and the Portuguese colonial state (Cleveland 2008: 47), entire villages were fleeing to resist the brutality of recruitment processes and mining.

Despite the efforts of the Diamang to increase local collaboration by giving gifts and extra money to colonial *Chefes de Posto* and to Sobas and their populations (Cleveland 2008: 59), and although the wage conditions in the neighboring colony were even harsher than at Lunda, all along the colonial period residents were fleeing and living there. The rate at which people fled from labour recruitment increased dramatically after Belgian Congo's independence in 1960 (idem: 46). In that context, and as stated in the beginning of this paper, I first interpreted this song as a compliment to the courage of a man named *Mwambwambwa*, as well as a message to all villages to speed up the process of fleeing. However, in Angola, where I brought some of those songs to be listened to and commented upon by Angolans, I realized that this was not the case. Accordingly, to my Cokwe interlocutors, the Portuguese translation missed some vernacular, linguistic and contextual meanings, and therefore an ambiguous and complex dimension.

```
                        Muambuâmbua.
                     The name of a man.
                                                                    beautiful
                               [manuscript comment in blue ink by the reviewer]

Uó iaia Muambuâmbua é, ------------Uó brother Muambuâmbua é,
Iaia Muambuâmbua é,-------------- Brother Muambuâmbua é,
Tângua meza txipale,--------------On the recruitment day to the cipale,
Canatxinhine é, ------------------ He fled é,


CORO:-                                CHORUS:-


Ai mama Muambuâmbua é,------------ Oh my mother Muambuâmbua é,
SOLISTA:-                             SOLOIST:-


Uó iaia Muambuâmbua é, ----------- Uó brother Muambuâmbua é,
Iaia Muambuâmbua é,-------------- Brother Muambuâmbua é,
Tângua meza txipale,-------------- On the recruitment day to the cipale,
Canatxinhine é, --------------------He fled é,


CORO:-                                CHORUS:-


Ai mama Muambuâmbua é,------------Oh my mother Muambuâmbua é,


SOLISTA:-                             SOLOIST:-


Iátuè cumahieto txótxo,-------------At our village we behave like this,
Canatxinhine é,---------------------He fled é,


CORO:-                                CHORUS:-


Ai mama Muambuâmbua é,------------- Oh my mother Muambuâmbua é,


[This lyric's structure repeats 2 times]


The colonial authority had to recruit people for the contract labour. Muambuâmbua, an
inhabitant from the village of Soba Txitopo situated in Txilombe river, a tributary of
Lóvua, fled and someone else had to replace him. It is the story of this festive and
danced song, of txianda. The soloist is Faila, it has a feminine choir, and it is
played with txingufo, 3 micundo, 3 micupela and micacala. This song is originally from
the sobado of Txitopo.
```

Table 1. UC. 5R MRFM (1954: 173–174)

The musical structure is a kind of a dialogue between the soloist *Faila* and the choir composed only by women. The soloist begins by talking about the escape of a man through the words: "*Uó iaia Muambuâmbua é*". The voice of this woman seems to leave no doubt: Through an ironic and derisive way—that the interjection

"*Uó*" means, in conjunction with *iaia Muambuâmbua*—this woman was performing someone who was angry, sad and in disagreement with something (enhanced by the interjection "é"). The sense of anger of the woman may be interpreted as an alert to the village, a kind of question put by women and addressed to men. Then, the chorus highlights the lament beneath her saying—"*Ai mama-Muambuâmbua é*"—to which the soloist replies with the main message of the song: "*Iátué cumahieto txótxo*".

In a literal sense, this expression "*Iátué cumahieto txótxo*" means 'In our village we behave like this', as rightly translated by the Mission. But as told by Mateus Segunda Chicumba, in that contextual Cokwe universe, and taking into account the ironic, metaphorical and sarcastic emphasis of those words, it has precisely an opposite sense, that is: "In our village we don't behave like this" (MSC, Lisbon, 15 April 2015), which means 'we do not run away' or shortly 'we must not flee'. In the same sense, when José Domingos Mutambi[35] listened to this song he realized that this Cokwe song is saying that people were fleeing and at the same time is advising people to stop doing that. I asked why, and José explained:

> They talk of someone who has to go to the labour contract. [. . .] But who did run away. She says, 'instead of going to work you are a lazy man! Then others will work but not you? Are you running away from work? '[. . .] Everyone was under the authority of the colonial system at the time. So people had to submit, if you do not submit . . . in a way you would stay invalid, because there's no escape! How will you survive? It was even making the 'Boss's game' ('o jogo do patrão') there's no other way. (Saurimo, 7 August 2014)

It would be a dead end: the men had to go to *cipale*. In fact, the story that was told to the Mission refers that *Mwambwambwa* fled but that "someone else had to replace him" (UC. 5R MRFM 1954: 174). So, what really means doing 'the Boss's game' through which José Domingos Mutambi is interpreting this song?

---

35   JDM was born in the commune of Cacimo, North Lunda, in 1964. He is son of a worker at the Diamang's Storages. He is a journalist at Catoca diamond mine, and musician and vocalist of the folk music band lead by him, 'Os Moyowenos da Lunda Sul', at the city of Saurimo.

3.1. Fleeing from *cipale*

Traditional Cokwe society, namely in the rural areas, is characterized by a subsistence economy where wealth is produced through vast webs of kinship defined by matrilineal lineage and clan solidarity (Sousa 2012: 53–54). This means that within a common clan shared by a set of families, the social prestige, property and political heritage are transmitted and activated through the uterine family—the lineage of women. Based on that logic, the duty of the man is to lead and constitute family while women are responsible for raising children. Also, the different contribution of both genders to the village is reflected in the sexual division of work. In short, men were hunters, did commerce, constructed houses, prepared the fields for cultivation; women did farming, cooked, and raised the children (Redinha 1966: 111–113). Thus, those societies were structured around values of collective solidarity since all economic organization, kinship, gender relations, social and political structures, and personhood, were structured around the sense of belonging to one community, to a family, to a *cihunda* (village) (Sousa 2012). Opposed to that social and political organization, the new colonial reality was characterized by industrial labour where the social power was linked to the accumulation of capital and rooted in an individualistic logic.

As in other Bantu African societies, the conception of a person is inscribed in a communitarian dynamics of cosmology, ideas about nature and society and defined by reference to the environing community (Menkiti 1984: 180). Here is implied the *Ubuntu* philosophy as an African spiritual ideal of thinking and action, which contains the emblematic African concept of identity: "I am because we are, and since we are, therefore I am" (Mbiti 1970 cited in Menkiti 1984: 171). To that extent, communal individual action as well as the individual interests was compromised by the introduction of individualism. In this regard, and in contexts of colonial oppression, the 'we' would always suffer when the 'I' refused to cooperate with colonial rule. Catele Jeremias refers to it when he told me about the decision to flee:

> If you run away somebody has to replace you. If you do not go, your village will suffer reprisals. The 'we' will suffer. When nobody wanted to go for the *contrato*, my grandmother told me that to preserve the integrity of the 'we' the whole village would flee. All of them would escape. Nobody goes [to *cipale*] and no one suffers. (Lisbon, 15 April 2015)

Thus, prior to the arrival of the *cipaios* to the village, the Soba would be meeting the headmen of each village at *cota*[36] and together they would decide about the men able to go to *cipale* to join who would be chosen by the *cipaios* (who choose firstly who had failed to pay their *impostos* [taxes]). At the same time, the families of the men chosen would deliberate if they would bring with them their wives and children, or if not the Soba needed to make sure that the wives left behind would have the support of their brothers and mothers, and that they would not commit adultery, come under permanent vigilance and with new duties owing to new social status of contract worker's wife. Domingos Cutwnga[37] stated that

> When a woman is alone at home, the husband's relatives must watch over her [laughs] . . . They are watching her to not commit adultery. [. . .] Even when the husband is in the contracted labour, his woman that stays in the village is under the control of the Soba, no one can abuse his house. If you abuse the house of the *contratado*, and the woman is committing adultery, the fine was so high! . . . She must to pay. (Saurimo, 1 September 2014).

Also if he had more than a wife, he could opt to go with one, or at least flee alone, knowing that his family would have a stronger support in the village. In the same way, the sexual division of work within the village would be reorganized in relation to the absence of the men during one or two, or more years.

So, fleeing unexpectedly from the labour recruitment implied different kinds of violence that could have deep repercussions for different parts of the village. For example, if we interpret what *Faila* is singing as the lamentation of a woman (because she can be

---

[36] *Cota* [*Txota* in colonial Portuguese language] is a round housing that is usually at the center of the village or in the *Bairros* at the suburbs, and where the Soba and his counselors and headmen decide together about village issues that need collective consensus.

[37] DC was born in the municipality of Kakolo, South Lunda, in 1965. His father was *cipaio* and his uncles were contract labourers in Diamang mining, during the 1950 and 1960 decades. He is journalist at National Radio of Angola (Radio Saurimo, South Lunda) in the city of Saurimo.

performing the voice of another member of the community) regretting the flight of her brother (*iaia* [*yaya*]) *Mwambwambwa*, that would pose a kinship issue with social, economic and political implications to her family and the social balance of the entire village.[38] But if *Faila* is talking about her husband, we can think about the processes of social differentiation within gender issues. This is what Domingos Cutwnga says about this song:

> At that time, when the cipaios arrived in the *bairro* [it means village], those who ran away were only men, and the women stayed at the village. [. . .] men who stayed in the *bairro* and who had fled from the contract labour couldn't work nor live in the *bairro* . . . [...] [they] have to flee to the forest because they were undocumented [...].[39] So a woman preferred a man or husband who had gone to the labour contract to live in peace at *bairro* during and after that forced labour. [. . .] When the Portuguese people came to the *bairro* they asked women who had husbands doing the labour contract. And they were respected at that time. And the women of those men who fled, stayed in the *bairro* with no way of expressing themselves before the others! They were without social status. [Laughs] In fact, at that time, despite the less bright side [of flee] there was a side that was worth pondering over. (Saurimo, 17 August 2014)

Also after a man's escape, the *cipaios* returned to villages and demanded that Sobas replace escapees, or just look indiscriminately for strong healthy men. In those situations, and when the Sobas refuse to choose their relatives to go to *cipale*, even Sobas would go to forced labour or suffer from corporal punishments at *Posto* where they would be humiliated and their powerlessness publicly exposed. In addition, entire villages would escape namely to the Belgian Congo (a decision previously decided at *cota* as told by Catele) in a mixed sense of collective solidarity and individual

---

[38] In a matrilineal system the children (in particular the uterine male nephews and cosins) are fundamental to the political continuity of the linage and family property, and the maternal uncle has the legal rights on children and is responsible for their formal education. (Redinha 1966: 77) In that context, the uterine family has the duty to support the women in the absence of their brothers and husbands. (idem)

[39] He is talking about the *Caderneta do Indígena*, an *indigenous* booklet where the Government would register the identification and the labour obligations of the native, including working places, labour contracts (at least one contract labour) and the payment of the native taxes. It was imposed to all indigenous from all the Portuguese colonies beginning in 1928 by the *Código do Trabalho dos Indígenas* (Indigenous Labour Law) (Cruz 2005: 154–155).

survival. And other possible scenarios: the burden on women in the farms and the lack of men for hunting, that together could lead to bad times of harvest and famine periods; the punishment of the fugitive's family and their arrest[40], together with Sobas as a mechanism of labour coercion, blackmail and intimidation; the pursuit of undocumented men; the decreasing of births and marriage breakdowns.

3.2. Why you should not flee from cipale

The name *Mwambwambwa* can be a pseudonym, a false name used in those songs to cover the real identities of the persons, and if so, it was chosen to make sense of a certain person's character or situation. Mateus Segunda Chicumba told me that the name *Mwambwambwa* signifies a person who talks a lot but who does nothing to solve problems, and who easily flees (Lisbon, 15 April 2015). In addition, to Neto Bernardo[41] that name signifies "warning someone, grabbing someone's attention" but also "conspiring against someone".[42] (Saurimo, 14 August 2014) He informs me that this song is talking about the anxieties raised by new ambitions and social expectations, namely the fear of returning from

---

[40] The imprisonment inside the mining area was done by the colonial administration but only after the will and interference of Diamang: the *cipaios* brought the *indigenous* inhabitants (namely the family members of the fugitive, and Soba) to *Posto* and Diamang informed *the Chefe de Posto* about the situation of transgression that occurred, and he would decide what to do with them. UC. Box 15. *Folder 1º, Serviço de Representação. Informações Diversas. 4/11/41–31/12/45*. "Despacho da Administração do Chitato na nossa informação de 25/2/42" de 25/2/42, "Informação da SR para o administrador do Chitato da Secção de Representação" de 2/8/43.

[41] NB was born in the municipality of Saurimo, South Lunda, in 1982. He was the grandson of a worker at the Diamang's Storages and the uncle of his grandfather was *cipaio*. He worked as a mechanical technician in a car workshop at the city of Saurimo.

[42] Morphologically, this word is constituted by the interjection *mbwa* that means "disdain, scorn, derision" (Barbosa 2012: 135), and also expresses the sound of "a bump, shock or fall, burst or crackling" (Barbosa 1989: 322). It can appear as "*mbwa-mbwa*" and "*mbwa-mbwa-mbwa*" which also means the idea of repetition of something noisy and the state of "emptiness, containing nothing, empty-handed" (Barbosa 1989: 323). It can further originate a personal name with the locative prefix *Mwa* that identifies a specific situation, condition or place, and in this case the one that is at *mbwa-mbwa-mbwa* situation.

cipale without goods and money. That situation would imply several processes of violence among the contract workers at the mines. That violence was not only physical but also emotional and symbolic:

> NB: When the *cipaio* arrived, people had to go, but sometimes they could not get property. They only worked, were beaten, most of them without strength and starving...and those who returned without anything were poorly spoken about. [...]
>
> CSV: The songs' report tells that this man fled from *cipale*. Do you think he fled or returned without anything from there?
>
> NB: I mean it can be both: flee or return without anything from *cipale*. [Laughs]
>
> CSV: And which one is worse?
>
> NB: If he didn't run away... he must go to *cipale* and [maybe] return with nothing. Because... when you go there... It was a very hard work. The mining work was divided in several deep wells [named *ndombe*]. Each man had to excavate it.[43] [...] So when the time ended, and one man ends the job and the other does not that person automatically signed an agreement with each other to not give him a beating: 'if you do my job, you keep my goods that I will receive or if you don't like that way you can have my wife for a while'. [...] All this was done to avoid the punishment [from the *capitas*]. [...] And if that does not happen, the only way was to just get away, back to the *bairro* [to village]. But if he escaped he had to hide because the white man would catch him and he was taken again back to *cipale*. (Saurimo, 14 August 2014)

Therefore, as José Domingos Mutambi said, the *cipale* was a kind of a dead end. All this violence around the coercive recruitment and forced labour practices reveal some of the tactics used by natives in negotiating and managing the new colonial reality. These labour tasks systems [working by *ndombe*], Todd Cleveland concedes, "benefited stronger workers, while weaker ones struggled to avoid the physical punishment that inevitably came if they failed to complete the daily task assignment" (2008: 101). It is precisely

---

43   The *tarefa* (task) was the removal of an amount of overburden and/or *cascalho* during a time until they reach to the diamonds. This manual system was introduced by Diamang since 1940 decades in mining and was done at the same time of the mechanical excavation gradually introduced by Diamang after 1937 (Cleveland 2008: 101).

this violence and these strategies to survive the violence that Neto Bernardo is referring to, but above all the possible scenario of returning to the village without anything and being barely spoken to by their community members.

The importance of bringing goods and money to the village is remembered through memories of the great festivals that were organized in villages for two or three days to give thanks to the men who had returned with health, goods and money from *cipale,* in a display of a kind of reciprocity. During a conversation with Sekulu[44] Celeste Natália Gomes[45], she remembers herself with enthusiasm:

> [...] We took five chickens or six goats to kill and eat. There were drinks. Everything. [...] And music. [. . .] She had to wait for her husband. She knows very well where he was. He will return with a lot of things to her: *pano* [cloth], silk tissues... [laughs] [...] and money. (*Bairro* Sakhombe, 22 August 2014)

Those celebrations were organized to welcome the *mukwa-cipale* (the people who were doing *cipale*)—called *Salukombo* and no more *Phembe*. In a linear sense, *Salukombo* means the Mr. Broom. According to Pinho Silva, the men who were going to *cipale* were *Phembe* (a goat) because they did not know anything about life and they were just following the others. In contrast, the men who returned from *cipale* were "smarter and knowledgeable" (UC. 5R MRFM 1954: 277).[46] At the same time, as stated by Mateus Segunda Chicumba, *Salukombo* can also mean a name assigned to a father who will not have more children. It means that

---

[44] *Sekulu* is a traditional authority. Like Sobas, it can be managed by a woman.
[45] CNG was born in the municipality of Saurimo, South Lunda, in 1964. Her father was a contract labour at Diamang mining, and later a cipaio, during the 1960 decades. She is Sekulu at *Bairro* of Nzagi, municipality of Saurimo.
[46] Accordingly to the Mission, originally *Salukombo* was given to the native men who were successful in helping their boss in the rubber trading within the long-distance trade caravans (idem, 276–77). Those ethnographical data were collected by Pinho Silva at Lovwa (North Lunda) in 1954 owing to another song called 'Salucombo'. During my fieldwork, no one of the elders (*mais-velhos*) knew exactly the meaning of this word, and some of them say that was a soldier at the colonial war. What I noticed was that José Manuel Salukombo was one of the Governors of the Province of Lunda Sul during the post-independence, from 1991 to 1992, and (maybe because that or not) nowadays "Salucombo" is a name of a street in the city of Saurimo.

those men that were returning from cipale would have achieved the respect of the community and thus stability and social prestige, similar to the status reached by paternity.

Thus, the new social status of the returned men derived from the qualities that those men needed during *cipale*: courage, physical strength, psychological resistance, survival skills, solidarity, bravery, resilience and perseverance. However, the social prestige came also from the distribution of goods and money between their family and entire community. Those goods were clothes [*panos*], shoes, gramophones, radios, mirrors, clothing, blankets, as well as bicycles and European axes and hoes that were used to facilitate the work tasks within the village. Xavito Mwana Kakolo[47] told me about a particular song that they used to sing in those moments. After singing that song, he reveals to me the meanings juxtaposed within it:

> You are welcome. This [the celebration] is for God to protect you. We know that the expedition was tough, but against all odds, you managed it, we are all to be congratulated. What you get is not just for you, it is for the whole community. We are pleased and grateful to you. The most important is health, not wealth. *Wasamba weza,* Your return is praiseworthy. (Saurimo, 30 August 2014)

Nevertheless, as mentioned by Neto Bernardo, not always, the *Phembe* returned as *Salukombo*, and accordingly to other Angolan interlocutors, not always returning from *cipale* would meet the needs that motivated those who wanted to go there, or those who were forced to. The meagre sum of money earned mostly for one or two years (and only partially paid when they arrived to *Posto* where the *Chefes* 'steal' an amount of it) would be needed to fulfill all family and collective needs, as well as individual duties to communal life. These included the buying of some goods to bring to honor the *Soba* and headmen and also to give it to wives and uterine family; to marry; to establish a village; to pay the *Imposto*

---

47   XMK was born in the municipality of Kakolo, South Lunda, in 1978. He is son of a contract labourer at Diamang mining in the 1960s. He is a musician and vocalist at the folk music band leaded by him, '*Minungu Kufunga Tchako, Xavito Mwana Kakolo*', in the city of Saurimo.

Indígena (native tax)⁴⁸; or to be able to migrate to another region or country.

But despite the poor salary earned and all the violence, the experience of waged labour (free or forced) became intertwined with native social dynamics by responding to both customary values of reciprocity and solidarity and to new individual desires, needs, and ways of social prestige and differentiation. At the same time the emancipatory dimension of the waged labour experience produced within different, apparently contradictory and ambivalent experiences continues to be concurrent with the feeling of injustice and violence lived by native populations and from which they never stop resisting—by escaping out of national borders or by negotiating the advantages taken from that system.⁴⁹ It becomes clear that the symbolic universe around the *cipale* and the money earned by wage labour seems to have produced important reasons around the decision to go or flee from *cipale*.

This is precisely what the *Mwambwambwa* song is talking about: the need for negotiation, cooperation, wariness and prudence to live in colonial realities where anyone needed to survive. The singing word *kumahethu* [writen in colonial language as "*cumahieto*"] means 'at our village' and is highlighting precisely the deep balance between the sense of collective belonging and solidarity, and the individual decisions and identities. However, at the same time, men were continuously leaving behind their villages by fleeing alone in order to survive or to reach other ambitions, as-*Mwambwambwa* did. In addition, as stated before, the collaboration with the colonial system implied a renewed balance between the collective and individual interests to obtain some kind of bene-

---

48   Since 1920 a *per capita* tax must to be paid every year instead of the *Imposto de Palhota* (hut tax), and made by black and mixed-race Angolan inhabitant, under the same racial logics of the *Estatuto do Indigenato*. (Neto 2012: 115)

49   I agree with Todd Cleveland that although the salary offered by Diamang was lower when compared with the rest of the colony, natives had no other choice and accepted it because they were obligated to (Cleveland 2008: 225). But I don't agree that the amount of salary earned is irrelevant for understanding their employment decisions (idem). It becomes relevant to inquire through the levels of subjectivities that are under and within that labour process, where wage labour produced ambiguous feelings between pragmatic, emotional and symbolic meanings around the decision of going or fleeing *cipale*.

fits from the colonial regime, such as material (money and goods) or symbolic (individual social status, collective empowerment and internal cultural balance) alongside both African and western values. Yet this could be a difficult situation made by concurrent voices, dilemmas and anxieties, as told by the *Mwambwambwa* song, it is not a clash of rival rationalities between Western individuality and African communal life and rather a sensitive negotiation between them. Therefore, if possible, they had to learn how to deal with different knowledge models and methods, articulating both western and traditional/native rationalities.

Like other societies colonized by the European metropolis, the indigenous populations were under political submission and subjected to a metonymic rationality based in a selective, exclusivist and dichotomist model of thinking that imposed on them a universal and totalizing truth (Santos 2002: 242). To that extent we need to go beyond a reified and essentialist perspective that conceives African cultures both as passive containers without active response or resistance, and as communal societies radically opposed to western individualistic cultures, having in consideration (in both cultures) issues of power and agency as well as ethnographic details about the actions themselves (Karp and Masolo 2000: 88).[50] Furthermore, the idea of African personhood needs to be understood rather "as descriptive of the varying ways in which human beings experience the world according to widely varying needs and interests" (Jackson and Karp 1990: 17). In a sense, the colonial encounter produced transformations in the Angolan local knowledge system which developed what can be called a poli-rationality logics (Masolo 2009) in order to survive in a new world.

---

[50] Those two models of experience were extremely polarized in reaction to colonial dichotomist thought that distinguish between western and African societies opposing individualistic and communitarian logics. That essentialist thought was used to highlight the capacity of African societies in having, like western cultures, complex and valid models of rationality and philosophy. For instances, see Placide Tempels's *Bantu Philosophy* (1959), John Mbiti's *African Religions and Philosophies* (1970) and Ifeanyi A. Menkiti's "Person and Community in African Traditional Thought" (1984).

4. Final remarks

It can be observed that the *Mwambwambwa* song, together with others collected, is not merely a song. Despite the fact that this sound piece has passed as 'folklore' for all its life, it functioned as a public discursive space in which people could make sense of their lived experience. This song reveals a creative engagement with colonial rule; it contains multiple messages, and shows some hidden and complex layers of meaning and logics. This song is about Cokwe people's experiences with colonial labour policies and how they straddled ambivalent tactics and strategies of compliance but also resistance to colonial rule, and articulated issues of violence, gender relations, kinship, family, cultural identity, property, individual and collective action, and social status. Pursuing an antireductionist research position, in this paper I suggested that those colonial complexities can be interpreted by the theoretical and methodological use of the so called Sociology of Absences, and its balance with the concept of Concurrences.

The Mission turned this song into a colonial representation that simultaneously highlighted the modern European, the civilized and evolved, as it naturally relegated the African societies to the condition of passiveness, primitiveness and subalternity. Such epistemological and ontological representations, based in monocultural logics turn other cultures and people into an ethnographic curiosity and into an economic resource to be exploited, transforming them into social absences. In that sense, Dundo Museum produced scientific knowledge about the native expressive cultures not only to study them but also to justify the inevitability and the importance of Portuguese colonial rule at Angola. In that attempt the native songs had to be converted into 'native folklore'—I mean a traditional, tribal, pristine, static, pure, exotic knowledge and culture—apart from (western) modernity to be better colonized. Towards that end, this epistemological and cognitive perspective overshadowed native cultures as well as their complex ways of resistance through self-definition and self-determination.

As registered in the colonial archive by the ethnographic expedition, the *Mwambwambwa* song is an aesthetically "beautiful" song about a man who fled from forced labour recruitment and was replaced by another man. However, this is not that the whole story about this colonial past and lived experience. Thus the notion of the Sociology of Absences can help us to realize that important silences produced by the processes of colonization in the world through creative 'abyssal lines' that legitimized and strengthened colonial rule and obfuscated agency and resistance processes to those who were submitted to it. Nevertheless, despite the recognition of the political construction of the 'absences', we need to interpret the intersections and overlaps between different logics to make sense of the 'abyssal lines' as fragile and porous walls.

Cokwe people were kept within their own traditions by the Dundo Museum to become a passive container for the Diamang decisions and subjects of colonial rule. However, at the same time, their culture and knowledges (turned into 'colonial folklore') were, in fact, important creative tools to transcend the bounds imposed on them and to achieve a sense of empowerment. Therefore, those populations could collaborate with the colonial rule not in agreement with it but to take the advantages from that system to improve the native systems of value and to reach new kinds of desires and ambitions. In that process, different agents in diverse places and through different ways of the same colonial process, showing interwoven colonial and native logics nourished by a diversity of motivations, expectations and collective and individual needs, appropriated this song. It was part of the native drumming festivals in villages, namely to receive the *Salukombo*; it traveled with the *contratados* between the villages and the *cipale*; it was recorded, appreciated, desired, studied, used, and preserved by European and Portuguese elite; selected by the *indigenous* populations to be sung to the Mission of Dundo Museum, and it was offered to scientific and cultural institutions in Europe, South and North America and Africa in magnetic tapes. This song reflected and produced colonial relations underpinned by complex webs of hierarchical relations among different social actors and between different places: women and men; Sobas, colonial staff and population; villages and the urban centers; the labour tasks and the colonial administration; the Diamang and the world.

Furthermore, all of that diversity of experiences were produced within power relations that could shift owing to constant negotiation and readjustment made within situated identities and processes of differentiation: the contract labors' wives, the escapee's wives, the Sobas, the *Salukombo*, the village's members, the miners' colleagues, the colonial officials, the Mission of Dundo Museum. The colonial relations were held together by concurring, complementary and cooperative actions, as well as by conflicting and concurrent constraints, purposes, logics and agendas, **thus producing simultaneous and juxtaposed contradictory and ambivalent discourses and viewpoints.**

It becomes clear that the notion of Concurrences help to dismantle the dichotomic character of colonial relations and to realize that there were multiple and interwoven power relations and veiled mechanisms of oppression and resistance which implied sensitive and situated engagements both with the colonial rule and the native system of value to achieve varying needs and interests. The colonial encounter was built by the colonizer and the colonized through reciprocal engagements in a tangled web of meanings and negotiations. It means that those social categories are a shifting pair and mutually constructed, and that power can always be subverted in both convert and overt ways.

Although memories about the Mission of the Dundo Museum has faded away, the songs have stayed where they have always been, that is in North and South Lunda. Although some of these songs continue to be part of the popular music and rhythmic repertoires mostly in the villages or in semi-urban settings, and to inspiring groups of contemporary popular Cokwe music at Lundas, the lived contexts had changed and thus also some of the rhythms, lyrics, meanings and messages performed by them. Rather, some of these rhythms and songs were gone and others are played with other instruments, and that most of these traditional songs that talk explicitly about *cipale* are no longer performed, as well as some other songs, rhythms and dances. Thus these particular old songs are sung from the memories of old people (*kotas* or *mais-velhos*) when they reminisce about the colonial past. So, these collected songs functioned as a reflection of colonial life and as a comment upon those particular realities. In this sense, these songs reflect not only life but also what it should or could be in a specific time and place. In a sentence, and following the memories of my interlocutors, playing, singing and dancing those Cokwe songs helped them to overcome colonial violence by making their voices heard even when their songs were not listened to.

Bibliography and Sources

Alexandre, Valentim. 2004. "O império português (1825–1890): ideologia e economia", Análise Social, vol. XXXVIII (169): 959–979.

Barbosa, Adriano. 1989. *Dicionário cokwe-português*. Coimbra: Instituto de Antropologia, Universidade de Coimbra.

_____2011. *Dicionário Cokwe-Português*. Luanda: Gestgráfica, SA.

___2012. *Noções básicas de gramática Cokwe*. Lwena: Edição da Diocese de Lwena.

Bastin, Marie-Louise. 1992. "Musical Instruments, Songs and Dances of the Chokwe (Dundo Region, Lunda district, Angola). *African Music*, Vol. 7, 2: 23–44.

Bendix, Regina. 1997. *In Search of Authenticity: The Formation of Folklore Studies*. Madison, Wisconsin: The University of Wisconsin Press

Brydon, Diana, Peter Forsgren and Gunlög Fur (Eds.), 2014 "Culture Bound and Unbound: Concurrent Voices and Claims in Postcolonial Places", in *Culture Unbound*, Vol 6, 1253–1257.

Cleveland, Todd. 2008. *Rock Solid: African labourers on the diamond mines of the Companhia de Diamantes de Angola (Diamang), 1917–1975*. PhD Thesis. Minnesota: University of Minnesota, ProQuest LLC.

Cruz, Elizabeth C. V. 2005. *O Estatuto do Indigenato—Angola. A Legalização da Discriminação na Colonização Portuguesa*. Luanda: Edições Chá de Caxinde.

Dirks, Nicholas B. 1995 [1992]. "Introduction: Colonialism and Culture", *in* ed. Nicholas B. Dirks. *Colonialism and Culture*. Ann Arbor: The University of Michigan Press.

Fabian, Johannes. 1978. "Popular Culture in Africa: Findings and Conjectures. To the Memory of Placide Tempels (1906–1977)", *Africa: Journal of the International African Institute*, Vol. 48, 4: 315–334.

Fernando, Manzambi Vuvu. 2013. "Origem, Expansão e Fixação das populações Ruund, Cokwe e comunidades aparentadas." in ed. Samuel Carlos Victorino et al. *A Rainha Lueji A'Nkonde e o Império Lunda. Actas da Conferência Internacional sobre a Rainha Lueji A'Nkonde*. Dundo: Lueji Editora, 34–45.

Fur, Gunlög. 2017. "Concurrences as a Methodology for Discerning Concurrent Histories.", in Brydon, Diana, Forsgren, Peter & Fur, Gunlög (eds.). *Concurrent Imaginaries, Postcolonial Worlds: Toward Revised Histories*. Amsterdam: Brill/Rodopi, 33–57.

Fur, Gunlög. 2015. "Concurrences.", paper from the Keynote presentation at Conference 'Concurrences in postcolonial research-perspectives, methodologies, engagements', 20 August 2015, Kalmar, Sweden.

Guerra-Marques, Ana Clara. 2006. *Sobre os Akixi a Kuhangana entre os Tucokwe de Angola: a performance coreográfica das máscaras de dança Mwana Phwo e Cihongo*. Dissertação de mestrado em Performance Artística-Dança. Faculdade de Motricidade Humana da Universidade Técnica de Lisboa.

_____. 2012. "Entre a arte e educação: manifestações culturais na sociedade tradicional Cokwe", in Ana Clara Guerra-Marques (coord.), *Memória viva da cultura da região leste de Angola. Catálogo da exposição permanente do Museu Regional do Dundo*. Luanda: Ministério da Cultura, 129–155.

Hall, Stuart. 2001 [1992]. "The West and the Rest: Discourse and Power", in Stuart Hall e Bram Gieben (orgs.), *Formations of Modernity*. Cambridge: Polity, 275–320.

Janmart et al. 1967. *Folclore Musical de Angola. Volume II, Povo Quioco (Área do Camissombo)*. Lisboa: Publicações Culturais da Companhia de Diamantes de Angola.

_____. 1961. *Folclore Musical de Angola. Volume I, Povo Quioco (Área do Lóvua)*. Lisboa: Publicações Culturais da Companhia de Diamantes de Angola.

Jackson, Michael and Ivan Karp. 1990. "Introduction" in Michael Jackson and Ivan Karp (ed.), *Personhood and Agency: The Experience of Self and Other in African Cultures*. Uppsala Studies in Cultural Anthropology 14. Washington, D. C.: Smithsonian Institution Press, 15–30.

Jerónimo, Miguel Bandeira. 2010. *Livros Brancos, Almas Negras. A missão «civilizadora» do colonialismo português c. 1870–1930*. Lisboa: ICS.

Jordán, Manuel. (Ed.) 1998. *Chokwe!: Art and initiation among Chokwe and related peoples*. Munich: Prestel.

Karp, Ivan and A. Dismas Masolo. 2000, "Introduction: Power, Personhood, and Agency" in Ivan Karp and D. A. Masolo (eds.), *African Philosophy as Critical Inquiry*. Bloomington: Indiana University Press, 83–88.

Lander, Edgardo (Org.). 1993. *La colonialidad del saber: eurocentrismo y ciencias sociales: perspectivas latinoamericanas*. Buenos Aires: CLACSO.

Masolo, Dismas A. 2009 [2003]. "Filosofia e Conhecimento Indígena: uma perspectiva africana" in Boaventura Sousa Santos and Maria Paula Meneses (org.), *Epistemologias do Sul*. Coimbra: Edições Almedina, 507–530.

McClintock, Anne. 1995. *Imperial Leather. Race, Gender and sexuality in the colonial contest*. London: Routledge.

Menkiti, Ifeanyi A. 1984. "Person and Community in African Traditional Thought" in Richard Wright (ed.), *African Philosophy, an Introduction*. Lanham, Md.: University Press of America, 171–182.

Mignolo, Walter. 2000. *Local Histories/Global Designs: Coloniality, subaltern knowledges, and border thinking*. New Jersey: Princeton University Press.

Mudimbe, Valentin-Yves. 1988. *The Invention of Africa. Gnosis, philosophy and the order of knowledge*. USA: Indiana University Press.

Naithani, Sadhana. 2010. *The Story-Time of the British Empire: Colonial and Postcolonial Folkloristics*. Jackson: University Press of Mississippi.

Neto, Maria da Conceição. 2012. *In Town and Out of Town: A Social History of Huambo. (Angola), 1902–1961*. PhD Thesis, SOAS, London: University of London.

Porto, Nuno. 2004. "Under the gaze of the ancestors—photographs and performance in colonial Angola", in Elizabeth Edwards and Janice Hart (orgs.), *Photographs, Objects, Histories*. London, New York: Routledge.

Porto, Nuno. 2009. *Modos de objectificação da dominação colonial: o caso do Museu do Dundo, 1940–1970*. Lisboa: Fundação Calouste Gulbenkian, FCT.

Porto, Nuno and Cristina Sá Valentim. 2015. "'A Terra Rica' Colonialidade e propaganda no cinema colonial português em Angola" in Gisela M. Bester, Hermes A. Costa, e Gloriete M. Hilário (eds), *Ensaios de Direito e de Sociologia a Partir do Brasil e de Portugal: Movimentos, Direitos e Instituições*. Curitiba: Instituto da Memória Editora. Centro de Estudos da Contemporaneidade, 498–526.

Quijano, Anibal. 2000. *Colonialidad del Poder y Clasificación Social*. Journal of World-Systems Research, Pittsburgh, V. 6, N. 2, 342–386.

Ranger, Terence. 1992 [1983]. "The invention of tradition in colonial Africa" *in* Eric Hobsbawm e Terence Ranger (eds.), *The invention of tradition*. Cambridge: Cambridge University Press, 211–262.

Redinha, José. 1988. *Instrumentos Musicais de Angola: sua construção e descrição*. Coimbra: Instituto de Antropologia da Universidade de Coimbra.

_____. 1966. *Etnossociologia do Nordeste de Angola*. Lisboa: Agência Geral do Ultramar.

Roque, Ricardo and Kim A. Wagner. 2012. "Introduction: engaging colonial knowledge" in ed. Ricardo Roque and Kim A. Wagner. *Engaging colonial knowledge: reading european archives in world history*. Hampshire: Palgrave Macmillan, 1–32.

Santos, Boaventura de Sousa. 2002. "Para uma sociologia das ausências e uma sociologia das emergências", *Revista Crítica de Ciências Sociais*, 63, outubro: 237–280.

_____. 2007. *Beyond Abyssal Thinking: From Global Lines to Ecologies of Knowledges, Review*, XXX, 1: 45–89.

_____. 2014. *Epistemologies of the South: justice against epistemicide*. London: Paradigm Publishers.

Scott, James C. 1990. "Voice under domination: The arts of political disguise", in *Domination and the Arts of Resistance: Hidden Transcripts*, Yale University Press, New Haven, 136–182.

Sousa, Fonseca. 2012. "Organização social e política dos Tucokwe", in (coord.) Ana Clara Guerra-Marques, *Memória viva da cultura da região leste de Angola. Catálogo da exposição permanente do Museu Regional do Dundo*. Luanda: Ministério da Cultura, 51–72.

Stoler, Ann Laura. 2009. *Along the Archival Grain: Epistemic Anxieties and Colonial Common Sense*. Princeton: Princeton University Press.

Stoler, Ann Laura and Frederick Cooper (eds.) 1997. *Tensions of empire: colonial cultures in a bourgeois world*. Berkeley: University of California Press.

Thomas, Nicholas. 1994. *Colonialism's Culture: Anthropology, Travel and Government*. Princeton: Princeton University Press.

Thomaz, Omar Ribeiro. 2001. "'O bom povo português': usos e costumes d'aquém e d'além mar", *Mana*, 7 (1): 55–87.

Valentim, Cristina Sá. 2012, "Um som que silencia. Ciência e colonialidade nos estudos musicológicos da música cokwe da Lunda, 1961 e 1967.", *Realis. Revista de Estudos AntiUtilitaristas e PósColoniais*, 2, 2, 132–151.

_____. 2015 "Músicas com experiências lá dentro. A 'Missão de Recolha de Folclore Musical' da Diamang, Angola/[Songs with experiences inside. The 'Folk Music Collecting Mission' of Diamang, Angola]", *Kult, Journal for Nordic postcolonial studies. Beyond the Empires*, 12, 67–95.

_____. 2015b "À procura da 'autenticidade indígena'. Tradição, tradução e transformação nas recolhas etnomusicais do Museu do Dundo em Angola", *Africana Studia*. Número temático: *"África: arqueologia e paisagem". Revista Internacional de Estudos Africanos/International Journal of African Studies*, 24, 107–128.

_____. 2016, "'Ciwewe'. Cultura y poder en una canción 'cokwe' del este de Angola colonial, 1955", *Revista de Antropología Social*, 2, 25, 281–316.

Vansina, Jan. 2010. *Being Colonized. The Kuba Experience in Rural Congo, 1880–1960*. Wisconsin: The University of Wisconsin Press.

Wolf, Eric. 1982. *Europe and the People without History*. Berkeley: University of California Press

Interviews/Conversations

Angola

Alberto Rosa, 27 August 2014, Dundo
Celeste Natália Gomes, 22 August 2014, *Bairro* Sakhombe
Domingos Cutwnga, 17 August and 1 September 2014, Saurimo
Domingos Liange Sawlimbo, 21 August 2014, *Bairro* Mwangeji
José Domingos Mutambi, 07 August 2014, Saurimo
Neto Bernardo, 14 August 2014, Saurimo
Xavito Mwana Kakolo, 30 August 2014, Saurimo

Portugal

Catele Jeremias, 15 April 2015, Lisbon
Mateus Segunda Chicumba, 15 April 2015, Lisbon

Archives sources

Diamang Archive at University of Coimbra, Portugal (UC)
Serviços Culturais (Cultural Division):
Arquivo Documental (Documentary Archive)
RAMD *Relatório Anual do Museu do Dundo*, 1948, 1949, 1950. (available on www.diamangdigital.net)
MRFM *Missão de Recolha de Folclore Musical*. 1–7R, 1950–1963. (available until 1954 on www.diamangdigital.net)
NMFL *Notas da Missão de Folclore da Lunda*. Vol I, 1950–59: NR. 42, 28/02/1955, p. 1 (available on www.diamangdigital.net)
Arquivo Sonoro (Sound Archive)
Colecção Povo Quioco/Série QUI, nº 185, Disco nº 633, faixa 2 [Pasta 5R, disco_633_2] (digital archive but yet not available on www.diamangdigital.net)
Arquivo Fotográfico (Photographic Archive)
Fig. 2: Photo nº 7599. Box nº4

Fig. 3: Photo nº 18468. 1958. Box nº8
Fig. 6: Photo nº9400. 1950. Box nº1 (available on www.diamangdigital.net)
Fig. 7: Photo nº 15009. 1954. Box nº7
Fig. 8: Photo nº 11822. 1951–1952. Box nº4 (available on www.diamangdigital.net)
Fig. 9. Photo nº15567. 1955. Box nº8
Fig. 10. Photo nº13729. 1952. Box nº 8

Serviço de Mão-de-obra (Workforce Division):

Folder 86B, 6a, 1º. 'Mão-de-obra Indígena - Recrutamento, 25/08/61–31/12/61

Serviço de Informações e Diligências (Security Divison):

Box 15. Folder1º, *Serviço de Representação. Informações Diversas*. 4/11/41–31/12/45.

A Contradictory Encounter:
Swedish Missionaries and the Local Population in the Congo Free State

Pia Lundqvist
Department of Historical Studies,
University of Gothenburg, Sweden

Introduction

Protestant missions were an essential global movement in the era of European imperialism. As the anthropologist Peter Pels has claimed, "missionaries have been some of the most pervasive, powerful and persistent protagonists in the long story of globalization" (Pels 2009 cited in Nielssen et. al. 2011: 1). The missionary endeavour included not only the spreading of Christianity, but also the implementation of Western cultural and moral values. A key issue in this context is the connection between Christian missions and colonialism. Some have regarded missionaries as imperialistic actors, while others have claimed that the mission had entirely different motives (Cox 2002: 9–16). The position of the missionary has been described as "torn between a sense of universal brotherhood in Christ and their identification with an imperial overlordship that accepted no such equality" (Beck 2007: 11). Even if the missionaries disassociated themselves from those in power in the colony, they were by definition part of a foreign influence on the indigenous population and culture. It should, however, be kept in mind that the collective body of missionaries cannot be considered as one uniform actor; instead, they represented different opinions and actions. Historically, the character of the mission and its organization also changed over time.

Today, historians, anthropologists and scholars of religion put great emphasis on complexity and inconsistencies in the intertwined history of mission and colonialism. This "struggle with the conflicts between universalist Christian religious values and the imperial context of these values" is the point of departure in Jeffrey Cox's historical study on missionary work in the Punjab (Cox 2002: 6). The historian Andrew Porter has stressed the importance of considering both history of religion and imperial history when mission is studied, and he argues in his synthesis on British protestant missions that the relationship between the missionary movement and empire was far more complex and ambiguous than previously recognized (Porter 2004). Another interpretation that captures the ambiguity, and the gradual transformation of missionary culture, is historian Richard Price's study of the encounter between British missionaries and the Xhosa people in nineteenth century South Africa. Although initially openminded and optimistic, the missionary culture was destabilized in its clash with the indigenous population. Some of the missionaries shifted their approach from blaming the failures they experienced on themselves to accusing the indigenous people. According to Price, this "closing of the missionary mind" can be seen as the beginning of the creation of a colonial discourse, which was basedon the idea ofa fundamental difference between the Europeans and Africans (Price 2008).

The colonial invention was legitimized by universalistic ideals; Western civilization and Christianity were supposed to be embraced by the colonized. There was, however, also an opposite idea, namely, that the colonized must remain different, "almost the same, but not quite", as Homi Bhabha concisely has expressed the ambiguous desire for a reformed, recognizable "Other". (Bhabha 1994: 122).

In recent studies, Swedish participation in the colonization of the Congo Free State has been highlighted (Tell 2005; Granqvist 2008). The case of the Congo is of interest, since the conflict between the colonial power and the population appears to be so obvious, and Swedish participation in its colonization was relatively significant. Various professional categories from Sweden were involved in the Congo; some even worked directly for the state as military officials. The largest group consisted of, for example, naval officers, seamen, and machinists, all involved in navigation on the Congo River. The second largest professional category included the missionaries.

This chapter assumes that the missionary encounter was multifaceted, complex and contradictory. A study at the micro level, based on individual stories, can hopefully capture the complexity of the relations between missionaries and the Congolese. There are several studies which focus on missionaries' view of the "Other", from Said's perspective (Said 1993). My intention is to include Congolese views on the missionaries, despite the imbalances in the depictions of the encounter discussed below. The following study is based on a reading of narratives about the first encounter between Swedish missionaries and indigenous villagers. Sweden was not a colonial power and the mission emanated from a democraticmovement where the idea of brotherhood was essential. In the Congo, these emancipatory ideals were confronted with a colonial system with a completely different approach to human equality. The Swedish Congo mission may therefore represent an interesting example of the field of tension where the mission operated.

As previously mentioned, there has been a tendency to consider the mission and the missionaries as a unified and coherent actor in the colonial context, which risks an unnuanced presentation of the situation. Furthermore, the indigenous population was not a homogenous group. This text is a preliminary attempt to grasp the complexity of the missionary encounter by including some voices of the indigenous people. The empirical cases and themes highlighted should be seen as starting points for further research. In other words, the purpose of this article is twofold; firstly to point out a number of themes that are worth developing, and secondly to discuss various aspects of the complexity of the missionary encounter. Initially, attention is paid to the problem with *disparities in the depiction of the encounter*. Then, three empirical examples of *the character of the encounter* are discussed, and, finally, different aspects of *the ambivalence and contradictions within the missionary encounter* are discussed. First, the historical context must be defined.

The Congo Free State and protestant missions

H. M. Stanley's travels in 1877 on behalf of the Belgian king Leopold II were the beginning of the so-called "opening" of Congo to colonial exploitation. This led to the establishment of the Congo Free State as the personal fiefdom of King Leopold in 1885. The world's interest was directed towards Congo, and hordes of European explorers, businessmen, military officers and missionaries arrived in the country. At least 650 Swedes settled or worked in the Congo between 1885 and 1908.[1] Under Leopold's administration, the Congo Free State was known as an international scandal in the early 20th century. Abuses committed against the indigenous people, forced labour and corporal punishment in connection with the extraction of ivory and rubber turned international opinion against King Leopold's rule. By 1908, public pressure by humanitarian interests led to the end of the Congo Free State. The country was transformed into a Belgian colony in 1908.[2]

During the same historical era, the protestant revivalist movements in Sweden grew strong, together with the temperance movement and the labour movement. Members were recruited mostly from the middle and lower classes. In previous research, it has been pointed out that these popular movements functioned as channels for popular protest against traditional authorities (Lundkvist 1977). Within the popular movements in general, two main ideas were highlighted as essential: brotherhood and the idea of civilization. Ideally, in this system, individuals were organized according to a horizontal structure, rather than a vertical, which

---

[1] Per Erik Tell (2008) counts 522 Swedish military men, seamen, etc. working in the Congo Free State. In addition to these, there were 124 Swedish missionaries working for SMS, but also Swedes working for other international missionary organisations, such as the American Baptist Missionary Union (see also Jenssen-Tusch 1903–1905).

[2] The Congolese historian Georges Nzongala-Ntalaja writes, however: "the transformation of the Congo from Leopold's personal possession to a Belgian colony in 1908, did not represent a major advance for the Congolese people and the quest for freedom and self-determination. For no radical change took place as a result of the action taken by the Belgian parliament ending the King's exclusive rule and territorial rights. The Leopoldian system was replaced by a colonial regime that was just as oppressive, albeit in a less brutal manner. " (Nzongola-Ntalaja 2002: 26).

suggests that its configuration was different than the patriarchal. It is also often stressed that these popular movements worked together in the struggle for universal suffrage, equality and the democratization of the Swedish society in general (Ambjörnsson 1988: 249–266).

For the dissenters, it was urgent to spread the Christian message to all parts of the world. From the very beginning, the Swedish Missionary Society (SMS) sent out missionaries to distant places.[3] One of the most important fields was the Congo Free State. The first Swedish missionary was sent out to the Lower Congo Basin in 1881. Five years later, the Swedes required their first missionary station, Mukimbungu, from American baptists via the British *Livingstone Inland Mission*. Between 1881 and 1908, 124 missionaries, 65 women and 59 men, worked in the Congo for the Swedish Missionary Society (Lundahl and Sjöholm 1911). Around fifteen different protestant missionary societies were established in the region between 1878 and 1907. The Swedish Missionary Society was the second largest missionary organization and played an essential role in relation to other Protestant missions (Stenström 2009: 207–8, 213–14).

Imbalances in the depictions of the encounter

Christian missions in the 19th century have generated an extensive range of detailed historical sources. It is important, however, to keep in mind that colonial archives as well as the records kept by missionaries exclude a great deal of information (Stoler 2002). Considering the existing power relations in missionary communities, there are very few written records emanating from the indigenous and the Christian converts, whereas the archives of missionary organizations provide good possibilities to analyse the encounter from the missionaries' point of view. In addition, women are often excluded in the records, although female missionaries domi-

---

[3] The name of the denomination in Swedish was Svenska Missionsförbundet (SMF). It was founded in 1878. The official name in English was later changed to *The Mission Covenant Church of Sweden*, but in the historical records of the mission, the organization is usually called the *Swedish Missionary Society* (SMS). In this text, the latter abbreviation SMS is used.

nated most missionary organizations in terms of numbers (Cox 2002: 5). This exclusion is also the case when it comes to the encounter between the Congolese people and the Swedish missionaries in this study; both female missionaries and indigenous women are more or less invisible in the archive material as well is in printed publications.

How then can colonial and missionary encounters be described from both sides when the written sources from the indigenous are so few? Some researchers have tried to overcome this problem by using the few written sources that exist in the missionary or colonial archives in which the voices from indigenous people are heard in one way or another (Axelson 1970; Gordon 2014). This approach has also been applied in this study, however, this is not an archival source but a printed publication; the sources representing the Congolese are stories, written by Congolese converts, in *Vildmarkens vår* (Spring of wilderness). This publication was aimed at a Swedish audience, and was printed in 1928. Published material is generally edited material and parts of the text may have been deleted for different reasons, and this is also true in this case according to the preface of the book. The foreword seems to be a kind of apology on the authors' behalf, and it reflects the opinion that the Congolese needed to be reshaped. It is mentioned that the authors "have been under the influence of the Gospel and civilization for only a relatively short time." They have very little education and "great difficulties in communicating their thoughts in written language" (*Vildmarkens vår* 1928: 5).

The missionary press and its associated literature are in general clearly marked by the evangelical culture and reflect the patterns of thought in the missionary discourse. These publications have been considered as a form of propaganda, which was legitimizing and supporting the missionary endeavour. One of the purposes was to spread knowledge about, and increase engagement for the foreign mission; another purpose was to promote funding for missionary work and confirm for the donors that their money was useful (Johnston 2003; Haggis and Allen 2008; Jensz and Acke 2013). It is clear that *Vildmarkens vår* belongs to this literary genre. The problems with these texts are, of course, that they are often adapted to the ideology of the missionary organizations and are structured by genre conventions defined by missionaries (McLisky and Vallgårda 2015: 12). Despite this bias, the various individual stories in *Vildmarkens vår* appear as authentic, each with its own voice. Furthermore, it has been claimed that memoirs of indigenous converts often challenge the conventions of the genre (Van Gent 2015: 243). It should, however, be said that these stories cannot be taken as representative for the Congolese people in general, as they are stories told by converted indigenous teachers.

With regard to the missionaries, there are a wide range of different kinds of historical sources that highlight their thoughts and their attitudes towards the indigenous people. The records consist of official documents such as reports, missionaries' correspondence with their mission associations and minutes from missionary conferences. This category of sources reflects the official policy of the Swedish Missionary Society. The texts clearly emphasize the commitment to evangelization, but principles for religious and moral rules are also discussed. Published letters, articles and books by missionaries belong to the same genre of religious literature as *Vildmarkens vår*, discussed above. The missionaries were obliged to regularly write reports from the missionary field. These letters were edited and published in the missionary periodical *Missionsförbundet*, aiming to promote missionary work. Diaries and private letters offer another kind of depiction of the missionary encounter. These sources give insights into individual experiences of personal meetings with the Congolese people and include descriptions of emotions that do not fit in the official narrative of the mission.

To sum up, the depictions of the first encounters between Congolese villagers and Swedish missionaries are described in disparate types of sources: The diaries used were written parallel to or shortly after the events. They were not intended for publication, instead they reflect personal experiences and reflections. Some published letters by missionaries have also been used, and these are presumably adjusted to the genre conventions of pious literature and its purpose to give an image of the successes of the mission. The narratives of the Congolese converts are memories, of which some are written several years after the events. Moreover, these have been edited and published, aiming for a Swedish audience who were supporting the mission. Regarding the missionaries, we have thus access to various stories from different sources, while the written material by the indigenous is limited to one secondary source. Despite of these disparities, a comparison between these sources could be fruitful, since the missionaries and the converts depict the encounter from different perspectives. Even if the stories in *Vildmarkens vår* are edited, they appear still as genuine. By paying attention to the variations between the narratives, and by keeping the different genre coventions in mind, a more complex picture can be revealed.

The character of the encounter

A fundamental question concerns the overall character of the early encounter between missionaries and Congolese people. What then can be said about its character? One answer to that question is that it depends on what case you investigate and from which perspective you look at it. The historiography of missionary encounters includes narratives of cultural imperialism, missionary offensive and indigenous resistance, as well as mutual exchange, openness and friendship (Cox 2002: 14). Highlighted below are three different cases, which indicate that the encouter may be interpreted in different ways. The first include the contacts between European and African cultures in the early modern era, which can be seen as an example of amalgamation of Christian and indigenous religious beliefs in the Kongo Kingdom. This example is followed by two descriptions of the first contacts between Swedish missionaries and Congolese villagers in the late 1880s, as they are depicted by congolese converts and the missionaries, respectively. Although these events occurred during the same time period, their character are rather different.

Early missions and hybridization

There is a long history of Christian evangelization in the lower Congo. As early as in 1491, the sovereign of the Kongo Kingdom, Nzinga Nkuwu, was baptized by Portugese missionaries (Axelsson

1971: 37). Contacts were established between the Kongo Kingdom and Rome, and Kongo continued to receive Catholic missionaries until the mid 1800s (Covington-Ward 2007: 75). In the mid-17th century, Italian Capuchin missionaries arrived.

Concerning cultural encounters, the term hybridization has become a concept of central importance. Originally used as a biological term, hybridization means a cross-breeding of two different species, the result of the hybridization is something new and different. In a transferred sense, it refers to "transcultural forms within the contact zone produced by colonization" (Ashcroft, 1998: 118). The term has been associated with the work of Homi Bhabha, who has used the concept in order to describe authentic, but ambivalent, non-western encounters with imperialism (Bhabha 1994: 38).

Of special interest, in terms of hybridization, is the prophet Kimpa Vita, also known as Dona Beatrice. She was the creator of the Antonian movement in the 17th century, which used Christian symbols and emanated from traditional Kongan cultural roots. Kimpa Vita believed that she was possessed by the spirit of the popular Catholic saint St. Anthony of Padua. In her belief, Jesus, Mary and other Christian saints originated from the Congo. Kimpa Vita strove to give the Congolese people dignity and self-respect by adapting the Christian faith to African conditions, but she also criticized the pope and the Catholic Church and its dogmas: "We black people have saints too [...] but the white man won't let us. The Church does everything to hamper us. So we have no use for its baptism, nor for its marriage, or for its confession, or its prayers, or its good deeds" (Quotation in Axelson 1970: 142).

Kimpa Vita was burned at the stake for heresy in 1706, at the instigation of the Capuchin Franciscan Friar missionaries (Brockman 2015). Nevertheless, the ideas of Kimpa Vita remained among the people in the Congo, later appearing in various messianic cults. There are several similarities between Kimpa Vita and the preaching of Simon Kimbangu, whose religious revival was an amalgamation of Christian and indigenous beliefs, and appeared two centuries later (Covington-Ward 2007). The examples of Kimpa Vita's Antonian movement and Kimbanguism, and possibly even the early contacts between Europeans and the Congolese in general, might be seen as early examples of cultural reciprocity and interpreted in terms of hybridity and creolization (Lingna Nafafé 2012). However, it must be noted that Kimpa Vita was, in the end, executed by the Capuchins and Kimbangu's revivalist movement was condemned by the both the Catholic and Protestant missionaries and considered by the colonial authorities to be a political problem that might provoke an insurrection. Kimbangu was sentenced to life imprisonment and died after thirty years of captivity in 1951 (Covington-Ward 2007: 81–4; Stenström 2009: 232–5).

First meetings in Kibunzi

A second wave of Christian mission began in the 1870s, just before the arrival of H. M. Stanley. This time, Protestants were also among those evangelizing. The first actors were the British Livingstone Inland Mission (LIM) in 1878, followed by the Baptist Missionary Society of England (BMS) and the Swedish Missionary Society, both in 1881 (Covington-Ward 2007: 252).

The first encounters between the Swedish missionaries and the people of the village of Kibunzi in 1887 was described by both a Congolese man, Eliza Nkambulu, and a Swedish missionary, Johan Nilsson. The people were very surprised when they saw white men with a large entourage and many burdens approaching. The first "white men" who arrived in the village were, according to Nkambulu, Karl Johan Pettersson, a veteran among the Swedish missionaries who also spoke the local tongue, and Nilsson. Nkambulu tells further that as the group of white men came closer, the women and children ran into the houses and shut the doors, because they had heard that these strange men were particularly powerful in witchcraft and might capture their shadows and bring them to their country (Nkambulu 1928: 50). Nilsson also mentions the fear of the people in his diary (Nilsson 1887–08–05). According to Nilsson's diary, however, it were he and Henning Skarp who arrived in the beginning of August, while Pettersson arrived on September 24, accompanied with twenty workers from Luango (Nilsson 1887–08–05 and 1887–09–24).

Nkambulu relates further that, when the white men had pitched their tents, the oldest men in the village approached to watch them and ask where they came from and where they were heading. Messages were sent to the neighbouring villages. Altogether, six chiefs and their men arrived the following day to negotiate with Pettersson and Nilsson. Missionary Pettersson had a servant from Tundua who knew a little English, and he served as interpreter. The missionaries used English, and the servant translated into the local language *Kikongo* (Nkambulu 1928: 50–51). "The white men explained that they had come to build in their land, and that their task was to teach people of the word of God, teach reading and writing and to introduce better morals in the country. They did not want to 'eat people', nor do them any harm" (Nkambulu 1928: 52). The chiefs went aside to consider. Some of them were willing to welcome the strangers; others were afraid that they would buy slaves and destroy them all. In the end, the missionaries got permission to stay and to build houses in the village. After this agreement, the missionaries distributed gifts to the chiefs: cloths, blankets, beads, metal spoons, knives and some other things that were new and strange to them. The chiefs expressed their wish to make the ties of friendship strong and solid (Nkambulu 1928: 51–53).

Nkambulu describes the chiefs as in a position of authority, negotiating with the white newcomers and offering them land. But, according to a state regulation, every square meter of land belonged to the Belgian king in person. Thus, it appears that both the local chiefs and the colonial administration considered themselves entitled to transfer the land. The missionaries seem to have ascertained that they had support from both parties (Stenström 2002: 67). These negotiations with the chiefs are not at all mentioned in Nilsson's diary, it is not clear why. Instead, Nilsson refers to his visits to the surrounding villages to evangelize, the purchase of a temporary house and the beginning of construction work for the new missionary post. He also describes in his diary how they very soon started to arrange worship services. He writes that "one of our men", a convert who accompanied them, preached to about fifteen people on the first Sunday (Nilsson 1887-08-07). Besides from practical issues and events, Nilsson is often concerned about his state of mind. Some days, he seems to be filled with optimism and confidence; but there are also more examples of pessimism and self-reproach. Notations such as "My spirit is not satisfied. How to glorify God among this people? Days come and go, and little gets done." (Nilsson 1888–08–26) or "I am like a man without strength, like an extinct volcano." (Nilsson 1888–09–29) are frequently occurring. On New Years Eve 1888, he writes: "When I have seen my many weaknesses, I have sometimes almost felt ready to crawl under the earth, never to be seen again" (Nilsson 1888–12–31). Statements like these, that reveal doubts and vulnerability, were of course not possible in the official writings. The genre of the missionary texts instead emphasized the successes of the missionary project and described the missionaries as heroes.

In the missionary press and related publications of SMS, missionary Karl Johan Pettersson appears to be the greatest pioneer and a true hero. According to Nkambulu, he was highly respected in Kibunzi. It is not unlikely that Nkambulu's positive image of Pettersson had been influenced by his good reputation. Nkambulu records that Pettersson was called *Tata Mayendo* (= Father Beard) by the locals, because of his big beard (Nkambulu 1928: 49). He further writes that "Missionary Pettersson's conduct among us was like a chieftain, as a true Nsundi-prince. He loved his people. He was patient and merciful. He helped the orphans. He took care of those who were doomed to be killed by witchcraft or poison. He devised building plots to the persecuted and homeless, on his own land." (Nkambulu 1928: 58). The villagers in Kibunzi thought that the missionary Pettersson was the chief of the Nazulumongo-family, who had died long ago, and was then resurrected and returned to visit his relatives (Nkambulu 1928: 49–50, 54).

According to several narratives in *Vildmarkens vår*, the arrival of white people was interpreted in terms of religious beliefs. It was believed that the Europeans were in fact dead men who, after their death, had changed skin (like some snakes) and had therefore become white.[4] Others believed that they were animals that "ate people", took away the life force, and caused death (Makundu 1928: 28). Even if the Congolese initially looked upon the white

---

[4] Ragnar Widman discusses these beliefs, that dead people became white, in his dissertation on the belief systems in the lower Zaire (Congo), see Further Widman 1979: 100, 113–116.

people with fear due to indigenous religious beliefs, some of them later turned to interpreting the missionaries as their ancestors who had returned to the world. It was, however, not until the arrival of white women in the village that the people really believed that the white people were born like other human beings (Nkambulu 1928: 57–58). In February 1889, the first Swedish missionary woman arrived in Kibunzi. Nkambulu comments on this and explains that one reason why the people in those days believed that the white people were resurrected from the dead was because there were no women among them. "But then, came the first woman—it was Mama Mina [Wilhelmina Svensson]—to help the men to cook and to teach in the school". A couple of days after her arrival in Kibunzi, Mina writes in her diary: "The women have already taken their white sister under consideration, they are curiously watching every movement I make. In their opinion, I'm probably worth seeing. I wish they knew you, Lord Jesus, as their Saviour!" (Svensson 1889–02–16).

In Nkambulu's narrative, the encounter seems to be characterized by reciprocity and friendship. Also according to Nilsson's writings, a spirit of benevolence and respect towards the villagers in general can be discerned. He has, however, a strong aversion to their religion and the manners and customs of the villagers, which he did not understand at all. Complaints of people drumming and dancing are constantly repeated in his writings: "It causes pain in my heart to see and hear the miserable lives of the people. They have brought noise throughout the day" (Nilsson 1887–08–18). Nilsson writes that he went to the village Kiazi, where he got to see the *bangangas* (he uses the word "fetish priests") giving medicine to the people.[5] He found it "both ridiculous and disgusting." (Nilsson 1887–10–09). He cites a poem or hymn, commencing with the words: "It is dark in the valleys of Congo, it is dark in people's hearts…" (Nilsson 1887–09–04).

It is obvious that the missionaries were just as influenced by *their* beliefs as the Congolese. In accordance with the rhetoric in

---

5   *Banganga* is a Kikongo word used to describe priests or healers in the Congolese traditional religion. See Axelson 1971: 12; Covington-Ward 2007: 254, note 36.

the missionary press, their view of the world was generally based on dichotomies such as light–darkness, Christianity–paganism and civilization–barbarism. The missionaries were driven by their vocation and had come to the Congo because they were convinced that the people, deeply sunken in paganism and sin, had to be saved. While the Congolese saw the Europeans and their customs, such as photography and reading, with great suspicion, the Swedish missionaries looked upon the *bangangas*, religious rituals, drumming and dancing with disgust. The missionary Karl Theodor Andersson reports that there is "a complete pagan darkness in these regions. European culture, civilization and education are quite unknown. One of Africa's greatest curses is the cunning fetish priests who seduce the people to eat poison. My heart cried when I saw this" (MF 1889: 80–84, letter dated Diadia 1889–03–25). The missionaries interpreted the world from a pietistic perspective; it was possible to hate paganism but still love the "heathen". The dividing line went between Christians and non-Christians, not between races (Claesson 2001: 209; Odén 2012: 71).

It appears like both parties characterize the encounter between missionaries and villagers in Kibunzi as interactive, and not in terms of missionary offensive and indigenous resistance. Instead, an image of the missionaries' dependence on the benevolence of the chiefs and the people emerges. As Porter has concluded, the missionaries were not automatically welcome; permanent acceptance could be won only by negotiations and acceptance (Porter 2004: 321). Furthermore, one can draw the conclusion that religion was crucial for both parties' perception of the other, whom they interpreted according to their religious beliefs. According to at least some Congolese interpretations, the Europeans were returning deceased ancestors. According to the pietistic worldview of the missionaries, the Congolese were urgently in need of salvation.

Conflicts at Diadia

In August 1888, the missionaries Karl Johan Pettersson and Henning Skarp led the expedition for SMS's third missionary station. The founding of Diadia was, from the very beginning, more fraught with conflict than the founding of Kibunzi. Skarp's young servant, Abeli Kiananwa (born in ca. 1870), reported that they were met by armed men when they approached the village in August 1888. A respected man, Nsiama Kungienda, was guiding them. When the chief from a nearby village explained that the foreigners were "God's white men", they were let into Diadia and were offered shelter (Kiananwa 1928: 79–80). Skarp writes in his diary that they first met a man who told them, that the villagers were going to fight against them, because of fear: "All the men were standing with loaded guns, but they calmed down when they saw that we were unarmed. One of the chiefs welcomed us, but he could not give us any promises to stay, since there were several chiefs in the village."[6] The following day gifts were exchanged. After negotiations with the chiefs, the missionaries were allowed to establish themselves in the village. Henning Skarp reports in *Missionsförbundet*, official organ for SMS, that the missionaries often suffered from fever and other diseases, and that the villagers took care of them (MF 1889: 7, letter dated Diadia 1888–10–22). However, relations between the missionaries and the local people, particularly the *bangangas*, were complicated. Skarp reports in May 1889 that it seems like this "tribe" has a more powerful character and a greater self-confidence than the indigenous in other villages (MF 1889: 93, letter dated Diadia 1889–05–28). The villagers were especially hostile against Pettersson, who was considered practicing sorcery. He was forced to leave the village. After a smallpox outbreak in the autumn of 1889, the antagonism between the missionaries and their antagonists in the village developed into violent unrest. The men from Diadia and the surrounding villages agreed to kill the white men (Kiananwa 1928: 84). Kinanwa asked his master if they should leave the village because of the threat, but Skarp told him not to fear: "God himself will protect us, we shall only believe in him, he will guard us, and no one will be able to hurt us" (Kiananwa 1928: 85). Nevertheless, the missionaries called for military protection from the colonial army. Skarp also sent a message to Johan Nilsson at Kibunzi, asking him to succour them. On the way to Diadia, Nilsson was anxious, but at

---

[6] Henning Skarp's diary 1888–08–08, cited by Nilsson 1888–11–14.

the arrival he became aware of the fact that only two of the chiefs who were against the missionaries, not the entire village (Nilsson 1889–10–24). The following night, a violent thunderstorm passed over the village. The missionaries saw this as a divine intervention; they were not attacked because of the heavy rain (Kiananwa 1928: 85–86). "Bula Matadi" and his soldiers arrived the next day and started fighting against the villagers.[7] Because of Skarp's appeal, the villagers were not killed, but the soldiers looted whatever they could find in the villages: goats, pigs, chickens, household items and food. They left the next morning. After a few days, a Belgian-officer with 24 soldiers returned with orders to imprison the rebellious chiefs and bring them to court. If this failed, they would take people's possessions and burn the village. The people fled, and the soldiers took their weapons and other belongings. One of the rebellious chiefs was imprisoned. Kiananwa tells that the armed conflict claimed several deaths (Kiananwa 1928: 86–7). Henning Skarp commented on the incidents in a report in the periodical *Missionsförbundet*: "This was painful, but we have no right to oppose, for rulers do not bear the sword for no reason. They are God's servants, agents of wrath to bring punishment on the wrongdoer." (MF 1889: 38–40, letter dated Diadia 1889–11–26).[8]

The violent incidents in Diadia are depicted in Nilsson's and Skarp's diaries as well as in Skarp's report in *Missionsförbundet* and in Kiananwa's memory in *Vildmarkens vår*, published several decades later. Kiananwa's description of the sequence of the events is, however, strikingly consistent with the two diaries in the details. Kiananwa emphasizes his fear and his own vulnerable position as allied with the missionaries. It is worth noting that his story is the only one that explicitly states that several people were killed. The missionaries seem to be have decided not to use violence themselves. Skarp told them not to shoot anyone, "but if necessary, only in the legs" (Kiananwa 1928: 85). Obviously, also the missionaries felt threatened and afraid, which is confirmed by the

---

[7] *Bula Matadi* (or Bula Matari) referred originally to H. M. Stanley, meaning "the crusher of rocks" and refers to his brutal methods. It was also the indigenous people's name for the white men of the colonial state in general.

[8] This is a reference to Romans 13: 20.

fact that they asked for military protection. This missionary fear can, however, only be inferred implicitly.

In his report in *Missionsförbundet*, Skarp refers to the Bible, stating "rulers do not bear the sword for no reason". Still, his description of the violent incidents reveals a sense of ambivalance; since he also writes that "We have always been very reluctant to engage the men of the state to sort out our affairs with the indigenous" (MF 1889: 38, letter dated Diadia 1889–11–26). The evangelical rhetorics is even more evident in a later comment on the conflicts in Diadia, in the same periodical, by the missionary Magnus Rangström (who was not present at the incidents): "Their evil conspiracy was lost, and paganism must give way to the breaking light. In the past, they attacked us with all possible means, but now they stand helpless [...] It is now our turn to attack, not with lies or with external force, like them, but with the saving Gospel of God" (MF 1890: 197, letter dated Diadia 1890–07–04). In this statement, no ambivalce can be seen. Instead, this is the rhetorics of combat.

***

The two latter stories, concerning the founding of the missionary stations Kibunzi and Diadia, show that the missionary encounter could include the exchange of gifts, negotiations and displays of kindness—and perhaps even friendship—as well as fear and violence. In general, the descriptions in the periodical *Missionsförbundet* are optimistic and unambiguously tell the story of the missionaries' struggle against paganism, while the missionary diaries and the narratives in *Vildmarkens vår* reflect contradictory aspects on the encounter. These narratives also appear more nuanced. For example, in some of the depictions from Diadia it is clearly described that there were different attitudes to the missionaries among the chiefs. It was discussed whether or not they should be received. In Kiananwa's story, it becomes also clear that the people separated "God's white" (the missionaries) from other white people in the Congo. Needless to say, resistance against the missionaries is not expressed in any of the written sources available. Moreover, very few women are mentioned. The main actors are the male missionaries, the male chiefs and, to some extent, the male converts. The arrival of the female Swedish missionaries is admittedly discussed, but Congolese women are hardly mentioned at all. It is, however, noted that the women in Diadia fled from Bula Matadi and that the soldiers tried to abduct a woman from the village (MF 1889: 38, letter dated 1889–11–26; Nilsson 1889–11–09).

Furthermore, it is evident that the encounter was characterized by strong emotions on both sides. A general observation is that emotions in colonial mission contexts were often characterized by polysemy and ambivalence (McLisky and Vallgårda 2015: 10). Initially, fear seems to have been a dominating emotion among the Congolese people. There are plenty of examples in *Vildmarkens vår*: Makundo relates the rumour that said that missionaries took children, especially boys, in order to teach them to sing hymns and read. It was believed that their square houses must have been built by magic (Makundu 1928: 30). When people heard that the white people were nearby, they began to build small huts well hidden in the woods, to conceal themselves and their possessions (Ndibu 1928: 15–16). Nbidu recalls that when a white man finally arrived, he hid to avoid seeing him and hear him speak. His heart beat hard, and all his body trembled with fear. When he, despite all his attempts to avoid them, was forced to look at a white person, he tried with all his might to dispel all of his aversion and fear of seeing a white person (Ndibu 1928: 22). Incidents like these are also commented on in the writings of the missionaries. Johan Nilsson writes in his diary, under the title *Sad*: "When I arrived at the market place, the majority of the people became frightened and tried to escape. I was later informed that the people thought I was Bula Matadi Stanley, who had passed the other day, insulting the people cruelly" (Nilsson 1887–04–13). Missionary Andersson reflects "We, white men, must be terrible creatures in their eyes, since they hide when we arrive. But when you socialize on a daily basis, it becomes something else" (MF 1889: 84, letter dated 1889–03–25). The missionaries were also afraid at times. Feelings of vulnerability and discomfort characterized Svensson's experience as the first white woman in Kibunzi. It is also hard to imagine that fear was an insignificant factor when the colonial army was sent for in Diadia, even if Skarp told Kiananwa otherwise. However, feelings of fear are not very often reflected in the missionaries' diaries, instead, several diaries frequently reveal feelings of discouragement, often in combination with self-reproach, as previously mentioned.

Another reflection on the encounters is the significance of indigenous actors. In the missionaries' diaries and reports, it appears as if the missionaries were alone when they arrived in Kibunzi. However, according to Nkambulu, they were accompanied by a whole caravan of carriers when they came. In addition, it was a native speaker, their Congolese servant, who preached to the people. A notation in Nilsson's diary reveals further that on one Sunday, "Ntambu was leading the prayer, Pettersson was preaching in English, with Nsiku as an interpreter, and finally Nsenga closed the service with a prayer" (Nilsson 1887–10–09). Kiananwa mentions that Henning Skarp did not know the language yet (Kiananwa 1928: 80). The missionaries were undoubtedly highly dependent on the indigenous; as porters, servants, workers, guides, interpreters and evangelists and these facts challenge the image of the solitary heroic missionary (Porter 2004: 327). Instead, the image of the vulnerable missionary can be glimpsed here. This is most evident in the fact that the missionaries fell ill and were cared for by the villagers of Diadia. This dependence of support from indigenous people is hardly explicitly discussed in the official writings of the mission, such as the published letters in the missionary press. It has, however, been assumed that missionary dependence on the skills, knowledge and empathy of the indigenous people were more openly admitted in early stages of missionary operations than in the later stages (Van Gent 2015: 244).

Ambivalence and contradictions within the missionary encounter

When summing up the empirical examples above, it is clear that a reading of the records reveals a complex image, with numerous ambiguous conflicts and contradictions concerning the role of the missionary.

The missionaries and colonial power

What makes this case different from colonial settings discussed by Porter, Cox, Price, and others is that Sweden was not an imperial state with its own colonies. Nonetheless, the relations between missionaries and representatives for the colonial state were still complicated. As seen in the example of Diadia, missionaries could, and did sometimes request armed protection from the state army. Henning Skarp's statement after the violent military intervention in Diadia reveals, in retrospect, a naïve confusion of regarding God's protection and the dreaded Bula Matadi. SMS was dependent on the colonial administration for permission to work in the country and to gain access to land and services. The mission's correspondence with the colonial officers in the Congo sometimes contains an ingratiating tone and readiness for cooperation. In other situations, individual missionaries expressed criticism against the colonial state's abuse and oppression of the population. When the Congo Reform Association first tried to sway international opinion against king Leopold's cruel rule in 1904, they based their critique on the testimonies from missionaries to a high degree, as can be seen in the *Casement Report* (Slade 1955; Lagergren 1970; Hochschild 2000). The SMS-missionary Ernst Storm signed the ecumenical petition against king Leopold in 1904 as an official representative of the SMS. Due to Storm's signing of the protest, other missionaries had to take over his contacts with the colonial authorities (SMS Missionary Conferences 1907–07–04).

The relations between the three parties, the colonial state, the missionaries and the indigenous population, were complex. There are examples of both common interests and conflicts between the government and missionaries, as well as between people and missionaries (Covington-Ward 2007: 76, 99–100). However, the criticism that missionaries and others targeted against colonial rule was directed at the cruel and inhumane *methods* used, and not colonialism itself. This has been pointed out by many but should still be emphasized (Said 1994: 176; Holmberg 1988: 517; Stenström 2009: 222). Thus, one could presumably agree with Beck's description of the missionaries' situation as torn between the idea of brotherhood and the imperial agenda.

Civilization and brotherhood

Civilizing the indigenous population was a part of colonization. It seems as if all European actors shared the same civilizational agenda, at least on an ideological level (Njoku and Korieh 2007: 3). The Swedish missionary C. W. Lembke writes that the Congolese people, through the missionaries, was "provided with knowledge about state laws and regulations to quite a considerable degree, which are very helpful in the suppression of the unrighteous and cruel pagan customs and practices in favour of civilization" (Lembke 1911: 388). The structures of thought that involved a sharp distinction between the civilized, Europe, and the primitive, Africa, were obvious to the majority of the missionaries. On the other hand, the missionaries had been raised in a popular movement with strong emancipatory features. The idea of universal brotherhood was central to the evangelical structure of thought in that evangelism was infused with a democratic tone. The indigenous population contained potential brothers and sisters, if they became Christians. At the same time, the missionaries still considered the indigenous people to be in need of control and education, and they were often treated like children. Despite the potential for brotherhood, it is hard not to come to the conclusion that the encounter was on unequal terms.

Within the mission, there was both a contradiction and confusion between the Christian ideal of brotherhood and love on the one hand, and the imperialistic task to civilize "inferior savages" on the other. In retrospect, it is easier to see that this position "between universal egalitarian ideals and an exploitative imperial presence" (Cox 2002: 6) might have constituted the very essence of the missionary's contradictory role. The paradox of universal equality and deep differences seems to have been a blind spot in the missionary mind.

Humble origins and white supremacy

Furthermore, the tension between the missionaries' often very simple background and their position of authority in the missionary field was in a way a paradox. The missionaries in SMS often came from poor circumstances in the countryside, or belonged to the lower middle class. Out of the 124 SMS missionaries working in the Congo Free State until 1908, nearly a half of them (61) had their origins in the rural peasant or other group. Another third (39) came from the families of workers or craftsmen. Only two female missionaries can be considered to have belonged to an educated middle or upper class. As Europeans in the Congo, the missionaries inevitably, and by definition, became part of the prevalent circumstances favouring white supremacy, which was a role that often made them feel uncomfortable. The first missionaries who were sent to Congo were hardly prepared for what they would meet. Almost none of them had any higher education, except from the missionary training courses. Moreover, practical skills in farming, construction and carpentry were requested. Among the evangelical dissenters in general, the foremost qualification for missionary work was the experience of conversion, not formal education. "Plain men from forge and farm, well read in the Bible and full of faith", were preferred over university-educated men (Sidenvall 2009: 41; Price 2008: 19–20). However, SMS subsequently requested medical and educational skills, to meet the needs of mission work.

The position of the female missionaries appears to have been even more complex. It is often argued that missionary work provided an opportunity for women to step outside of the prescribed gender patterns of the time (Okkenhaug 2003: 8). Despite the fact that they soon constituted the majority of the missionaries and carried out work close to the people, their formal influence was limited. Missionary women were primarily engaged in activities that did not challenge the prevailing gender order: teaching, orphanages, and health care. Thus, dual power hierarchies can be observed interacting with each other. As white Europeans, they were superior to the indigenous, but as women, they were subordinate to the male missionaries.

Optimism and despair

The early missionaries encountered a world that was harsh and alien. They were driven by a personal calling, a divine task to preach to and convert foreign peoples. The soon return of Christ was stressed in the revivalist communitities "at home" and it was a fact that made the missionary work very urgent. The importance of a personal conversion and close relation with God, the absolute authority of the Bible and an universalistic view of mankind were other fundamental ideas among revivalists. Strong emotions—remorse and pity as well as exitement and enthusiasm—played a significant role in protestant revivalism. Initially, the missionaries were filled with a deep sense of optimism and confidence. This feeling risked giving way to pessimism when they failed in their work or when rapid conversion did not occur. It is likely that the missionaries were not mentally prepared for the totally different reality they met. The encounter was sometimes shocking and posed physical challenges in addition to cultural and psychological ones. It has been suggested that oscillation between naive optimism and darker pessimism was a pattern that was to become typical of missionary culture. In the first place, self-introspection about the source of failure in their evangelization work often pointed to themselves (Price 2008: 74). As mentioned, the diary of Johan Nilsson provides a revealing insight into this aspect of missionary culture. These kinds of feelings of shortcomings, loneliness and anxiety are expressed in several diaries and private letters, while the official reports in missionary press and literature maintain the spirit of optimism.

***

On the basis of the many contradictions highlighted above, one could describe the missionary position as "in-between". Ambiguities existed within the missionary organization as a whole, and presumably also inside each individual missionary. The fact that the indigenous people's voice is absent from the records is a methodological problem, which is hard to overcome. Nonetheless, one can easily point out ambiguities among the Congolese Christians, which are similar to those of the missionaries. Many of the indigenous teachers or evangelists who are authors in *Vildmarkens vår* had been adopted by the missionaries and raised at the missionary stations. This group of converts generally played key roles as intermediaries between the mission and the local society (Price 2008: 60; Lindmark 2006: 120). Converting to Christianity meant, however, dissociating oneself from one's original family and culture, and this process was often filled with conflict. As seen in the example of Diadia, Kiananwa feared the threats against the missionaries with whom he was associated. The converts had their origins in the Congolese culture, but also within the culture of the missionaries. Their position was just as ambivalent as the missionaries'. As Ashcroft has expressed it, the relations were "ambivalent because the colonized subject is never simply and completely opposed to the colonizer [...] ambivalence suggests that complicity and resistance exists in a fluctuating relation within the colonial subject" (Ashcroft 1998: 12–13). In this particular case, one could say that both the missionaries and the converts were implicated in the ambivalence of colonial discourse.

Concluding remarks

In this essay, only a few examples from the earliest encounters between Swedish missionaries and the indigenous people in the Congo have been presented. These examples cannot be seen as representative for the relations between the SMS missionaries and the population of the Lower Congo. The character of the missionary encounter varied depending on the historical, political and geographical context. One assumption is, however, that the relations between the two groups and the missionary discourse might have changed over time. The pioneer missionaries seem to have shared the same living conditions as the local population to a much higher degree than their later successors (Stenström 2002: 138). However, the missionary enterprise became increasingly institutionalized and formalized, and later included more detailed regulations regarding the Congolese converts. In the minutes of the later SMS Missionary conferences, there seems to be very little evidence of the initial spirit of reciprocity and negotiation with the indigenous. A couple of decades after the arrival of the missionaries, some published texts on the mission reveal an entirely different mentality in which the differences between Europeans and Africans are much more stressed than in the early writings (Ollén 1919; Palmær 1931). In these texts, the differences between the missionaries and the indigenous population are explained in terms of race, whereas, at an earlier stage, these discrepancies were instead explained by religious and cultural disparity. If this discursive change can be seen as a parallel to what Price refers to as the "closing of the missionary mind" requires further investigation.

One should, however, keep in mind that missionary texts contain many different—and sometimes contradictory—voices and ideas, and that dichotomies and stereotypes are part of much more complex structures of thought (Gregersen 2010: 261). When discourses and relations are examined at different levels—ideological, political, as well as individual—and from different perspectives, the results become less predetermined. In her recent study of female missionaries in Tunisia and Swedish Lapland, Catarina Lundström concludes that differences in religion and culture were the starting points of these meetings between the Swedish missionaries and the Tunisians or the Sami, respectively. However, by using a personal and friendly approach, the encounter housed a potential change of relations. Sometimes the dichotomy between "us" and "them" was completely dissolved. Sometimes it was reinforced (Lundström 2015: 213). The same can be said about the encounters between the Swedish missionaries and the Congolese villagers. Once again, a contradictory and ambivalent picture emerges.

Bibliography

Archival and unpublished sources

Nilsson, Carl Johan. National Archives, Stockholm, Archive of Svenska Missionsförbundet-Missionskyrkan, Privata dagböcker [Private diaries] vol. 1:1, diary of Carl Johan Nilsson.

Svensson, Wilhelmina. National Archives, Stockholm, Archive of Svenska Missionsförbundet-Missionskyrkan, Privata dagböcker [Private diaries] vol. 1:3, diary of Mina (Wilhelmina) Svensson.

SMS Missionary Conferences. National Archives, Stockholm, Archive of Svenska Missionsförbundet-Missionskyrkan, Huvudarkivet [Main archive], Kongomissionen/Yttre missionen [Archive of the Congo Mission], vol. 146, "Svenska missionskonferensen i Kongo" [SMS Missionary conferences in the Congo].

Printed sources

Kiananwa, Abeli. 1928. "Några minnen från Diadias första tid". In *Vildmarkens vår: skildringar från Kongo av infödda lärare*, 79–87. Stockholm: Svenska missionsförbundet.

Lembke, C. W. 1911. "Missionens förhållande till Kongostaten". In *Dagbräckning i Kongo: Svenska Missionsförbundets Kongomission: illustrerade skildringar av Kongomissionärer*, eds. Jakob Emanuel Lundahl and Wilhelm Sjöholm, 384–389. Stockholm: Förbundet.

Lundahl, Jakob Emanuel & Wilhelm Sjöholm, eds. 1911. *Dagbräckning i Kongo: Svenska Missionsförbundets Kongomission: illustrerade skildringar av Kongomissionärer*. Stockholm: Förbundet.

Makundu, Tito. 1928. "Våra fäders avgudadyrkan och förhållandena nu". In *Vildmarkens vår: skildringar från Kongo av infödda lärare*, 61–78. Stockholm: Svenska missionsförbundet.

Missionsförbundet (MF) (Periodical, official organ for SMS).

Ndibu, Josefi. 1928. "Mina tankar förr och nu om de vita människorna". In *Vildmarkens vår: skildringar från Kongo av infödda lärare*, 12–26. Stockholm: Svenska missionsförbundet.

Nkambulu, Eliza. 1928. "Några minnen från Kibunzi stations första tid". In *Vildmarkens vår: skildringar från Kongo av infödda lärare*, 49–60. Stockholm: Svenska missionsförbundet.

Ollén, J. M. 1919. *Svenska missionsbragder: skildringar ur svenskt missionsliv i Afrika och Asien. D. 1, Ostafrika och Kongo*. Stockholm: Svenska missionsförbundet.

Palmær, Georg, ed. 1931. *I fetischmannens spår: förr och nu i Kongo.* Stockholm: Svenska missionsförbundet.

Vildmarkens vår: skildringar från Kongo av infödda lärare. 1928. Stockholm: Svenska missionsförbundet.

Secondary sources

Ambjörnsson, Ronny. 1988. *Den skötsamme arbetaren: idéer och ideal i ett norrländskt sågverkssamhälle 1880–1930.* Stockholm: Carlsson.

Ashcroft, Bill. 1998. *Key concepts in post-colonial studies.* London: Routledge.

Axelson, Sigbert. 1970. *Culture confrontation in the Lower Congo: from the old Congo kingdom to the Congo independent state with special reference to the Swedish missionaries in the 1880's and 1890's.* Diss. Uppsala: Uppsala University.

Axelson, Sigbert. 1971. *Kulturkonfrontation i Nedre Kongo.* Uppsala: Tvåväga.

Beck, Roger B. 2007. "All things to All People: Christian Missionaries in Early Nineteeth Century South Africa." In *Missions, states, and European expansion in Africa*, eds. Chima J. Korieh and Raphael Chijioke Njoku, 11–34, New York: Routledge.

Bhabha, Homi K. 1994. *The location of culture.* London: Routledge.

Brockman, Norbert C. "Kimpa Vita", In *Dictionary of African Christian Biography*, http://www.dacb.org/stories/congo/kimpa_vita.html (2015-06-18)

Casement Report. 1904. https://archive.org/details/CasementReport (2015-10-25)

Claesson, Anna Maria. 2001. *Kinesernas vänner: en analys av missionens berättelse som ideologi och utopi.* Diss. Lund: Lund University.

Cowington-Ward, Yolanda. 2007. "Threatening gestures, immoral bodies. The intersection of church, state, and Kongo performance in the Belgian Congo." In *Missions, states, and European expansion in Africa*, eds. Chima J. Korieh and Raphael Chijioke Njoku, 73–100, New York: Routledge.

Cox, Jeffrey. 2002. *Imperial fault lines: Christianity and colonial power in India, 1818–1940.* Stanford, Calif. : Stanford University Press.

Gordon, David M. 2014. "Interpreting Documentary Sources on the Early History of the Congo Free State: The Case of Ngongo Luteta's Rise and Fall.", *History in Africa*, 41: 5–33.

Granqvist, Raoul J. 2008. "Med Gud och kung Leopold i ryggen: En berättelse om svensk mission i Kongo.", *Ord & Bild* 2008 (2): 98–117.

Gregersen, Malin. 2010. *Fostrande förpliktelser: representationer av ett missionsuppdrag i Sydindien under 1900-talets första hälft.* Diss. Lund: Lund university.

Haggis, Jane and Margaret Allen. 2008. "Imperial Emotions: Affective Communities of Mission in British Protestant Women's Missionary Publications c. 1880–1920". *Journal of Social History*, 41(3): 691–716.

Hochschild, Adam. 2000. *Kung Leopolds vålnad: om girighet, terror och hjältemod i det koloniala Afrika*. Stockholm: Ordfront.

Holmberg, Åke. 1988. *Världen bortom västerlandet. [1], Svensk syn på fjärran länder och folk från 1700-talet till första*. Göteborg: Kungl. Vetenskaps- och vitterhets-samhället.

Jenssen-Tusch, Harald. 1902–1905. *Skandinaver i Congo: svenske, norske og danske Mænds og kvinders virksomhed i den uafhængige Congostat*. Köbenhavn.

Jensz, Felicity and Hanna Acke. 2013." The Form and Function of Nineteenth-Century Missionary Periodicals: Introduction". *Church History*, 82: 368–373.

Johnston, Anna. 2003. *MissionaryWriting and Empire, 1800–1860*. Cambridge: Cambridge University Press.

Lagergren, David. 1970. *Mission and state in the Congo: a study of the relations between Protestant missions and the Congo independant state authorities with special reference to the Equator district, 1885–1903*. Diss. Uppsala: Uppsala University.

Lindmark, Daniel. 2006. "Pietism and Colonialism: Swedish Schooling in Eighteenth-century Sápmi", *Acta Borealia: A Nordic Journal of Circumpolar Societies*, 23 (2): 116–129.

Lingna Nafafé, José. 2012. "Europe in Africa and Africa in Europé: Rethinking postcolonial space, cultural encounters and hybridity", *European Journal of Social Theory* 16 (1): 51–68.

Lundkvist, Sven. 1977. *Folkrörelserna i det svenska samhället 1850–1920*. Uppsala: Uppsala University.

Lundström, Catarina. 2015. *Den goda viljan: kvinnliga missionärer och koloniala möten i Tunisien och västra Jämtland*. Lund: Nordic Academic Press.

McLisky, Claire and Karen Vallgårda. 2015. "Faith through feeling: An Introduction". In *Emotions and Christian missions: historical perspectives*, 1–21, Basingstoke: Palgrave Macmillan.

Nielssen, Hilde, Inger Marie Okkenhaug and Karina Hestad Skeie, eds. 2011. *Protestant missions and local encounters in the nineteenth and twentieth centuries: unto the ends of the world*. Leiden: Brill.

Njoku, Raphael Chijioke and Chima J Korieh. 2007. "Introduction". In *Missions, states, and European expansion in Africa*, eds. Chima J. Korieh and Raphael Chijioke Njoku, 1–10, New York: Routledge.

Nzongola-Ntalaja, Georges. 2002. *The Congo from Leopold to Kabila: a people's history*. London: Zed.

Odén, Robert. 2012. *Wåra swarta bröder: representationer av religioner och människor i Evangeliska fosterlandsstiftelsens Missions-Tidning, 1877–1890*. Diss. Uppsala : Uppsala University.

Okkenhaug, Inger Marie. ed. 2003. *Gender, race and religion: Nordic missions 1860–1940*. Uppsala: Svenska institutet för missionsforskning.

Pels, Peter. 2009. "Missionaries". In *Palgrave Dictionary of Transnational History*, eds. Iriye, Akira and Pierre Yves Saunier, 716–719, Basingstoke [England]: Palgrave Macmillan.

Porter, Andrew. 2004. *Religion versus empire?: British protestant missionaries and overseas expansion, 1700–1914*. Manchester: Manchester University Press.

Price, Richard. 2008. *Making empire: colonial encounters and the creation of imperial rule in nineteenth-century Africa*. Cambridge: Cambridge University Press.

Said, Edward W. 1993. *Orientalism*. Stockholm: Ordfront.

Said, Edward W. 1994. *Culture & imperialism*. [New ed.] London: Vintage.

Sidenvall, Erik. 2009. *The making of manhood among Swedish missionaries in China and Mongolia, c. 1890–c. 1914*. Leiden: Brill.

Slade, Ruth. 1955. "English Missionaries and the Beginning of the Anti-Congolese Campaign in England", *Revue belge de philologie et d'histoire* 33(1): 37–73.

Stenström, Gösta. 2002. *Vi möts vid Mukimbungu: berättelsen om Anna, Wilhelmina och Elisabeth, Svenska missionsförbundets tre första kvinnliga missionärer i Kongo 1886–1890*. Falköping: Kimpese.

Stenström, Gösta. 2009. *Archives de Bruxelles: 1922–1968: Bureau des Eglises et Missions Protestantes en Afrique Centrale, Bruxelles*. Uppsala: Swedish Institute of Misson Research.

Stoler, Ann. 2002. "Colonial Archives and the Arts of Governance", *Archival Science* 2: 87–109.

Tell, Per Erik. 2005. *Detta fredliga uppdrag: om 522 svenskar i terrorns Kongo*. 1. utg. Umeå: hström - Text & kultur.

Van Gent, Jacqueline. 2015. "Emotions, Missions and Colonial histories: An Epilogue". In *Emotions and Christian missions: historical perspectives*, 240–250, Basingstoke: Palgrave Macmillan.

Widman, Ragnar. 1979. *Trosföreställningar i Nedre Zaïre från 1880-talet*. Diss. Uppsala: Uppsala University.

"Lest the punishment of Ahab fall upon you":
The Psychic Impact of Concurrent Narratives in the Hawaiian Missionary Legacy

Catherine E. Hoyser
Director of Women's Studies,
University of Saint Joseph, West Hartford

Introduction

Nobody wants their paradise ruined with reality. Tourists cling to the fantasy of Hawaii as the land of skimpily clad hula girls and surfers, mai tais, breathtaking sunsets, and rainbows. All of that is accented with the stereotypes of overweight Hawaiian natives that exude aloha and ohana (family) while singing in lush falsetto and catering to their every need. Likewise, the descendants of missionaries who made the treacherous journey out to the, then, Sandwich Islands, to save the heathen natives and had children who became powerful landowners and entrepreneurs, do not want to recognize the impact of their families' actions on the people and land of Hawaii. Descendants cling to the image of their missionary relatives as saviors of a heathen people who were so disorganized that they were unable to recognize the commercial opportunities that their location and climate promised. These descendants block the reality that their ancestors brought chaos, death, and poverty to the majority of Hawaiian natives and ruin to the landscape amidst the development of capitalism, Christianity, and democracy. Indeed these outsiders saw only their fantasy of heathen people and missed the highly sophisticated system of sustainable agriculture and social organization that characterized Hawaiian life. Rather than bringing organization, the missionaries and their descendants brought a psychic disorganization that remains deadly for native Hawaiians and whites alike.

As a white woman, or haole or foreigner in Hawaiian, I will not presume to speak for Hawaiians and their psychic trauma. Others have done so and continue to do that work[1]. Gayatri Spivak and others have analyzed the issue of post colonialist critics silencing the subaltern (Spivak 1988, Parry, Loomba), and I do not wish to silence the native Hawaiian in this paper. The Hawaiian people protested and resisted the occupation of the Hawaiian Islands on multiple occasions. (For histories of those efforts see Silva, Kuykendall, Sai, Daws, Osorio, Haley.) Over the past five years, however, I have been compiling an oral history with a member of the fifth generation of New England missionary descendants. This project analyzes the entanglement of the concurrent narratives of contemporary life with the past trauma of missionary history localized in one missionary descendant's processing of trauma by challenging the historic narrative of missionary benevolence and compensating for the damage that her ancestors helped perpetuate. This study outlines the descendant's efforts to research her family's culpability in cultural genocide and land grabbing while enacting her own attempts at reparations to Native Hawaiians as an effort to break a cycle of loss and grief for Hawaiians and her own family.

When white people write about their role in Hawaiian history, the missionary descendants and others cite the advantages of civilization that they introduced to the Hawaiian people. Scholars have analyzed the complexity of this missionary narrative and its complicity with colonial and capitalist agendas (Dudley and Agard *A Call*, Prior, Spivak, *Postcolonial Reason*, Sugirtharajah). In fact, the financial backers for the ABCFM were prominent businessmen (Dudley, and Agard, *Hawai`i* 74). The dominant mission group was the American Board of Commissioners of Foreign Missions (ABCFM) of the Congregational Church, a Protestant New England church that recruited missionaries among students at Yale College and Andover Divinity School in Connecticut and Massachusetts. They dominated the Christian community so much that

---

[1] Several investigations of the impact of colonialism on the psyche and lives of Hawaiian peoples or Moale kanaka have been written. See Trask, *From a native daughter colonialism and sovereignty in Hawaii;* Kauanui, *Hawaiian Blood;* Silva, *Aloha Betrayed.*

the ABCFM hounded Catholic missionaries out of the Islands with physical violence, in some cases, so that they gained majority control.[2] They sent the first group of missionary couples to the Islands in 1820. Bachelors were not allowed to go out as missionaries, and so had to find a woman who would agree to marry and join the ABCFM cause. The Mission was to introduce the Natives to Congregationalist Christianity, which was a Puritanical version of the religion. The original charter for missionaries departing for what was then called the Sandwich Islands included a clause that mandated no interference in local politics or culture (McCullough 63).

The vow of no interference into local customs and organization, however, quickly slipped away. Besides introducing the Native Hawaiians to Christianity, ABCFM missionaries developed an alphabet for the Hawaiian language, which gave the Native peoples a written language and ability to read the Bible and record their history. Soon the Missionaries also began giving the Monarchy an understanding of more so-called democratic governance and capitalist concepts such as land ownership. The adage about the missionaries is that "They went out to do good, and did well." Even now, missionary descendants remain the dominant financial, political, and cultural leaders in the Islands. The Hollywood film, *The Descendants*, captures the power of such a family and includes actual members of one of those families in a pivotal scene (Payne).

The narrative of the Missionaries, therefore, sounds benevolent on the surface. The people sailed out to Hawaii with good intentions of saving souls and civilizing a people that had achieved the unification of the Islands into one nation under the leadership of King Kamehameha I who led a bloody war rife with massacres in his effort to create one sovereign nation able to defend itself against forces that would annex each individual island. He believed that not unifying the individual islands would endanger the Native population even more if they were not united to work together as one country. By the time the ABCFM missionaries arrived, the Hawaiian monarchy was already undergoing change in

---

[2] For the contentious history between Protestants and Catholics in Hawaii, see Kamakau, 326–329, 411; The first Catholic priests arrive in Hawaii in 1827 and Catholicism is outlawed in 1829, but Catholic priests return in 1836–7. See also Daws 80, 89–90, 102, 105, 140, and Haley, 123–25, *passim*.

its beliefs because of Western contact (Pfeiffer 270). Despite the fact that the transforming of Hawaiian spirituality was well under way, the Missionary population developed a narrative that featured them as saving the Native population and developing the Islands as a functioning Congregationalist, Christian, capitalist democracy with a titular monarchy. We hear this narrative from any power that has colonized a land—the colonizers "civilize" a nation of people that they claim has no culture, no civic organization, no spiritual system, and no intellectual, scientific or artistic achievements. In a 1900 commentary, the *Pacific Commercial Advertiser,* one of several newspapers in the Islands during the nineteenth and early twentieth centuries, demonstrates the civilizing and saving narrative that most whites subscribed to and continued to promulgate even eighty years after the arrival of the first ABCFM missionaries: "'In spite of the large number of Hawaiians and Orientals on these islands this is essentially an American community. White men, chiefly Americans, have built it up from nothing and have made it one of the most prosperous and modern and progressive places in the world' (Rohrer 39). Notice the "nothing" as the starting point for the white male Americans. This rhetoric represents the justification for the U. S. -backed Committee of Safety overthrow of the Hawaiian government in 1893, the incarceration of Queen Lili`uokalini in 1895, ending in the United States' Annexation of Hawaii in 1898.

Such justifications for the oppression and exploitation of a people abound throughout history. The legacy from this attitude haunts Hawaii still. In 1993, the President of the United States, Bill Clinton, signed a document called "Apology to the Hawaiian People Resolution," on the centenary of the United States' overthrow of the Islands. The United Church of Christ apologized to the Hawaiian people for the "Missionary Boys'," as the second generation of missionary children were called, support of the overthrow of the Hawaiian monarchy in 1993 as well[3]. This dominant

---

[3] It would, however, take until 2008 for the House of Representatives to draft an apology to African-Americans for slavery and Jim-Crow laws. Currently there are legal efforts underway to define Hawaiians one who has been born in the state of Hawaii rather than one who has the genetic marker of Hawaiian blood. Kēhaulani Kauanui has written about the blood definition of Hawaiian

civilizing narrative, however, has multiple concurrent narratives. I will briefly outline the impact of one of the dominant civilizing stories before concentrating on one dissenting voice—a Missionary descendant who eschews the savior narrative of her Missionary ancestors and regards the legacy as an actual curse still being enacted on her family.

One example of the benevolence narrative of the Missionary presence in the Islands is the "gift" of an alphabet that enabled Hawaiians to write and read in their language. Regina Pfeiffer describes the ABCFM's approach to converting the Hawaiians as two-pronged: literacy and prayers (275). One additional impact of this tactic was that literacy empowered the people to share information and to communicate among themselves. As was usual in missionary colonialist endeavors, the impetus for the alphabet was the translation of the Christian Bible into Hawaiian so that the Native people could access the "Word" of "God."[4] In fact Alexander Liholiho (1834–63), Kamehameha IV, translated the Anglican Book of Common Prayer into Hawaiian to encourage the observance of the new Catholic Episcopalian Church that he and his wife, Queen Emma, worked to import to Hawaii. The Hawaiian alphabet that the whites developed left out many sounds and, thus, words that were part of the Hawaiian spoken language. Apparently, the whites could not distinguish among pronunciations that for Hawaiians were ordinary. Consequently, the people lost concepts and methods of discussing abstract understandings about the universe that Hawaiians possessed, but haoles did not. As David Spurr observes, with the creation of an alphabet and, thus, vocabulary for the colonized people, the colonizing missionaries gain more control (31–32). With the loss of the vocabulary comes the loss of the concept, a common linguistic truism that philosophers

---

    in her book *Hawaiian Blood* (2008). Whites are using the case to gain entry into an exclusive school that was founded by a Hawaiian princess for Hawaiians only, claiming equal opportunity discrimination under U. S. law.

4   In her "Typology of Colonialism," Nancy Shoemaker notes that the colonial agendas shift among variant colonialist goals regarding Hawaii with the missionary colonialists as a later phenomena after transport and extractive colonialism were well under way. Planter colonialism roughly follows the mission colonialism. None are mutually exclusive.

and linguists claim: we cannot identify and discuss a phenomenon unless we have the vocabulary to do so. With this alphabet, then, Hawaiians lost their means of talking about their conceptions of space and time in their universe, among other abstractions (Kailihou). David Malo (1793–1853) who was educated by the Missionaries chronicled, in Hawaiian, the loss of Hawaiian knowledge as a result of the creation of a Hawaiian alphabet and the transition into a written language (Kailihou). Those white narratives erased for the Hawaiian an alternative means of thinking about the world. This example is one part of the cultural genocide that the missionaries orchestrated. Raphael Lemkin coined the word genocide and spent his life advocating for what became the U. N. Convention on the Prevention and Punishment of the Crime of Genocide. He wanted to include what he called cultural genocide. Among other impacts, cultural genocide erases collective memory, pride in one's culture, and a sense of identity.

The concurrent narrative that I want to explore focuses on a missionary descendant who believes that her ancestors were primary orchestrators of cultural genocide among the Hawaiian royalty. She connects the treatment of royal children by her ancestors, those included in that Hollywood film, with a curse on her family that is manifested in the premature deaths of two of her children, and other early deaths in her family. I will call her variously, the descendant, the interviewee, the informant, to create some variety and protect her anonymity. Whereas her siblings and other relatives regard their ancestors as noble educators and protectors of the royal children, her perspective raises the question of their responsibility for the tragic results of the past. Her subsequent efforts to compensate for the collusion of her ancestors in the decline of the Hawaiian monarchy not only raises questions about a legacy of responsibility, but also, about the efficacy of such personal initiatives from guilt. She exhibits a guilt that echoes that of descendants of Nazi officers and officials.[5]

---

[5] Nazi descendants' guilt has taken the form of converting to Judaism and moving to Israel as well as choosing sterilization. See Gold, Cronin, and Albeck, Adwan, Bar-On.

A direct descendent of the missionaries Amos Starr Cooke and Juliette Montague Cooke, the informant's efforts to purge herself and family of a curse may not be as bizarre as we think. At the time of the Annexation of Hawaii, the Kingdom's last monarch, Queen Lili`uokalani, published a history of her country. She ends her book, *Hawaii's Story by Hawaii's Queen* (1898), with a curse on the Missionary Boy overthrowers:

> Oh honest Americans, as Christians hear me for my down-trodden people! Their form of government is as dear to them as yours is precious to you. ... With all your goodly possessions, covering a territory so immense that there yet remain parts unexplored... do not covet the little vineyard of Naboth's, so far from your shores, lest the punishment of Ahab fall upon you, if not in your day, in that of your children, for "be not deceived, God is not mocked." (373)

The curse of Ahab is that his sons will suffer for Ahab's sins of murder, blasphemy and greed. Because Naboth will not sell his vineyard to Ahab, Jezebel, his wife, plots Naboth's death. Elijah announces the curse that Ahab's repentance spares him immediate death, but his sons will suffer. All men of the house of Ahab will die and have no offspring (I Kings 21–22 Revised Standard Version). In her curse, Queen Lili`uokalani demonstrates a tactic of resistance to the American overthrow by using the Americans' weapon of cultural dominance against them. The Queen's intelligent use of the master's language in hopes that she can destroy the master's house, as Audre Lorde's essay ("The Master's") would describe it, fails to stop the usurpation of her kingdom, but displays the depth of her intelligence and determination. Her curse of the usurpers and their descendants employs the weapon of American religious rhetoric against the Americans. Hawaiian resistance to the U.S. occupation of Hawaii manifested in other forms as well such as a petition signed by Hawaiians in protest of the treaty, which the U.S. Congress never passed, granting Hawaii to the United States. The curse comes to fruition partially for the family of Amos Starr Cooke, which will suffer premature deaths in future generations, causing the informant to re-examine the history of her family in relation to the Hawaiian people.

The descendant's ancestors were prime movers in the program to "civilize" Hawaiians because they directed the Chiefs' Children's

School. Amos Starr Cooke and Juliette Montague Cooke arrived in Hawaii after the long voyage around the Horn on the vessel the Mary Frazier on April 9, 1837 (usgwarchives). They were part of the eighth wave of missionaries sent over to save souls in Hawaii. The first group arrived in 1820, sailing from Boston Harbor and mostly coming from Yale College and Andover Divinity School. As was usual in the 19th century, Amos Starr Cooke as head of household would dictate the conditions that his wife, children and schoolchildren lived under. The Missionaries, according to George S. Kanahele, fought what they saw as licentious, sensuous, and depraved behavior such as the hula (36). The openness of the Hawaiians clashed with the guardedness of the missionaries who came from cold climates that had farms separated from other people by miles in many cases and a suspicion of sensory pleasure as the devil's playing field. King Kamehameha III and other island kings desired that the royal children learn Western customs and language so that they could interact with representatives and royalty from other countries, and asked the ABCFM missionaries to found a school for Hawaiian royal children. Cooke and his wife instructed the chiefs' children in Western European subjects, contributing to a near eradication of Hawaiian customs, arts, and beliefs in their charges.

Sixteen ali`i or royal Hawaiian offspring attended the school by the time it closed ten years later for lack of children from Hawaiian royalty, mainly from early deaths or infertility. The Cookes did not treat the children as royalty. Amos shares his view of the Hawaiians in a letter to his sister:

> One obstacle to the progress of this nation is the ignorance of their rulers, could they be taught the customs of civilised [sic] nations, & the reasons why & wherefore of such and such a change, they would soon be ranked among the civilised [sic] nations of the earth.
> Amos Cooke to sister Mary July 27, 1838. Ms 65905

Cooke Family

While reflecting the typical view of colonizers that the local people are heathens, Cooke demonstrates his awareness of the future roles of his students and his responsibility to make them leaders.

Among the pedagogical techniques the Cooke's used to help "civilize" the future leaders of the Hawaiian kingdom were regular beatings, withheld food, and solitary confinement for infringements of rules and disobedience. His diary entry for January 30, 1844 notes that "i put moses in the carpenter room and emma in the grass house and punished her with a rawhide for her several disobediences this day" (HMCS, ASC, vol. 7). The grass house was the location for solitary confinement. Cooke records many beatings of Moses, in particular. Moses will die at age 19, shortly after leaving the school. Emma will become queen, and Lili`uokalani, the last queen and royal ruler of Hawaii, will enter the school at age four. Meager food and food deprivation as punishment characterized the Cooke school. Despite nineteenth century perspectives on child rearing, royal children would have been spared such treatment in Europe, for example. Amos records in his journal in December of 1848 that he entreated Alexander and Lot not to follow the path of Moses, but to seek guidance from "the Almighty" to help them keep balance among the flatteries and temptations they might face as future kings. Further he writes that he apologized to Alexander and Lot "if his discipline had seemed too severe" (Richards 357–58). Despite his apology, the damage to his charges had been done.

Apparently, the Cookes and their staff succeeded, however, in "civilizing" the chiefs' children. An Island newspaper reports that "Nor do Mr. and Mrs. Cooke neglect to impress upon their pupils that the 'fear of the Lord is the beginning of wisdom, and religion the basis of all private and public worth" (*The Friend* August 1, 1844). Furthermore according to a report in *The Friend*, "There is nothing perceptible in their manner or habits that could strike a stranger as differing much from the manners and habits of young English or Americans of the same age" (August 1, 1844). In fact, among other accomplishments, Queen Emma was an excellent pianist of European classical music.

One of the informant's conclusions is that the royal children were more susceptible to the measles and other epidemics that killed so many Hawaiians because of their weakened condition from the meager nourishment and regular beatings that her ancestor perpetrated on them. A brief listing of those early deaths includes: Moses Kekuaiwa (1829–1848) who died at age 19, and Kaiminaauo, at age 4, both during the measles epidemic. (It is said that no infants born in 1848 survived because of the measles.) Queen Emma, who attended the school, lost her son Prince Albert Edward (1858–1862) at age 4. W. P. Kinau, (1842–1859) son of another student, Princess Ruth, was 17 when he died. William Pitt Leleiohoku (first husband of Princess Ruth; rheumatic fever) (1854–1877) age 23. The last heir apparent to the throne, Princess Victoria Kauilani (1875–99) died age 24. In addition was Victoria Kamamalu (1838–1866), who died at age 28. Among the monarchs who passed away prematurely were King Alexander Liholiho, who became Kamehameha IV, and died at age 29 (1834–1863); his wife, Queen Emma, who died at age 49 (1836-April 1885), King Lot, Kamehameha V, who died at age 36; King William Lunalilo (1835–1874), age 39. Many of the royals were unable to have children. The last two kings died without issue.

The Cooke family has had its own share of early deaths. When he was 23 years old, the interviewee's son, Dewey (November 1961-October 1985) was hit by a truck while out on a bicycle ride. Dewey spent 13 days in a coma before he died. Dewey was one of those rare individuals that people universally describe as wonderful, lovely, special, a prince. The informant describes him with the Hawaiian label of punahele or the chosen one. At his funeral, rainbows arced ground to ground and birds flew in a large flock up toward the rainbows, signs, according to Hawaiian belief, of a royal soul passing to the ancestors. The kahunas (wise person or shaman) watched for and saw this royal sign when the last queen Lili`uokalani was born in 1838. This extraordinary phenomenon nudged the interviewee to ponder if more than the random wastefulness of the universe accrued to her son's death.

While coping with this death and the symbolism at the funeral, the interviewee remembered that several Hawaiian ali`i, or Hawaiian royals, died young as well. This memory led her to connect Dewey's death to those of the young people whom her maternal ancestor had taught, supervised, and, since the children of the ali`i lived on the school premises, parented as well. She also began to recall other early deaths in her family.

In contrast, the Cookes lived longer lives: Amos (1810–1871) until he was 61; Juliette Montague Cooke (1812–1896), the mother of seven children, until she was 84. The average lifespan in the 19th century was 50 years old. The seven Cooke children survived into adulthood and had children of their own, except for one daughter who married but did not give birth. The eldest and youngest sons died early, however, with the first-born, Joseph Platt (1838–1870) dying at age 32, and the youngest, Clarence Warner (1856–80), at age 24, just a bit older than the age when the informant's son died. The informant's maternal grandmother lost her first child who died in its infancy. The interviewee's cousin, Peter, died at age 26 and another cousin, Teddy, died at age 4. She was extremely close to Teddy who died when she was 13 years old. Like Dewey, Teddy was the punahele of her parents' generation. When thinking about percentages of infant or early deaths in a family, Douglass's has had more than their share, especially considering the decrease in infant mortality in the twentieth century. Of course, it does not match the multitude of early deaths the Hawaiian ali'i and people endured.

Her cousin Teddy died at one of the family properties in Luakaha, built, as the interviewee describes it, "on the land of the King which our Cooke family usurped. On every land that has been usurped—that's a nice word—it really is stolen, a child has been taken. That has been part of my research" (interview 1/6/2012: 10). In part, the descendant is referring to vast land acquisitions by the missionaries and their offspring. When the ABCFM decided to close its Hawaiian mission, it sold land at deep discounts to the missionaries, thus, beginning or augmenting missionary financial advantages. The informant's family is a common example. After running the Chiefs' Children's School, which the chiefs desired in 1839, and teaching the children of the ali`i, Amos Starr Cooke partnered with Samuel Northrup Castle in 1851 to found the lucrative supply firm known as Castle & Cooke. [6] Cooke and Castle, as many missionaries did, continued to amass land holdings on Oahu and Maui, among other islands. These descendants remain highly influential in real estate and Hawaiian society with controversial developments of holdings on Maui and Lanai as recently as 2014.

The interviewee for my project can serve to inspire others to recognize the connections between a family's legacy of privilege, power, and wealth and the individual's responsibility to action once they realize that history. Her actions raise the perennial question of responsibility for the behavior of one's family, no matter the length of time between the events and one's generation. Her intense identification with the Hawaiian people parallels the behavior of descendants of Nazis who convert to Judaism and move to Israel (Gold). She claims that she always had felt more comfortable with Hawaiians than her own people (Interview 9 Jan 2010). It also demonstrates that the personal is the political or public.

Is all of this early death a fluke or a curse? Her reaction could be interpreted in multiple ways: as a delusion because of her belief in a curse; guilt over the death of her son, even though she had nothing to do with the cause; a mid-life crisis, since she changes from an anti-authoritarian blackjack dealer into a crusader for Hawaiian rights and culture during her middle age; or a grief reaction that assigns meaning for her son's death by making it a karmic retribution for her ancestors' treatment of the people of Hawaii and the land.

To cement further the descendant's sense of a need to redress the wrongs her ancestors committed and her belief in a curse on her family is an incident in a flower shop in Paia on Maui. The informant tells the story with a hushed voice. She enters the shop, looking for a coconut bracelet, and walks to the counter. As she describes the scene, she says that a little old Hawaiian lady handles the transaction rather coldly. After her purchase, the woman becomes a bit warmer. The descendant says to the woman,

> 'I am of the Cooke family.' I just put it out like that, you know, and then she goes, 'Yes' (whispery). And I go, 'Do you know that family?' 'Yes.' You know with an "e" at the end? . . . Do you know that they taught the royal children in the 1840s? She goes, 'Yes, dear, they had a little funeral for someone.' And I said, 'Oh. Do you know that they also beat the royal children?' 'Yes, dear.' 'I feel it right now.' . . And she says, 'Yes, dear' . . . My family was telling me that it wasn't really true. My family was telling me that I was nuts. . . . So I said to her, 'Don't you think that your people, if they ever put a curse on my family, they would put it on the family of the man who did that?' And she said, 'Yes, dear, that happened.' Then she reached over and held my hand on that cold glass countertop and she says, hurry, dear, tell the story.' (9 Jan 2010)

This encounter solidified the descendant's resolve to trace the story deeper and deeper, and share it with the Hawaiian people. In addition she decided to support programs contributing to the revival of Hawaiian values and culture.

Another incident fueled the interviewee's belief that she must embark on a path of reparation to break the curse. It functions symbolically as giving up the legacy of gold gained from her ancestors' treatment of native Hawaiians. When she married, she took all of the wedding presents that she did not want to a jeweler and purchased a gold necklace with the money she received for them. It was two heavy ropes of gold, but a plain necklace—she asked them to remove the jeweled clasp at the back—that she wore constantly for years. As she journeyed through the processing of her son's death and her family's complicity with the missionary exploitation of the resources in Hawaii, she met a couple who took her to a kahuna who did spiritual cleansing. The informant gave the kahuna the necklace in exchange for the ceremony. Feeling lighter and freer as soon as she removed it, she realized that the necklace had been symbolic and that giving it to the healer was a natural gesture. We could interpret it as an albatross around her neck, representing the ill-gotten wealth that her relatives and friends had showered upon her with their wedding gifts. Conversely, we could interpret this episode as another incidence of the missionary exploiting the special gifts of the native Hawaiian kahuna; the interviewee, however, does pay for the service with an offering of particular emotional significance and high value. Giving away the necklace signifies her rejection of the emphasis on wealth that dominates her ancestors' and other missionary family histories. Additionally, it represents her conviction that the gold necklace was ill-gotten gains that she should not use, either as decoration or as a source of income. Because she was financially living month to month at this time, she could have used the money that selling the necklace would have given her. Instead she gives it away in appreciation of a spiritual purification that many people would debunk as superstition or as the exploitation of a gullible public.

As her research proceeded she launched, what we could call, a one-woman reparations program to native Hawaiians. Coincidentally the informant's projects focus on six areas that the Hawaiian people, but especially the ali`i children, lacked or lost: food, history, culture, land, water and sovereignty. She has supported the restoration of a taro farm and a community center to educate Hawaiian children about their cultural heritage and host guest speakers for the adults. She has underwritten the production of, produced and promoted CDs and DVDs of Hawaiian artists and educational programs about native rights. Although these efforts sound as if she is only giving money (until recently her own existence has been on a minimal income), she donates much time, energy, physical labor and archival materials that she has discovered to local activists.

This series of events leads the interviewee to connect with grassroots native Hawaiian projects. One of those projects is the unearthing of Amos Cooke's diaries and journals among other primary documents. Unaware of scholarly dictums in feminist scholarship about the intellectual colonialism of speaking for people who are perfectly capable of speaking for themselves and who would say something entirely different or have other priorities that they would communicate to the world, the descendant, has practiced them.[6] As Hobson and Spivak have analyzed, the question of who speaks for whom forces a recognition of the uneven power dynamics between and among groups and people (Spivak passim, 1988; Hobson 65–66). She will not publish or write about the copious material demonstrating the cruelty and exploitation by the Missionaries, especially in her family line, of the native peoples of the Hawaiian Islands because she believes that the Hawaiian people must tell their story. Instead she shares the material from the Bishop Museum, the State Archives, the Mission Houses Museum and other sources that she has unearthed with Hawaiian activists and students to do with as they see fit. According to the informant, when native Hawaiians go to private museums they may be told that documents she has seen are unavailable or available only as translated excerpts, demonstrating that a two-tier system of privilege remains. With our interviews, she told me she has passed on to me the kuleana, or responsibility, of sharing her ancestors' actions, the story of her journey, and her growth in consciousness.

The descendant's policy of sharing her research with local activists has received acknowledgement in the community, and her endeavors make her a valued and respected resource among Hawaiians. A native Hawaiian activist describes the informant's role in a response to a woman coming to Hawaii to research her genealogy. She writes that the informant "has become a very important source of guidance and counsel to me." She adds that "The Cooke family, I am sure you are aware, is a very prominent family here in Hawaii," and that "She is lovingly and respectfully called by so many people on our island, in our country, auntie." The activist further describes the informant as telling "the story from a very different place than that of the history books has caused her to research and gather information that is invaluable to this work of correction. She freely offers her collection of information to all of us and has become a very stable bridge not only between us and the past but also between both sides of the story" (Willard email 2011). As the message confirms, the informant's sharing of information and resources garners much respect in the Islands and provides needed communication between the "both sides" that Willard mentions. Her policy of sharing the information that she has gathered with Hawaiians and researchers rather than publishing it herself makes her a respected liaison on the border between Hawaiians and haoles.

We will turn now to another category of projects that the descendant's work supports: food. As mentioned earlier, her ancestors regularly deprived the royal children of food. When Amos and Juliette ran the chiefs's children's school, the children had to keep journals just like Amos did. No one has found a journal by Juliette; letters are all that establish her responses and experiences. As mentioned earlier, the informant has discovered in these documents that multiple times Amos records switching, beating, and punishing his charges, often by withholding food and locking them in the grass house.

Efforts to control the royal children and enforce Western behavior on them could reach extremes. Amos recorded in his journal on 4 October, 1842 that "just before supper Moses was punished and he was quite angry and had no supper." (HMSC/asc vol. 7). He records many missed dinners by Moses and the other students. In her history of Hawaii, Queen Lili`uokalani reports about the school:

> The family life was made agreeable to us, and our instructors were especially particular to teach us the proper use of the English language; but when I recall the instances in which we were sent hungry to bed, it seems to me that they failed to remember we were growing children. A thick slice of bread covered in molasses was usually the sole article of our supper, and we were sometimes ingenious, if not over honest, in our search for food: if we could beg something of the cook it was the easier way; but if not, anything eatable left within our reach was confiscated. As a last resort, we were not above searching the gardens for any esculent root or leaf, which (having inherited the art of igniting a fire from the friction of sticks), we could cook and consume without the knowledge of our preceptors. (5)

Lili'uokalani's comment shocks first because these are children and second they are royalty. We do not expect them to scavenge for food. Keep in mind that Lili'uokalani was 4 years old when she entered the school and is 10 when the measles swept through the island in 1848, taking Moses and Kamaauno to their graves. We could say that perhaps the Cookes were feeding them just as they would feed their own children, according to the austere allowances of the ABCFM followers, but would the measles epidemic have killed two of the children so easily if they had had better nutrition? The Hawaiians had no natural immunity to measles. Although they did become ill, none of the Cooke's seven children died during the epidemic, perhaps because of antibodies imbibed from their mother's milk, if Juliette nursed them (Richards 351). Were the early deaths of the others hastened by this poor nutrition while at the school? We will never know the answer to those questions. The interviewee believes so.

Coincidentally, as part of the descendant's work and in contrast to her ancestors rather than depriving Hawaiians of food, she supports, among other projects, the reclamation of a taro farm on Maui. The farmers, who are Hawaiian, built their house on land that the wife's family received from the king, as was common practice before the mahele, a change in Hawaiian land practice that enabled the private ownership of land (Van Dyke 5). The king would reward loyal followers with tracts of land. Her family, like many Hawaiian families, lost their taro fields, but she and her husband have reclaimed them, digging out the patches and planting indigenous fruit trees. Cultivating taro or *kalo* is a radical act. Hawaiians believe that humans came from *kalo* and that humans have these roots as their origin. Hawaiian psychological practice aims to restore a person's balance by reconnecting the individual to their roots in the earth (Rezentes *passim*). A healthy psyche requires *pono*, balance between Nature and human. Cultivating taro challenges the hegemony of big agribusiness and promotes sustainability among the Hawaiian communities.

Taro is also a challenge to authorities because it enables a degree of independence. As the cultivator explains to visitors, the taro is a whole food that satisfies nutrition needs with little processing. Therefore, people could subsist on taro or poi, which is the word for the processed food. By reclaiming land for taro, Hawaiians free themselves from corporate and governmental dependence, enhancing their sense of agency. In theory they would not need commercial food companies or food stamp programs. They would re-connect with their roots by working the land and processing their own food. Their pride and sense of self would raise as they enter a rebalancing with Nature. The informant helps support this effort to reinstate food production and easy access to healthy traditional Hawaiian nutrition.

Water access is another issue that Hawaiian activists have taken to court. The informant is involved with that work as well. The taro patches need flowing water that originates from the mountain heights. Traditionally the access was portioned out fairly by the family who lived at the top of the hill. The farm owner's family was one such regulator of the waterway and was responsible for keeping the stream flowing for farmers all along the stream bed. Now that golf courses, resorts, and sugar plantations have commandeered the water on Maui, the cultivators, and many others, participate in fighting for and reclaiming water flow. They host school classes that come to the farm and learn the traditional practices of their ancestors, clearing the taro patches, eating lunches that have been cooking in the trenches, or umi, dug by previous students, and digging the holes for the next group's lunches. The children learn to reconnect with the land and traditional practices at the taro farm. Additionally, they recognize that they must plan for the people who come after them. If the people could plant their taro patches, receiving the requisite water to do so, they could feed themselves and others at very little expense with a healthy diet. Many Hawaiians live squatting on beaches or in parks because they cannot afford the housing prices on the islands. Therefore, healthy and inexpensive food is a necessity. The informant's support of the taro project is just one step in her effort to be a behind-the-scenes catalyst for redressing the wrongs of the Missionaries. Make no mistake: she is not claiming any kind of credit for these projects. The local people are the doing the hard political and physical labor to make these projects bloom. The informant provides some financial or informational fertilizer when she perceives a need or receives a request. She even contributes her hands-on labor in the taro patches, but her goal is sharing the information her research provides and her resources. To further this sharing of information and promotion of the activists, her partner has created DVDs of the school groups coming to the farm and of activists clearing land to re-establish waterways. These are shown on public access television to communicate with the Hawaiian community. More over, teachers and professors are using the DVDs in their classes.

Ultimately her reaction and subsequent efforts to support Hawaiian sovereignty and cultural groups demonstrate a zeal that perhaps echoes the missionary fervor of her ancestors with the crucial difference that she intends not to impose her beliefs on others, but to support the beliefs and efforts of a wronged people. Her cultural projects, however, often reflect what Spivak, in *A Critique of Postcolonial Reason,* calls the financializing mission equivalent to the past civilizing missions (ftnte 42, 223). One example is the financing of a campaign for the singer/songwriter Cosma Pekelo who died in 2011. She and her partner provided the funds for preparing the nomination of one of his songs for the annual Hoku Award in 2007 when "Ni'ihau," co-written with Ileialoha Beniamina, won in the Haku Mele category for the best newly written Hawaiian language composition. Despite this award and the acclaim for his debut album *Going to Hana Maui* (1991), Pekelo did not want to pursue the intense high profile life of a musician, but maintained a less capitalist career as a musician, receiving the 2011 Ki Ho'alu Foundation Legacy Award for his contributions to the maintenance and perpetuation of Hawaiian slack key guitar a few months before his death. His resistance to the pressures from the informant and the award becomes his way of speaking, recalling Spivak's analysis of the subaltern (1988). His values were not the same as the informant's. He was successful because he lived the life he wanted to live, but from her perspective he failed to follow Western capitalist definitions of success. Consequently, to her, she failed in her agenda, which was to cultivate his career and Hawaiian cultural legacy. As another example of Hawaiian voices asserted by resistance, a Hawaiian cultural center to educate Hawaiian children about their history, philosophy, and culture that she underwrote lasted about four years. It did not become self-sustaining, which reflects her Western capitalist perspective that it should become so.

Few descendants would admit that their families colluded in the destruction of Hawaiian life, culture, and environment for their financial gain. In fact, most relatives of this descendant will not speak to her because of her outspoken criticism of the family's ancestors and continued exploitation of Hawaii. I should note that she does not regard herself as particularly noble or special; she does not take credit for the accomplishments of the different individuals or organizations that she may support or provide with information. She would say that they do all the work, and they do most of it. Their success or failure rests on their own efforts, however, the political and economic powers that resist their projects impact their outcomes as well, just as they do in any activist projects. Most interesting is that after some success, her efforts usually fail and are flawed from an NGO or TED Talk perspective. These limited outcomes, however, are an effort to make amends. Do we scoff at them or honor their intentions even though we recognize their limitations?

She acknowledges that the land and wealth that her family has because of the ancestors, including the Missionary Boys, comes from the exploitation of native peoples. The following conversation with one of her brothers reflects her understanding of Native Hawaiian anger about the overthrow. She tries to evoke empathy from him for the Hawaiian Sovereignty Movement by asking him what he would feel if someone took over his land; anger, he answers. She responds:

> That is a human feeling. It's not your own feeling. Everybody feels that way if somebody comes in and takes away their land. Right from under you? Illegally? Hundreds of years later, it's acknowledged to be an illegal act and not even a "sorry" from our people who did it? Never mind if the church says "sorry." What about us? We should, every one of us, be trying to help make things a little more even. If everybody did a little bit, we would make these two societies that are in the same land—totally haves and the have nots, right?—make more equal. And then the children, there's no other way we're gonna make the children at peace for the future because some have everything and some have nothing. And, it's not their fault! It's from the past.
>
> It's the continuation of the illegal, dishonest, immoral; they betrayed the people who helped them. So, for today, if we reinstate the motto, or whatever you call it—mantra or what—admission, of those original guys, they took a vow when they left Boston everyone of 'em, "Ye shall abstain from all interference in the cultural, political, personal," you know, there are about three words there. (Interview 2010)

In this conversation, the informant connects her brother's anger toward the possibility of someone stealing the land he possesses and the feelings the Hawaiian people must have about the usurpation of their system of land management and communal ownership by the Missionary Boys, and demands that Missionary descendants work to create parity in the distribution of land and money or, at the least, stop the destruction of the land.

Echoing the descendant's comments, one Hawaiian archivist said to me after she learned that I was writing about this family that the least they could do is apologize for what their ancestors have done to Hawaiians. As the descendant stated in the earlier quotation, though, that is not enough without action. Feeble as we may see her efforts, she has done more than many others who continue to live in denial, smug in the thought that their ancestors were so clever and successful. Yes. Their ancestors did work hard, but the Hawaiians worked harder as field hands and factory workers in the sugar mills and pineapple estates of the Islands. Many now live in tents on the beaches, commuting to jobs in the hotels in Waikiki. Now Hawaiian culture has become a commodity that the haoles exploit for their income in the tourist industry.

Overall, the impact of the ABCFM missionaries, however, was a suppression of a civilization's culture and cultural memory until it became economically useful in later generations as a means for luring tourists to bolster their economic ventures. Ultimately, the informant believes that as director and teachers of the Chiefs' Children School, Amos and Juliette Montague Cooke were prime movers in this suppression of Hawaiian culture and, perhaps the premature deaths of the royal children. In *From a Native Daughter: Colonialism and Sovereignty in Hawai`i*, Haunani-Kay Trask uses the term cultural hegemony to describe the pervasive embracing of American culture. Her critique of the co-optation of Hawaiian values—the spirit of aloha, the extended family, and the hula—in the service of the tourist industry demonstrates the twisted commercialization of Hawaiian values that suddenly become valuable to the white descendants of the missionaries after being banned and rejected as too open and promiscuous.

Beside the missionary narrative of saving "heathen natives" is the parallel narrative of contemporary missionary descendants who refuse to recognize that their relatives participated in an exploitive co-optation of the Hawaiian people and territory. The interviewee's alternative narrative is one of giving back, recognizing wrongs, and reparation. Her efforts may fail, but her attempts are positive steps toward a reparation for the damage her family has done. Rather than personally self destructive as some Nazi descendants have been, this descendant has chosen a positive means for the lifting of Queen Lili`uokalani's curse.

Bibliography

Albeck, Joseph H., Adwan, Sami, and Bar-On, Dan. 2002. "'Dialogue Groups: TRT's Guidelines for Working through Intractable Conflicts by Personal Storytelling.'" *Peaceand Conflict: Journal of Peace Psychology* 8. 4: 301–322.

Bailey, J. Martin, and W. Evan Golder, (eds.). 2006. *UCC@50: Our History—Our Future*. Cleveland, Ohio: United Church of Christ.

Carey, Hilary M. 2010. "Lancelot Threlkeld, Biraban, and the Colonial Bible in Australia." *Comparative Studies in Society and History*, 52. 2 (April): 447–478.

Cooke, Amos Starr. 1810. Journal. HMCS ASC. vol. 7. Honolulu, Hawaii.

Daws, Gavin. 1974. *Shoal of Time: A History of the Hawaiian Islands*. 1968. Honolulu: University of Hawaii, Print.

Dudley, Michael Kioni, and Keoni Kealoha Agard. 1993a. *A Call for Hawaiian Sovereignty*. Honolulu: Na Kane O Ka Malo P.

———. 1993b. "Hawai`i Under Non-Hawai`ian Rule" in Maaka, and Anderson: 72–90.

Gold, Tanya. 2008. "The Sins of Their Fathers." *The Guardian*. 6 Aug. http://gu.com/p/xzjct/sbl Web.

Haley, James L. 2014. *Captive Paradise: A History of Hawai`i*. New York, N. Y: St. Martin's Press.

Hobson, Barbara. 2003a. "Recognition struggles in universalistic and gender distinctive frames: Sweden and Ireland" in Hobson: 64–92.

———. 2003b. Recognition Struggles and Social Movements: Contested Identities, Agency and Power. Cambridge, UK: Cambridge UP.

Kailihou, Aolani. 2014. "The Role of Missionaries in 19th Century Hawaii." N. p., video recording. http://gu.com/p/xzjct/sbl Web.

Kamakau, S. M. 1992. *Ruling Chiefs of Hawaii*. Revised. Honolulu: Kamehameha Schools Press.

Kanahele, George S. 1999. *Emma. Hawaii's Remarkable Queen : A Biography*. Honolulu, Hawaii: Queen Emma Foundation.

Kauanui, J. Kehaulani. 2008. *Hawaiian Blood : Colonialism and the Politics of Sovereignty and Indigeneity*. Durham: Duke University Press.

Kuykendall, Ralph S. 1938–67. *The Hawaiian Kingdom*. 3 vols. Honolulu: University of Hawaii Press.

Lorde, Audre. 1984. "The Master's Tools Will Never Dismantle the Master's House,".

———. 2007. *Sister* Outsider*: Essays and Speeches*. Berkeley, CA: Crossing Press, 110–114.

Lili`uokalani, and Glen Grant. 2004. *Hawaii's Story by Hawaii's Queen*. Honolulu, Hawaii: Mutual. Print.

Loomba, Ania. 1998. *Colonialism/Postcolonialism*. London: Routledge

Maaka, Roger CA, and Chris Andersen, (eds.). 2006. *The Indigenous Experience: Global Perspectives*. Toronto: Canadian Scholars' Press.

McCullough, Charles. 2015. "Why Our Church Apologized to Hawai`i." in *UCC@50—OurHistory, Our Future*. N. p., 2006. Web. 5 Aug.

Osorio, John K. K. 2002. *Dismembering Lahui: A History of the Hawaiian Nation to 1887*. Honolulu: University of Hawaii Press.

Parry, Benita. 1987. "Problems in Current Theories of Colonial Discourse." *Oxford Literary Review* 9. 1–2: 27–58.

Payne, Alexander. 2011. *The Descendants*. Fox Searchlight Film.

Pfeiffer, Regina. 2012. "Christianity Builds a Nest in Hawai`i" in Putney and Burlin: 269–286.

Putney, Clifford, and Paul T. Burlin, (eds.). 2012. *The Role of the American Board in the World: Bicentennial Reflections on the Organization's Missionary Work 1810–2010*. Eugene, OR: Wipe & Stock.

Rezentes, William C. 1996. III. *Ka Lama Kukui: Hawaiian Psychology*. Honolulu, HI: "A"ali'i Books.

Richards, Mary Atherton. 1941. *Amos Starr Cooke and Juliette Montague Cook : Their Autobiographies Gleaned from Their Journals and Letters*. Honolulu: Daughters of Hawaii.

Rohrer, Judy. 2010. *Race & Ethnicity in Hawaii*. Honolulu: University of Hawaii Press.

Sai, David Keanu. 2011. *Ua Mau Ke Ea: Sovereignty Endures: An Overview of the Political and Legal History of the Hawaiian Islands*. Honolulu: Pū`ā Foundation.

Shoemaker, Nancy. 2015. "Typology of Colonialism." *Perspectives on History* Oct. 2015. Web. 10 Nov.

Silva, Noenoe K. 2014. *Aloha Betrayed : Native Hawaiian Resistance to American Colonialism*. Durham: Duke University Press.

Spivak, Gayatri Chakravorty. 1988. "Can the Subaltern Speak?" in *Marxism and the Interpretation of Culture*. Cary Nelson and Lawrence Grossberg, eds. Urbana: U of Illinois P, 271–316.

———. 1999. *A Critique of Postcolonial Reason: Toward a History of the Vanishing Present*. Cambridge, MA: Harvard University Press.

Sugirtharajah, R. S, (ed.). 2005. *The Bible and the Empire: Postcolonial Explorations*. Cambridge: Cambridge University Press.

Spurr, David. 1993. *The Rhetoric of Empire: Colonial Discourse in Journalism, Travel Writing, and Imperial Administration*. Durham, NC: Duke University Press.

Trask, Haunani-Kay. 1999. *From a Native Daughter Colonialism and Sovereignty in Hawaiì*. Honolulu: University of Hawaiì Press.

USGWarchives. 2013. "State of Hawaii Archives Biographies." Web. 24 February.

Van Dyke, Jon M. 2008. *Who Owns the Crown Lands of Hawaii?* Honolulu: University of Hawaii Press.

Willard, Donna Lanakila. 2011. Re: Ivanka. Message to L Douglass. 20 Jan. Email.

Policy Lending or Imposition:
An Assessment of the World Bank's Education Policy influence on Development in Africa

Terence Y. Yong
Faculty of Management,
University of Tampere, Finland

1. Introduction

This chapter evaluates the relationship between the World Bank (WB) and developing African countries concerning policy lending and implementation towards economic growth and development. It draws on a wide range of secondary data and literature across the institutional theory framework. In addition, with emphasis on the constructionist and constructivist paradigms, it establishes that the policy discourses of the bank promote myriad activities, which justify major shifts in national and institutional practices and processes in African countries that for the most part remain de-contextualized, unexamined and unspecific. Furthermore, the bank's propagation of a global education policy agenda for economic growth and development is subjecting developing African countries to a position of perpetual weakness and complete dependency on her and other donor institutions. The paper also explores the character of higher education from independence in the 1960s up to the 1990s when education policy gained compelling WB influence in the African region. Hence, it suggests that economic growth and development is possible for the region if education and development policies take into consideration specific country attributes and directly reflect their needs, aspirations and priorities.

As an international organization, the WB has eventually gained the mandate and legitimacy to dominate global education and development policy. The African continent has particularly gained a wide range of challenging education and development aid policy influence from the bank. Until recently, the bank in her education policy discourse did not seem to recognize higher education as important for the production and advancement of knowledge, and as fundamental for economic growth and development. Her recent position recognizes that universities are training centers for high-level skills and personnel with necessary capacity for inducing growth and development in their societies. Therefore, between 2000 and 2015, the WB invested over 1 billion in US dollars in support of HE in Africa (Macgregor, 2015). However, her increased involvement has meant that education policies for developing African countries have to be shaped by a 'globally structured educational agenda' (Dale, 2000). Undoubtedly, Lindgard and Ozga have argued that this kind of practice which amounts to policy borrowing and lending, promotes varied activities which justify major shifts in national, institutional and individual practices and processes that for the most part remain de-contextualized, unexamined and unspecific (Lindgard and Ozga, 2007).

The hypothesis of this paper suggests that humanity is so diverse and distributed into regions and countries with distinctive experiences and situations that are shaped by different forms of civilization and historical accounts. These variables (civilization and historical accounts) amongst others constitute the basis from which different social structures and systems that determine economic growth and development would emerge. Therefore, the reason why some social structures, systems and policy frameworks take center stage in world polity would be twofold. The first reason is the pursuit of hegemony within the context of socio-cultural, political and economic dominance. Such is the attitude that led to colonialism and eventual subjugation of most African countries to foreign cultures and philosophies. This happens when a society fails to look within her nature, uphold ger socio-cultural lineages to the extent that it should reflect on her needs, priorities and aspirations. Consequently, that society is coerced to depend on borrowed knowledge and policies within her distinct fabric for growth and development. Secondly, successful micro level policy measures from some social structures, international and supra national organizations or countries may present as a model or prototype, providing a framework for identity enactment at both the macro and micro (the world and national) levels. In both cases, policy borrowing and lending or transfer will eventually become the norm within the institutional theory framework. How these practices unfold and affect developing African countries, in particular, known to often be at the receiving end of policies, is of keen interest to this study.

The study, therefore, explores education policy borrowing and lending/transfer through the bank's initiative to developing African countries within her converging global economic framework. It examines how policy borrowing and lending or transfer resonate in the local context in some of these countries. In the process, questions relating to how the Bank manages her development mission are addressed. For instance, does the bank accomplish her mission through some form of democratic principles whereby developing countries freely decide on what policies to borrow and how to adapt or contextualize them? In other words, does the bank force education policy and implementation on these countries through her mandate and legitimacy, politics, subversion or contestation? While using the institutional theory approach to examine this practice of education policy borrowing and lending in developing African countries, the study relies on the constructionist and constructivist paradigms to evaluate the relationship between the WB and these countries on the practice. The constructionist model asserts that reality and knowledge are socially constructed. By a further stretch, this implies that the current realities of people, which could be characterized by needs, values, interests, priorities or expectations and so on, eventually determine the kind of knowledge regime to influence their growth and development. By arguing that reality and knowledge reside in the minds of individuals, constructivists compliment constructionist view with the claim that knowledge may be uncovered by unpacking individual, societal or country experiences. Therefore, by investigating, knowing and understanding the civilization, history and culture of people in tandem with their experiences, circumstances, needs and priorities, we might set the right precedence for deciding the most appropriate policy measures for their growth and development.

To accomplish its objectives therefore, the paper quickly explores post-colonial higher education in sub-Saharan Africa. The reason is to demonstrate how Eurocentric and WB influences have dominated and are still influencing the reality and knowledge shaping economic growth and development in most of the African countries. Secondly, it examines the education policy impacts of the bank in the development of higher knowledge in the region. The focus is on the bank's preference for primary education over HE, and her insistence and promotion of the knowledge for development program (K4D) as measures for guaranteeing economic growth and development in the region. Thirdly, the paper examines the outcome of the bank's policy imposition on some Africa countries. It discusses the effects of university entrepreneurialism, academic capitalism, university partnership and collaboration as offshoots of the bank's imposed neoliberal policies on developing African countries. Finally, the paper discusses on what policy measures could be drawn from the successful Finnish case that experienced similar challenges like most African countries in the 1960s yet emerged quite successful by the first half of the 2000s.

2. Post-Colonial Higher Education in Africa

Even though most African universities immediately after independence seemed autonomous in design, structure and purpose, they were Eurocentric. Before independence, colonial powers had started to educate and create new African elites to whom they assigned administrative and political responsibilities within Eurocentric ideals and principles. The French colonial policy of assimilation was for example enforced through higher education (HE). First introduced in 1837 by Chris Talbot (philosopher), it aimed at expanding French culture to her trust territories in the 19th and 20th centuries (Zeleza, 2006: see Woldegiorgis & Doevenspeck, 2013, p. 37). To achieve this aim, France trained few Africans through French universities into an elite class so that they could act as catalysts in spreading their culture and influence in the entire sphere of their interest. That notwithstanding, for most African countries south of the Sahara, HE began at the advent of independence in the 1960s. sub-Saharan Africa, for instance, had only 6 universities for a population of 230 million by the end of 1960 (Teferra & Altbach, 2004: see Woldegiorgis & Doevenspeck, 2013,

p. 36). The creation of modern universities with the influence of European colonialists was part of a plan to accomplish their mandates as United Nations (UN) trustees of their respective trust territories towards self-determination of the colonized people.

The vision for creating higher education institutions (HEIs) was to educate the African masses and train them with skills necessary for managing their affairs and administering their countries toward economic growth and development. But questions as to whether HE was rooted in the spirit and being of the African society are addressed in the course of the discussions. Worth knowing, however, is the fact that, the French Foundation for Higher Education was created shortly after independence in the 1960s, to cater for the higher education systems of French African colonies. It was charged with the affairs of French teaching and the provision of administrative personnel for the upper school system, which they eventually administered as extensions of universities in the French metropolis. Additionally, university students received bursaries, and the states bore the entire cost of their education. Graduates were expected to spearhead post-independent nation building and development of their countries. In spite of that, the French were only able to produce four graduates in the field of agriculture between 1952 and 1963 in all of French speaking Africa (Eisemon, 1982: see Woldegiorgis & Doevenspeck, 2013: 37). In the specific case of Cameroon, the first institutions addressing some specific needs of the people were created between 1976 and 1977, as university centers. The Buea university center was designed to cater for translation and interpretation; Douala was set up for business studies and teacher training; and Dschang for Agricultural Science and Ngaoundere for Food science and Food technology. Since then, the number of HEIs has continued to rise. HE, in this case, includes universities, professional higher institutions of learning (teacher education, and other special schools for the training of persons at post high school level), polytechnics, and higher vocational and technical institutions (above high school level).

By 1990, the number of tertiary students by regional average per 10.000 was less than 50 for Africa compared to Asia that ranked second from bottom with over 100 students per 10.000 (Schofer & Meyer, 2005). The low participation rate for Africa was first and foremost due to the general perception of higher education as meant for an elite class destined for public service positions. Another reason would be that there was not enough infrastructural and financial capacity to enrol, support and sustain high numbers into HE. Additionally, education at this time was not considered as a fundamental right for Africans. However, some governments (like that of Cameroon) were able to entirely fund HE and absorb its graduates into public service positions. Most of the training was offered through special higher institutions of learning until the early 1990s. Things changed from the 1990s when the Bretton Woods organizations (WB and IMF) introduced and imposed on these countries, their structural and sectoral adjustment policies. With WB loan conditionality to some African countries, the HE sector was liberalized with the intention to relieve governments from too much public expenditure and to increase HE participation rates. In 2009 the WB reported that there were already more than 250 public and 420 private higher education institutions in Africa (Woldegiorgis & Doevenspeck, 2013, p. 36). The number of student cohort has also continued to rise. Comparatively, however, HE participation rates for Africa is quite low compared to world average amidst a myriad of challenges for national governments, students, guardians/parents and other stakeholders.

The dominant view here is that the establishment of Eurocentric post-colonial universities and the influence of international development organizations like the WB and IMF are still the primary determinants of the reality and knowledge shaping the socioeconomic and educational structure of most developing African countries. For example, the Structural Adjustment Programmes (SAPs) of the WB and IMF have in a powerful way influenced the socioeconomic and educational landscape of most African countries in the early 90s and thereon. These structural and sectoral adjustments policies marked the beginning of a clear policy "imposition" plan in these countries within the framework of policy lending/transfer in the socioeconomic and educational sphere of global polity.

3. World Bank Education Policy Lending/Transfer on Africa

Shortly after independence, African countries thought they would determine for themselves new standards for economic growth and development by investing heavily on HE. By 1990 most of them experienced economic difficulties that forced them to seek development funds from the WB and IMF to direct and rebuild their economies towards their own needs and aspirations. Bound by the need to borrow funds from these institutions, most African countries eventually and overtly, lost the independence to make and decide their own education policies. The SAPs conditioned them on specific education policy measures. Most strategic was the demand by the WB and IMF for state governments to revise their HE funding strategy. They urged national governments through imposed conditions to drastically reduce their funding responsibilities over HE. In Cameroon for instance, bursaries were abolished, and university students were asked to pay a substantial amount of fees. Attention was then directed to primary/basic education, which development donor organizations had determined as more beneficial for poverty reduction, growth and development. Besides, education had been declared as a fundamental human right at the World Conference on Education for All (WCEFA) held in Jomtien, Thailand from 5–9 March 1990 (WCEFA, 1990).

One major question surrounding the ambiguity in education policy lending to Africa in the 1990s and onward is simple. Why would education be declared as a fundamental human right and at the same time, the HE sector is liberalized for capitalist competition? Therefore, considering the interaction and collaboration between development donor organizations and developing countries within this dispensation, this paper conceptualizes policy lending/transfer as "Policy Imposition" on developing African countries. This is primarily because the education policies of this category of countries have been enforced through loan conditionality from the WB and the IMF. The paper, therefore, seeks to understand how these education policy impositions on developing African countries are affecting the performance and contribution of HE to economic growth and development in the region. But first, a synopsis of the African university in the era of colonization.

3.1 Universal primary education in Africa

In her release, *Accelerating Catch-up: Tertiary Education for Growth in Sub-Saharan Africa*, the World Bank reassesses her stance on education policy for developing African countries. She argues that social and private "returns to tertiary education have risen appreciably" and that private returns to tertiary education in low-income countries are now frequently on par with the returns from primary education" (2009, xxi). Using some macro data, the bank also affirms that "research and development (R&D) raises productivity", and that "a one-year increase in average tertiary education levels would raise annual GDP growth in SSA by 0.39 percentage" (ibid). My assumption is that the correlation between private return to education (most especially higher knowledge) and research output have forever remained indispensable to economic development. Most importantly, research at the level of HE is the foundation upon which knowledge is created and developed. Hence, the preference for primary education over HE as a means to spur economic development at any one point in time remains overly ambiguous. However, the bank's justifications enhance the need for greater attention on sustainable forms of organisation and management of universities in most of Africa. They highlight the need for appropriate financial support on public universities. Appropriate organisational and financial support would for example, enhance the research and development capacities of most African universities in ways that would leverage their response ability to the demands and needs of their societies. Notwithstanding, the United Nations' 2015 Sustainable Development Goals (SDGs) apparently still present universal pre-primary, free equitable and quality primary, and secondary education as more important than the output of HE in Africa. Conversely, most of the SDGs require university-level education and training to implement.

Apparently, the MDG of universal primary education, which has retained high recognition in the SDG, was established based on higher social and private rates of returns for primary education compared to HE. Accordingly, while studying the potential of tertiary education for growth in SSA, the bank lays emphasis on education rate of return as a big factor to economic development. She observed that the worldwide average private rate of return to HE and primary education were 19 and 26.6 percent respectively by 2004 (World Bank 2009, 7). This demonstrates why the bank used her conditional loan scheme to constrain national governments of most African countries to divert funding from HE to primary education in the 1980s and 1990s. Concurrently, she reduced HE loans to these countries to levels lower than they were in the 60s through the 80s (Samoff & Carrol, 2004, 25). Underlying the actions of the bank is the question of why she would discourage HE at a time when demand was rising at a much higher rate (average annual rate of 16 percent 1991-2006: World Bank 2010) than it was in the 1960s through the 1980s. Also questionable is the fact that while the bank's HE lending declined in Africa between 1990–1995, her global lending increased during the same period (ibid). In fact, this attitude demonstrates how donor organisations use their avowed financial power to set agendas and priorities for developing countries. Consequently, in addition to depending "on hindered capacities to mediate supranational policy pressures", developing countries have become "the object of a more intense flow of external pressures" (Grek et al. 2009, as in Verger et al. 2012, 2&3) as the global education governance theory demonstrates.

In relation to the developing world, the legitimised monopolistic position of the bank over financial and development aid issues still gives her the presumptive power to impose policy conditions on developing countries. In a reflection on how the bank uses her legitimatized monopolistic position to influence/impose education policies in most developing African economies, the former Secretary of State for Education of the Republic of the Gambia Hon. Mrs. Ann Therese Ndong-Jatta observed the following:

> A condition for qualifying for World Bank assistance in the education sector was for African countries to divert resources from higher education and channel them instead towards primary and basic education . . . . African Governments protested that in the matter of providing education to their

people, it was not a question of either primary or secondary, or indeed higher education . . . . Needless to say, with the tremendous pressures that come along with World Bank and IMF conditionalities, they lost the battle, and higher education in Africa virtually went under. To this day, many countries have not been able to recover from that onslaught on African higher education. Some of our finest institutions have thus almost been destroyed, thanks to the imposition of bad policies from partners who, in the first place, came out professing to help us. What we received from them was the kiss of death (see Samoff & Carrol 2004, 1)[1].

In connection with the SAPs imposed on most African countries, this assertion points to the fact that global education policy contexts are a "fluid and risky" approach pushing for continuous "dependence on neo-liberal principles of system redesign" (Ozga and Jones 2006, 3). Quoting Luke (2003), Ozga and Jones affirm that the neo-liberal perspective of global education policy does not provide a consistent agenda for situations that demand "a strong normative vision of what might count as just and powerful educational systems in new economic and social conditions, in increasingly complex, risky and unjust transnational contexts" (ibid). Further to that, Ozga and Jones express the concern that, even though the global context is "risky, complex and unjust", international and donor agencies still choose to rely on "restricted forms of evidence, on performance measurement and management, and on superficial and contradictory acknowledgements of difference and diversity" in country specific contexts (2006, 3).

Additionally, some institutional theorists have ascertained the fact that, "institutional formations are borne of temporal historical circumstances" within some "context and scope conditions" that eventually determine the outcome of their objectives (Thelen 1999; as in Suarez and Bromley 2014, 142). This implies that setting policy agendas based on "some arbitrary sequence of past events or characteristics of key actors" or "self-interested players" do not take into account the "salience of dynamic thresholds, unintended consequences, and unexpected events" of the receiving organisation (Rueschemeyer and Stephens 1997; Mahoney 2000; see Sua-

---

[1] Statement by Hon. Mrs. Ann Therese Ndong-Jatta, Secretary of State for Education of the Republic of The Gambia (Economic and Social Council 200 2 High-Level Segment: The contribution of Human Resource s to Development, 200 2). www.un.org/esa/coordination/ecosoc/hl200 2/gam bia.pdf

rez and Bromley 2014, 142). Therefore, even if global education policies are deemed appropriate for developing African countries, they face a high chance of failure due to contextual institutional/organisational exigencies. Hence, the conclusion follows that, the acceptance and implementation of global education policies are simply accomplished within the coercive framework of institutional isomorphism.

Also, within the period of his tenure as president of the WB (1995-2005), James D. Wolfensohn experimented the CDF as a mechanism for poverty reduction. The objectives of the framework were country-focused and particularly stressed on "enhanced country ownership of development goals" (World Bank 2000, 5). To complement this strategy, the bank prescribed for long-term country vision and strategy towards development, encouraged more strategic partnership among country stakeholders and emphasized on institutional accountability for development results (ibid). Suitably, the CDF advocated that long term vision and strategy should be built on sound macro-economic framework and institutions including governance, effective legal and financial systems, and social safety nets and programs of the specific country. This approach suggests that the bank was interested in enhancing country ownership of her own development, rather than outsourcing the responsibility to supranational agencies. Hence, the need for all stakeholder involvement and enhanced strategic partnership among them in the development process.

Even though the experiment recorded lots of success stories and was adopted by many countries across Africa, the bank did identify a host of remaining challenges accompanying the scheme. Most important of the challenges contends that global governance remains the dictate of supranational development organizations. For instance, within the framework of enhanced ownership of country development goals, the bank and her development partner agencies are still demonstrating lack of confidence in country ownership capacity, and so, are unwilling to let go. Primarily, this is because of the belief that developing countries do not have the required capacity to effect "changes in the policies, practices, and procedures of the wider development community to nurture what is often a delicate process" towards country specific development goals (World Bank 2000, 9). Consequently, the entire process through policy design and implementation are determined by these agencies with a system-wide policy approach. Similarly, the eleventh president of the World Bank, Robert B. Zoellick expressed the intention to foster a comprehensive bank approach for developing countries that would rather "encompass the experiences of successful developing countries-not with ordered templates, blueprints, or prescriptions-but with inquiry, innovation, cooperation, and openness" (World Bank 2011, V). In a somewhat controversial statement, he set out the bank's development agenda in the following words:

> World Bank Group that plays a catalytic role in linking up data, information, and ideas with those in search of development solutions-in ensuring that knowledge for development is readily available to citizens, civil society, opinion makers, researchers, and government policy makers at all levels (ibid).

Underpinning the statement is the knowledge for development (K4D) concept that predominates the discourse of global development within the current development agenda of the bank. In the following section therefore, we examine the influence of the K4D concept within the education framework of some developing African countries.

3.2 The knowledge for development (K4D)/ knowledge economy (KE) and economic development

Although knowledge has always been at the helm of every premise of socio-political and economic development, the new global K4D programme creates the impression of a whole new proposition about the relationship between knowledge and economic development. Important to note that the KE framework is the end result of the K4D programme. The concept emphasizes the creation, dissemination and use of knowledge in every area of human involvement in the direction of economic development. A KE is therefore one that achieves economic development through the use of special knowledge (the K4D). In order to make a distinction between traditional scholarship and the now heralded global K4D/KE concept in relation to economic development, the bank contends that contemporary societies can only achieve economic development if they consider knowledge over capital (including natural resources) as key factor of development. Consequently, this is the new global policy concept that shapes the organization and management of most universities in the world, including those in developing African countries. However, there is growing concern over the kind of effects that the new global KE policy has on specific national or regional contexts. To this effect, Ozga and Jones concur (with Kenway et al. 2004) that, the KE concept has heralded in a global trend "prioritising techno-scientific research and its modes of operation and organization-concentrated in centres of excellence" (2006, 5). The highlight here is that the KE policy operates within a one-size-fits-all principle.

Consequently, the bank's recent support for education in Africa is based on the new KE framework, with focus on the science and technology fields. Within the framework, the bank approved US$150 million to finance 19 university-based centers of excellence in 7 countries in West and Central Africa in 2014. The project is intended "for advanced specialized studies in science, technology, engineering and mathematics (STEM)-related disciplines, as well as in agriculture and health".[2] Notwithstanding, the policy option is based on the premise that successful and competitive contemporary economies are based on the increasing use and exploitation of intangible assets such as knowledge, skills and innovative potentials (Brinkley 2006, p. 4). It sustains the idea that, these variables are of central importance to achieving economic growth and development for African countries. However, this proposition renders ambiguous the intentions of the bank on the interest she has for the development of African countries. For example, in 2009 the bank posited, in relation to Sub-Saharan African (SSA) countries, that the gross domestic product (GDP) growth from "an average annual rate of 2.0 percent during the 1990s, to over 6.0 percent during 2002-07" was due to "rapidly

---

[2] The World Bank Press Release, April 15, 2014: World Bank to Finance 19 Centers of Excellence to Help Transform Science, Technology, and Higher Education in Africa. http://www.worldbank.org/en/news/press-release/2014/04/15/world-bank-centers-excellence-science-technology-education-africa (Accessed 05.10.2017).

increasing global demand for the natural resource-based commodities exported" by countries in the region (2009, xix). Additionally, the bank affirms that the phenomenon was responsible for accelerated investment in "the primary sector, infrastructure, and urban housing and services" for some African countries (ibid). Consequently, she suggested for appropriate investments in physical capital as another solution towards a sustainable development growth rate for Africa. The approach used by SSA countries between 2002 and 2007 is illustrative of an adaptive approach towards economic growth and development, informed by specific country circumstances and characteristics in terms of available variables that account for growth and development in the region.

Apparently, the availability of enormous amounts of natural resources and the absence of physical and human capital (e.g. machinery and infrastructure, skills, knowledge and experience) in most of Africa, demand for a KE concept that reflects the particular context of the region. This is more so because, the attempt at a global KE perception is nothing different from the 19th century creation of mass systems of schooling linked to the creation of "imagined community" in many Western countries (Anderson 1991; see Ozga and Lingard 2007, 70). Similarly, according to some researchers, the KE concept only "works as a powerful economic imaginary or a political condensation that frames the preferences of political actors and guides the way they intervene in society" (Jessop et al. 2008 and Ball 1998; see Verger et al. 2012, 12). Furthermore, Barrow et al. (2004) argue that the imaginary attribute of the KE concept "puts education at the centre of the economic strategies of governments due to its crucial contribution to the formation of knowledge-intensive manpower, applied research and knowledge transfer" (Verger et. al 2012, 12). Consequently, the idea is influencing most African universities to pursue goals as illustrated by the concept. For this reason, the programme structures and curricula do not often reflect the development needs and priorities of most African societies. Also, the mission statements of most universities in the region are unrealistic as they claim a global dimension of their goals. Quite often, they highlight their involvement in international research and cooperation; and the development of skills for the local and global markets. According to Carney (2009), this attitude is influenced by the KE concept which is "associated with an educational reform jargon based on the principles of quality, learning, accountability and standards" (ibid).

Likewise, in 2007 the bank concluded that the KE revolution is leading the entire world "into a post-industrial age in which brains, not brawn, are the best means of coping with intensified competition and new challenges, including those related to human development and the global environment" (WB 2007, xiv). This claim substantiates the idea that in global education perspective (governance), states, international organisations and other agents have policy responsibilities over the essence of education policy as they find different reasons to express ownership of education through funding and other support measures (Verger et. al 2012). At the same time, the declaration of the bank coincided with the affirmation that, the global HE policy idea was a European illustration within the context of "the expanding role of new technologies, including cross-border electronic delivery" and "the political emergence of the notion of the knowledge economy which emphasised the importance of knowledge in creating economic growth and global competitiveness" (Margison and Marijk 2007, 10). It is apparent that knowledge has assumed greater importance for economic growth and development compared with natural resources, physical strength and low-skill labour in Western industrialized countries over the past two decades. However, considering the contextual origins of the KE ideology, it does not seem quite appropriate to enforce it as an economic growth and development policy for developing African countries simply because of its success experiences in western industrialized countries.

As suggested in the opening paragraph of this section, knowledge in all its forms (tacit or explicit) has always been at the centre of economic development. This opinion is reiterated to cast a shadow of doubt over the judgemental premise of the KE idea (global education tool) for economic growth and development for African countries. Considerably therefore, Margison and Marijk (2007) argue that the KE idea is simply based on a broader political framework including the possibility of a more diversified cross-border education provision due to demographic factors in some countries. Ozga and Jones add that, the concept is "a policy meta-narrative that assumes the commodification of knowledge in a system of global production, distribution and exchange" (2006, 6) based on a revived human capital theory, new forms of work organisations and the idea that "knowledge will replace labour and property as the key building blocks in society" (Peters 2001; see Ozga and Jones 2006, 6). Furthermore, the KE policy idea promotes more, the creation and development of the enterprising individual than the effective promotion of knowledge as a public good for economic development. For instance, international collaboration in HE within a neoliberal frame of the KE idea would influence the development of research skills, innovative and technological capacity of entrepreneurial individuals, but not necessarily enhance macro-level economic growth and development of developing African countries. Most shockingly, internationalization in HE seems to be enhancing the brain drain phenomenon with mass exodus of intellectual capacity flow from Africa to the West.

Compared to the KE proposition, there are propositions that industrial development remains fundamental to the economic development of most African countries. Based on the economic principle of comparative advantage which states that "the gains from trade arise from specialization" (Rodrik 2007, 9), it is imperative for the bank to rather assist SSA to effectively and efficiently make use of her comparative advantage position of natural resources. Besides other measures, Finland for example "developed a wood-based industry (furniture factories, paper mills, and so on) and other industries of comparative advantage (such as the manufacture of ice breakers)" (World Bank 2007, 48) in order to boost her economic development. In the same vein, besides advocating a strong science and technology base for low income African countries, the bank should concurrently enable for them a support scheme for comparative specialisation on manufacturing exports through industrial activities. Unfortunately, development aid agencies like the bank, "frown upon" economic policies that promote "manufacturing, or some manufacturing subsectors over others" (Rodrik 2007, 8). The current economic thinking of the KE policy reform that "pays scant attention to structural transformation and industrial development" (ibid) seems a perfect justification to the claim. Even though this policy option is informed by the knowledge that "there are many service activities that are tradable, and many non-traditional natural-resource based products which provide potential for high growth" (ibid), the opposing argument is that, African countries should be rather encouraged to explore and exploit effectively and efficiently all that which is naturally and readily available to them for economic transformation. The reference is made of the abundant natural resource endowment in Africa. To this effect, Rodrik makes allusion to a large volume of literature "that ascribes the underperformance of developing nations to their failure to let domestic resource flows be guided by the forces of comparative advantage" (2007, 9).

4. Outcomes of policy imposition on developing African countries

Given the challenges in the relationship between the WB and developing African countries, this section examines in a more specific way, some of the outcomes of the bank's lending approach and policy influences on higher education in some developing African countries. Most importantly, it examines the neo-liberal impacts of the bank's imposed reform measures. That is those reform measures that influenced the transformative and public perception role of the modern African university, turning it into the entrepreneurial university with an academic capital character. And as part of the neo-liberal influence, it examines the partnership and collaboration existing between African universities and the external environment. Secondly, it makes and assessment of the acceptance and implementation of borrowed policies by some developing countries.

4.1. The entrepreneurial university and academic capitalism

University entrepreneurialism in higher education explains the situation when a university chooses to break away from imposed constraints specifically due to restrictive funding systems or the bureaucratic conventions of state-run higher education systems

(Clark, 1998: see Shattock, 2009). Public funding restrictions to universities in Africa have served as the primary catalyst for such university attitude. At this instance, therefore, we maintain that the bank's acclaimed neoliberal position and education policy influence on African countries is the reason why most African universities adopted the entrepreneurial university position. The entrepreneurial attitude of schools involves actions within the threshold of innovative academic behaviour that engage the university into wide-ranging partnerships with the external environment. However, the functional objective of this partnership is to generate non-state resources that can cross-subsidize its activities and be used to incentivize further independent academic activities (ibid). This explains the market orientation and capitalistic perspective of most African universities. Apparently, this perspective is gaining increasing attention as a reference for both international and African-level policy for growth and development with emphasis on institutional self-reliance and less dependence on public support. This suggests that when universities go entrepreneurial, they eventually gain freedom from all sorts of constraints that may limit academics from the exercise of duty towards scholarship and new ideas. It also allows for them, the freedom of organization and rearrangement of the structures of the university to suit their specific agendas. This constitutes a very good idea within the constructivist perception about economic growth and development. That is, contextualizing the attributes of growth and development than drawing from a global level perspective. However, the focus is more on how academic freedom through neoliberal principles imposed on developing African countries from the 80s is affecting higher education scholarship towards economic growth in the region.

According to Shattock (2003; 2005), the entrepreneurial university is conceptualized within the scope of freedom and capacity to identify and handle issues of individual and shared interests. The wonder is whether "individual and common interests" of academics would eventually be synonymous to, or representative of general societal interests. The expectation is that given the opportunity, it is incomprehensible that academics would act in the same interest for the general public as they would for themselves within a competitive market dispensation. Also ambivalent is the expectation for universities to divert hard earned resources from their private endeavours into public interest after losing the comparative advantage of public support to other sectors due to the bank's imposed neoliberal education policy reforms. While sourcing for resources in the global competitive market place, universities would rather strive to meet their specific goals. For example, they would endeavour to keep pace with institutional peers, respond to the expectations of their other partners and struggle to execute some public responsibility that is only commensurate to the limited public support they receive from the government. Therefore, the diversion of public support from universities has rather encouraged more universities to consider higher knowledge more like a private than public good. Thus a systematic transition from the 'public good knowledge/learning regime' to 'academic capitalist knowledge/learning regime' (McClure 2014, 1). Consequently, the inclination of scholars to teach and do research for their interests, and for universities to raise money for their activities effectively complicates and compromises the public essence of their existence. Accordingly, when personal interests gain precedence over public interests, societal growth and development are compromised.

4.2. Partnership and Collaboration in University entrepreneurialism/academic capitalism

In spite concerns over limited public support for universities, Slaughter and Leslie (1997) point to 'academic capitalism' as remunerating from the relationship between the university and its external environment. Academic capitalism explains the proactive and innovative procedures used by schools to raise funds for their activities, boost institutional prestige and enhance their standing in a competitive and global environment. Patents and licensing, external grants, distance education and consulting are major characteristics defining this concept. It is indicative of the type of activities that academics and universities choose to invest their time and other resources on (Kniola, 2009). Induced by the liberalization and privatization of higher education in Africa, more and more universities are therefore transforming themselves from traditional universities to institutions responding more to specific demands and needs of the private sector in return for financial and other resources. The situation is made even more complex as academics of most public African universities continue to face diverse challenges relating to their salaries as public servants. Consequently, university research in most developing countries has become more of a capitalist endeavour than serving as a public mechanism guarded by poverty reduction strategic papers (PRSP) reflecting the needs, expectations and aspirations of societies. Consequently, the curiosity that drives most research in Africa is also influenced by the desire to gain promotion in the professorial rank, determined by a number of scientific publications.

That notwithstanding, Shattock (2009, 3) argues that entrepreneurialism 'reinforces academic performance by attracting additional resources and widening the research agenda'. This is about the expression of academic freedom as influenced by academic neoliberalism of the Structural Adjustment Programmes (SAPs) in some African countries. With insufficient public support and government regulation of HE, universities and other HE institutions have the freedom to operate within the limits of their chosen satisfactory levels. Thus the liberty to diversify their activities towards multiple goals. However, the bone of contention is on the relevance of the university to the public interest; for example, on the growth and development of communities.

Given that funding is fundamental in the pursuit and execution of education policies both at the system and institutional levels, universities with the autonomy that is backed by effective and independent sufficient financial capacities are now able to wield considerable power over their vision and mission. The nature of this power is often determined by the amount and type of funding they receive from other stakeholders, especially corporate businesses. For example, adequate funds will put in place the right infrastructure, acquire the right and needed equipment, provide an enabling environment and attract the best capacity for execution of research and other activities that government would not provide. When private sector donors make available these infrastructures and other amenities, they effortlessly influence policy both at the system and institutional level in favour of those specific projects whose outcome will benefit them the most. This situation is compelling most universities in the developing countries and regions to deviate from country PRSPs, as they mainly align their mandate and vision with those of influential stakeholders. This is common when corporate businesses propose vast sums of money for research and other projects that have nothing to do with the mission and vision of a university that is starved of funding.

Similarly, Pouris and Ho (2013) indicate that there is heavy dependence on Africa countries on international scientific collaboration. This has proven to have a far reaching effect on the third mission role (influence of university on growth and development) of universities on communities of most developing African countries. According to Pouris and Ho, scientific collaboration between universities of developing African countries and Western industrialized countries is unbalanced in the sense that the outcome of the collaboration is far less profitable to African countries compared to their counterparts. For example, there is increasing the involvement of academics of African universities in research and collaborative activities funded by Western industrialized countries that have no particular relevance to the needs, expectations and aspirations of the African communities. Scientometric analysis for research collaboration between African academics and their international partners indicate that between 2007 and 2011, collaboration was most emphasized in tropical medicine, parasitology and infectious diseases which are respectively 12.5, 6.5 and 4.6 times larger than expected from the scientific size of Africa (Pouris and Ho, 2013). Besides, one major reason why some African universities and academics engage in research activities with the external environment is due to attractive financial and other remunerations.

African academics for instance easily fall for research grants from private and external funding agencies due to low salaries. And the financial difficulties of most African universities is compounded by the fact that salaries of teachers (who are civil servants) of public institutions of learning in developing countries account for 80–90% of the national education budget (Steiner-Khamsi, 2012). Added to this is disagreement among the policy actors, and between academics as to what the level of compensation and structure of the salary should be and structure of the salary should be (ibid). In need of funding, therefore, universities and academics often engage in research activities with organizations or corporations, even in areas not prioritized within the PRSP of the country. Consequently, the need for extra earnings incentivizes academics to minimise their role and responsibilities as public service employees. In this circumstance, chances are very slim for higher knowledge production and development to be accomplished within the framework of the development and welfare need of the community/Society. In the most part, higher knowledge are influenced by institutional, individual and corporate quest for financial power. Even in the capitalist USA where university entrepreneurialism and academic capitalism are mostly practised, college and university managers are required '...To examine the way they operate, reconsider their many functions, and, even question some of their most cherished values such as academic freedom and access' (Kozeracki, 1998: see Rubins, 2007, 8).

4.3 Implementation and Management of Borrowed Policies

4.3.1 Universal Primary Education

The essence of this study necessitates that besides discussing policy borrowing and lending, we should assess the implementation and management of such policies. Using Cameroon as a case study, we assess the implementation and management of the universal primary education policy agenda of the UN. Our assessment uses data on a study carried out in the Far North, Littoral and North West regions of Cameroon (siteresources. worldbank. org), and on 30 public schools by Transparency International Cameroon (TIC) in the Centre region which includes the capital of Cameroon, Yaounde (TIC, 2013 Report on Teacher Absenteeism). Results from both studies point to sufficient governance challenges that are linked to the inefficient management of the education system and the lack of accountability in the allocation of public resources for primary schools.

In spite of massive public support for primary education and the elimination of fees within the concept of universal primary education, significant challenges remain in the face of achieving equitable access and quality in educational outputs. A lot of these challenges relate to the implementation and governance approaches used by receiving countries. Implementation and governance approaches of borrowed policies determine the outcome of expected results. In the case of Cameroon, results of the implemented UN's universal primary education policy reflect rather, the subjective intention of the government and not, the accepted institutional and functional objectives of such borrowed policies. Upon accepting the UN's universal primary education agenda, one would suggest that the government of Cameroon quickly adapted its implementation and governance approach with, for example, the use of Parent Teacher Associations (PTAs). The global call for universal primary education stipulates that every child has the right to go to school. It includes 'entering school at an appropriate age, progressing through the system and completing a full cycle' (UNESCO). This implies amongst others that, state governments have to create schools to accommodate the growing population of the age cohort, recruit and train more teachers to take care of their needs, provide didactic materials, infrastructural, social and other required assistance to make sure that the goal is attained. In line with these expectations, the government of Cameroon has created a myriad of primary schools through presidential decrees. For the records, nearly 3.4 million children, that is, more than 90% of school-age children enrolled in primary education in 2009, up from just under 2 million, an equivalent of 69% in 1991 (Africa Region, 2012-Report No. 67201-CM).

However, Cameroon's constituted governance approach has subjected school administrative effectiveness, consistency and sustainability into several challenges. The very first difficulty in the implementation procedure of universal primary education has to do with the recruitment, deployment, transfers, and remuneration of teachers. The 2012 Africa Region report on Governance and Management in the Education sector of Cameroon, indicates that decisions about the allocation of teachers across schools are partly arbitrary and mired in political interventions. The same document reports that nearly 35% of appointments of the primary level teachers are unrelated to total enrollment. Besides, rural areas which display the greatest needs of teachers are less desirable by teachers who frequently request for transfers. The lack of health and other basic facilities such as housing in rural areas is just one of many reasons that scare teachers away from schools in rural communities. Ngwe (2013) notes that in the Centre Region of Cameroon, teacher absenteeism by 2013 was at an average of 15.1%. It was 13% for civil servants, 22.2% for contracted teachers and 10% for PTA teachers. Based on 7 hours a day times 5 working days a week, 15.1% absenteeism translates to 5.25 hours of absence per teacher a week. This equals 21 hours a month, the equivalent of 3 working days of absence per teacher per month (Ngwe 2013). Contract teachers lose almost a full week every month, which implies that pupils lose almost a quarter of expected learning time in a month. In this case, we assert that the functional objectives of universal primary education do not seem to be of primary importance to the state.

Furthermore, severe teacher shortages across the country have caused the state to technically transfer some of her governance responsibilities to PTAs. The organization of PTAs gives parents and guardians constituted rights as stakeholders of education, and thus, involves them comprehensibly in the management of schools. In most cases, especially in rural areas, PTAs recruit and remunerate teachers from contributions and levies donated by parents and guardians of students. This is how they make up for the severe teacher shortages and other challenges, including infrastructures and other school facilities. Therefore, through the concept of the PTA, parents have subsequently assumed a substantial responsibility with regards to providing funding for the running of these schools. This particular influence is "complicating the process of budget planning and fund allocations" for schools (Africa Region, 2012-Report No. 67201-CM, Vii). For instance, it accounts for a blurred system of accounting and reporting concerning financial transfers from the centralised education authority to schools; a situation which accounts for under-financing of some school budgets and facilitates the misuse of education funds. Consequently, the responsibility of providing infrastructure and its development, mostly in rural communities, is mostly left in the hands of poor parents and guardians of school children. Concurrently, since these schools are created simply by presidential decrees most of them end up without structures. When civil service teachers are posted to such schools, they end up some times in the cities where they adopt other profitable assignments for themselves. So, inexperienced and ill-trained PTA teachers with insignificant and non-motivational pay packages are recruited to "under-teach" school pupils. This contributes negatively to the teaching quality and educational output of these schools. Consequently, the essence of primary education in the region is compromised.

4.3.2 Knowledge Economy and Knowledge for Development Programs

We have seen that the K4D and KE framework of the bank were policy instruments adopted as measures for effective poverty reduction. They advocate for the practical use of knowledge, including the use of the CDF to encourage sound macro-economic framework and institutions for developing countries. K4D/KE promote the development of skills and competencies that would equip humans as better workers, managers, entrepreneurs and innovators. This calls for extensive investments in education, a pre-requisite for institutional quality and the production of relevant technology (World Bank, 2007). Through higher knowledge, institutions would be able to recognise opportunities and turn them into competitive advantages for the creation of wealth. As a follow-up measure, therefore, the bank instituted the concept of the PRSP as part of her aid negotiation condition. These measures should add meaning to the endeavour of developing African countries towards increased access to HE. This is because successful knowledge economies are those that have expanded especially on their higher knowledge base, which determines levels of innovation systems, including solid information and communication technology infrastructures. A high quality economic and institutional regime is also dependent on the availability of an effective and efficient higher knowledge base that is adapted to a country's needs and aspirations.

Developed from the bank's CDF, the PRSP of Cameroon is also adopted in respect of the bank's economic growth and loan strategy for developing countries. The essence of these measures is to encourage knowledge based strategies that would leverage the strength of countries towards attaining their development goals. This would not happen in the absence of a well organised and managed HE system. Therefore, Cameroon's HE liberalization policy is a continuous effort to increase access to HE and expand its higher knowledge base for growth and development, in conformity with the K4D/KE framework of the bank. How this program is implemented and governed determines to what extent government wants to attain its development goals. In Cameroon, the liberalization of HE sector seemed mainly to cater for the continuous and exponential increase in student enrolment into higher education as experienced in the 1980s and 1990s. However, there is no concrete evidence to suggest that much was done by the government to assist in affordability. On the contrary, austerity measures were put in place to rescue the country from economic crisis. Public support for HE dwindled; bursaries were stopped, and until date, no student support or loan schemes are available. Therefore, the burden of education is mainly on students, their parents and guardians. Unfortunately, salaries are extremely low that parents and guardians of students are unable to effectively take care of themselves, their families and simultaneously sponsor their children through HE. Besides, unemployment is rife, a situation that makes it hard for students to afford side jobs, temporary or holiday jobs for extra money to assist themselves in their studies.

The above analysis suggests that the government of Cameroon accepts and implements borrowed policies without giving due considerations to the functional objectives of such policies, and the contextual circumstances that would determine their effectiveness. This implies that the intention of the government is most probably often backed by ill-conceived and inappropriate agendas. In her PRSP, for example, Cameroon adopts a Growth and Employment Strategy Paper (GESP), a reference framework for government action over the period 2010–2020. In its human development agenda, government amongst others plans to improve the quality of education at all levels. Her plan for HE is to encourage fields that are of priority to development, a university education with professional focus and measures to improve the quality and working conditions of teachers. However, Government has not identified those fields that are of priority to national development and growth. Besides, teachers continue to strike in demand for better working conditions and salaries. Even though the government pledged to promote universal primary education, there was only a 'timid increase in education provision', and the situation remained almost stagnant between 2001 and 2007 with only a slight increase of 0.3 points (IMF, 2010). Accordingly, the IMF (2010) reports that 'the main reason for failure by children of primary or secondary school going age to attend school (6–19years) is a refusal by their parents or tradition (26.4 per cent).' Additionally, she claims that this is true irrespective of the standard of living of the household. This translates to the fact that the government of Cameroon is not entirely committed in its endeavour to achieve a hundred percent enrolment in primary education. They would otherwise have adequately convinced parents of the imperatives to educate their kids freely. Government by such attitude is yet to recognise its children and youths as products of the society and future custodians of the state. This explains why there are 'frequent complaints of the high cost of education' in the southern parts of the country (ibid).

Teacher shortage at all levels, especially in HE, ascertains the fact that government is practically not ready to emerge through the K4D/KE principles. The absence of modern libraries and other enabling research facilities both for students and academics is another indication of government's ill intention on the implementation of the KE agenda. The fact that Cameroon was recently a victim of the recent international food crisis suggests that government is ineffective in its use of higher knowledge for greater economic good. The absence of well-defined study programs adapted to specific economic needs and circumstances of the people of Cameroon is fundamentally part of the reason why Cameroon in the first half of 2008 financial year, imported cereals worth CFA 120 billion francs. It is also important to note that this happened at a time when the tax on the import of basic grains had fallen (ibid). This explains why in 2010, the IMF encouraged Cameroon to enhance university training with a professional focus and foster vocational training based on the mastery of technical skills that would prioritise the satisfaction of local needs.

5. Policy learning from Finland

Finland is one of those countries that have excelled from a middle-income economy in the 1960s to be recently recognized among the high-income countries concerning growth and development in the world. Like most developing African countries today, Finland in the 60s operated an ineffective and inefficient higher education sector with low research and development output, depended on raw materials and cheap labour force and experienced low industrial and general productivity levels. By the mid-2000s, Finland had made giant strides and was recognized as a knowledge economy (KE) with high economic growth delivery levels through the use of ICTs and other innovative mechanisms. She also attained high levels of R&D and general education output, which boosted a diversified industrial base. Depending on the type of policy frameworks, implementation and evaluation processes, most developing African countries can draw useful lessons from the Finnish case. The most recognizable virtue about the Finnish success story is the fact that in exploring partnership and collaboration frameworks, and inclusive engagement with international experts, her government threads along the path of her unique history (Pradhan: see Halme et al., 2014). This approach falls within the ontological and epistemological design of the constructionist and constructivist paradigms where policies are designed from the realities and knowledge distinctive of the history, culture, needs and expectations of the concerned society. This comprehensive pathway to policy design for growth and development is in contrast to the subjective approach of the one size fits all global knowledge construct of a poverty free world.

Particularly, the 1990s marked the point of transformation for Finland. In this period, Finland was able to achieve more as an innovative-driven economy. This happened because of increased public support for higher learning. While the bank constrained borrowing African countries to reduce funding for higher education activities in the midst of severe economic crisis in the 90s, Finland was able to cut public expenditure on all other sectors, 'except those for education and for research, development and innovation (RDI)' (Halme et al., 2014). In pursuit of growth and development, the Finnish government unlike developing African countries made more funding available for R&D and higher education institutions (ibid). In line with these actions, they were able to establish and adequately fund Science and Technology Policy Council (STPC) with emphasis on information and communication technology (ICT). Even though the Finnish KE (ICT and innovative knowledge bases) has recently suffered a backlash, there is an indisputable view that investment in intangible resource activities such as education, RDI (the national base of Finland's knowledge regime) formed the foundation for its economic development for 20 years prior to the world economic crisis of 2008 (ibid). Unlike most developing African countries that conditionally depended heavily on the WB for financial and policy support to revive their crumbling economies, Finland was more able to decide the policy measures she thought were appropriate for solving her problems. Therefore, Finland's success is a reflection of the notion that a single development knowledge base for all countries of the world beset by a myriad of diverse, complex problems would not make a good recipe for solving individual country problems.

The general trend of education policy framework represented by the World Bank and her KI for developing African countries has mainly been towards imposition and standardization. On the other hand, Finland and other Scandinavian countries are more flexible and adaptive in the design, choice and implementation of their education policies. In the area of primary education, for instance, Finland has taken a shift from the global trend 'towards a narrowed focus on literacy and numeracy' to emphasizing 'broad learning combined with creativity' (Lingard, 2010). In the 90s, Finland introduced an entirely new system of polytechnics that offered programs tailored at imparting students with skills (achievements, understandings and attributes) according to labour market demands. The training of this new set of human resources was aimed at enhancing growth and development in the aspiration and needs of the Finnish society at the time. These new institutions and the programs they offered 'adsorbed roughly four-fifths of system growth between 1995 and 2010' (Orr, Wespel & Usher, 2014, 12) and consequently fulfilled the development needs of the state of Finland. Similarly, the Finnish higher education system does not charge tuition fees to her nationals. It disposes of a substantial student support system that enhances participation rates, which in turn favours a high rate of needed human resources for the country (Orr, Wespel & Usher, 2014, 13). The idea is that where policy is designed taking into consideration the history (experiences), culture and needs of people (constructivist paradigm) and implemented within the right institutional frame, the results are often beneficial. The reverse is true when policies are designed and imposed as loan conditionality on receiving developing African country against the backdrop of some imaginary context.

Compared to most developing African countries, Finland is a small country with a higher GDP and low Gini coefficient of social inequality. It is relatively an egalitarian society with a high degree of equality (ibid). That notwithstanding, the burden of cost is still with the government as its universities are slowly and publicly funded towards achieving a more inclusive, more effective and more sustainable higher education system. A 2014 comparative study on cost sharing for nine countries including Finland indicates that, even when 'private funding for institutions increased, public revenues did not tend to decrease, bringing about an overall increase in institutional income'. Also, when countries such as Austria, England, Germany and Portugal instituted tuition fees in the 1990s, 2000s, they aimed at providing the system with more funds 'without fundamentally altering the predominance of the public sector in higher education funding' (Orr, Wespel & Usher, 2014). This attitude expresses the fact that higher education is so important and fundamental to economic growth and development. Hence, the imposition of cuts in public support for higher education accompanied by high student fees in developing countries pose real threats to economic growth and development. In other words, lack of adequate funding enhances ineffectiveness and inefficiency towards higher education output. Similarly, a rise in the cost of university education for the student cohort interferes with affordability, access and equity; a situation that limits student enrollments and increases poverty rates.

Most important for developing African countries at the education level would be the freedom for them to be able to adapt policy choices to their specific contexts in a manner that would determine an appropriate way forward for economic growth and development in these countries. Like Finland, most of them have the potential to thread the growth and development path that is unique to their histories, cultures and specific needs. Therefore, no matter how good the mandate and objectives of transnational organizations in promoting education policies to ensure economic growth and social well-being of the people of Africa, there are concerns relating to the idea that lumps up the economies of different developing Africa countries into one small economic unit. This perspective indicates that general development policy trends are void of the distinctive characteristics and diverse priorities of various national systems that determine a country's transformation process. And looking at the trends followed by industrialized economies (moving from primary through manufacturing industries to the new knowledge economy concept of technology and innovation), one would raise a concern on the prioritized relevance of ICT and innovation to the economic growth of countries endowed with a myriad of natural capital and physical labour. Abundant natural capital for example, added to global education policy, gives developing African countries a wide range of education policy choices towards economic growth and development. Indeed, growth would be attained if significant attention is focused on the science and development of extractive industries given the abundance of natural capital that is embedded in countries of the Central Africa sub region. There is strong evidence that economic growth and development would be stimulated through the promotion of primary and secondary economic sectors productions in the path followed by Western industrialized economies. For them, the new knowledge economy concept fills the gap created by the decline in primary industry activities due to insufficient supply of natural capital.

6. Conclusion

This essay has discussed the influence of the world's institutional view on the economic growth of developing African countries within the framework of the global development agenda. It contends that global development models defined by international and supra national organizations construct the knowledge regime and activities that determine the growth and development of developing African countries. It argues that growth and development in African nations are in fact not solely influenced by the strategic pursuit of their inherent self-interest (needs and aspirations) or by the clear functional objectives of their national governments. In particular, the education policy of these countries are rather constructed and constituted by external influences of world polity views. The policy ideas and impositions of the WB and IMF through the SAPs and the bank's knowledge Institute are perfect examples. These organizations strive to shape developing countries in ways that conform to their perception of countries and world development. They, therefore, generate isomorphism in the structures and policies of nation states through international standard constructions such as the K4D etc.

In addition, we sought explanations as to why the Bretton Woods institutions and other organizations continue to impose the same education policy measures to different African countries with distinct histories, needs and priorities. Most countries in the CEMAC region of Central Africa, in the African continent, are endowed with a myriad of natural resources. We question why the same set of growth policy measures would be emphasized for all categories of developing countries. Undoubtedly, Suarez and Bromley (2014) argue that 'the highly abstract character of world models allows them to spread to unexpected locations and beyond the specific context where they emerged'. The paper then maintains that this knowledge regime emanates from within the subjective research perspective where the reality and knowledge that determines policies are limited to the values and perceptions of the mandate of legitimized organizations. It demonstrates that there is a need for a diverse range of knowledge regimes where reality and knowledge for policies are derived from the histories, sociocultural perspectives, experiences, local circumstances and natural capital base of people. Consequently, it is plausible for African countries to achieve growth and development through a comprehensive support of contextualized education policy and natural resource-based initiatives; and exploiting low-skill labour via primary and secondary industry endeavours. At the most, when governments of developing countries adopt world polity tradition it is to gain recognition by conforming to the expectations and mandate of legitimized international organizations. Unfortunately, this conformist stance does not usually match the experiences, needs, expectations and priorities of their society.

References

Africa Region. 2012. Cameroon-Governance and Management in the Education Sector. Report No. 67201-CM. Available at: http://siteresources.worldbank.org/INTCAMEROON/Resources/governance-and-management-in-the-education-sector-march2012.pdf. Accessed on 08.01.2017.

Brinkley, Ian. 2006. Defining the knowledge economy. Knowledge economy programme report. London: The Work Foundation. Available at: http://www.theworkfoundation.com/assets/docs/publications/65_defining%20knowledge%20economy.pdf. Accessed on 03.06.2016.

Bromley, Patrica & Meyer, John W. 2016. *Hyper-organization. Global organizational expansion,* excerpt. London: Oxford University Press.

Chen, Derek H C & Dahlman, Carl J. 2006. The Knowledge Economy, The KAM Methodology and World Bank Operations. World Bank Institute, Washington, D. C.

Dale, Roger. 2000. Globalization and Education: Demonstrating a "Common World Educational Culture" or Locating a "Globally Structured Educational Agenda"? Educational Theory, 50: 427–448. doi: 10.1111/j.1741-5446.2000.00427.

H Halme, Kimmo, Lindy, Ilari, Piirainen, Kalle A., Salminen, Vesa & White, Justine. (Eds.) . 2014. Finland as a Knowledge Economy 2.0: Lessons on Policies and Governance. Washington DC: The World Bank. Available at: https://openknowledge.worldbank.org/bitstream/handle/10986/17869/869430PUB0Finl00Box382171B00PUBLIC0.pdf. [Accessed on 09 June 2016].

International Monetary Fund. (IMF). 2010. Cameroon: Poverty Reduction Strategy Paper: Country Report No. 10/257, August 2010. Washington DC: International Monetary Fund.

Kniola, David J. 2009. *Constructing an Estimate of Academic Capitalism and Explaining* Faculty *Differences through Multilevel Analysis*, Ph. D. dissertation, Virginia Polytechnic Institute. Available at: https://theses.lib.vt.edu/theses/available/etd-11062009-133835/unrestricted/Kniola_DJ_D_2009.pdf. [07 July 2015].

Ling Cristian & Dawn, Robert. 2007. *Formative Assessment of the Knowledge for Development Program*. Report No. EG07-136. Washington, DC: World Bank Institute. Available at: http://info.worldbank.org/etools/docs/library/241419/EG08-136%20Formative%20Assessment%20of%20the%20Knowledge%20for%20Development%20Program.pdf. Accessed on 09.06.2016.

Lingard, Bob. 2010. Policy borrowing, policy learning: testing times in Australian schooling, Critical Studies in Education, 51: 2, 129–147, DOI:10.1080/17508481003731026. Available on: http://dx.doi.org/10.1080/17508481003731026. McClure KR (2014) *Beyond Academic Capitalism: Innovation and Entrepreneurship as Institutional Ethos at a Public Research University*, Ph. D. dissertation, University of Maryland. Available at: http://drum.lib.umd.edu/bitstream/1903/15233/1/McClure_umd_0117E_15028.pdf [10 July 2015].

Marginson, Simon., & Van der Wende, Marijk. 2007. "Globalisation and Higher Education", OECD Education Working Papers, No. 8, OECD Publishing, Paris. http://dx.doi.org/10.1787/173831738240

McGrath, Simon. 2012. Education and development in Africa: lessons of the past 50 years for beyond 2015. In *CAS@50, 6–8 June 2012*, Edinburgh, UK. (Unpublished Version).

Macgregor Karen. 2015. *Higher Education is Key to Development*. World Bank, University World News: Global Edition, Issue no: 362 http://www.universityworldnews.com/article.php?story=20150409152258799. [14 September 2016].

Ngwe, Gabriel. 2013. Teacher absenteeism in primary schools in Cameroon. In: Sweeney G., Despota K and Lindner S (eds) Transparency International: *Global Corruption Report: Education*. Oxon/New York: Routledge 2013, p. 74.

Orr, Dominic, Wespel, Johannes, & Usher, Alex. 2014. Do changes in cost-sharing have an impact on the behaviour of students and higher education institutions? European Commission, Education and Training - Luxembourg: Publications Office of the European Union.

Ozga, Jenny & Jones, Robert. 2006. Travelling and embedded policy: the case of knowledge transfer *Journal of Education Policy* 21(1), 1–17. DOI: 10.1080/02680930500391462

Ozga, Jenny & Lingard, Bob. 2007. Globalisation, Education Policy and Politics. In: Lingard, Bob and Ozga, Jenny (eds.) *The Routledge Falmer reader in education policy and politics*. London/New York: Routledge, pp. 65–82.

Pouris, Anastassios and Ho, Yuh-Shan. 2014. Research emphasis and collaboration in Africa. In: *Scientometrics* Vol 98(3), pp 2169–2184. Available at: DOI 10.1007/s11192-013-1156-8

Robertson, Susan L. 2008. 'Producing' Knowledge Economies: The World Bank, the KAM, Education and Development, published by the Centre for Globalisation, Education and Societies, University of Bristol, Bristol BS8 1JA, UK, available: http://susanleerobertson.com/publications/.

Rodrik, Dani. 2007. Industrial development: Some stylized facts and policy directions. In *Industrial Development for the 21st Century: Sustainable Development Perspectives*. (pp. 7–28. United Nations publication, Sales No. 07. II.A.1.

Rubins, Ira. 2007. *Risks and Rewards of Academic Capitalism and the Effects of Presidential Leadership in the Entrepreneurial University*, Available at: http://www.asu.edu/mpa/Entre%20University.pdf. [Accessed 10 September 2016].

Samoff, Joel & Carrol, Bidemi. 2004. Conditions, Coalitions, and Influence: The World Bank and Higher Education in Africa. http://www.eldis.org/vfile/upload/1/document/0708/DOC17679.pdf. [Accessed 14 September 2016].

Schofer, Evans & Meyer, John W. 2005. The World-Wide Expansion of Higher Education: Center on Democracy, Development, and The Rule of Law Stanford Institute on International Studies. Standford: Standford University. https://fsi.stanford.edu/sites/default/files/Schofer-Meyer_No3 2.pdf. [Accessed19 October 2016].

Schriewer, Jürgen & Martinez, Carlos. 2004. Constructions of Internationalityin Education. In Gita Steiner-Khamsi, ed., *The Global Politics of educational borrowing and lending*, chapter 2, pp. 29–53. New York: Teachers College Press.

Science, Technology and Innovation Strategy for Africa 2024. Available at: http://www.hsrc.ac.za/uploads/pageContent/5481/Science,%20Technology%20and%20Innovation%20Strategy%20for%20Africa%20-%20Doc ument.pdf. [Accessed 03June 2016].

Shattock, Michael. 2003. *Managing Successful Universities*, Buckingham: SRHE.

Shattock, Michael. 2009. Entrepreneurialism and organizational change in higher education in Entrepreneurialism in Universities and the Knowledge Economy Diversification and Organizational Change in European Higher Education M. shattock (Ed.) The Society for Research into Higher Education and Open University Press.

Slaughter, Sheila & Leslie, Larry L. 1999. *Academic Capitalism, politics, policies and the Entrepreneurial University*. Baltimore, London: The John Hopkins University Press.

Smith, Keith. 2000. What is the 'Knowledge Economy'? Knowledge Intensive Industries and Distributed Knowledge Bases. STEP Group, Oslo. DRUID Summer Conference. Available at: http://www.druid.dk/uploads/tx_picturedb/ds2000-123.pdf. [Accessed 06June 2016].

Steinberg, Shirley R. 2014. "Critical Constructivism" In: *The SAGE Encyclopedia of Action Research*. Coghlan, D & Brydon-Miller, M (Edts), London, SAGE Publications Ltd. DOI: http://dx.doi.org/10.4135/978144629 4406.

Steiner-Khamsi, Gita. 2012. The global/local nexus in comparative policystudies: analysing the triple bonus system in Mongolia over time. *Comparative Education,* 48 (4), 455–471.

Suárez, David F. & Bromley, Patricia. 2014. Institutional Theories and Levelsof Analysis: History, Diffusion, and Translation. Draft May 2014.

Sørensen, Eva & Torfing, Jacob. 2009. The Politics of Self-Governance inMeso Level Theories. In Eva Sørensen and Peter Triantafillou (eds). *The Politics ofSelf-Governance*, chapter 3. London: Ashgate.

Takayama, Keita. 2010. 'Politics of externalization in reflexive times: Reinventing Japanese education reform discourses through "Finnish success"', *Comparative Education Review,* 54(1): 51–75.

The World Bank. 2000. Comprehensive Development Framework Country Experience March 1999–July 2000. Available at: http://web.worldbank.org/archive/website01013/WEB/IMAGES/CEXP_WEB.PDF. [Accessed on 07 June 2016].

The World Bank. 2007. *Building Knowledge Economies: Advanced Strategies for Development*. Washington, D. C: WBI Development Studies. Available at: http://siteresources.worldbank.org/KFDLP/Resources/461197-1199907090464/BuildingKEbook.pdf.

The World Bank. 2009. *Accelerating Catch-up: Tertiary Education for Growth in Sub-Saharan Africa* (Washington DC, World Bank).

The World Bank. 2010. *Financing higher education in Africa*. Africa Regional Educational Publications; Directions in development. Human development. Washington, DC: World Bank. Retrieved from: http://documents.worldbank.org/curated/en/497251467990390368/Financing-higher-education-in-Africa (Accessed 02.05.2016).

The World Bank. 2011. The State of World Bank Knowledge Services: Knowledge for Development. Results connectivity openness. Available at: http://siteresources.worldbank.org/PROJECTS/Resources/40940-1316471060185/KnowledgeBookletcomplete.pdf

The World Bank Institute, K4D Newsletter, The Knowledge for Development Program 2006, Volume 2(4). Available at: http://siteresources.worldbank.org/KFDLP/Resources/K4D_Newsletter_Jan_2006.pdf. [Accessed on 09 June 2016].

The World Bank Group - SKU 32857. Available at: http://www.un.org/esa/ffd/ffd3/wp-content/uploads/sites/2/WBG-UN-Brochure.pdf. [Accessed on 13 October 2016].

The World Bank Annual Report 2009, Year in Review. Annual Report, Office of the Publisher, External Affairs, The World Bank, Washington D. C.: International Bank for Reconstruction and Development, 2009.

The World Bank – Knowledge for Development. The World Bank Institute's program on building knowledge economies. Available at: http://siteresources.worldbank.org/KFDLP/Resources/461197-1199907090464/k4d_bookletjune2008.pdf. [Accessed on 05.12.2016]. UNESCO - The Eight Millennium Development Goals. Available at: http://www.unesco.org/new/en/education/themes/leading-the-international-agenda/education-for-all/education-and-the-mdgs/goal-2/. [Accessed 04.01.2017].

Verger, Antoni., Novelli, Mario & Altinyelken, Hulya Kosar. 2012. Global education policy and international development: An introductory framework. In Verger, Antoni., Novelli, Mario & Altinyelken, Hulya Kosar (Eds.), *Global education policy and international development: New agendas, issues and policies* (pp. 3-32). London, England: Continuum International Publishing Group. Retrieved from: http://ww.geps-ua b.cat/sites/default/files/publicacions-adjunts/Verger%20et%20al%20GEP_introduction.pdf [Accessed 18.09.2017].

Woldegiorgis, Emnet Tadesse& Doevenspeck, Martin. 2013. The Changing Role of Higher Education in Africa: A Historical Reflection. *Higher Education Studies*, 3(6): 35–45.

World Bank Institute. 2013. Measuring Knowledge in the World's Economies: Knowledge Assessment Methodology and Knowledge Economy Index. Knowledge for Development Programme. Available at: http://siteresources.worldbank.org/INTUNIKAM/Resources/KAM_v4.pdf. [Accessed on 07June 2016].

World Conference on Education for All. 1990. Meeting Basic Learning Needs: A Vision for the 1990s. New York, NY: UNICEF House. Available at: http://unesdoc.unesco.org/images/0009/000975/097552e.pdf. [Accessed on 02.12.2016].

World Conference on Education for All. 1998. World Declaration on Higher Education for the Twenty-First Century: Vision and Action and Framework for Priority Action for Change and Development in Higher Education. Available at: http://www.unesco.org/education/educprog/wche/declaration_eng.htmtemple.jpg. [Accessed on 02.12.2016].

ibidem.eu